THE
TIMECHART
OF THE
CIVIL
WAR

The assault on Fort Fisher, January 15, 1865, after bombardment from land and sea. The Union capture of the fort closed the Confederate's last port. (Nav.Ac.)

THE
TIMECHART
OF THE
CIVIL
WAR

MBI Publishing Company

This edition first published in 2001 by
MBI Publishing Company, Galtier Plaza, Suite 200,
380 Jackson Street, St. Paul, MN 55101-3885 USA

The information in this book is true and complete
to the best of our knowledge. All recommendations are made
without any guarantee on the part of the author or publisher,
who also disclaim any liability incurred in connection with the
use of this data or specific details.

We recognize that some words, model names and
designations, for example, mentioned herein are the property of
the trademark holder. We use them for identification purposes
only. This is not an official publication.

MBI Publishing Company books are also available at
discounts in bulk quantity for industrial or sales-promotional
use. For details write to Special Sales Manager at Motorbooks
International Wholesalers & Distributors, 729 Prospect Avenue,
PO Box 1, Osceola, WI 54020-0001 USA.

Library of Congress Cataloging-in-Publication Data
Available.

ISBN 0-7603-1122-6

Printed in China

EDITORIAL CONSULTANTS
James R. Arnold and Roberta Wiener

Timechart Compilation by Paul Kincaid
Battle Chronologies by C. J. Davies
Cartography by MACArt

Designed by David Gibbons

PRODUCTION TEAM
David Gibbons
Anthony A. Evans
Meredith MacArdle
John Gilbert
and
Boxharry Design Associates

Picture Credits

Author	James R. Arnold and Roberta Wiener	NA	National Archives
ASKB	Anne S. K. Brown Military Collection	NavAc	Courtesy of the U.S. Naval Academy Museum
B&L	*Battles and Leaders of the Civil War*	NGB	Courtesy of the National Guard Bureau
Harper's	*Harper's Weekly*	NHC	Naval Historical Center, Washington, D.C.
ILN	*The Illustrated London News*	NPS	National Park Service
LC	Library of Congress	WP	West Point Museum Collection, U.S. Military
Leslies	*Frank Leslie's Illustrated Newspaper*		Academy
M	*The Photographic History of the Civil War*,	VMI	Virginia Military Institute
	edited by Francis Trevelyan Miller	Wilson	Courtesy of the artist, Robert W. Wilson,
MARS	Moores' Military Archive and Research Services		Woodruff, S.C.

ORIGINS OF THE WAR

In 1776, American rebels resolved that "these United Colonies are, and of right ought to be, free and independent states." Thereafter, soldiers from all thirteen colonies marched side by side to win the War of the American Revolution. They fought with the rallying cry "United we stand, divided we fall." During this time they thought of themselves not as northerners and southerners, but as Americans. After they won their freedom, they called their new nation the United States.

Yet, in 1860 the grandsons of the men who fought in the Revolutionary War were fighting again, this time against one another in a terrible civil war that pitted North against South. Both sides believed that they fought for the same principles that had motivated the Founding Fathers to create the United States.

The divergent beliefs came about because after the Revolutionary War the North and South rapidly became very different and developed different ways of life. Slavery became essential to the economy and culture of the states south of the Mason-Dixon line. Simultaneously, southern political leaders came to believe that each state government had the right to make important decisions without interference from the national government. They called this belief "states' rights."

Most northerners agreed with the idea of states' rights, but many thought that slavery should be an exception. Whereas slavery became the foundation of the southern economy, the North gradually abolished slavery.

Southerners feared that the rest of the nation would force them to give up slavery. Southern politicians saw that the best way to resist anti-slavery pressure was to maintain a political balance in the United States Congress. Essential to this balance was parity between free and slave states. Because the United States expanded constantly during the first half of the nineteenth century, preserving the balance became a source of enormous friction. Political leaders averted disunion by repeated compromise, most notably the 1820 Missouri Compromise and the Compromise of 1850.

By 1850 Americans were more alike than different. White Americans from the North and South all shared one language, English, the same Constitution and legal system, the same history, and the same memory of a war for independence. Most were of British ethnic heritage and called themselves Protestants. In spite of all of this common ground, the division over slavery caused northerners and southerners to emphasize their differences instead of their similarities.

TO THE BRINK: THE 1850S

The Compromise of 1850 proved merely the first in a series of political crises that took place over the next decade. By the terms of this compromise, the people living in the new territories were to decide for themselves whether to form a free or a slave state. Consequently, these territories became political battlegrounds between supporters of the South and supporters of the North and West. In the minds of southern leaders, it was very important to win these battles because they saw that as the nation's population increased, they were becoming increasingly outnumbered. Only in the Senate was the political balance level. Southern leaders clung desperately to the equality of votes in the Senate.

These facts set the stage for conflict when, in 1854, a Democratic senator from Illinois named Stephen A. Douglas proposed a bill to establish a new territorial government for the vast land between the Missouri River and the Rocky Mountains. His proposal became the Kansas–Nebraska Act. It proved to be one of the most important single events that pushed the nation into civil war. The Kansas–Nebraska Act gutted the Missouri Compromise, a national covenant that had bonded the nation for 34 years. Across the North, citizens met at hundreds of "anti-Nebraska" meetings to protest. Northern voters formed many new political parties, all of them based on opposition to slavery. The party that rose above the others was the Republican Party.

Meanwhile, after 1854, Kansas became not just a political battleground, but also a place where rival sides fought ruthlessly with gun, knife, and fire. An

Left: One of the most important legacies of the American Civil War was the abolition of slavery. To abolitionists, the institution itself was abhorrent. The brutal treatment meted out by some slave owners drove many reformers to join the abolitionist cause. (NA)

Right: Photographed in Richmond in 1861, these young, cheerful, and confident Confederate soldiers have yet to face the shocking battles of the early stages of the war. (M)

Far right: Richard Watson Gilder, born in 1844 in New Jersey, was not a military man by inclination, having been involved in publishing his own newspaper from the age of twelve. During Lee's invasion of the North, however, Gilder enlisted for the emergency, and became a cadet with Landis's Philadephia battery in 1863, helping defend Carlisle, Pennsylvania. In 1864, Gilder returned to journalism, becoming an editor as well as a poet and social reformer. He died in 1909. (M)

abolitionist zealot named John Brown wanted to "strike terror into the hearts of the pro-slavery people" in Kansas. Brown lived along the banks of Pottawatomie Creek. During the night of May 24—5, 1856, Brown and a small group including four of his sons stalked up to the cabins belonging to five pro-slavery men. They abducted and executed them in cold blood by splitting open their skulls with swords. The killings at Pottawatomie Creek naturally goaded the pro-slavery forces in Kansas to respond. So continued a cycle of violence and revenge. "Bleeding Kansas" became a battleground with hit and run raids, ambushes, and murder in the night.

The civil war in Kansas was the most important issue during the presidential election of 1856. The Republican Party managed to unite voters who opposed the repeal of the Missouri Compromise and the extension of slavery. A politician named Abraham Lincoln gradually emerged as the party's most articulate spokesman. Although a Democrat named James Buchanan won the 1856 election, it was clear to all that the Republican Party was the power of the future.

THE ELECTION OF 1860

National crisis came in 1860. Four decades of compromise between North and South had failed. Four honorable men representing four different ideas about the future of the nation competed to become president of the United States. Northern and western Democrats wanted Senator Stephen Douglas to be the Democratic candidate. Many southern Democrats bitterly disliked Douglas because they did not share Douglas's views on slavery. An Alabama editor wrote that Democrats should condemn Douglas and cast aside "his loathsome carcass." Democrats like this man preferred to lose the election rather than have Douglas be their candidate. They succeeded in splitting the party in two. About one-third of the delegates, almost all from the South, left the party and nominated John C. Breckinridge as their candidate. Breckinridge's platform was pro-slavery.

The Republican party selected Abraham Lincoln. A fourth candidate was John Bell of Tennessee. He repre-sented a new party called the Constitutional Union party that tried to bridge the gap between North and South. Bell's party recognized no political principle other than "the Constitution ... the Union ... and the Enforcement of the Laws." It avoided taking a substantive stand on the issues of the day.

The election of 1860 became two separate contests: Lincoln versus Douglas in the North; Breckinridge versus Bell in the South. Lincoln received only 40 percent of the nation's popular vote, but it comfortably gave him enough electoral votes to become president.

Few doubted the importance of Lincoln's election. Virginia had been a moderate southern state. A majority of its voters had voted for Bell, the compromise candidate. Now, a Richmond newspaper gloomily wrote, "A party founded on the single sentiment ... of hatred of African slavery, is now the controlling power." A New Orleans paper called the Republicans a "revolutionary party." Anti-slavery people agreed that the election did mark a revolution. "We live in revolutionary times," wrote an Illinois man, and "I say God bless the revolution."

SECESSION

Because they believed in states' rights, southern politicians believed that states had the right to secede from the United States and form their own nation. Because of their fear of the new United States president, Abraham Lincoln, seven southern states seceded: South Carolina (December 20, 1860), Mississippi (January 9, 1861), Florida (January 10, 1861), Alabama (January 11, 1861), Georgia (January 19, 1861), Louisiana (January 26, 1861), and Texas (February 1, 1861). In February, delegates from these states met in Montgomery, Alabama to form a new nation, the Confederate States of America. The Confederate Convention chose Jefferson Davis as president and Alexander Stephens as vice-president.

In his inaugural speech, Davis calmly described the new nation as an established fact. He showed no interest in reconciliation with the North. He said that the new nation faced perilous times, but that he had confidence that southerners were willing

to make whatever sacrifices necessary to preserve "honor and right and liberty and equality." Along with other secessionist leaders, Davis believed that the Confederate States of America represented the Founding Fathers' true principles. Consequently, secessionist leaders believed it quite natural to copy most of the language of the U.S. Constitution when writing a new Constitution for themselves. However, the Confederate version stated plainly that slavery was to be "recognized and protected" by both the federal government and the territorial government. There would be no confusion about the legality of slavery when people settled on the western frontier.

Two weeks after the Davis inaugural came Abraham Lincoln's inaugural. Lincoln well knew that the entire nation, but most particularly the southern states, would listen carefully to his words. Lincoln said that he had no intention of interfering with slavery in the states where it existed. But he denied that a state possessed a constitutional right to secession. Furthermore, a president's most important duty was to see that the laws of the Union be faithfully executed. A president's solemn duty was "to preserve, protect, and defend" the United States. Therefore, Lincoln pledged to use the power given him as president to defend all government property. He called southerners "my dissatisfied fellow countrymen" and said that "the momentous issue of civil war" was in their hands. The government would not attack them. War could only come if they attacked first.

Both Davis and Lincoln knew that the future depended greatly upon what took place among the eight neutral states that lay between the South and North. Neither president wanted to strike the first blow because such an action would likely drive the neutral states into the opposing camp. In addition, Lincoln knew that many northerners did not support the idea of using force to compel the seceded states to return to the union. If the southerners attacked first, if they were the aggressors, Lincoln believed that northerners would unite to defend themselves.

FORT SUMTER

The greatest likelihood of conflict involved four Federal forts still flying the Stars and Stripes near the Confederate coast. Three were off the coast of Florida, and the fourth, Fort Sumter, was in Charleston harbor. The fact

that here, in the cradle of secession, the flag of the United States still flew above the fort's ramparts served as a test for Confederates. How could a nation be respected if it could not even control its own territory?

After seceding, South Carolinians had placed artillery around Charleston harbor and prevented any ships from bringing supplies to Fort Sumter. Hotheads shouted for action. A Virginia politician begged a Charleston crowd to "strike a blow!" so that Virginia and the other still neutral southern states would join the Confederacy. The *Charleston Mercury* agreed: "Border southern States will never join us until ... we have proven that a garrison of seventy men cannot hold the portal of our commerce ... The Fate of the Southern Confederacy hangs by the ensign halliards of Fort Sumter." For the moment, however, calmer men remained in charge.

The day after his inauguration, Lincoln received a dispatch from the officer who commanded at Fort Sumter, Major Robert Anderson, stating that there was only enough food to last another six weeks. Lincoln faced a huge decision: should he order a force to carry supplies to Fort Sumter?

On April 6, 1861, Lincoln signed an order for a naval expedition to relieve Fort Sumter. He informed the governor of South Carolina that this expedition was only carrying food. There would be no attempt to reinforce the fort with men or weapons. Lincoln had shrewdly put Confederate leaders in a bind. Either they would have to back down from their threats or fire the first shot at a ship carrying food to hungry men.

Now it was the turn of Davis and his cabinet to make a momentous decision. Robert Toombs was a fire-eater, a politician who had helped push his state to secede. Yet he understood the significance of the issue and

Right: The opening act of the war on April 12, 1861: the bombardment of Fort Sumter in Charleston Harbor by General Beauregard's command. From floating batteries and forts around Charleston Harbor, the shelling was so intense that they were shrouded in smoke. (ASKB)

There can be no neutrals in this war, only patriots — or traitors." New York City, which had a pro-south tradition, held a patriotic parade that brought out 250,000 people. The Stars and Stripes flew from nearly every house top, dome, and steeple. "The change in public sentiment here is wonderful," wrote one businessman. A New York woman observed that there was so much excitement that the "time before Sumter" was like another century.

Northern states quickly enrolled the required number of militia and more. Lincoln asked Indiana for six regiments, the governor offered twelve. Ohio's governor telegraphed Lincoln to plead for permission to enlist additional units because so many men were volunteering. More than 100,000 volunteers responded to Lincoln's initial call.

Lincoln's request backfired in the South. It caused a bitter outcry from the four southern states which had yet to secede. The Governor of Virginia replied that Lincoln had chosen to begin civil war; he would send no troops. The Governor of Arkansas answered that his people "will defend to the last extremity their honor, lives, and property" against the North. In response to Lincoln's call, Virginia (April 17, 1861), Arkansas (May 6, 1861), North Carolina (May 20, 1861), and Tennessee (June 8, 1861) joined the Confederacy.

The vice-president of the Confederacy, Alexander Stephens, cried, "Lincoln may bring his 75,000 troops against us. We fight for our homes, our fathers and mothers, our wives, brothers, sisters, sons, and daughters! We can call out a million of peoples if need be, and when they are cut down we can call another, and still another, until the last man of the South finds a bloody grave." President Davis was more restrained. He announced, "All we ask is to be let alone."

SINEWS OF WAR

At first glance it seemed that the 23 states of the Union held overwhelming advantages versus the 11 seceding states. About 22 million people lived in the North compared to 9 million in the South, of whom 3.5 million were Negro slaves. The North had about a two to one superiority in available military manpower. Some 2.1 million men served in the Federal military during the war while between 800,000 and 900,000 served the Confederacy. Peak strengths rose to about 1,000,000 and 600,000, respectively.

There were about 110,000 manufacturing plants in the North versus 20,631 in the South. Viewed differently, the 11 states that seceded produced manufactured goods in 1860 that amounted to about 53 percent of the value of manufactured goods produced in Massachusetts alone in 1855. The South was particularly poor when considering only the manufacture of essential military supplies. In 1860 the North produced 97 percent of the country's firearms, 94 percent of its cloth, 93 percent of its pig iron, and over 90 percent of its boots and shoes.

The South could feed itself, but its transportation network depended upon outside manufacture. Nearly all rails came from the North or from Great Britain. In 1860 the North built 470 locomotives, the South 19. Almost all replacement machine parts for steam engines, the motive power for locomotives, ships, and riverboats, came from the North. The South possessed 30 percent of the nation's rail lines, but inevitably both the rails themselves and the trains that ran on them would deteriorate due to the lack of replacement capacity. Moreover, the North had more horses and mules, essential to haul military supplies from rail and river heads.

When the war began, the North had a functioning government that enjoyed international recognition and a small but efficient army and navy. The South had no internal revenue service to levy and collect taxes, no foreign service to conduct international relations, and no established professional military force. Lastly, and not to be overlooked, the North had a tremendous preponderance in commercial and financial resources.

The South's major physical advantage was its geography. The Confederate coastline ran for 3,500 miles, a

Below: Alert on the horizon, by the closing stages of the war a line of Union blockaders guarded every important Southern harbor. Blockade-running, delivering all sorts of war supplies and collecting cotton in return, was so lucrative – and so essential to the resource-poor South – that foreign merchantmen as well as Southern patriots continued to try to slip through the net. At first ineffectual in preventing the trade, the Union navy grew in strength until blockade-running became particularly dangerous. (M)

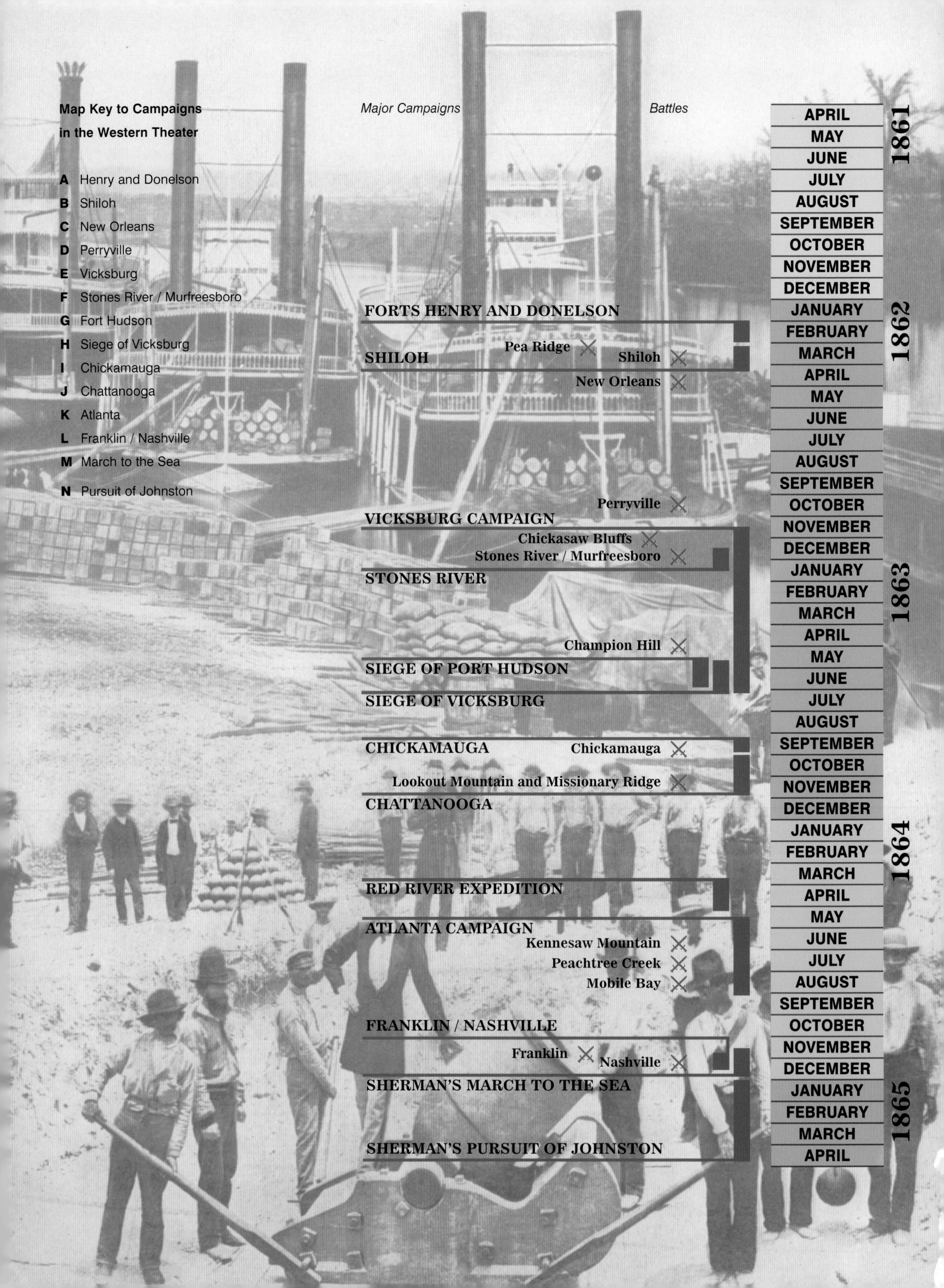

Map Key to Campaigns in the Western Theater

A Henry and Donelson
B Shiloh
C New Orleans
D Perryville
E Vicksburg
F Stones River / Murfreesboro
G Fort Hudson
H Siege of Vicksburg
I Chickamauga
J Chattanooga
K Atlanta
L Franklin / Nashville
M March to the Sea
N Pursuit of Johnston

Major Campaigns   *Battles*

FORTS HENRY AND DONELSON

SHILOH   Pea Ridge ✕   Shiloh ✕
                                               New Orleans ✕

                                      Perryville ✕
VICKSBURG CAMPAIGN
                              Chickasaw Bluffs ✕
                    Stones River / Murfreesboro ✕
STONES RIVER

                              Champion Hill ✕
SIEGE OF PORT HUDSON

SIEGE OF VICKSBURG

CHICKAMAUGA   Chickamauga ✕

        Lookout Mountain and Missionary Ridge ✕
CHATTANOOGA

RED RIVER EXPEDITION

ATLANTA CAMPAIGN
                          Kennesaw Mountain ✕
                          Peachtree Creek ✕
                          Mobile Bay ✕

FRANKLIN / NASHVILLE

                Franklin ✕   Nashville ✕
SHERMAN'S MARCH TO THE SEA

SHERMAN'S PURSUIT OF JOHNSTON

1861
APRIL
MAY
JUNE
JULY
AUGUST
SEPTEMBER
OCTOBER
NOVEMBER
DECEMBER

1862
JANUARY
FEBRUARY
MARCH
APRIL
MAY
JUNE
JULY
AUGUST
SEPTEMBER
OCTOBER
NOVEMBER
DECEMBER

1863
JANUARY
FEBRUARY
MARCH
APRIL
MAY
JUNE
JULY
AUGUST
SEPTEMBER
OCTOBER
NOVEMBER
DECEMBER

1864
JANUARY
FEBRUARY
MARCH
APRIL
MAY
JUNE
JULY
AUGUST
SEPTEMBER
OCTOBER
NOVEMBER
DECEMBER

1865
JANUARY
FEBRUARY
MARCH
APRIL

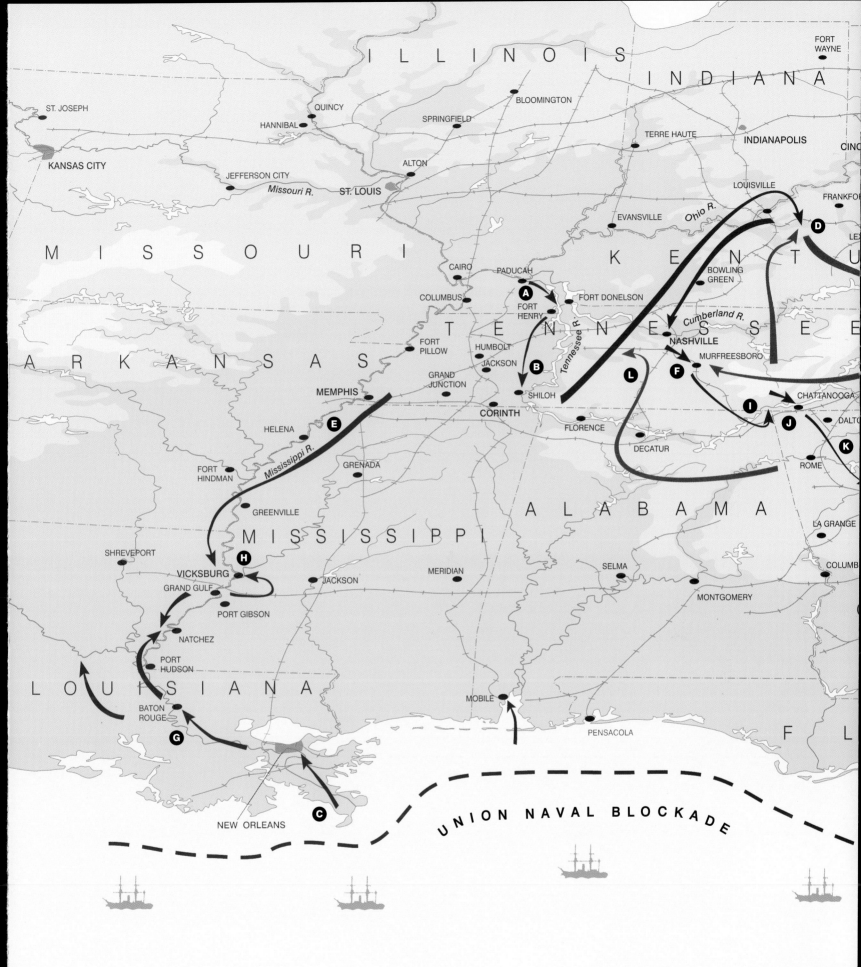

STRATEGIC PANORAMA OF THE CIVIL WAR

showing the major campaigns (schematic)

said, "The firing on that fort will inaugurate a civil war greater than any the world has yet seen." Davis believed that the entire world would realize that it was Lincoln who had forced the issue by sending the relief fleet. The neutral states would see that Lincoln had been the aggressor. The Confederate president sent orders to open fire against the fort.

At 4:30 on a Friday morning, April 12, 1861, the first gun fired. Soon there were 47 artillery pieces bombarding Fort Sumter. The defenders could only survive by staying inside the brick casemates where the smoke was so thick that they had to breathe through wet handkerchiefs. The defenders fired back not because their fire was very effective but rather to show defiance, to show that they still lived. Confederate gunners pounded Fort Sumter with more than 4,000 shots fired from cannons, howitzers, and mortars.

There could be no doubt about the outcome. Having satisfied honor, Major Robert Anderson — a slave-owning Kentuckian who understood the meaning of duty — surrendered the fort. No one had been injured in the fighting. Unfortunately, an accident after the surrender caused an explosion that killed a U.S. private named Daniel Hough. His death was the first fatality in a war that would claim more than 620,000 soldiers' lives.

Lincoln had skillfully maneuvered the rebellious states into firing the first shot. The rash Confederate attack removed many difficulties from Lincoln's effort to preserve the Union.

On April 15, 1861, he requested the states still in the Union to supply 75,000 militia to meet the emergency and put down the rebellion. This call aroused the nation. Just as Lincoln had hoped, it united patriots in the north. Republicans and Democrats, bitter foes just a half year earlier, found common ground. Lincoln's old rival, Stephen Douglas, told a huge crowd in Chicago, "Every man must be for the United States or against it.

strategic viewpoint it was a decidedly secondary region. Both sides had to invest most of their strength east of the Mississippi. The trans-Mississippi received the leftovers.

The 3,500-mile-long Confederate coastline was another theater of war. There were some 189 harbors and navigable river mouths. Because this lengthy coastline was so difficult to blockade effectively, Union strategists decided that the best policy was to capture the ports themselves. Thus, the major southern ports were the scene of many Union army-navy amphibious operations.

SOUTHERN WAR STRATEGY

When the war began, southerners believed that they held a trump card that ensured victory. "King Cotton," they called it. The South supplied at least 85 percent of the cotton Europe consumed. Southern leaders thought that cotton could be used to coerce England and France to intervene in the war. They decided to embargo cotton to hasten the happy day when foreign recognition would come.

Events proved the hollowness of the King Cotton strategy. First of all, in recent years the British cotton industry had begun to decline in importance relative to the overall British economy. Second, the cotton industry was overwhelmingly concentrated in one area of England, which meant it had limited representation in Parliament and thus limited influence upon British policy. Third, Europe in 1861 had just imported a bumper cotton harvest from the South and this buffered the impact of the southern embargo. Lastly, other cotton-producing areas such as Egypt and India proved eager and capable of replacing southern cotton.

By 1862 the South's need for foreign supplies necessitated a policy reversal. The South had little money to purchase supplies. The only commodity the South possessed was cotton. So the Confederate government sanctioned running cotton through the blockade in order to obtain rifles, artillery, and all the other war supplies produced by the manufacturing world. Southern leaders hoped that this was a temporary expe-

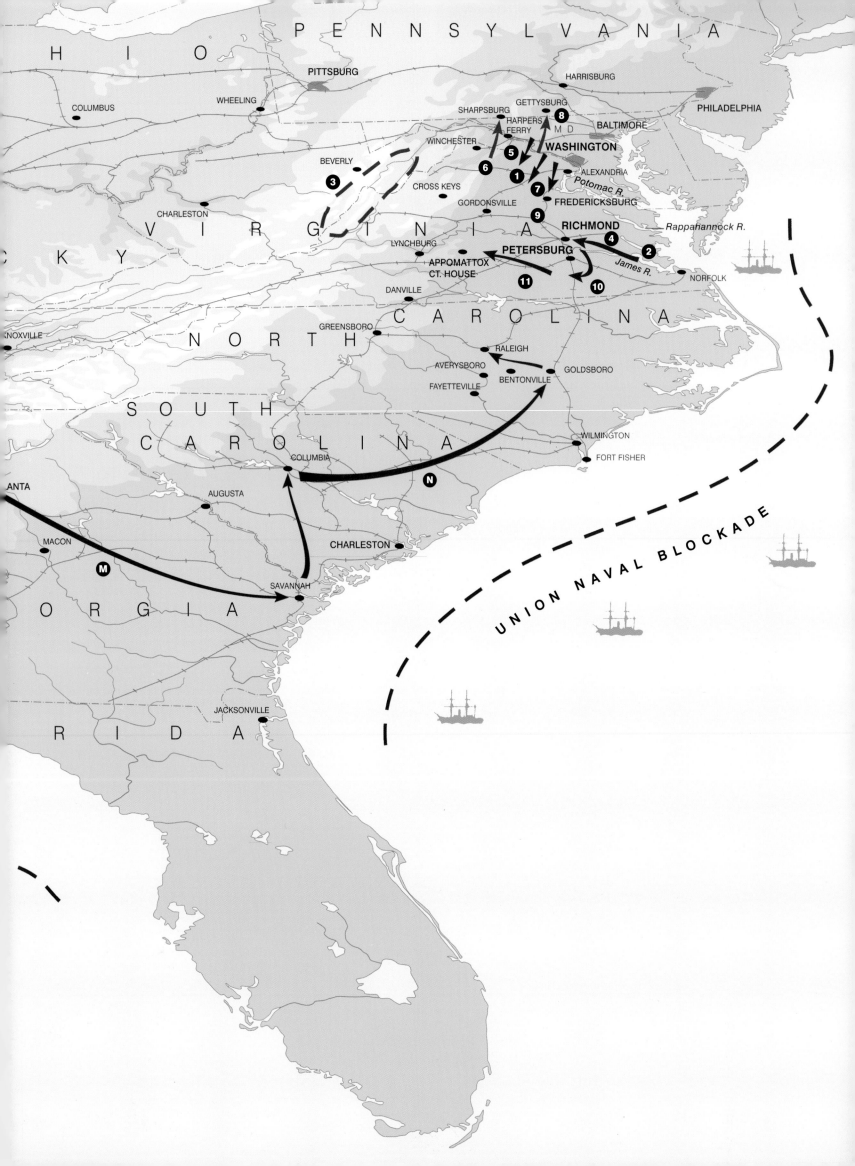

PENNSYLVANIA

HIO

PITTSBURG

HARRISBURG

COLUMBUS

WHEELING

PHILADELPHIA

SHARPSBURG

GETTYSBURG

HARPERS
FERRY

8

M D

BALTIMORE

WINCHESTER

WASHINGTON

5

BEVERLY

ALEXANDRIA

6

1

Potomac R.

3

CROSS KEYS

GORDONSVILLE

7

FREDERICKSBURG

CHARLESTON

VIRGINIA

9

RICHMOND

Rappahannock R.

LYNCHBURG

PETERSBURG

4

2

APPOMATTOX
CT. HOUSE

James R.

KY

11

10

NORFOLK

DANVILLE

CAROLINA

KNOXVILLE

NORTH

GREENSBORO

RALEIGH

AVERYSBORO

SOUTH

FAYETTEVILLE

BENTONVILLE

GOLDSBORO

CAROLINA

WILMINGTON

COLUMBIA

FORT FISHER

N

ANTA

AUGUSTA

MACON

M

CHARLESTON

ORGIA

SAVANNAH

UNION NAVAL BLOCKADE

RIDA

JACKSONVILLE

1861	
	APRIL
	MAY
	JUNE
	JULY
	AUGUST
	SEPTEMBER
	OCTOBER
	NOVEMBER
	DECEMBER

1862	
	JANUARY
	FEBRUARY
	MARCH
	APRIL
	MAY
	JUNE
	JULY
	AUGUST
	SEPTEMBER
	OCTOBER
	NOVEMBER
	DECEMBER

1863	
	JANUARY
	FEBRUARY
	MARCH
	APRIL
	MAY
	JUNE
	JULY
	AUGUST
	SEPTEMBER
	OCTOBER
	NOVEMBER
	DECEMBER

1864	
	JANUARY
	FEBRUARY
	MARCH
	APRIL
	MAY
	JUNE
	JULY
	AUGUST
	SEPTEMBER
	OCTOBER
	NOVEMBER
	DECEMBER

1865	
	JANUARY
	FEBRUARY
	MARCH
	APRIL

Battles

Major Campaigns

First Bull Run

Roanoke Island
Hampton Roads   **PENINSULA**

Siege of Yorktown   **JACKSON'S VALLEY CAMPAIGN**

Seven Pines   **SEVEN DAYS**

Second Bull Run   **SECOND BULL RUN**

Antietam   **ANTIETAM**

FREDERICKSBURG
Fredericksburg

Charleston Harbor
Chancellorsville   **CHANCELLORSVILLE**
                     GETTYSBURG
Gettysburg

WILDERNESS AND SPOTSYLVANIA
Wilderness   Spotsylvania
Cold Harbor
Petersburg   The Crater

SHERIDAN'S VALLEY CAMPAIGN
Winchester
Cedar Creek

Five Forks   **SIEGE OF PETERSBURG**

Map Key to Campaigns in the Eastern Theater

First Bull Run / Manassas	1
Peninsula	2
Jackson's Valley Campaign	3
The Seven Days	4
Second Bull Run	5
Antietam	6
Fredericksburg / Chancellorsville	7
Gettysburg	8
Wilderness / Spotsylvania / Cold Harbor	9
Petersburg	10
Pursuit to Appomattox Court House	11

span that seemed to defy blockade. On land, the main military front from the Mississippi River to the Atlantic Ocean was about 400 miles long. The front's depth was about 500 miles. To win the war the North had to invade and conquer this vast territory, roughly the size of western Europe, save Italy and Scandinavia. Meanwhile, the Confederates would enjoy the physical advantage of fighting on interior lines and the morale edge of fighting in defense of their homeland.

The Civil War marked a transition from limited to total war. The neat distinction between the civil and the military blurred. The process of mobilizing, supplying, and transporting thousands of men distorted all aspects of the economy. Historic patterns of production and consumption altered beyond all recognition. Armies drafted factory workers and farmers, including those whose special talents — rail workers, iron smiths, wagon and harness makers — produced the sinews of war. Their absence from productive society caused huge changes in wages and profits. On the consumption side, armies were like open maws, receiving money, food, munitions, clothes, and always demanding more. When supplies did not arrive, the armies took from the area around their camps, leaving desolation where there had been plenty.

THEATERS OF WAR

Military operations naturally divided into two main theaters and numerous secondary fronts. The eastern theater was Virginia, a 100-mile-long front from the Allegheny Mountains to the coast. From a military standpoint, the region looked like a triangle with the apex pointed at the Federal capital, Washington, D.C. The Potomac River and the lower Chesapeake Bay formed the triangle's right leg. The Blue Ridge Mountains and adjacent Shenandoah Valley formed the left leg. The James and Appomattox Rivers formed the

base of the triangle. Halfway along this base was the Confederate capital at Richmond. The major rivers ran west to east through the triangle and so provided the rebels with a succession of good defensive positions.

The rival capitals lay a mere 90 miles apart. Neither side could afford to lose its capital, so the eastern theater received first call on men and material. For three and one-half years northern leaders suffered defeat on the legs and in the center of this triangle as they tried to capture Richmond. During this time, northern Virginia witnessed titanic clashes. Three adjacent counties in northern Virginia saw more Americans die in battle than in the Revolutionary War, the War of 1812, the Mexican War, and all the Indian wars combined. Only with hindsight could it be seen that the east was a strategic dead end. A defeated army, whether Union or Confederate, could and did retire from the field to the safety of its capital's fortifications. Protected by these all but impregnable fortifications, the defeated force licked its wounds and prepared for new battles.

The western theater extended for about 300 miles from the Mississippi River to the Allegheny Mountains. In the West the major rivers — the Mississippi, Tennessee, and Cumberland — ran north and south. This gave the Union natural avenues to follow to invade the South. There were some other important differences between the east and west. There were fewer big cities and fewer railroads. These facts made it harder for western armies to receive logistical support. As soon as the Union forces moved away from the rivers, their supply lines became increasingly vulnerable to raiders and guerrillas.

West of the Mississippi lay a vast area stretching all the way to the Pacific Ocean. Although the trans-Mississippi theater provided the Confederacy with manpower, mules and horses, and grain, from a

dient that would delay but not negate the effect of the cotton embargo. It proved a false hope.

In 1861 southern leaders understood that it would take time for the King Cotton strategy to work. In the meantime, the new nation had to endure the inevitable Union attack. Confederate President Jefferson Davis was the prime architect of southern war strategy. He was West Point educated, a Mexican War veteran, a former U.S. Secretary of War, and fancied himself a top-drawer military thinker. Davis devised a strategy that he called the "offensive-defensive." The defensive aspect of this strategy relied upon the South's interior lines to position troops to block Yankee thrusts. The offensive aspect involved waiting for, or maneuvering to create, an enemy blunder and then exploiting it by a hard blow.

Periodically, southern generals, most notably Pierre T. Beauregard, proposed a grand offensive; a war-winning strike north. This required a concentration of force and it fell afoul of political considerations. No southern politician wanted to see his area stripped of forces so that some distant place could be reinforced. In 1862 a desperate situation in Tennessee compelled the South to send every available man to reinforce Albert Sydney Johnston so he could attack U.S. Grant's army. Five thousand infantry dutifully departed New Orleans. In their absence New Orleans, the South's largest city, fell to a Federal naval force. Thereafter, southern politicians pointed to New Orleans's fate whenever the Davis Administration requested local leaders to send forces to address distant threats. At moments of great crisis – Lee's 1863 Invasion of Pennsylvania and Joseph Johnston's abortive relief of Vicksburg are two notable examples – Davis managed to pry away forces from covetous local leaders, but political reality compelled a wider dispersal of scarce Confederate manpower than was ideal.

In time, the King Cotton strategy proved fallacious and the hope of foreign intervention ephemeral, while the grand offensives proved unsustainable logistically and politically. A third promising southern path to victory emerged. Whereas the North had to win the war by invading and subjugating the South, the South could win by simply outlasting the North. This path to victory became more apparent in 1864 when Lincoln's re-election depended upon votes from a war-weary nation.

In 1861 the South had a plausible path to victory, namely Jefferson Davis's "offensive-defensive."

Success depended upon the patience and skill of southern generals and the fortitude of southern people. It also depended upon the ineptitude of northern leaders. For the first third of the war, the North provided the ineptitude in full measure.

NORTHERN WAR STRATEGY

Unlike Jefferson Davis, Abraham Lincoln had no formal military education. Lincoln possessed a great deal of common sense and proved capable of penetrating military insights. From the beginning he understood that the North possessed advantages in manpower, resources, and naval strength. How to employ these advantages effectively proved vexing.

At the beginning of the war only General-in-Chief Winfield Scott produced a practical strategy. Scott recommended that Lincoln take time to raise and train an 85,000-man army. Meanwhile, he recommended a naval blockade of the entire Confederate coast. Then, the trained army would move south, down the Mississippi River, to divide the Confederacy in two. A waiting period was to follow in the belief that the constricted South would eventually succumb. The northern press ridiculed Scott's strategy, calling it the Anaconda Plan.

Regardless of the plan's real merits, Lincoln knew that it was politically impossible. Northern politicians and the public wanted fast action. They demanded an immediate advance on Richmond. In 1861, Lincoln succumbed to the pressure. After initial failure in Virginia, Lincoln turned to George McClellan to develop and guide Union strategy. When McClellan proved unfit, he summoned the successful manager of the western war effort, Henry Halleck, to Washington to provide strategic direction. Halleck also disappointed. He was, in Lincoln's words, merely a "first rate clerk." Frustrated by his generals' inability to bring the North's superior force to bear, Lincoln tried issuing his own strategic directions. This effort merely earned him the scorn of his generals. Finally, the emergence of U.S. Grant brought Lincoln a capable strategist who also possessed the moral courage to see the war through to final, albeit bloody, victory.

By the middle of 1864 it was clear that two cornerstones of Union strategy, the naval blockade and the advance on Richmond, could not produce victory. The blockade usefully weakened the South, but did not fatally wound the Confederacy. The advance against

Left: Burnside's assault across Antietam Creek confronted well-sited Confederate batteries on nearby hills as well as rebel defenders sheltered in quarry pits along the crest of a hill overlooking the stone Rohrbach Bridge. At the cost of many lives, he finally crossed the bridge, which became known afterwards as Burnside Bridge. (MARS)

Richmond stalled against the city's nearly impregnable fortifications and the line of the James and Appomattox rivers. It took William T. Sherman's northward march through the Carolinas and toward the rebel rear to uncover this line.

The evolution of Union strategy followed four phases: a naval blockade; a division of the Confederacy by gaining control of the Mississippi River; control of Chattanooga, Tennessee (the gateway to the Confederate heartland) followed by a drive across Georgia to split the eastern Confederacy; closing the pincers (Sherman in Atlanta, Grant before Richmond) to crush the remaining rebel armies.

CONTEST FOR THE BORDER STATES

Following the second wave of southern secession, four "neutral" states remained: Delaware, Maryland, Kentucky, and Missouri. Even though Delaware was nominally a slave-holding state, geography decreed that it would remain Union-loyal. The other three neutrals were the great prize of the early war. Together they contained about 517,000 men of military age.

After Virginia seceded, the northern limit of the Confederacy in the east was clearly marked as the line of the Potomac River. In the west, the protracted struggle for the key border states of Missouri and Kentucky created great uncertainty among southern strategists. During the war's early months, they did not know where to commit resources and where to prepare a defensive position. This paralysis greatly helped the Union cause.

Lincoln believed that Kentucky was the key. If it seceded, he worried that Missouri and Maryland would follow. This would be disaster. Neither the North nor the South wanted to enter Kentucky first. Both sides worried that a violation of Kentucky's neutrality would drive the state into the opposite camp. But in the summer of 1861, Jefferson Davis gave one of his old

"Plenty of Fighting Today": The 9th Illinois at Shiloh. Part of the Union army caught napping by Albert Sidney Johnston at Shiloh, the 9th Illinois Infantry was told: "There is going to be plenty of fighting today; there must be no cowards." Sent to reinforce the Union left south of the Peach Orchard on the first day of the battle, the regiment raced Confederates for the cover of a ravine, managed to get there first, and held their ground for 90 minutes, long enough to help save the left of the Union army. Johnston commented on the soldiers' "stubborn stand," despite heavy losses of 103 killed and 258 wounded. Founded in 1809, Abraham Lincoln was a company commander in the regiment during the Black Hawk War, so the 9th Illinois joined the president's call for a Union army immediately in 1861. A National Guard Heritage Painting by Keith Rocco. (National Guard Bureau)

friends, Major General Leonidas Polk, discretionary powers as commander in the Mississippi River Valley. Polk knew that some time a Union drive would come down the Mississippi River. The best defensive position to block such a drive was about 20 miles north of the Tennessee–Kentucky border at Columbus, Kentucky.

On September 3, 1861, Polk ordered a rebel force to occupy Columbus. This was a serious blunder. Heretofore, Kentucky had acted like a great shield protecting Tennessee and the deep south from any Federal attack. Polk's action removed the shield. Three days later, a then-obscure Union brigadier general named Grant responded by moving a force to Paducah, Kentucky. Grant acted on his own initiative because Paducah was a strategic point controlling river movement on the Ohio and Tennessee Rivers. Control of Paducah was the first link in a long chain that eventually led to Union control of the entire Mississippi River Valley.

Union and Confederate forces poured into Kentucky. Confederate sympathizers organized a new state government and proclaimed secession on November 18. It was a hollow act. Although Kentucky contributed about 25,000 men to the Confederate cause, more than three times that number served in the Union army.

Missouri contained a sizable disloyal element. Southern sympathizers controlled the Missouri militia, called the Missouri State Guard. In early 1861, a Union officer, Nathaniel Lyon, and a cagey politician, Frank Blair, Jr., collaborated to save the St. Louis armory from rebel hands. On May 10, 1861 they proceeded to disarm a nearby rebel force. Their decisive action saved Missouri for the Union.

Missouri would contribute thousands of hard-fighting men to both sides during the war. It would witness several large battles, including Wilson's Creek on August 10, 1861, and endure bitter guerrilla warfare. But the South would never seriously threaten Federal control of St. Louis and the northern half of the state. Thus, the Union flank was secure while the main advance proceeded down the Mississippi River.

Maryland too fell to Union control. Officially it would remain neutral. Like the other border states, it contributed men to both sides. The hope of recruiting more men was one of the bases for Lee's 1862 Invasion of Maryland. This hope proved ephemeral.

In sum, the Lincoln government — aided by Confederate blunder in Kentucky and Union initiative in Missouri — won the very important opening round of the war, the contest for the border states.

LEADERSHIP

In the spring of 1861 neither the North nor the South was ready to fight a war. Professional soldiers understood this fact. Civilians and politicians did not. The young northern and southern volunteers needed time to make the change from civilian to soldier. They needed time to learn how to march and to fight, and they needed to learn these things from professional soldiers. There were hardly enough professionals to do the teaching.

When the war started there were only about sixteen thousand professional, or regular, soldiers in the United States Army. Most of them were dispersed in the west where they fought against the Indians. About fifteen thousand of the regular soldiers were enlisted men. Only twenty-six of them deserted to join the Confederate Army. The rest stayed loyal to the United States. The U.S. Regulars could have been dispersed and used as cadres to train the volunteers. Instead, the Federal government blundered by keeping the existing regular units intact.

There were 1,080 army officers on active duty when the war began. Six hundred and twenty were from the North and 460 from the South. All but sixteen of the northern-born officers stayed loyal to the Union. The sixteen who left the U.S. Army were all married to southern women. Of the officers from the South, about two-thirds of them left the U.S. Army to join the Confederacy while one-third remained loyal to the Union side.

Both sides employed retired West Point graduates to help meet the huge demand for experienced military men. These proved a mixed blessing. For example, the 34-year-old George McClellan had resigned in 1857 to pursue business opportunities. Thus his knowledge of war was up to date when he returned to the army. In contrast, Leonidas Polk had graduated from West Point in 1827, gone on furlough, and decided to discard his uniform to become an Episcopal minister. Since that time he had neither studied war nor seen a battle. Yet, when "Bishop" Polk offered his services to the Confederacy, Davis made him a general and assigned him to command the defense of the Mississippi River. Polk's subsequent strategic blundering unhinged the entire Confederate defense of the west.

Foreign-trained officers also sought and were given positions of responsibility. They too proved a mixed blessing. Some showed great merit. Irish-born Patrick Cleburne served as a non-commissioned officer in the British army before emigrating to Arkansas. He developed into one of the South's outstanding combat generals. Alfred Duffié was a St. Cyr graduate and combat veteran. He came to the U.S. at war's onset and secured the rank of captain in the 2nd New York Cavalry. Duffié's impressive résumé eventually led to divisional command, yet he never exhibited any notable leadership qualities. The same could be said about many other foreign-educated officers.

Moreover, for every capable foreign-trained leader there were two or three like Louis Blenker — whose division became lost, nearly starved, and fell to looting for food during a six-week march behind friendly lines — or Alexander Schimmelfennig, who became lost in Gettysburg during his unit's rout and spent the balance of the battle hidden in a stable. Because most former German officers settled in the North, the Union forces found themselves saddled with many such men. In addition, the Lincoln administration appreciated the ability of the German officers to recruit among their fellow immigrants. Franz Sigel, a graduate of the German Military Academy, was the best known. German volunteers proudly boasted, "I fights mit Sigel." Yet, Sigel gave an unblemished record of ineptitude and defeat from Wilson's Creek in 1861 through to New Market in 1864.

In addition to military professionals, the South called upon two other sources to find leaders. Unlike the North, the South had better maintained its militia in the years before the war. They provided a trained nucleus around which were built many regiments and batteries. Even more important were the South's private military academies. The Virginia Military Institute (VMI) contributed 18 generals, 95 colonels, 65 lieutenant colonels, 110 majors, 310 captains, and 221 lieutenants to the Confederate cause. Graduates of the South Carolina Military Academy (the Citadel) and the Georgia Military Institute also served the South. Almost all of these men took part in the critical early war training programs. Even VMI students, teenagers

17 and 18 years old, gathered at a camp of instruction on the Richmond Fair Grounds in 1861 to train and drill new recruits.

Because neither the North nor the South had enough men with military education and experience, both sides employed officers who began the war wholly ignorant of all military craft. Most northern junior officers in particular knew no more about military matters than the volunteers they were supposed to teach. The system of raising units contributed to this problem.

Typically, individual state governments were responsible for raising units. Usually some prominent citizen would organize a company in his town or county. Then the recruits held an election for company captain, junior officers, and non-commissioned officers. Popularity rather than merit played a large role. Too often volunteers voted for lax officers who allowed them too much freedom as opposed to sterner task masters.

Then the newly elected captain offered his unit's service to the state governor. The companies moved to designated camps of instruction where they merged to form regiments. At this point either the entire regiment, or all of the officers, again voted for the regimental officers. A wealthy man who distributed a rum ration before the election, or a smooth-talking lawyer, stood a better chance than a poor or inarticulate budding Napoleon. Consequently, the training and combat efficiency of new units varied widely from good to very poor. However, by the end of 1861, officers had to prove their qualifications before examining boards.

The selection of generals followed a different procedure. Lincoln usually appointed West Point graduates or men who had held volunteer commissions during the Mexican War. But he knew that northern support for the war was precarious. Consequently, he followed the advice of governors and congressmen in selecting leading politicians in order to enlist a broader base of political support. Men like John Frémont, Nathaniel Banks, and Benjamin Butler held army command even though they all proved woefully inept. Jefferson Davis never faced the same acute political pressure that Lincoln faced. He never gave higher than a brigade command to a Confederate volunteer officer until that officer proved himself in battle.

Civil War soldiers expected their officers, at least up to the rank of brigadier general, to lead from the front.

Right: Intense fighting in the Union center on July 3, 1863 at the Battle of Gettysburg. (LC)

Officers paid with a lavish expenditure of blood. As one Confederate officer described it, "every atom of authority has to be purchased by a drop of your blood." Thus, attrition depleted the supply of capable officers. By 1864, Robert Lee was deliberately leaving colonels in command of brigades because he could find no qualified replacements. A year earlier, a British observer had predicted this outcome when he told a Confederate friend that the Army of Northern Virginia was magnificent, but it could not endure. "Your system feeds on itself," he said.

Neither the North nor the South developed a good system to replace losses. As battle losses mounted, the ranks thinned. Commanders had to send veterans home to recruit. If they failed to attract enough replacements the unit was disbanded. Thus, unit esprit de corps was not promoted. Moreover, northern governors welcomed the opportunity to raise new units rather than sustain existing ones. This gave them fresh opportunities to appoint officers and thereby earn favors and votes. On balance, southern regiments did better at maintaining strength and thereby retaining veteran units, but Confederate leaders also faced daunting political problems. Early in the war, units were reorganized so that brigades comprised regiments from the same state. There was the expectation that same-state officers would command these brigades regardless of military capacity. When Georgian James Longstreet examined the command roster of the newly reorganized army, he muttered, "too much Virginia."

The war showed that men lacking pre-war military training and experience performed less well as generals that those who had the benefit of some previous connection with the military. There were notable exceptions such as the southern generals Nathan Bedford Forrest, John B. Gordon, and Wade Hampton. Political appointees usually were real hindrances, although again there were exceptions such as Union generals John Logan and Frank Blair, Jr.

TACTICAL COMBAT IN THE CIVIL WAR

The typical Civil War battle took place in wooded terrain at extremely close range. Cavalry contributed little on the battlefield, artillery was decidedly a supporting arm. It was the rival infantry who decided the day. Combat centered around the infantry firefight.

This was an affair of opposing lines — both sides deployed in loose, two-deep formation — blazing away at one another until one or both wavered and withdrew. It was a time, recalled one officer, "when all consideration for tactics is lost." In a Civil War firefight there was no substitute for raw courage.

In past wars, infantry wielding smoothbore muskets had little chance of hitting an enemy soldier standing 200 yards away. Civil War soldiers carried improved weapons. A French captain named Minié developed a conical bullet with a tapered hollow, the base of which was fitted with a small iron cap. When a soldier squeezed the trigger the force of the explosion drove the cap into the hollow, thereby expanding the bullet so that it engaged the rifling tightly. This reduced the windage, the difference between the bullet's and the gun-bore's diameter. Minié's bullet appeared in 1849. With it, a trained rifleman on a proving ground could hit a man-sized target at 500 yards at least half the time. A decade of improvement gave Civil War marksmen a deadly weapon capable of killing at a heretofore unsurpassed distance.

However, three factors prevented soldiers from killing every enemy encountered. First, the accuracy a tester achieved on the firing range was very different from that achieved when the shooter was himself under fire. Secondly, the Civil War-era weapons had low muzzle velocity compared to modern weapons. This meant a

Below: Front-line positions were often hastily constructed mazes of trenches and burrows. This rabbit warren was the forward position of Major General John Logan's division investing Vicksburg in 1863. Although the Confederates no longer had artillery to defend the city with, sharpshooters were in wait behind a strong breastwork near the brow of the hill. (M)

Right: A week after the Battle of Chattanooga, which Grant had overseen from afar, he went to view the site of the "Battle Above the Clouds" from Lookout Mountain itself. Hooker had waved the Stars and Stripes from the mountain peak to signify his victory, and for a long time afterwards the mountain was a well-visited tourist spot. Grant was, unusually, wearing a sword, but as usual he was smoking a cigar. With him, left to right, were General John.A. Rawlins, General Webster, Colonel Clark B. Lagow, and Colonel William S. Hillyer. Seated by the path farther up the hill is an orderly. (M)

soldier had to fire high to reach a distant target, in effect lobbing his shot at his foe. This required precise assessment of range, and few shooters had that ability. Lastly, regardless of theoretical ranges, since most battles occurred in wooded, uneven terrain, sighting ranges were often less than 100 yards. This greatly reduced the tactical impact of Captain Minié's invention.

Shoulder arms, whether smoothbore or rifled, were by far the war's biggest combat killers. Medical statistics for the whole war showed that bullets caused 94 percent of all wounds with artillery fire responsible for most of the rest. At Cold Harbor (June 3, 1864), General Lee heard the sounds of his artillery opening fire against the charging Union soldiers. Then came the tearing sound of massed infantry fire. He remarked, "It is that that kills men."

In theory, the bayonet was an even more lethal killer. Experienced Mexican War officers believed that a spirited bayonet charge could win the day every time. They acquired this belief for some reasons that did not apply to the Civil War. A close-order bayonet charge presented a terrifying sight to those on the receiving end. In the overwhelming number of cases a defender would not wait to feel a bayonet rammed home but rather would flee. Officers did not understand that a bayonet charge was formidable because of the psychological stress it placed upon the defender. In the Mexican War, the Mexican defenders were generally low-morale troops. Many U.S. officers had seen the Mexican infantry run

from their trenches when the American infantry pressed home a bayonet charge. They expected the same to occur in the Civil War. Consequently, at the beginning of the war they became obsessed with the physical aspects of bayonet drill without realizing that the usefulness of the drill was to teach the recruit confidence and discipline. During the war, edged weapons produced only 0.4 percent of all casualties.

The standard tactical manuals used by both sides were inappropriate to the emerging conditions of the Civil War battlefield. The manuals carefully prescribed three different movement paces: common time at 70 yards per minute; quick time at 86 yards per minute; double quick time at 109 yards per minute. Conscientious officers drilled their men to use these three paces only to find that in combat they were irrelevant. Likewise, drill manuals specified with great detail frontages, intervals, and the like. But on the battlefield, formal shoulder to shoulder maneuvering was as irrelevant as parade ground pacing. To take just one example among hundreds: at Shiloh in April 1862, when the 30th Indiana received fire for the first time, the entire regiment "treed" itself with the men scattering to take shelter behind tree trunks.

This scattering for shelter was not the result of lack of drill or lack of experience. Rather, veteran units quickly learned how to disperse to take advantage of all available cover while retaining sufficient cohesion to respond to their officers' orders. But the drill

manuals never reflected such tactical realities. Consequently, close-order bayonet assaults against waiting lines of equally determined defenders produced the staggering casualties characteristic of offensive action during the early part of the Civil War. Brave men could and did pierce the enemy position, but at terrible cost. John Bell Hood's charge at Gaines's Mill on June 27, 1862, set the offensive tone for Lee's Army of Northern Virginia. One in four participants in the two assault brigades fell. In the 4th Texas, Hood's old regiment, all the field officers were killed or wounded. This battle, the first major engagement of the Seven Days' Campaign, foreshadowed what was to come. Lee's relentless assaults cost the South some 20,141 irreplaceable casualties during the Seven Days' Campaign.

Over time, individual officers and units acquired valuable combat experience and devised tactical innovations. Yet it remains striking how neither the North nor the South had a system to circulate tactical lessons. Instead, officers continued to train the soldiers with the same tactics used when the war began and to employ the same formations. From the beginning to the end of the open battle phase of the war, in other words before the comprehensive use of fieldworks, there was little tactical evolution despite the fact that the tactical challenge remained unchanged. No one figured out how to maintain command and control in wooded terrain that typified Civil War battlefields. Generals continued to try to maneuver long battle lines through thick woods without using tactical reconnaissance. The situation reached a terrible climax in Virginia in 1864 when two utterly determined, bloody-minded commanders — Lee and Grant — opposed each other. Given the paucity of tactical thinking, all the advantages went to the defender. The advent of trench warfare in 1864 accelerated this trend.

By the end of 1863 there was sufficient evidence to show a discriminating onlooker that the era of open battle was giving way to a new kind of warfare in which the defenders fought exclusively from behind fieldworks and fortifications. In the west, the Army of the Cumberland did not entrench before the Confederate attack at Stones River in December 1862. It preferred fighting in the traditional "stand up" style. After the first day of its next battle, along Chickamauga Creek in September 1863, it spent the night felling trees and preparing a long line of breastworks. In the east,

neither side prepared extensive fieldworks during the July 1863 Battle of Gettysburg. Less than five months later, Lee's army responded to a Federal advance by immediately building an imposing line of works along Mine Run. It then challenged Meade's army to attack, an assault the Union general wisely declined to make. By the spring of 1864, western and eastern armies alike immediately constructed works whenever they were in the enemy's presence.

A handful of forward-thinking officers tried to develop assault tactics appropriate to the new conditions. The simplest, most effective was to order the men to charge with uncapped weapons so they could not stop to shoot during the advance. This compelled the soldier to charge through the lethal zone more quickly before the build-up of losses stopped him. Another alternative, used most famously by the brilliant Union officer, Emory Upton, at Spotsylvania in May 1864, was to form a deep but narrow assault column. Only the

leading rank carried rifles ready to fire. Upton's first assault on May 10 featured twelve regiments formed in four lines of three regiments each. The charge overran the Confederate works but eventually failed due to lack of support from adjacent units. Two days later, an entire corps employed Upton's formation with the leading division advancing in a solid rectangle some forty ranks deep. The subsequent breakthrough led to the bitter fighting at the Bloody Angle.

Such breakthroughs were the exception during the late war. Veteran soldiers, if not their generals, understood the futility of charging enemy works. They would still perform their duty, by their own lights, by rising from their trenches and advancing. Upon receiving first fire, they halted and lay down. Even as late as the Siege of Petersburg green troops did not understand the wisdom of such behavior. In June 1864, the 1st Maine Heavy Artillery, with 950 men serving as infantry, charged the rebel works and lost 115 killed,

489 wounded, and 23 missing within 10 minutes. A notable late war exception to the veterans' pronounced reluctance to charge fortifications occurred at the Battle of Franklin (November 30, 1864). Hood had recently impugned the courage of his army. They responded with suicidal courage in their attack against the Union works. Of 26,897 rebels engaged, 6,252 were lost including five generals killed.

ARTILLERY DOCTRINE AND ORGANIZATION

American officers had learned artillery theory at West Point from Professor Dennis Hart Mahan. Had they been about to refight the Napoleonic wars, these officers would have been well prepared. Mahan promoted the deployment of artillery in such a manner as to silence the enemy guns and pave the way for the infantry assault. This was reasonable enough as far as it went. Where Mahan went astray was in his advice to have cannon accompany the assault infantry by positioning some guns on the infantry flanks and a two-gun

section 100 paces ahead of each infantry column. In an era where infantry employed rifled shoulder arms, this was unworkable.

Fortunately for the Federal cause, in 1858 an officers' board revised artillery instruction. The resultant manual, *Instruction for Field Artillery*, was generally excellent and greatly contributed to the performance of Union artillery. Still it had some serious flaws. It recommended deployment intervals that packed a six-gun battery into a target box 82 yards wide by 47 yards deep. This failed to take account of the accuracy of rifled artillery with a maximum effective range of 2,500 yards and the improvement in explosives. Consequently, counter-battery fire could accurately bombard a battery-sized target box of regulation dimensions. Gunners on both sides quickly learned to ignore the recommended deployment intervals. Instead, they moved vulnerable limbers, caissons, and teams into nearby woodlots, reverse slopes, and small ravines.

The most important component of effective artillery fire was a good firing position, which meant a good field of fire. If necessary, gunners sacrificed defensive security to obtain a better field of fire. Artillery proved most effective firing in enfilade or at the oblique. Skilled gunners sought battlefield positions from where they could deliver such fire. Battle accounts are full of reports of aggressive battery commanders deploying in an exposed position in order to bring their guns to bear. Much depended upon a battery commander's sense of ground. Ideally, his position was far enough away from covered terrain that might conceal lurking enemy marksmen and had access to an escape route should things go badly.

At war's onset, both sides assigned batteries to individual brigades. This proved a poor tactical choice. Infantry generals concentrated on the regimental firefights and often overlooked their batteries. This left

Above: Sherman and his staff. On the March to the Sea, he was described by one of his officers thus: "[In the early hours he would be] poking around the camp fire … bare feet in slippers, red flannel drawers … woollen shirt, old dressing gown with blue cloth (half cloak) cape." After rising at 3:30 in the morning he would often cat nap beside the line of march. He never wore boots, always low-cut shoes with only one spur. In this photograph with the major generals who accompanied him through Georgia and then north through the Carolinas, Sherman is wearing uniform, but is still more untidy than any of his staff. Left to right: Oliver Otis Howard, John Alexander Logan, William B. Hazen, William Sherman, Jeff C. Davis, Henry Warner Slocum, and Joseph Anthony Mower. (LC)

Left: Longstreet's assault against Fort Sanders on November 29, 1863 confronted wire entanglements and a steep-sided ditch in front of the fort. The botched effort cost the Confederates over 800 men. (WP)

batteries to deploy wherever chance dictated that the accompanying infantry deploy. Forced into a location with restricted field of fire, the battery would be exposed to concealed enemy infantry. If adjacent or supporting friendly infantry retired or broke, the battery could be taken in flank or rear before the gunners knew what had happened.

Lee's Army of Northern Virginia was the first major organization to address this problem. Officers reorganized the batteries into artillery battalions, generally with four batteries each, and also created corps and army reserve batteries. Highly qualified artillery officers commanded the artillery battalions. This modern practice gave Lee and his lieutenants the ability to mass their artillery fire better than the old practice of dispersing batteries. The Army of the Potomac followed suit by organizing its artillery into battalions to support each corps along with an army reserve. Artillerists in the western armies were slow to copy this practice. Not until the winter of 1863—4 did the Confederate Army of Tennessee abandon the practice of assigning batteries to infantry brigades.

Pre-war artillery doctrine, as described by Mahan, decreed that artillery support the other arms by "keeping the enemy from approaching too near" and by silencing the opposing artillery so that the infantry could advance. Throughout the war, artillery proved

more useful in the defense than in the attack. An efficient battery, firing at the rate of two to three rounds per minute, sent shot and shell at long range and then switched to the devastating canister rounds — tins filled with musket balls — as opposing infantry came closer. A canister round fired from a 12-pdr. Napoleon sent out a 20-yard wide swath of flying lead balls. Typically fired at ranges of 300 yards and closer, these shotgun-like blasts inflicted terrible losses. Artillerists figured that a battery should be able to defend its own front by employing canister fire. In practice, because infantry often enjoyed partially or completely concealed approaches through the woods, determined infantry could overrun a battery. Frequently the attackers shot down the battery horses, making it impossible for the gunners to withdraw their guns.

Offensively, the concept of counter-battery fire worked better in theory than in practice. There were several technical reasons for this. Civil War artillery fire was line of sight fire; indirect fire was a development that came in the future. Range-finding depended upon the human eye. Lastly, the explosive charges contained within the artillery shell were relatively small. Still, rifled cannon could and did achieve impressive long-range accuracy. However, they seldom drove opposing gunners from their position. Furthermore, supporting artillery had to cease fire when friendly infantry drew near the enemy. In other words, just when the charging infantry most needed help, the friendly guns stopped providing that support. Because of the long killing range of rifled muskets, artillery seldom could move forward in the classic horse artillery style to give close-range fire support. Lastly, because so many battles took place in wooded terrain, artillery often did not have adequate fields of fire. Once infantry began to entrench routinely, offensive artillery proved even less useful. Artillery fire simply lacked the explosive capacity to knock down breastworks or bury earthworks.

THE ROLE OF CAVALRY

Before the Civil War, the United States army possessed only a slight tradition of mounted combat. America's leading pre-war thinker, Mahan, wrote in a widely read tactics book that by itself, cavalry could accomplish little. Still, West Pointers had also studied the Napoleonic tradition of massed saber charges and found the image hard to discard. Successful charges against infantry came about when the infantry was already wavering due to other causes. One of the most famous occurred early in the war at First Bull Run (July 21, 1861) when Jeb Stuart's 1st Virginia charged the 11th New York (Fire Zouaves). The Zouaves routed at first sight of the advancing cavalry. Battlefield reality soon made a mounted cavalry charge against formed infantry a rare occurrence. The gallant try of the 5th U.S. Cavalry at Gaines's Mill (June 27, 1862) demonstrated the futility of cavalry charges against rifle-armed infantry. Six of the seven Union officers were hit and the charge quickly dissolved into a stampede of fear-stricken, riderless horses.

At the war's onset, the South enjoyed a considerable cavalry advantage over the North. This was most true in the east where relatively few Union soldiers had sufficient equestrian skills. Here the Confederate cavalry quickly asserted a psychological edge that persisted until the spring of 1863. The emergence of capable Federal cavalry leaders and the experience gained from practice brought the Union cavalry to near parity by the summer of 1863. Thereafter, Lee's cavalry physically weakened while the arrival of Phil Sheridan energized the Army of the Potomac's mounted arm. By mid–1864, Union troopers in the east clearly held the advantage. Sheridan molded them into a dominant battlefield weapon that spearheaded the victory at the Third Battle of Winchester (September 19, 1864) and again at Five Forks (April 30 to May 1 1865).

In the more rural west, both sides benefitted from tapping experienced riders. Organizational problems — as in the east, the dispersal of troopers for courier and escort duty — and the lack of outstanding leaders inhibited the western Union cavalry. Consequently, rebel cavalry led by such dashing leaders as Earl Van Dorn, Joseph Wheeler and, most especially, Nathan Bedford Forrest, generally bested their mounted foes. Not until the latter stages of the war in the west did the Union cavalry equal the Confederate mounted force. James Wilson assembled a 12,500-man force of cavalry and mounted infantry in northwest Alabama in February 1865. The ensuing Selma Campaign featured a combination of mobility and firepower that foreshadowed the mechanized tactics of the Second World War.

FOREIGN INVOLVEMENT

In 1860, the young and brash United States was growing into a power that threatened the economic dominance of western Europe. Moreover, England had no particular affection for its rebellious former colonies. Thus, many European statesmen greeted the apparent implosion of a disliked rival with some satisfaction.

The Union naval blockade became a critical foreign policy issue. European powers (but not the United States) had signed a legal agreement stating that to be binding, blockades had to be maintained by forces strong enough to prevent access. This condition manifestly did not prevail in 1861. Blockade runners easily passed through the U.S. Navy's loose cordon. Confederate diplomats sought to persuade Great Britain that the blockade was therefore illegal. Thus, the Royal Navy should intervene to protect British trade with the South.

Prime Minister Palmerston's government was too cagey to become embroiled in a war on mere legal pretext. Then, on November 8, 1861, a U.S. warship stopped the British mail steamer *Trent*, removed two Confederate diplomats, James Mason and John Slidell, and sent them to prison in Boston. This outrage provoked war fever in England. Wisely, the Lincoln Administration released the diplomats and so averted hostilities.

Thereafter, British merchants enjoyed the benefits of neutrality. They maintained a very lucrative blockade-running trade with the South. When Confederate raiding ships drove American merchantmen

Above: Fort Morgan, at Mobile Point on the eastern side of Mobile Bay, was a strong, well-defended fortress, originally built as part of the United States coast defenses. Its garrison formed part of the ring of defenses round Mobile Bay, which all proved in vain in August 1864 as Admiral Farragut damned the torpedoes and proceeded to bombard the Bay's forts. After enduring two weeks of continuous battering, and firing back with its 60 guns, Fort Morgan surrendered. (M)

from the seas, British merchantmen happily picked up the trade. Crop failures in western Europe in 1860—2 compelled the import of American grain and flour. Union states doubled their grain export, supplying nearly half of British imports, and sent much of this grain aboard British merchantmen.

In spite of the economic advantages of neutrality, the Palmerston regime came close to intervention in the late summer of 1862. It was the time of greatest British labor unrest caused by unemployed textile workers suffering from the absence of southern cotton. Lee had just driven the Yankees out of Virginia and stood poised to invade Maryland. In the western theater, Bragg was beginning his move north into Kentucky. Foreign Minister Lord Russell predicted to Palmerston that in the next month "the hour will be ripe for the Cabinet" to discuss intervention. Lee's subsequent defeat at Antietam and Bragg's retreat from Kentucky ended all serious talk of intervention for the remainder of the war.

Just as British merchants took advantage of American difficulties, so Louis Napoleon of France sought to benefit from American internal preoccupation. He sent French soldiers to Mexico to overthrow Mexico's government and establish the Hapsburg Archduke Ferdinand Maximilian as Emperor of Mexico. Napoleon's motive related to the shifting alliances and balance of power in Europe. In the event, 35,000 French soldiers captured Mexico City in June 1863. This attracted Lincoln's attention. He was determined to assert the Monroe Doctrine and accordingly, after Grant captured Vicksburg in July 1863, ordered forces to move into Texas as a counterpoise to the French presence in Mexico. Again, when the 1864 campaign

season began, Lincoln ordered resources diverted to Texas to check the French. Thereafter, Napoleon lost interest in Mexico.

The rest of the world, excepting Canada, watched the American Civil War unfold either with indifference or, like Russia, supported the North diplomatically because of the slavery issue. Some 50,000 Canadians walked south over the border to enlist in the Union army. Some sought adventure, most were attracted by the lure of the recruiter's bounty payment.

THE CIVIL WAR'S LEGACY

Passion about the American Civil War remains high in America today. The city of Vicksburg, which surrendered to Grant on July 4, 1863, refused to observe the national July 4 Independence Day celebration for decades after the event. It took World War Two to change Vicksburg's attitude. Even today, many southerners do not use the term Civil War to describe the conflict. Rather, it is "The War Between the States" or, particularly among the older generations, "The War for Southern Independence." Academic and popular interest is such that each year witnesses numerous books dissecting the people and events of that terrible conflict. The questions of how the North won and why the South lost have of themselves produced a veritable cottage industry of publications.

For the United States, the most obvious legacy of the war relates to race relations. The great tragedy of Lincoln's untimely death was its effect on national attitudes. Lincoln might have been able to heal the war's wounds. His assassination passed that responsibility to a vindictive group of radical politicians who took great delight in extracting several more pounds of flesh from the weakened South. In response, southern nationalism flourished. A group like the Ku Klux Klan, founded originally as a quasi-veterans organization, changed into an ugly and murderous anti-black terrorist organization. Since the war, only slowly and with great difficulty has the nation come to grips with its racism.

The other major legacy of the war stems from the North's March 3, 1863 Enrollment Act. Late in 1862, Union governors found that they could no longer raise enough troops to meet the war's demands. Congress passed the Enrollment Act, a law that made able-bodied males between 20 and 45 years of age liable for national service. The law provoked great unrest, including the New York City Draft Riots (July 13—16, 1863). It also marked a sea change in American history. It firmly established the principle that every citizen has the obligation to defend the nation and that the Federal government can impose that obligation without mediation of the states. Implicitly, the act recognized that the nation's historic reliance on militia and volunteers was inadequate to fight a modern, total war.

WHY THE SOUTH LOST

The American Civil War was a modern war. Modern war demands centralized efficiency (at odds with the South's adherence to states' rights) and a subordination of everything to the war effort. When the war began in 1861, no one could anticipate all of this. But the North had sufficient resources to buffer against misstep and muddle. The South's margin for error was wafer thin. The genius of Robert E. Lee, his mastery of the art of defensive warfare, staved off defeat for four long years. Once Lincoln found the right men to lead the Federal armies, with Grant at the apex of command, the North brought to bear a decisive superiority in manpower and economic resources.

A massive rebuilding and reconstruction program was needed in the South after the war. Once proud cities lay in tatters. Below: Atlanta's large and gracious railroad depot was deliberately torn down by Sherman on his March to the Sea. Having evacuated the civilian population, he needed to safeguard himself from attack from behind, so he ensured that the city's essential services were destroyed. The railroad and its buildings were a natural target for his men. (M)

Top to bottom: Pierre Beauregard (NA),
Braxton Bragg (LC), John Breckinridge (LC),
Simon Buckner, Patrick Cleburne, and
Jefferson Davis (M).

BEAUREGARD, Pierre Gustave Toutant
Born New Orleans, Louisiana, May 28, 1818.
Graduated West Point (1838) and distinguished himself in several battles of the Mexican War, including Veracruz (March 1847), Cerro Gordo (April 1847), Contreras (Aug 1847) and the assault on Mexico City (Sept 1847). Appointed superintendent of West Point (Jan 1861) but held the post less than a week before resigning to become brigadier general in the Confederate army. Directed the bombardment of Fort Sumter (April 1861), one of the heroes of the day at First Bull Run (July 1861), and assumed command at Shiloh (April 1862) when A.S. Johnston was killed. Forced to turn his command over to Bragg due to ill health, he assumed command of coastal defenses and repulsed numerous Union assaults, notably at Charleston. Defeated Butler's Army of the James at Drewry's Bluff (May 1864) and constructed the defenses around Richmond and Petersburg that Lee would use. Served with Johnston in the Carolinas and surrendered April 1865. Thereafter he was a railroad president and commissioner of public works in New Orleans. Died in New Orleans, Feb 20, 1893. A capable officer hampered by grandiose ideas of his own importance.

BRAGG, Braxton Born Warrenton, North Carolina, March 22, 1817. Graduated West Point (1837) and served in the Seminole War and the Mexican War, where he played a decisive role in the victory at Buena Vista (Feb 1847). Appointed brigadier general in the Confederate army (Feb 1861), promoted major general (Jan 1862), fought at Shiloh (April 1862) and promoted full general shortly after. Commander, Army of Mississippi (renamed Army of Tennessee, Nov 1862), he led invasion of Kentucky but withdrew after Perryville (Oct 1862), forced to withdraw again after Stones River (Dec 1862–Jan 1863), he was out-manoeuvred by Rosecrans and lost Chattanooga. Won victory at Chickamauga (Sept 1863) and established siege of Chattanooga, but routed by Grant (Nov 1863) and removed from command. Appointed military advisor to his friend, President Davis, and was with Johnston when he surrendered to Sherman (April 1865). Returned to civil engineering after the war and died, Galveston, Texas, Sept 27, 1876. Indecisive and a poor commander, he lost the loyalty of nearly all his subordinates, who actively campaigned against him. He would have been removed from command

long before he was if not for the personal friendship and support of Davis.

BRECKENRIDGE, John Cabell Born Jan 21, 1821, Lexington, Kentucky, a lawyer who served briefly in the Mexican War, he was U.S. congressman (1851–55), vice president (1857–61), a losing presidential candidate (1860) and briefly a U.S. senator before accepting commission as brigadier general in Confederate army. Led the reserve at Shiloh (April 1862), oversaw defenses at Vicksburg and Port Hudson, fought at Stones River (Dec 62–Jan 63), Jackson (May 1863), Chickamauga (Sept 1863), Chattanooga (Nov 1863), won distinguished victory at New Market (May 1864), fought at Cold Harbor (June 1864) and with Early during Washington raid. Appointed Confederate secretary of state (Feb 1865), he fled to Cuba and England, returning after 1868 to resume his law practice. Died Lexington, Kentucky, May 17, 1875. Breckenridge was one of the few politicians on either side who proved able as a military commander.

BUCKNER, Simon Bolivar Born Kentucky, 1823, graduated West Point (1844), served in Mexican War and taught at West Point. Organized Kentucky State Guard (1860) then joined Confederate army as brigadier general. Surrendered Fort Donelson to his old friend Grant (Feb 1862), fought at Perryville and Chickamauga, critical of Bragg so sent with Longstreet to siege of Knoxville, later transferred to Trans-Mississippi under Kirby Smith. A pallbearer at Grant's funeral, he entered politics, governor of Kentucky, and Democrat vice-presidential candidate (1896). Died 1914. Buckner was a solid divisional and corps commander.

CLEBURNE, Patrick Ronayne Born March 17, 1828, in County Cork, Ireland. Served as officer in the British army for several years before emigrating to America to become a druggist and property attorney. Brigadier general, he fought at Shiloh (April 1862) and Corinth (Oct 1862) and was wounded at Richmond, Kentucky and at Perryville (Oct 1862), division commander at Stones River (Dec 62–Jan 63) and Chickamauga (Sept 1863), covered the retreat from Chattanooga (Nov 1863). He proposed that the Confederate government should temporarily free slaves in order to fight in the army. The proposal was rejected. He was promoted corps commander just before the

battle of Franklin, where he was the most senior of six generals killed, on Nov 30, 1864. One of the most popular of Confederate division commanders, Cleburne proved himself fully capable of higher command.

DAVIS, Jefferson Born June 3, 1808, in southwest Kentucky. Graduated West Point 1828 and saw active service in the Black Hawk War (1832). Entered Congress 1845 but resigned to fight in the Mexican War (1846–8), playing a distinguished and heroic role at Monterrey (Sept 1846) and Buena Vista (Feb 1847). Elected senator for Mississippi (1848) and served as able and innovative secretary of war under President Franklin Pierce (1853–7). Re-entered Senate 1857, but resigned (Jan 1861) to side with secessionists. Unanimously chosen as President of the Confederate States of America at the Montgomery convention (Feb 1861) though he accepted with reluctance. A handsome and intelligent man, and gifted orator, he played a major part in holding the Confederacy together throughout the war, though ill-health often made him seem cold and remote. He was prepared to let his most gifted generals, such as Lee, get on with the job, but his military background often led him to interfere with the plans of other generals, and friendship with Bragg and personal antipathy to Joseph Johnston often led him to make unpopular and unfortunate decisions in terms of command. Fled Richmond with his government (April 1865), unable to accept defeat, he was captured at Irwinville, Georgia (May 10, 1865). After two years of imprisonment he was released on bail (May 1867) and the case against him was quietly dropped, but he never regained his U.S. citizenship. Died at Beauvoir on the Gulf Coast, Dec 6, 1889. Though probably the best person for the Confederate Presidency, he lacked the subtlety and flexibility of a Lincoln.

EARLY, Jubal Anderson Born Virginia 1816, graduated West Point (1837) and fought in the Mexican War before taking up law and politics. He voted against secession but nevertheless joined the Confederate army. Led brigades at First Bull Run (July 1861), Williamsburg (May 1862) and Second Bull Run (Aug 1862). Given division command under Ewell at Antietam (Sept 1862), Fredericksburg (Dec 1862), Chancellorsville (May 1863) and Gettysburg (July 1863) where he was on the left wing of the Confederate army that failed to take Culp's Hill on

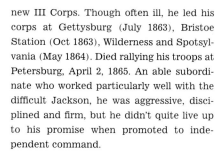

Top to bottom: Jubal Early, Richard Ewell, Nathan Forrest, William Hardee, A. P. Hill, (M) and John Hood (NA).

Jackson standing "like a stone wall" at First Bull Run. (Wilson)

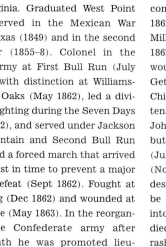

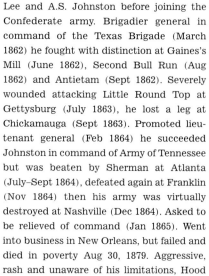

the first day. He took temporary control of Hill's corps at Spotsylvania, and of Ewell's corps at Cold Harbor (May–June 1864). Sent to command in the Shenandoah Valley he led raid on Washington and then suffered a series of defeats by Sheridan culminating at Cedar Creek (Oct 1864). In March 1865 he was removed from command. After the war he led the feud against Longstreet until his death in 1894. Always irascible and eager to find other people to blame for his failings, he was a fiery subordinate who proved unsuited to command.

EWELL, Richard Stoddert Born Washington D.C., Feb 8, 1817. Graduated West Point (1840), served in the Mexican War then went on to fight Apaches. Despite being a Unionist, he joined the Confederate army and commanded a brigade at First Bull Run (July 1861). Played a key role in several of Jackson's victories in the Shenandoah Valley (May–June 1862) and in the Seven Days (June–July 1862). Lost a leg at Groveton (Aug 1862) but returned to duty after Jackson's death as lieutenant general commanding his corps. Fought without much distinction at Gettysburg (July 1863) and at the Wilderness and Spotsylvania (May 1864) before ill health forced him to hand over command to Early. After the war he retired to Maury County, Tennessee and died there on Jan 25, 1872. Though a resourceful and intelligent commander, his physical condition should never have allowed him to resume active command.

FORREST, Nathan Bedford Born July 13, 1821, near Chapel Hill, Tennessee. Self-educated, he worked in various jobs acquiring a fortune as a slave dealer and cotton farmer. Volunteered as a private (April 1861), he raised his own cavalry regiment and became its lieutenant colonel (Aug 1861). Led his men in a daring escape from Fort Donelson before its surrender (Feb 1862) and won distinction for bravery at Shiloh (April 1862). Commanding a cavalry brigade under Bragg he led a series of daring raids behind Union lines, capturing a Union cavalry brigade near Rome, Georgia (April 1863). Fought at Chickamauga (Sept 1863). At capture of Fort Pillow (April 1864) he was blamed for the massacre of black troops attempting to surrender. Defeated a superior force at Brice's Cross Roads (June 1864), commanded the cavalry on Hood's Nashville campaign and fought a brilliant rear guard

action after the defeat at Nashville (Dec 1864). Promoted lieutenant general (Feb 1865), he was defeated in the last major action of the war at Selma, Alabama (April 1865) and surrendered at Gainesville (May 9, 1865). A plantation owner and railroad president after the war, he founded and became Grand Wizard of the Ku Klux Klan. Died Oct 29, 1877, in Memphis, Tennessee. Without any military training, Forrest was one of the few authentic military geniuses produced by the war, though his brilliant reputation was stained by instances of brutality, especially against blacks.

HARDEE, William Joseph Born near Savannah, Georgia, Oct 12, 1815. Graduated West Point (1838) and served in Second Seminole War and Mexican War, published the standard manual on *Rifle and Light Infantry Tactics* (1855), commandant of West Point (1856). Raised Hardee's Brigade in Arkansas and fought at Shiloh (April 1862), Perryville (Oct 1862), Stones River (Dec 62–Jan 63). Promoted lieutenant general Oct 1862, commanded left flank at Chattanooga (Nov 1863) and temporarily replaced Bragg as commander, Army of Tennessee (Dec 1863). Corps commander during Atlanta campaign but asked to be relieved when Hood took command. Transferred to South Carolina he abandoned both Savannah and Charleston to Sherman before surrendering with Johnston (April 1865). Retired to Selma, Alabama and died Nov 6, 1873, at Wytheville, Virginia. His nickname, "Old Reliable", describes his abilities. He was respected rather than loved by his men.

HILL, Ambrose Powell Born Nov 9, 1825, Culpeper, Virginia. Graduated West Point (1847) and served in the Mexican War (1847–8), in Texas (1849) and in the second Seminole War (1855–8). Colonel in the Confederate army at First Bull Run (July 1861), served with distinction at Williamsburg and Fair Oaks (May 1862), led a division in heavy fighting during the Seven Days (June–July 1862), and served under Jackson at Cedar Mountain and Second Bull Run (Aug 1862). Led a forced march that arrived at Antietam just in time to prevent a major Confederate defeat (Sept 1862). Fought at Fredericksburg (Dec 1862) and wounded at Chancellorsville (May 1863). In the reorganization of the Confederate army after Jackson's death he was promoted lieutenant general and given command of the

new III Corps. Though often ill, he led his corps at Gettysburg (July 1863), Bristoe Station (Oct 1863), Wilderness and Spotsylvania (May 1864). Died rallying his troops at Petersburg, April 2, 1865. An able subordinate who worked particularly well with the difficult Jackson, he was aggressive, disciplined and firm, but he didn't quite live up to his promise when promoted to independent command.

HILL, Daniel Harvey Born July 12, 1821, York District, South Carolina. Graduated West Point (1842) and served with distinction in Mexican War. Professor of mathematics, Washington College (1849), superintendent, North Carolina Military Institute (1859). Fought at Big Bethel (June 1861) and won rapid promotion. Held South Mountain passes against long odds (Sept 1862) and involved in heavy fighting at Antietam (Sept 1862) and Fredericksburg (Dec 1862). Corps commander under Bragg at Chickamauga (Sept 1863) and largely responsible for Bragg being removed from command after Chattanooga (Nov 1863). Unpopular with Davis, he was himself removed from command until final months of the war. Involved in publishing, president University of Arkansas (1877–84), president Georgia Military College (1885–9). Died Charlotte, North Carolina, Sept 24, 1889. A courageous, energetic and talented commander, his career was blighted by political opposition.

HOOD, John Bell Born Owingsville, Kentucky, June 1, 1831. Graduated West Point (1853) and saw service in Texas under Lee and A.S. Johnston before joining the Confederate army. Brigadier general in command of the Texas Brigade (March 1862) he fought with distinction at Gaines's Mill (June 1862), Second Bull Run (Aug 1862) and Antietam (Sept 1862). Severely wounded attacking Little Round Top at Gettysburg (July 1863), he lost a leg at Chickamauga (Sept 1863). Promoted lieutenant general (Feb 1864) he succeeded Johnston in command of Army of Tennessee but was beaten by Sherman at Atlanta (July–Sept 1864), defeated again at Franklin (Nov 1864) then his army was virtually destroyed at Nashville (Dec 1864). Asked to be relieved of command (Jan 1865). Went into business in New Orleans, but failed and died in poverty Aug 30, 1879. Aggressive, rash and unaware of his limitations, Hood was out of his depth as an army commander.

Top to bottom:
Daniel Hill,
Thomas Jackson,
Albert Johnston,
Joseph Johnston, and
Robert E. Lee. (M)

JACKSON, Thomas Jonathan Born Clarksburg, Virginia, Jan 21, 1824. Graduated West Point 1846 and served with distinction at Veracruz (March 1847), Cerro Gordo (April 1847) and Chapultepec (Sept 1847), where he was brevetted major. Professor of artillery tactics and natural philosophy at Virginia Military Institute (1851–61), he was commissioned colonel of Confederate volunteers (April 1861) and promoted brigadier general in June. His defense of Henry Hill, which prevented Confederate defeat at First Bull Run (July 1861) won him the nickname "Stonewall". In the Shenandoah Valley (Nov 1861 to June 1862) he fought a masterful campaign against superior forces, gaining a reputation for rapid marches and unexpected attacks which brought victories at Front Royal, Winchester, Cross Keys and Port Republic (May–June 1862). His efforts during the Seven Days (June–July 1862) were lacklustre, but he was again brilliant in the campaign against Pope leading to the victory at Second Bull Run (Aug 1862), and fought with distinction at Antietam (Sept 1862) and Fredericksburg (Dec 1862). Promoted lieutenant general and given command of II Corps, Oct 1862. He led a brilliant flanking maneuver that contributed to the defeat of Hooker at Chancellorsville (May 1863) but in the confusion was wounded by his own men and died of wounds and pneumonia May 10, 1863, at Guinea Station, Virginia. An eccentric and strict disciplinarian, he worked his men hard but was idolized by them for bringing victories. Though unpredictable, he played a significant part in Lee's success in the early part of the War.

JOHNSTON, Albert Sidney Born Feb 2, 1803, Washington, Kentucky. Graduated West Point (1826), fought in Black Hawk War (1832), fought for Texas against Mexico (1836), secretary of war, Republic of Texas (1838), fought in Mexican War (1846), commander of the Mormon Expedition (1857–8). Second ranking Confederate general. Raised Army of Mississippi, and placed in command of too extensive Western department. Killed in action at Shiloh, April 6, 1862. Jefferson Davis considered him the South's ablest general. His death early in war makes it impossible to assess his ability.

JOHNSTON, Joseph Eggleston Born near Farmville, Virginia, Feb 3, 1807. Graduated West Point (1829), he served against the Seminoles (1836 and 1838), in the Mexican War, and in the Mormon Expedition (1857–8). Appointed brigadier general and quartermaster general (1860), he resigned to become Confederate brigadier general (April 1861). After his victory at First Bull Run (July 1861) he fought a skillful campaign against McClellan in the Peninsula (1862) until wounded at Fair Oaks (May 1862) and replaced by Lee. He returned to duty in the West, but was unable to prevent Grant's victory at Vicksburg (May–July 1863). Replacing Bragg after Chattanooga, he fought an impressive defensive campaign against Sherman, including victory at Kennesaw Mountain (June 1864) but when Sherman closed in on Atlanta, Johnston was replaced again. Given command in the Carolinas against Sherman (Feb–April 1865) he again fought a clever defensive campaign until his surrender at Durham Station (April 26). After the war he worked in insurance, and served as a congressman (1879–81). An honorary pallbearer at Sherman's funeral, he caught a cold and died March 21, 1891, in Washington D.C. A brilliant strategist, Johnston often found himself working with inferior forces which caused him to decline battle frequently and meant he could not be as aggressive as his superiors wanted. This led to frequent quarrels with President Davis.

LEE, Robert Edward Born Jan 19, 1807, at Stratford, Virginia, to a distinguished military family, and when he married (July 5, 1831) the great-granddaughter of Martha Washington he confirmed his position as one

Top to bottom:
James Longstreet,
William Loring,
John Pemberton,
Sterling Price, and
Edmund Kirby Smith. (M)

of the aristocrats of the U.S. Graduated second in his class at West Point (1829), he gained a high reputation as an engineer and served with great distinction throughout the Mexican War (1846–8). Superintendent at West Point (1852–5), then promoted colonel commanding 2nd Cavalry (1855), he commanded the troops who captured John Brown at Harpers Ferry (Oct 1859). At the outbreak of the Civil War he was invited to command the Union army, but resigned to go with his native state, Virginia. Appointed military advisor to President Davis, he was defeated at Cheat Mountain (Sept 1861), but replaced Joseph Johnston when the latter was wounded at Seven Pines (May 31 to June 1, 1862). Though initially not well regarded by his troops (he was known as "Granny Lee") he quickly became very popular as he led the Army of Northern Virginia to a series of spectacular victories, driving back McClellan during the Seven

Days (June–July 1862) and winning at Second Bull Run (Aug 1862), Fredericksburg (Dec 1862) and Chancellorsville (May 1863), though he was less successful when he invaded the North, being forced to withdraw at Antietam (Sep 1862) and decisively defeated at Gettysburg (July 1863). He skillfully held off Grant's attacks from the Wilderness to Cold Harbor (May–June 1864) but his lines were stretched too thin at Petersburg and when Grant outflanked him at Five Forks (March 1865) he retreated to Appomattox Court House where he surrendered (April 9, 1865). He became president of Washington College (Sept 1865) and died there (Oct 12, 1870). Personally brave, inspiring immense loyalty, he acted quickly whenever necessary and was prepared to take risks in the face of the enemy that often resulted in great victories. Lee is now recognized as one of the great generals of military history.

LONGSTREET, James Born Jan 8. 1821, in Edgeville District, South Carolina. Graduated West Point (1842) and was twice brevetted promotions during the Mexican War. He was promoted captain (1852) and major (1858), before resigning to accept a commission as Confederate brigadier general (June 1861). The most senior Confederate general not from Virginia, he won victory at Blackburn's Ford (July 1861) and performed with distinction during the Peninsula Campaign. His intervention at Second Bull Run (Aug 1862) was decisive, and though opposed to the invasion of Maryland he fought well at South Mountain and Antietam (Sept 1862). Promoted lieutenant general and given command of I Corps, Oct 1862, his men did most of the fighting at Fredericksburg (Dec 1862). Though he disagreed with Lee's strategy at Gettysburg (July 1863), he bore the brunt of the fighting there and was later criticized unfairly for being slow to act. Detached to the West he arrived in time to play a decisive part in the victory at Chickamauga (Sept 1863), but was then sent to besiege Burnside at Knoxville and missed Chattanooga. Wounded in the Wilderness (April 1864), he rejoined the army in Oct 1864 despite a paralyzed arm and was with Lee until the surrender at Appomattox (April 1865). After the war he was the most prominent Confederate to support the Republicans, serving among other things as U.S. minister to Turkey (1880), U.S. marshall in Georgia (1881) and U.S. railroad commissioner (1898). He died in Gainesville, Georgia, Jan 2, 1904. Certain die-hard Confederates tried to make Longstreet the scapegoat for their defeat, though he served with bravery and ability throughout the war and gave Lee the solidity he relied on for most of his victories

LORING, William Wing Born Wilmington, North Carolina, Dec 4, 1818, volunteered for Seminole War at age 14, studied law and elected to Florida legislature, fought in Mexican War, fought Indians in Texas, took part in Mormon Expedition. Served under Jackson in Shenandoah Valley, under Pemberton at Champion Hill, replaced Polk as corps commander on Atlanta campaign, Hood's second in command at Franklin and Nashville. Commissioned in army of the Khedive of Egypt (1869) and fought in Abyssinian War (1875–9). Died New York, Dec 30, 1886.

Lee in Richmond after the war. This photograph is one of a number taken by Matthew Brady in 1865 in the basement below the back porch of Lee's Franklin Street house. On his right is General G. W. C. Lee (Robert's son); on his left Colonel Walter Taylor. (M)

Top to bottom:
Leonidas Polk,
Raphael Semmes,
Jeb Stuart,
Richard Taylor (M), and
Earl Van Dorn (NA).

PEMBERTON, John Clifford Born Philadelphia, 1814, graduated West Point (1837) and served in Seminole War, Mexican War and Mormon Expedition. Married a Virginian and went with that state after secession. As lieutenant general he held Vicksburg against Grant, but suffered series of defeats and eventually forced to surrender (July 1864). Suspected of treason because of his Northern birth, resigned his commission and offered to serve as a private. Recommissioned as lieutenant colonel of artillery until end of war. Retired to a Virginia farm and died 1881.

PICKETT, George Edward Born Jan 28, 1825, Richmond, Virginia. Graduated West Point 1842 and won distinction at storming of Chapultepec (Sept 1847) where he was the first over the parapet. Fought with distinction at Williamsburg, Fair Oaks and Gaines's Mill where he was severely wounded (May–June 1862). Promoted major general (Oct 1862) and given a division in Longstreet's Corps, which he led at Fredericksburg (Dec 1862). Arrived late on the field at Gettysburg and his division formed the core of the final day attack known as Pickett's Charge (July 1863); he ever after blamed Lee for the heavy casualties he suffered. After detached service in North Carolina, he rejoined his old division at Cold Harbor (June 1864). His defeat at Five Forks (April 1865) initiated the final Confederate collapse and Lee's surrender (April 9). He turned down a commission in the Egyptian Army, and worked as an insurance agent until he died in Norfolk, Virginia, July 30, 1875. Pickett was brave but vain and not very clever; he was ill-suited to the command roles he was given.

POLK, Leonidas Born April 10, 1806, Raleigh, North Carolina. Graduated West Point (1827), ordained in Protestant Episcopal Church (1830), first bishop of Louisiana (1841-61), founder, University of the South (1860). Confederate major general, his impetuous violation of Kentucky's neutrality was a strategic blunder. Defeated Grant at Belmont (Nov 1861), fought at Shiloh, Perryville, Stones River, Chickamauga. Removed from command due to disagreements with Bragg. Killed in action, Kennesaw Mountain, June 14, 1864. Polk was well liked but proved an inept general.

PRICE, Sterling Born Sept 20, 1809, Prince Edward County, Virginia. Missouri state

legislator (1836-8, 1840-4), U.S. congressman (1844-6), resigned to fight in Mexican War, governor of Missouri (1852-6). Won victory at Wilson's Creek (Aug 1861), defeated at Pea Ridge (March 1862), fought at Iuka, Corinth, (Sept–Oct 1862), defeated at Helena (July 1863) and Pine Bluff (Oct 1863), attempts to take St. Louis repulsed (Sept–Oct 1864), his army destroyed at Westport (Oct 1864). Fled to Texas then Mexico. Died St. Louis, Sept 29, 1867.

SEMMES, Raphael Born Maryland, 1809, entered the Navy 1826 and rose to the rank of commander, though he also qualified as a lawyer. After obtaining naval supplies from the north before the outbreak of actual hostilities, he was commissioned commander, C.S.N., and converted a packet steamer into commerce raider *Sumter*. Captured 18 prizes before *Sumter* was blockaded and abandoned at Gibraltar. Promoted Captain and given command of CSS *Alabama* (Sept 1862), the most successful of all Confederate commerce raiders. Her 69 prizes included Union gunboat *Hatteras* sunk in a naval battle. *Alabama* finally sunk in battle with USS *Kearsarge* at Cherbourg (June 1864). Promoted rear admiral (Feb 1865) and given command of James River Squadron but forced to destroy his vessels. Elected to judgeship in Mobile, but authorities removed him from office. Resumed his law career and died, Mobile, Alabama, 1877.

SMITH, Edmund Kirby Born St. Augustine, Florida, May 16, 1824. Graduated West Point (1845), served in Mexican War, taught mathematics at West Point, fought in Southwestern Indian Campaigns. Commanded brigade at First Bull Run (July 1861), led Bragg's invasion of Kentucky (July–Oct 1862), fought at Perryville and Stones River. Appointed commander of Trans-Mississippi Department (Feb 1863) which, when cut off by the fall of Vicksburg, became known as "Kirby Smithdom" under his almost independent authority. Defeated Red River Campaign (March–May 1864). Surrendered at Galveston, May 26, 1865). President and professor of various universities. Died Sewanee, Tennessee, March 28, 1893.

STUART, James Ewell Brown Born Feb 6, 1833, in Patrick County, Virginia. Graduated West Point 1854 and served in Texas and

Kansas before resigning his commission to join Confederate army. Appointed colonel and commander of 1st Virginia Cavalry (July 1861) and after serving at First Bull Run (July 1861) and Williamsburg (May 1862) won praise for his actions at Fair Oaks (May 1862). Led 1,200 men on a ride all around McClellan's Army of the Potomac (June 1862). Promoted major general and commander of Lee's cavalry (July 1862). Raided Pope's H.Q. and supply base (Aug 1862), fought at Second Bull Run (Aug 1862) and Antietam (Sept 1862), commanded right flank at Fredericksburg (Dec 1862) and discovered vulnerability of Hooker's flank at Chancellorsville (May 1863). His attempt to ride around the Union army once more during the Gettysburg campaign (June–July 1863) left Lee without vital intelligence in the crucial days before the battle. Mortally wounded during cavalry battle at Yellow Tavern (May 11, 1864), he died in Richmond, May 12, 1864. Flamboyant and daring, "Jeb" Stuart was the very image of the Southern Cavalier. His brilliance as a cavalryman gave Lee a crucial advantage early in the war, but his love of a grandstand gesture became a liability when the North later found cavalrymen of similar ability.

TAYLOR, Richard Born Louisville, Kentucky, Jan 27, 1826, son of General Zachary Taylor and future brother-in-law of Jefferson Davis. Graduated Yale (1845), with his father during Mexican War, Louisiana state legislature (1856-61). Served with Jackson in Shenandoah Valley, with Lee in Seven Days, bottled up Union forces in New Orleans, repulsed Red River campaign, replaced Hood in command of Army of Tennessee (Jan 1865), surrendered Citronelle, Alabama, May 4, 1865. Died New York, April 12, 1879. Taylor was a fine tactical and grand tactical combat leader.

VAN DORN, Earl Born Sept 17, 1820, Port Gibson, Mississippi. Graduated West Point (1842), took part in occupation of Texas (1845-6), fought in Mexican War and saw action against Indians in Texas. Succeeded Jefferson Davis as commander Mississippi State Militia, major general in Confederate army and commander of Trans-Mississippi (Jan 1862), defeated at Pea Ridge (March 1862) and Corinth (Oct 1862), captured Union supply depot at Holly Springs (Dec 1862). Shot and killed by a jealous husband in Spring Hill, Tennessee, May 8, 1863.

Top to bottom:
Nathaniel Banks (M),
Don Carlos Buell (NA),
Ambrose Burnside,
Benjamin Butler, and
Joshua Chamberlain (M).

BANKS, Nathaniel Prentiss Born Jan 30, 1816, Waltham, Massachusetts. Elected to Congress (1853), speaker of the House (1854-7), governor of Massachusetts (1857-60). A political general given Corps command in Shenandoah, defeated at Winchester (June 1862) and Cedar Mountain (Aug 1862), replaced Butler in New Orleans (Nov 1862), captured Port Hudson (July 1863) then led ill-fated Red River expedition (April–May 1864), removed from command, he resigned (Aug 1865). Active in state politics and Congress (1888–91), died Sept 1, 1894, in Waltham, another political general who proved unenterprising and ineffective in command.

BUELL, Don Carlos Born Ohio, 1818, graduated West Point 1841, fought in Seminole and Mexican Wars. Helped organize Army of the Potomac under McClellan (Oct–Nov 1861), then given command of Army of the Ohio. Captured Nashville, then moved to support Grant at Shiloh (April 1862) bringing vital reinforcements for the second day of battle. Involved in the slow advance on Corinth, then fought the indecisive Battle of Perryville (Oct 1862) but condemned for not chasing the retreating enemy. Relieved of command, he received no further orders and resigned, June 1864. Worked as an industrialist in Kentucky and died 1898. Full of his own importance, he was a slow and ineffective leader.

BURNSIDE, Ambrose Everett Born May 23, 1824, in Liberty, Indiana. Graduated West Point 1847, but left the army 1853 to run a firearms company where he designed a breech-loading carbine (1856) but was bankrupted 1857. Brigade commander at First Bull Run (July 1861) then organized amphibious force to capture Roanoke Island (Feb 1862) and New Bern (March 1862). In command of left wing at Antietam (Sept 1862), and replaced McClellan in command of Army of the Potomac (Nov 1862). Repulsed by Lee at Fredericksburg (Dec 1862) and replaced by Hooker (Jan 1863). Sent west to clear Cumberland Gap and hold Knoxville against Longstreet (Sept–Dec 1863), then returned to lead IX Corps in Army of the Potomac. Blamed for disaster at the Crater (July 1864), he resigned (April 1865). Governor of Rhode Island (1866-9) and U.S.Senator (1874–81), national commander of Grand Army of the Republic (1874). Died Sept 13, 1881, at Bristol, Rhode Island. A flamboyant char-

acter noted for his extravagant sideburns (which are named after him), he recognized his limitations but was promoted well beyond his limited abilities and proved unequal to the challenge of independent command.

BUTLER, Benjamin Franklin Born Nov 5, 1818, in Deerfield, New Hampshire, he was a successful lawyer when elected to the Massachusetts assembly (1853) and senate (1859). As a leading pro-war Democrat, he was one of the most important of the Union's political generals, leading the militia that occupied Baltimore (May 1861). After a defeat at Big Bethel (June 1861), he commanded the troops that captured Fort Hatteras (Aug 1861), where he proclaimed runaway slaves to be "contraband of war." After capturing New Orleans (May 1862) he became military governor of the city until unpopularity (he was called "Beast" Butler after issuing Order Number 28 and became the most reviled Northerner throughout the South) made him too much of a liability and he was relieved (Dec 1862). As commander of the Army of the James he was bottled up in the Bermuda Hundred (May 1864) and after successive failures was relieved from command (Jan 1865). Member of the House of Representatives (1867–75 and 1877–9), governor of Massachusetts (1882–3) and failed presidential candidate (1884), he died in Washington D.C. Jan 11, 1893. He was sluggish and inept as a commander, unpopular as an administrator, but wily as a politician.

CHAMBERLAIN, Joshua Lawrence Born Maine 1828, was professor of rhetoric and received religion at Bowdoin College, Maine, when war broke out. Denied permission by his college to enlist, he took a sabbatical, supposedly for study in Europe, and enlisted anyway. Served with 20th Maine (which he came to command) at Antietam (Sept 1862), Fredericksburg (Dec 1862) where he was wounded, and Chancellorsville (May 1863). At Gettysburg (July 1863) his inventive defense of the extreme Union left on Little Round Top preserved the Union line and made him a national hero. Fought at Cold Harbor (May 1864), promoted to brigade command (June 1864) only to receive a wound that was expected to be fatal and promoted to brigadier general on the spot by Grant. Returned to duty to take part in Appomattox campaign and commanded the troops that received the

George Custer. (M)

Andrew Foote. (M)

David Farragut. (M)

formal surrender. Later served as governor of Maine and president of Bowdoin College. Died as a belated result of wounds Feb 24, 1914, in Portland, Maine. An unlikely hero, he proved to be a resourceful and energetic commander.

CUSTER, George Armstrong Born Dec 5, 1839, New Rumley, Ohio. Graduated West Point 1861 and fought at First Bull Run (July 1861), Antietam (Sept 1862), Fredericksburg (Dec 1862), Chancellorsville (May 1863). Won quick promotion as cavalry commander and gained distinction at Gettysburg (July 1863) and under Sheridan at Yellow Tavern (May 1864), Winchester (Sept 1864) and Five Forks (April 1865). Reduced in rank when army re-organized after war. Fought Indians in Kansas, court-martialed and suspended (1867), recalled by Sheridan and fought in Plains Indians Wars until killed at Little Big Horn, Dakota, June 25, 1876. Reckless, flamboyant, insubordinate and vainglorious, he revelled in battle but was unfit for high command.

FARRAGUT, David Glasgow Born as James G. Farragut July 5, 1801, near Knoxville, Tennessee, adopted by Commander David Porter (1810) and later changed his name to David to honor his foster father. Appointed midshipman (Dec 1810) and served under Porter aboard USS *Essex* in War of 1812. Appointed commander (Sept 1841) and given his own command, established Mare Island Navy Yard in California (1854–8). On outbreak of Civil War given command of West Gulf Blockade Squadron, captured New Orleans (April 1862) then went on to command Union ships on the Mississippi. Promoted rear admiral (July 1862), the first admiral in the U.S. navy. Led the bold attack on Mobile (Aug 1864) where he gave his famous order: "Damn the torpedoes! Full speed ahead." Promoted vice admiral (Dec

Left: Grant and staff, painted by H. A. Ogden. (NA)

Top to bottom: Henry Halleck (NA), U. S. Grant, Winfield Scott Hancock, Joseph Hooker (M), Abraham Lincoln NHC), and John Logan (NA).

1864) but no longer involved in active operations due to ill health. Promoted to newly-created rank of admiral (July 1866) and died at Portsmouth, New Hampshire, Aug 14, 1870. Farragut was probably the boldest, most aggressive and most able commander in the Union navy.

FOOTE, Andrew Hull Born Sept 12, 1806, New Haven, Connecticut, the son of a Senator. Appointed midshipman (Dec 1822) and his distinguished naval service included leading role in suppressing the slave trade. Command of naval forces on the upper Mississippi (Aug 1861), instrumental in rapidly building fleet of gunboats, took part in capture of Forts Henry and Donelson (Feb 1862) and Island No. 10 (March–April 1862), retired June 1862, promoted rear admiral (July 1862), died New York City June 26, 1863. A capable and energetic naval commander who played a fundamental role in Union control of the Mississippi.

GRANT, Ulysses Simpson Born April 27 1822, Point Pleasant, Ohio, as Hiram Ulysses Grant, name changed by clerical error when he enrolled at West Point (1839) and U.S.G. never corrected it. Graduated West Point 1843, commissioned 2nd lieutenant in 4th Infantry. Mexican War: served with distinction at Palo Alto (May 1846), Veracruz (March 1847), Molino del Rey (Sept 1847, brevetted 1st lieutenant for gallantry), Chapultepec (Sept 1847, brevetted captain). Resigned his commission 1854, but failed in various business ventures before joining family leather business in Galena, Illinois. Civil War: commissioned colonel of Illinois Volunteers (June 1861) then promoted to brigadier general. His demand for "Unconditional Surrender" at Fort Donelson gave him his popular nickname. Victory at Shiloh, then given command of Western Armies (July 1862); after victory at Vicksburg

promoted to major general and given command of Military Division of the Mississippi; after victory at Chattanooga promoted to lieutenant general with command of all Union armies. Overland campaign against Richmond led to siege of Petersburg, then surrender of Lee at Appomattox. Promoted to new rank of general (July 1866), secretary of war (1867–8), president (1869–77), went bankrupt through unwise investments, wrote memoirs to provide for his family and died of throat cancer four days after finishing them (July 23, 1885). U.S.G. was stubborn, able to learn from mistakes, and an effective strategist. He grew bored and took to drink when away from fighting, but was tenacious and quick thinking in action. His presidency was marked by corruption scandals, though he was not implicated. He was probably the most successful general on either side in the Civil War.

HALLECK, Henry Wager Born Jan 16, 1815, Westernville, New York. Graduated West Point 1839, an authority on fortifications, also instrumental in drafting constitution of California (Sept 1849). Commander, Department of the Missouri (Nov 1861), led Army of the Ohio during Corinth campaign (May–June 1862), transferred to Washington as general in chief (July 1862), became chief of staff to Grant (March 1864), later commanded Divisions of the Pacific and of the South. Died Jan 9, 1872, at Knoxville, Kentucky. An able administrator but poor field commander, he was often at odds with field commanders, especially Grant.

HANCOCK, Winfield Scott Born Feb 14, 1824, Montgomery County, Pennsylvania. Graduated West Point 1844, served in Mexican War, Third Seminole War and Kansas disorders. Brigadier general of volunteers (Sept 1861), served in Seven Days (June 1862), division commander at Antietam (Sept 1862), major general of volunteers (Nov 1862), fought with distinction at Fredericksburg (Dec 1862) and Chancellorsville (May 1863), wounded leading the repulse of Pickett's Charge at

Gettysburg (July 1863), corps commander at Wilderness, Spotsylvania, Cold Harbor and Petersburg (May–June 1864), ended the war as commander of Washington defenses. Fought Indians in Kansas (1866-7), then commanded various military divisions. Ran as unsuccessful Democratic presidential candidate 1880. Died at his H.Q. on Governor's Island, New York, Feb 9, 1886. Personally exceptionally brave, Hancock was one of the most energetic and able divisional and corps commanders in the Union army.

HOOKER, Joseph Born Nov 13,1814, Hadley, Massachusetts. Graduated West Point 1837 and served with distinction in Seminole War and Mexican War. Divisional commander in Peninsula campaign (April–May 1862) and Second Bull Run (Aug 1862). Promoted corps commander, Army of the Potomac (Sept 1862), wounded at Antietam (Sept 1862), grand division commander at Fredericksburg (Dec 1862), promoted to commander Army of the Potomac (Jan 1863) but defeated at Chancellorsville (May 1863) and relieved. Served under Grant in Chattanooga and won victory at Lookout Mountain (Nov 1863), then served under Sherman in Atlanta campaign (May–Aug 1864) but passed over for command of Army of the Tennessee. Retired as major general (Oct 1868), died Oct 31, 1879, Garden City, New York. A brave and talented subordinate, Hooker was not suited to independent command.

LINCOLN, Abraham Born Feb 12, 1809, near Hodgenville, Kentucky. Moved to Indiana (1816) then Illinois (1830), received little formal education. Volunteered for Black Hawk War (1832) but saw no action. Moved to Springfield 1837 to practice law. Served in Illinois state legislature (1834–40) and U.S.House of Representatives (1847-9). Joined the newly formed Republican Party (1856), ran for Senate against Stephen A. Douglas and lost after a series of high-profile debates which made him a national figure. Chosen as presidential candidate (May 1860) and elected following split in Democratic Party. Though he was ambiguous on slavery, his election prompted secession and war. Repeatedly disappointed by the inactivity or incompetence of his generals, he constantly interfered by urging positive action. This rarely produced the results he wanted, but he became quick to fire those generals who displeased him. His Emanci-

John Pope. (M)

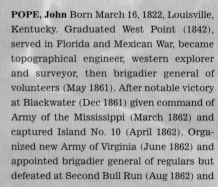

William Rosecrans. (M)

David Porter. (M)

Top to bottom:
George McClellan,
John McClernand,
Irvin McDowell, (M)
James McPherson (NA),
and George Meade (M).

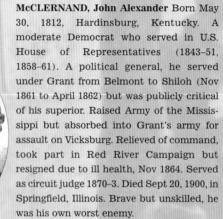

pation Proclamation (Sept 1862) and his eloquence, especially in the Gettysburg Address (Nov 1863) gave the Union a new moral purpose. Re-elected Nov 1864. In meetings with Grant and Sherman toward the end of the war he advocated generous terms toward the losers, but within days of the surrender at Appomattox he was shot while watching a performance at Ford's Theater and died the next morning (April 15, 1865). One of the most able presidents America has known, he was intelligent, compassionate, insightful, fast to act and quick to learn from mistakes.

LOGAN, John Alexander Born Murphysboro, Illinois, Feb 9, 1826, served in Mexican War, elected to House of Representatives (1858, 1860), volunteered as private at outbreak of war then appointed colonel of an Illinois regiment under Grant. Fought at Belmont (Nov 1861), Henry and Donelson (Feb 1862), division commander in Vicksburg campaign (Jan–July 1863), then corps commander Army of the Tennessee, given temporary command of the army on McPherson's death at Atlanta. Congressman (1867–71) and senator (1871–7, 1878–86). Died Washington D.C., Dec 26, 1886. A fiery tactical leader and able corps commander who perhaps deserved the chance to lead the Army of the Tennessee.

McCLELLAN, George Brinton Born Dec 3, 1826, in Philadelphia, graduated second in his class from West Point, 1846, and served with distinction in the Mexican War then taught at West Point (1848–51). He was a U.S. observer at the Crimean War (1853–6) before becoming a railroad engineer and eventually president of the Ohio and Mississippi Railroad. A major general at the start of the war, he won an early minor victory for the Union in West Virginia, earning the undeserved name "The Young Napoleon", and was appointed commander of the Army of the Potomac (July 1861) and general in chief of the army (Nov 1861). After reorganising and resupplying the army, his Peninsula Campaign was marked by hesitation and though he won most of the battles of the Seven Days (June 1862) he still retreated. Persistently overestimating the enemy strength, he was slow to act even when in possession of Lee's plans but still emerged the victor at Antietam (Sept 1862). Failing to follow up, he was relieved of command (Nov 1862). Ran against Lincoln as Democratic candidate for president (Nov 1864); he was

defeated and resigned his commission. After the war he returned to engineering, and served as governor of New Jersey (1877–81). Died in Orange, New Jersey, Oct 29, 1885. A superb administrator and organizer, he was overly cautious in battle against an enemy able to see and exploit his weaknesses.

McCLERNAND, John Alexander Born May 30, 1812, Hardinsburg, Kentucky. A moderate Democrat who served in U.S. House of Representatives (1843–51, 1858–61). A political general, he served under Grant from Belmont to Shiloh (Nov 1861 to April 1862) but was publicly critical of his superior. Raised Army of the Mississippi but absorbed into Grant's army for assault on Vicksburg. Relieved of command, took part in Red River Campaign but resigned due to ill health, Nov 1864. Served as circuit judge 1870–3. Died Sept 20, 1900, in Springfield, Illinois. Brave but unskilled, he was his own worst enemy.

McDOWELL, Irvin Born Oct 15, 1818, Columbus, Ohio, graduated West Point 1838. Instructor at West Point, fought in Mexican War then held number of staff posts until given command of Washington area on outbreak of Civil War. Diligent in organising an army of raw recruits but pushed to attack at First Bull Run (July 1861) and his army not able to put his complex plan into effect. Became corps commander under McClellan and Pope, criticized for his role at Second Bull Run (Aug 1862) and relieved of command, he was later exonerated but his career was ruined. Commanded Department of the Pacific 1876–82. Died San Francisco, May 4, 1885. A capable officer hampered by commanding a green army.

McPHERSON, James Birdseye Born Nov 14, 1828, Sandusky County, Ohio. Graduated first in his class from West Point (1853). Chief engineer on Grant's expedition against Forts Henry and Donelson (Jan–Feb 1862), served with distinction at Shiloh (April 1862) and promoted brigadier general. Praised by both Sherman and Grant for his role in the Vicksburg campaign (Jan–July 1863) and given command Army of the Tennessee (March 1864). Distinguished himself at Dalton (May 1864) and Kennesaw Mountain (June 1864) but killed during Battle of Atlanta, July 22, 1864. Charming, intelligent and talented, his superiors were confident he would achieve great things.

MEADE, George Gordon Born Dec 31, 1815, in Cadiz, Spain, the son of an American naval agent. Graduated West Point 1835 and commissioned in the artillery, saw immediate service in the Seminole War. Resigned due to ill health 1836 to work as a civil engineer, he rejoined for the Mexican War and was brevetted 1st lieutenant for his actions at Monterrey (Sept 1848). At the outbreak of the Civil War he was promoted brigadier general of Pennsylvania volunteers. Wounded during the Seven Days (June 1862), he fought at Second Bull Run, Antietam (when he assumed command of I Corps after Hooker was wounded), and Fredericksburg, after which he received command of V Corps. Given command of the Army of the Potomac days before Gettysburg, he waged a masterly tactical defense making superb use of his ground, but failed to follow up the victory aggressively. Remained in command of the Army under Grant, though his role became effectively that of executive officer, he nevertheless played an important part in operations right up to Appomattox. After the war he served with fairness in the South, dying in Philadelphia, Nov 6, 1872 of pneumonia brought on by his wounds. Known as "Old Snapping Turtle" to his men for his fierce temper, he was tenacious and able, but overly cautious.

POPE, John Born March 16, 1822, Louisville, Kentucky. Graduated West Point (1842), served in Florida and Mexican War, became topographical engineer, western explorer and surveyor, then brigadier general of volunteers (May 1861). After notable victory at Blackwater (Dec 1861) given command of Army of the Mississippi (March 1862) and captured Island No. 10 (April 1862). Organized new Army of Virginia (June 1862) and appointed brigadier general of regulars but defeated at Second Bull Run (Aug 1862) and

Top to bottom:
John Schofield,
Philip Sheridan,
William Sherman,
Franz Sigel (M), and
George Thomas (NA).

relieved of command. Given command of various western Departments, fought Sioux in Minnesota, retired (March 1886). Died Sept 23, 1892, at Sandusky, Ohio. An able administrator but poor tactician whose abrasive character won few friends.

PORTER, David Dixon Born June 8, 1813, Chester, Pennsylvania, son of Captain David Porter and foster brother of Farragut. Midshipman in Mexican Navy (1826), then U.S. Navy (1829), served in Mexican War. Took part in Farragut's operations against New Orleans (April 1862) and Vicksburg. Promoted acting rear admiral (Oct 1862) and achieved spectacular success creating and leading Mississippi Squadron of gunboats against Vicksburg (April 1863) and Red River (May 1863), supported ill-fated Red River campaign (March–May 1864), commander North Atlantic Blockading Squadron (Oct 1864) and captured Fort Fisher (Jan 1865). Superintendent of Naval Academy (1865–9), vice admiral (July 1866), admiral (1870). Died still on active duty, Washington D.C., Feb 13, 1891. Bold, energetic and resourceful, he was, with Farragut, a highly effective commander.

ROSECRANS, William Starke Born Sept 6, 1819, Kingston, Ohio. Graduated West Point 1842 and taught there (1843–7). Early successes in West Virginia under McClellan (July–Sept 1861) then at Iuka (Sept 1862) and Corinth (Oct 1862) under Grant. Commander Army of the Cumberland (Oct 1862), victor at Stones River (Dec 1862) and outmaneuvered Bragg in Tullahoma campaign (June–Sept 1863) but defeated at Chickamauga (Sept 1863) and relieved of command. Resigned, March 1867. Minister to Mexico (1868–9), House of Representatives (1881–5), Treasury official (1885–93). Died Redondo Beach, California, March 11, 1898. A brilliant strategist, but not so effective tactician.

SCHOFIELD, John McAllister Born New York, 1831, graduated West Point 1853, taught physics at Washington University, St. Louis. Decorated for his services at Wilson's Creek (Aug 1861), commanded various departments in Kansas-Missouri until becoming corps commander under Sherman on Atlanta campaign (March–Oct 1864), defeated Hood at Franklin (Nov 1864) then rejoined Thomas for the overwhelming victory at Nashville (Dec 1864). Sent to Wilmington, N.C., to unite with Sherman

(Feb 1865) and served until surrender (April 1865). Secretary of war, superintendent of West Point, and commanding general of the army (1888–95). Died St. Augustine, Florida, March 4, 1906. A brilliant corps commander and perhaps the finest peacetime commander of the U.S. Army.

SHERIDAN, Philip Henry Born March 6, 1831, near Albany, New York. Graduated from West Point 1853 and served in Texas and Oregon. Promoted brigadier general for his raid on Booneville (July 1862), and thereafter advanced rapidly, gaining a reputation for hard fighting and fine leadership at Perryville (Oct 1862), Stones River (Dec 1862), Chickamauga (Sept 1863) and Chattanooga (Nov 1863). Given command of the Army of the Potomac's cavalry under Grant, he defeated Jeb Stuart at Yellow Tavern (May 1864) before leading a brilliant campaign in the Shenandoah Valley. When his army was surprised at Cedar Creek (Oct 1864) he rode 20 miles, rallied his men and turned defeat into a stunning victory. Promoted major general of regulars, Nov 1864. His victory at Five Forks (April 1865) precipitated Lee's retreat to Appomattox. Led successive campaigns against the Indians, 1868–9 and 1876–7, and appointed commanding general of the army Nov 1883. Died Nonquitt, Massachusetts, Aug 5, 1888. Blunt-spoken and popular with his men, he was a resourceful leader and sound tactician, though too aggressive to be a great strategist.

SHERMAN, William Tecumseh Born Feb 8, 1820, in Lancaster, Ohio. Graduated West Point 1840 and served in the Seminole Wars then on General Kearny's staff in the Mexican War (1846–7). Served in California, but resigned his commission (1850) and started a building company that went bankrupt. After practicing law he became superintendent of Alexandria Military Institute, Louisiana (1859) until secession when he returned to active service in Union army. Brigade command at First Bull Run (July 1861), then joined Grant's Army of the Tennessee and won distinction at Shiloh (April 1862) and by the Vicksburg campaign (Dec 1862 to July 1863) was Grant's friend and lieutenant. Promoted major general of volunteers (May 1862) and brigadier general of regulars (July 1863). After Chattanooga (Nov 1863) he succeeded Grant as commander of the Military Division of the Mississippi, captured Atlanta (Sept 1864), then launched his March to the Sea

(Nov–Dec 1864) followed by his march through the Carolinas until he received Johnston's surrender (April 1865). Was commanding general of the army (Nov 1869 to March 1883). Died New York, Feb 14, 1891. Though prone to depressions, Sherman was highly intelligent, aggressive and imaginative, making him one of the most effective generals in the war.

SIGEL, Franz Born Grand Duchy of Baden, 1824, served in the duke's army but forced to flee after 1848 revolutions, became teacher in St. Louis until Civil War. Fought at Wilson's Creek and Pea Ridge, division commander in Shenandoah, then corps commander under Pope at Second Bull Run (Aug 1862). Given command in the Shenandoah he was defeated by a smaller force at New Market (May 1864) and removed from command. Resigned May 1865 and died 1902. An ineffective commander given too high rank because of the spurious glamor of his European military experience and his popularity among German-Americans.

THOMAS, George Henry Born July 31, 1816, in Southampton County, Virginia, graduated West Point 1840 and served with distinction in the Seminole and Mexican Wars, promoted major at Buena Vista (Feb 1847). He taught at West Point and served in California, Arizona and Texas before becoming one of the few Southerners to remain in the Union army during the Civil War. Won the first Union victory in the West at Mill Springs (Jan 1862) and fought at Corinth (Oct 1862) and Perryville (Oct 1862) where he was second in command to Buell. Won distinction at Stones River (Dec 1862), and for his staunch defense which prevented a rout at Chickamauga (Sept 1863) won the nickname "The Rock of Chickamauga". Instrumental in the victory at Chattanooga (Nov 1863), he was Sherman's second-in-command on the Atlanta campaign, then went on to inflict a devastating defeat on Hood at Nashville (Dec 1864). After the war he commanded the Divisions of the Tennessee and Cumberland (1865–9) and the Pacific (1869), dying in San Francisco, March 28, 1870. A stolid, undemonstrative man, he was slow to move until certain of delivering an overwhelming blow. Though superiors often complained of his slowness, they could not complain of his achievements. He was a brilliant commander, though flashier colleagues often stole the limelight.

THE ARMY OF THE POTOMAC

ARMY OF THE POTOMAC
Organized March 3, 1862

- G. McClellan 03/03/62
- A. Burnside 11/07/62
- J. Hooker 01/25/63
- G. Meade 06/28/63
- J. Parke 12/30/64
- G. Meade 01/11/65

I CORPS
Organized March 3, 1862

- I. McDowell 03/03/62
Merged into the
Department of the
Rappahannock 04/04/62
A new I Corps organized in
September 1862
- J. Hooker 09/12/62
- G. Meade 09/17/62
- J. Reynolds 09/29/62
- J. Wadsworth 01/02/63
- J. Reynolds 01/04/63
- J. Wadsworth 03/01/63
- J. Reynolds 03/09/63
- A. Doubleday 07/01/63
- J. Newton 07/02/63
Corps disbanded 03/24/64

II CORPS
Organized March 3, 1862

- E. Sumner 03/13/62
- D. Couch 10/07/62
- J. Sedgwick 12/26/62
- O. Howard 01/26/63
- D. Couch 02/05/63
- W. Hancock 05/22/63
- J. Gibbon 07/01/63
- W. Hancock 07/03/63
- W. Hays 07/03/63
- G. Warren 08/16/63
- J. Caldwell 08/26/63
- G. Warren 09/02/63
- J. Caldwell 12/16/63
- G. Warren 12/29/63
- J. Caldwell 01/09/64
- G. Warren 01/15/64
- W. Hancock 03/24/64
- D. Birney 06/18/64
- W. Hancock 06/27/64
- A. Humphreys 11/26/64
- G. Mott 02/15/65
- N. Miles 02/17/65
- A. Humphreys 02/25/65
- F. Barlow 04/22/65
- A. Humphreys 05/05/65
- G. Mott 06/09/65
- A. Humphreys 06/20/65

III CORPS
Organized March 3, 1862

- S. Heintzelman 03/13/62
- G. Stoneman 10/30/62
- D. Sickles 02/05/63
- D. Birney 05/29/63
- D. Sickles 06/03/63
- D. Birney 07/02/63
- W. French 07/01/63
- D. Birney 01/28/64
- W. French 02/17/64
Corps disbanded 03/24/64

IX CORPS
Organized July 22, 1862

- A. Burnside 07/22/62
- I. Stevens (commanded
1 and 2 Div during Second
Bull Run Campaign)
- J. Reno 09/03/62
- J. Cox 09/14/62
- O. Willcox 10/08/62
- J. Sedgwick 01/16/63
- W. Smith 02/05/63
- A. Burnside 03/17/63
IX Corps sent to Department
of the Ohio 03/19/63,
Returned east in April 1864,
under Burnside, and served
directly under Grant, not as
part of Army of the Potomac

IV CORPS
Organized March 3, 1862

- E. Keyes 03/03/62
IV Corps discontinued
08/01/63

CAVALRY CORPS
Organized
February 12, 1863

- G. Stoneman 02/12/63
- A. Pleasonton 05/22/63
- P. Sheridan 04/04/64

V CORPS
Organized March 3, 1862

- N. Banks 03/03/62
Detached to Department of
Shenandoah March 15, 1862
A new V Corps provisionally
organized May 18, 1862;
confirmed July 22
- F. Porter 05/18/62
- J. Hooker 11/10/62
- D. Butterfield 11/16/62
- G. Meade 12/24/62
- C. Griffin 01/26/63
- G. Sykes 02/01/63
- G. Meade 02/05/63
- G. Sykes 02/16/63
- Humphreys 02/23/63
- G. Meade 02/28/63
- G. Sykes 06/28/63
- S. Crawford 10/07/63
- G. Sykes 10/15/63
- G. Warren 03/23/64
- S. Crawford 01/02/65
- G. Warren 01/27/65
- C. Griffin 04/01/65

XI CORPS
Organized
September 12, 1862

- F. Sigel 09/12/62
- J. Stahel 01/10/63
- C. Schurz 01/19/63
- F. Sigel 02/05/63
- A. Von Steinwehr 02/22/63
- C. Schurz 03/05/63
- O. Howard 04/02/63
- C. Schurz 07/01/63
- O. Howard 07/01/63;
1st Div transferred to
Charleston Harbor in August
1863
2d and 3d Div (O. Howard)
sent to Army of the
Cumberland 09/25/63

VI CORPS
Provisionally organized
May 18, 1862
Confirmed July 22

- W. Franklin 05/18/62
- W. Smith 11/16/62
- J. Sedgwick 02/04/63
- J. Ricketts 04/06/64
- J. Sedgwick 04/13/64
- H. Wright 05/09/64
- G. Getty 01/16/65
- H. Wright 02/11/65

XII CORPS
Organized
September 12, 1862

- J. Mansfield 09/12/62
- A. Williams 09/17/62
- H. Slocum 10/20/62
- A. Williams 07/01/63
- H. Slocum 07/04/63
- A. Williams 08/31/63
- H. Slocum 09/13/63
XII Corps sent to Army of the
Cumberland 09/25/63

THE APPROACH OF WAR

- **1776** The Declaration of Independence America's Founding Fathers declare that "all men are created equal," but retain the institution of slavery – though many believe it will soon wither away.

- **1784** Jefferson's Land Ordinance, including a provision for the abolition of slavery, is defeated by a single vote.

- **1793** The Cotton Gin. Eli Whitney's invention makes the cotton grown in the Southern states into a profitable proposition – and hence makes slavery particularly profitable.

- **1803** Louisiana Purchase. The United States acquires a vast swathe of territory from the Gulf of Mexico to the Pacific Northwest, beginning a rapid western expansion.

- **1807** African slave trade abolished.

- **1820** The Missouri Compromise. The debate over whether the new territory acquired in the Louisiana Purchase should be free or slave-holding is settled by a compromise: Missouri enters the Union as a slave state, but no further slave states north of the southern border of Missouri will be established.

- **1821** Cotton overtakes tobacco as America's most profitable trade commodity.

- **1822** Denmark Vesey, a free black man, nearly succeeds in organizing a mass slave revolt in Charleston, South Carolina.

- **1831** William Lloyd Garrison launches *The Liberator*, the most influential abolitionist newspaper.

- **1831** Nat Turner, a Virginia slave, leads a rebellion that kills 57 whites before he is captured and executed.

- **1837** The Republic of Texas asks to be admitted to the Union, but the petition is denied by Northerners anxious to avoid adding another slave state.

- **c.1840** The Underground Railway begins spiriting escaped slaves from the South to freedom in Canada.

- **1845** The U.S. approves the annexation of Texas, but a dispute breaks out with Mexico over the border.

- **1846-8** War with Mexico. The war proves an easy victory for the U.S. and an early training ground for many of the generals who will fight in the Civil War.

- **1846** Congressman David Wilmot introduces legislation to prevent the formation of slave states in any territory that might be acquired from Mexico. The Wilmot Proviso fails, but forms the basis for much debate over the following years.

- **1846** Henry David Thoreau, in common with most abolitionists, sees the Mexican War as an illegitimate design to extend slavery. He is arrested for refusing on moral grounds to pay a poll tax.

- **1847** Brigham Young establishes a Mormon settlement at the Great Salt Lake in what he calls Deseret.

- **1848** Treaty of Hidalgo. The treaty to end the Mexican War adds more territory to the United States, including New Mexico, Arizona, Utah, Nevada and California.

- **1848** Gold discovered at Sutter's Farm in California, initiating the great California Gold Rush.

- **1848** By the end of the year California, Deseret, Minnesota and Oregon are all on the point of asking for admission to the Union as free states.

- **1849** Thoreau publishes *Civil Disobedience*, a key text for abolitionists and for future nonviolent movements.

- **1850** Fugitive Slave Act. As part of a compromise to allow the admission of California to the Union as a free state, a punitive Fugitive Slave Act is enacted denying Congress any right to interfere with the slave trade between states. In effect, the law allows free blacks to be taken from the North to slavery in the South, galvanizing abolitionist sentiment.

- **1851** *Uncle Tom's Cabin* by Harriet Beecher Stowe appears. One of the most influential books in the history of literature, it has the immediate effect of hardening opinion on both sides.

- **1854** Kansas-Nebraska Act. Senator Stephen A. Douglas introduces the bill that overturns the Missouri Compromise, allowing settlers in Kansas and Nebraska to decide for themselves whether to be free or slave-holding.

- **1855** Pro-slavery Southerners flock into Kansas to win the territory for the South; clashes with free-state Northerners begin.

- **1856** Dred Scott Case. U.S. Chief Justice Roger Taney delivers a controversial judgement in the case of slave Dred Scott, who sued for his freedom on the grounds that he had lived for many years in free states. Taney's judgement against Dred Scott effectively makes slavery legal throughout the United States.

- **1856** Bleeding Kansas. Fighting between pro- and anti-slavery factions in Kansas grows to near civil war. On May 21 pro-slavery Border Ruffians from Missouri sack the free-soil settlement of Lawrence. Three days later John Brown and his followers hack five pro-slavery settlers to pieces in the Pottawatomie Massacre.

- **1856** Abolitionist Senator Charles Sumner of Massachusetts is beaten senseless by Congressman Preston Brooks on the floor of the Senate. Southerners inundate Brooks with new canes to applaud his act.

- **1858** Lincoln-Douglas Debates. Abraham Lincoln runs for the Senate against Stephen A. Douglas. Douglas wins, but the series of debates staged by the two turn Lincoln into a national figure.

- **1859** Harpers Ferry Raid. John Brown and his followers seize the government arsenal at Harpers Ferry, expecting to spark a slave revolt. The raid is unsuccessful and militia led by Colonel Robert E. Lee capture Brown and capture or kill all his followers. Brown and his surviving followers are hanged at Charlestown, Virginia, December 2, and are immediately proclaimed martyrs by Northern abolitionists.

- **May 18 1860** Lincoln wins the Republican presidential nomination.

- **Nov 6 1860** Abraham Lincoln elected as the first Republican president.

- **Dec 20 1860** South Carolina secedes, the first state to leave the Union.

- **Dec 25 1860** Major Robert Anderson, commander of the Federal garrison at Fort Moultrie in Charleston, South Carolina, withdraws his troops to Fort Sumter in the middle of the harbor "to prevent the effusion of blood."

JANUARY 1861

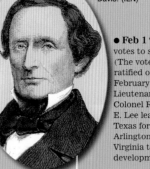

Left: Jefferson Davis. (ILN)

- **Jan 3** Delaware rejects a proposal that the state should secede.

- **Jan 9** Mississippi secedes.

- **Jan 9** An attempt to resupply Fort Sumter fails when shots are fired on the ship *Star of the West*. The ship is undamaged.

Above: Robert E. Lee in the 1850s. (NA)

- **Jan 10** Florida secedes.

- **Jan 10** Louisiana militia seize Federal forts and arsenals, prompting William T. Sherman to resign as head of the Louisiana Military Academy.

- **Jan 11** Alabama secedes.

- **Jan 19** Georgia secedes.

- **Jan 26** Louisiana secedes.

- **Jan 19** Virginia calls for a convention of all Southern states in Richmond. The Convention is to be held in early February but will achieve nothing.

Jan 29 Kansas is admitted to the Union as the 34th state.

FEBRUARY 1861

- **Feb 1** Texas votes to secede. (The vote will be ratified on February 23). Lieutenant Colonel Robert E. Lee leaves Texas for Arlington, Virginia to await developments.

- **Feb 9** Jefferson Davis of Mississippi is elected first president of the Confederacy, with Alexander Stephens of Georgia as his vice president. Davis will not learn the news until February 10.

Feb 4 A Convention of seceded states is held in Montgomery Alabama to form the Confederacy.

Feb 7 The Choctaw Indian Nation declares for the Confederacy.

- **Feb 11** President-elect Lincoln leaves his home in Springfield, Illinois for the journey to Washington, a journey that will crisscross the North via Pittsburgh, Cleveland, Buffalo, Albany, New York, Philadelphia and Baltimore.

- **Feb 18** Jefferson Davis inaugurated as Confederate president.

- **Feb 22** A mass meeting in San Francisco declares California for the Union.

- **Feb 23** Lincoln arrives in Washington.

- **Feb 28** Congress votes to form the Territory of Colorado as part of the Union.

MARCH 1861

- **March 2** Congress adds Territory of Nevada, Dakota Territory and most of Wyoming and Montana to the Union.

- **March 4** Lincoln inaugurated as 16th President of the United States.

- **March 4** The "Stars and Bars," the official Confederate flag, is raised for the first time.

Right: Abraham Lincoln. (B&L)

- **March 11** The Confederate Congress in Montgomery officially adopts the Constitution of the Confederacy. In all but a few details this is identical to the Constitution of the United States, except that it explicitly endorses slavery.

- **March 16** The Territory of Arizona declares itself out of the Union.

- **March 16** Lieutenant Colonel Robert E. Lee is promoted to Colonel of the 1st U.S. Cavalry.

- **March 18** In Texas, Governor Sam Houston refuses to take the oath of allegiance to the Confederacy.

- **March 29** Sam Houston is deposed as governor of Texas. He refuses a Federal offer to re-establish him in the post.

- **March 29** Lincoln orders an expedition to re-supply Sumter.

APRIL 1861

- **April 3** At Charleston, South Carolina a battery fires on Federal schooner *Rhoda H. Shannon*.

- **April 4** The Virginia State Convention rejects an ordinance of secession.

- **April 6** Lincoln sends an envoy to inform Governor Pickens of South Carolina that Sumter will be supplied with provisions only, not guns or reinforcements. The envoy delivers his message April 8.

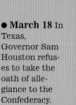

Below: The man who started the war. Private Edmund Ruffin, Confederate soldier who fired the first shot against Fort Sumter. (NA)

Below: December 1860. In the face of local hostility, the U.S. garrison abandons Fort Moultrie and holes up in Fort Sumter. (Leslies)

33

● **April 8** The *Harriet Lane* sails from New York loaded with supplies for Fort Sumter.

● **April 9** A Charleston, South Carolina newspaper declares that re-supplying Sumter means war. The Confederate government is less certain: they do not want to fire on the Union flag and be branded the aggressor.

● **April 10** USS *Pawnee* sails from Hampton Roads to relieve Sumter.

● **April 10** Confederate Secretary of War Leroy P. Walker instructs Gen. P.G.T. Beauregard to demand the surrender of Sumter before it could be re-supplied, and if refused to reduce the fort.

April 11 ●
Major Anderson refuses to surrender Sumter.

● **April 12** Just after midnight, Anderson offers to evacuate Sumter on the 15th unless re-supplied, unaware that a relief fleet is just outside the harbor awaiting daylight. A demand for immediate surrender is refused.

● **April 12** 4:30 a.m.: 67-year-old Edmund Ruffin fires the first shot upon Sumter. The Civil War begins.

● **April 12** Federal troops reinforce Fort Pickens at Pensacola, Florida. The Confederates are unable to prevent the landings, and the fort remains in Union hands throughout the war.

Above: Union troops burn the U.S. arsenal at Harpers Ferry on April 18, 1861. (Leslies)

April 18 ●
Colonel Robert E. Lee is offered command of all the Union armies. Still undecided where his loyalties lie, he refuses.

WAR IN THE EAST

● **April 18** The first troops arrive in Washington for the defense of the capital.

● **April 20** Finally deciding to go with his state rather than the Union, Colonel Robert E. Lee resigns from the Union army.

● **April 21** Robert E. Lee is given command of Virginia's defenses.

● **April 19** Massachusetts infantry, marching through Baltimore en route to Washington are attacked by a mob of southern sympathizers, and return fire. Four soldiers and 12 civilians are killed.

● **April 26** Major General Joseph E. Johnston, the highest ranking army officer to go with the Confederacy, is assigned command of all Virginia State forces around Richmond. Meanwhile Thomas J. Jackson of the Virginia Military Institute is promoted to Colonel and sent to Harpers Ferry.

WAR IN THE WEST

● **April 25** Captain Stokes of Illinois leads a raid on the St. Louis Arsenal which seizes 10,000 muskets and other stores before the Confederates know what is happening.

● **April 20** The USS *Merrimack* is burned and sunk at the Gosport Navy Yards before the Yards are handed over to the Confederacy. However, the Confederacy will be able to raise and restore the ship, renaming it the CSS *Virginia.*

THE NAVAL WAR

● **April 21** Telegraph and rail connections through Baltimore are cut, leaving Washington effectively cut off from the rest of the Union.

Below: Fort Sumter under bombardment. (LC)

● **April 13** After a bombardment which results in no casualties on either side, Major Robert Anderson surrenders Fort Sumter. The next day, as U.S. troops evacuate the fort, Anderson is permitted to fire a 100-round salute to his flag, during which a burning ember falls on powder causing an explosion which kills Private Daniel Hough and wounds two others. These are the first casualties of the war.

Above: The 65-man garrison of Fort Sumter attempts to fire back on the attackers. The fort is designed for a garrison of 650 men. (Leslies)

April 15 ●
President Lincoln issues a call for 75,000 volunteers to serve for three months.

● **April 16** Governor Harris of Tennessee rejects Lincoln's call for troops and takes the state into the Confederacy, despite the fact that voters had already rejected secession.

● **April 17** A Secession Convention in Virginia votes to join the Confederacy.

● **April 26** The governor of Georgia repudiates all debts owed to northern interests.

April 29 ●
The Maryland House of Delegates votes 53 to 13 against secession.

POLITICS

● **May 3** General George McClellan is placed in command of the newly-formed Department of the Ohio, covering Ohio, Indiana, and Illinois. When he later moves his army into western Virginia, McClellan will claim the credit for all the victories there, though the battles will be mostly fought by other subordinate generals.

● **May 6** Captain Nathaniel Lyon disguises himself as a woman, complete with veil to hide his red hair and beard, and tours militia camps in St. Louis, Missouri to gather intelligence.

● **May 10** Captain Lyon, with 7,000 troops, imprisons 700 pro-Confederate militia in St. Louis, causing a riot in which 28 men, women and children are killed.

WAR IN THE WEST

Left: Nathaniel Lyon after his masquerade as a woman. Promoted to general, he is killed at the Battle of Wilson's Creek, August 10, 1861. (M)

Right: An astute politician, General Ben Butler is the North's foremost political general. NA)

May 18 ●
Union ships blockade the mouth of the Rappahannock River.

Left: Harpers Ferry, scene of several momentous events. (NA)

WAR IN THE EAST

Left: A young Thomas "Stonewall" Jackson (ILN). Eccentric and austere, he suchs lemons all the time, even during battle, and will not eat pepper because it makes his left leg ache. He would stand rather than sit because sitting puts his internal organs "out of alignment". He is described as a "blue-eyed killer."

● **May 14** William Tecumseh Sherman returns to the army, accepting a commission as commander of the 13th Infantry. On the same day Irvin McDowell is promoted to Brigadier General.

Left: William Tecumseh Sherman. His middle name is that of the Shawnee war leader. Subject to deep depressions, in a 1880 speech he said, "war is hell." (LC)

May 17 ●
North Carolina is admitted to the Confederacy.

● **May 3** Lincoln expands his troop requirements, calling for 42,000 more volunteers to serve for three years.

● **May 3** Governor Jackson of Missouri declares the state for the South.

● **May 4** Pro-Union groups in western Virginia meet to discuss secession from Virginia.

● **May 6** Tennessee and Arkansas officially leave the Union.

● **May 13** Queen Victoria announces that England is strictly neutral in the conflict.

POLITICS

May 2
At Fortress Monroe Gen. Ben Butler refuses to re[turn] three slaves who escaped into his lines, calls them "contraban[d] war." From this point escaped slaves have a haven behind Union li[nes]

May 2[?]
Union troops c[ross] the Potomac R[iver] and s[eize] Alexan[dria,] Virginia. Col[onel] Elmer Ellswort[h of] the First [New York] Zouaves (11th [New] York) seiz[es a] Confederate [flag] from a hotel an[d is] killed by the ow[ner] James Jack[son.] Jackson is hi[mself] killed. Both bec[ome] martyrs for [their] respective s[ides.]

● **May 20** The Confederacy vot[es to] move its capital [from] Montgomery, Al[abama] to Richmond, V[irginia.]

● **May 20** Nort[h] Carolina official[ly] secedes from th[e] Union, the 11th [and] last state to do [so.]

● **May 20** Kent[ucky] declares itself n[eutral] and forbids the [move]ment of any tro[ops on] state soil, a po[sition] almost immedi[ately] violated by both [sides.]

● **May 20** Tele[graph] offices through[out the] North are raide[d by] U.S. Marshals [and copies] of all telegrams [from] the last year are [seized] in an attempt t[o iden]tify spies.

34

07 08 09 10 11 12 13 14 15 16 17 18 19 20 21 22 23 24 25 26 27 28 29 30 01 02 03 04 05 06 07 08 09 10 11 12 13 14 15 16 17 18 19 20 21 22 23

JUNE 1861

SUNDAY   SUNDAY   SUNDAY   SUNDAY

JULY 1861

SATURDAY

28 29 30 31 01 02 03 04 05 06 07 08 09 10 11 12 13 14 15 16 17 18 19 20 21 22 23 24 25 26 27 28 29 30 01 02 03 04 05 06 07 08 09 10 11 12 13

Below: Captain George Hollins, who along with his Union counterpart Nathianiel Lyon, uses the ages-old trick of dressing as a woman when in enemy territory. Beard regrown, he becomes commodore of the Confederate fleet at Island No. 10 in 1862. (M)

July 5 ●
Union General Franz Sigel attacks the forces of Missouri governor Claiborne Jackson. Jackson counter-attacks and Sigel retreats through Carthage, Missouri. Jackson then links up with Confederate General Sterling Price.

July 11 ●
A Union force under General Jacob Dolson Cox begins the ascent of the Great Kanawha Valley by boat. This is the second prong of the movement into western Virginia orchestrated by General McClellan.

Right: Raphael Semmes, who is promoted to Admiral in 1865. After the destruction of the Confederate navy that year, he transfers to land duty, and as a brigadier general, leads a marine brigade. (M)

bove left and right: In a war on the cusp of technological change, communications vary from the enturies-old to the most modern of devices. Lincoln often relies on telegrams from the front, made possible by the U.S. Military Telegraph Construction Corps stringing the insulated telegraph wire. Members of the core need good balance and a head for heights. (M)

● **June 29** Captain George N. Hollins, disguised as a woman, boards Union steamer *St. Nicholas* as it sails between Baltimore and Washington. With other Confederates, Hollins then seizes the ship and sails her down to Chesapeake Bay where she is used to capture three other Union vessels.

● **July 6** Commander Semmes arrives at Cienfuegos, Cuba having captured seven Union ships.

● **June 30** Commander Raphael Semmes aboard CSS *Sumter* breaks through the Union blockade at the mouth of the Mississippi to begin his career as the most successful commerce raider in the Confederate navy.

ove: Aides-demp and battlefield riers are an older hod of relaying ssages. They often e to ride through thick of the firing eep the battlefield . in touch with the t line. (B&L)

● **June 3** A strange turnabout at sea when, within the space of one day, Union brig *Joseph* is captured by Confederate privateer *Savannah*, which is in turn captured by the USS *Perry*.

● **June 10** The USS *Merrimack*, raised from the bottom at the Gosport Navy Yards, is renamed CSS *Virginia*.

Above: The the view from the Signal Camp at Georgetown Heights, outslde Washington. Traditional communication systems such as signal flags , backed up with up-to-date telescopes, are still used. (B&L)

Right: Converting the *Virginia* into an ironclad. The wooden hull is covered with two layers of two-inch-thick iron plate. A first attempt to float her proves she is unstable, and two hundred tons of pig iron have to be used as ballast. (M)

Right: The Battle of Rich Mountain. (LC)

● **July 2** Union General Robert Patterson moves into the Shenandoah Valley with the aim of keeping confederate General Johnston occupied while McDowell moves against Manassas.

● **June 1** Union cavalry are defeated by Confederate troops at Fairfax Court House, Virginia.

● **June 24** J.D. Mills of New York demonstrates what is effectively the world's first machine gun to President Lincoln. However, cost and indecision by senior army officers mean that few of the guns are ever purchased, and fewer still ever deployed.

● **June 29** General Irvin McDowell outlines his plans for attacking Confederate forces at Manassas Junction.

● **July 11** Union General William S. Rosecrans defeats Confederate army at Rich Mountain in western Virginia. At the same time, some miles to the north at Laurel Hill, Union General T.A. Morris forces Confederate General Robert S. Garnett to abandon his position.

low: General auregard, superndent of West nt for less than a ek when the war aks out and he gns to join the uth. (M)

● **June 2** General Pierre Gustave Toutant Beauregard takes command of all Confederate forces in northern Virginia.

● **June 8** All Virginia troops are transferred to the Confederate government, leaving Robert E. Lee with no command. He serves as an advisor to President Davis.

● **June 17** "Professor" Thaddeus S.C. Lowe ascends in a balloon to demonstrate its effectiveness for aerial observation and artillery direction.

July 13 ●
Garnett continues his retreat across the Cheat Mountains, but Union troops catch up with him at Corrick's Ford. Garnett is killed, the first general to be killed in the war, and 555 Confederate troops surrender. The northern part of western Virginia is now clear of Confederate troops.

● **June 3** Union troops in Philippi, western Virginia, take Confederate troops totally by surprise. The rebels flee with Union forces in hot pursuit. This becomes known as the "Philippi Races", and helps to establish the reputation of General McClellan.

● **June 10** The first serious battle of the war at Big Bethel, Virginia is a Confederate victory.

● **June 3** Stephen Douglas dies in Springfield, Illinois. Douglas's debates with Lincoln in 1860 had helped establish Lincoln as a national politician. Douglas was one of the Democrat candidates who ran against Lincoln for the Presidency, but when the war began he worked loyally for the Union.

● **June 15** Brigadier General Joseph E. Johnston, now in charge of troops at Harpers Ferry, evacuates the town and moves south toward Winchester.

Left: Federal Review of Troops on Independence Day, July 4, 1861. (ILN)

● **May 29** In Washington, Dorothea Dix is authorized to organize and establish military hospitals.

● **June 11** Pro-Unionists at Wheeling in western Virginia meet to form a separate state government.

● **June 19** Francis H. Pierpont is named provisional governor of what will eventually be West Virginia.

● **July 2** Lincoln suspends the writ of *habeus corpus* on or near any military line between Washington and New York.

JULY 1861

SUNDAY

AUGUST 1861

SUNDAY

14 15 16 17 18 19 20 21 22 23 24 25 26 27 28 29 30 31 01 02 03 04 05 06 07 08 09 10 11 12 13 14 15 16 17 18 19 20 21 22 23 24 25 26 27 28 29

Above: George Brinton McClellan. An excellent organizer and administrator, McClellan builds the magnificent Army of the Potomac but is cautious and hesitant in the field. (NA)

Right: General J. D. Cox. (M)

July 24 ●
General Cox reaches Charleston, western Virginia, and attacks the Confederates of General Henry A. Wise. Wise retreats.

July 25 ●
Major General John Charles Frémont assumes command of the Department of Missouri.

Aug 2 ●
General Frémont arrives in Cairo, Illinois with eight boats and reinforcements for General Lyon.

● July 31 Colonel Ulysses S. Grant is promoted to Brigadier General.

Aug 5 ●
Lyon retreats from Dug Springs, Missouri in the face of a larger Confederate force.

● July 25 General Cox occupies Charleston. The Union has now secured all the navigable headwaters of the Ohio River, gained control of valuable coal and salt mines, and ensured that the pro-Union counties of what would become West Virginia remain outside the Confederacy.

● July 28 The entire Seventh U.S. Infantry surrenders to Confederate troops at St. Augustine Springs, New Mexico, without a shot being fired.

Right: Ulysses S. Grant is a short, stubby man with light brown hair and beard, blue eyes, always smoking a cigar and, when there is no fighting to be done, a propensity for drink. He has no time for grand uniforms. (LC)

July 22 ●
Lincoln calls Major General George B. McClellan from western Virginia to assume command of all Union forces around Washington. Command of the Department of the Ohio goes to Rosecrans.

● July 15 Patterson skirmishes with Confederate cavalry north of Winchester.

● July 16 McDowell, with 35,000 men, the largest American army ever assembled, begins his advance toward Manassas. Undisciplined and ill-trained troops break ranks to sit in the shade or pick blackberries; much equipment is discarded along the way.

● July 25 Major General Banks replaces Patterson in command of Union troops in the Shenandoah Valley.

● July 27 McClellan assumes command of the newly formed Army of the Potomac.

● July 17 McDowell reaches Fairfax Court House. Meanwhile Patterson has defied orders to withdraw from Winchester, leaving Confederate General Johnston free to move his troops to join the main army at Manassas.

BULL RUN CAMPAIGN

● July 18 A Union reconnaissance clashes with Confederate troops near Centreville and is forced to retreat.

● July 19 General Thomas J. Jackson arrives with his troops at Manassas.

Below: Brigadier General Bernard Bee coins the nickname "Stonewall" for Thomas Jackson before he is killed at the Battle of Bull Run. (M)

● July 20 General Johnston with the main body of his army arrives at Manassas. McDowell and his officers reconnoiter the proposed battlefield.

Above: Ambrose Burnside's brigade attacks Confederate batteries during the First Battle of Bull Run. The original drawing, by Alfred Waud, was published in the *New York Illustrated News* on August 5, 1961. (LC)

Left: Irvin McDowell, whose inexperienced troops break at the Battle of Bull Run. (M)

● July 21 BATTLE OF BULL RUN (MANASSAS) (see page 98)
Several U.S. congressmen and their ladies bring picnics to Centreville to watch the battle, interfering with troop movements during the battle and creating even greater problems during the retreat.

Both armies begin by trying to turn the other's left flank, causing the whole battle to slowly turn. At first the Union have the better of it, but Jackson's men, in a relatively secure position on the crest of a hill, hold firm. General Bee, rallying his own men, cries: "There is Jackson, standing like a stone wall" and the name "Stonewall Jackson" sticks. Bee himself is killed shortly after. This is the turning point. In the confusion a Union retreat becomes a rout, but the Confederate forces are themselves so disorganized that there is no pursuit. In less than one day fleeing Union troops cover as much ground as it had taken them two and a half days to cover on the way to Manassas.

Aug 1 ●
Brazil recognizes the Confederate States as a belligerent, the first foreign nation to do so.

WAR IN THE WEST

Left: General Robert Anderson. (WP)

● Aug 14 General Frémont imposes martial law in St. Louis and closes two local newspapers with southern sympathies.

● Aug 15 Newly-promoted General Anderson, the hero of Fort Sumter, is named the new Commander of the Department of the Cumberland, consisting of Kentucky and Tennessee. He establishes his H.Q. in Cincinnati, Ohio.

Aug 30 ●
General Frémont decla[res] martial law throughou[t] Missouri, confiscates t[he] property of "those who ta[ke] up arms against the Unit[ed] States," and declares th[e] slaves free, all without co[n]sulting Lincoln. Lincoln ca[lls] these acts "dictatorial" a[nd] will later repudiate the[m].

Below: The Battle of Wilson's Creek. (MARS)

● Aug 10 Battle of Wilson's Creek, Missouri, the first major battle in the West. Union General Lyon, with 5,400 men, divides his force in the face of a Confederate army of 11,000, but General Sigel's attack on the Confederate rear comes to nothing and Lyon is killed leading his men. The Union army retreats to Rolla near St. Louis, leaving the Confederates in control of a large part of Missouri.

● Aug 8 Congress appropriates a sum of $1,500,000 for the construction of iron-clad ships The result of this investment will be the USS *Monitor,* and other ironclads called "monitors".

● Aug 17 The Departments of Northeastern Virginia, Washington and the Shenandoah are merged to form the Army of the Potomac.

Aug ?
After two days of shel[ling] which result in some phy[sical] damage but only light cas[ual]ties, Fort Hatteras, N[orth] Carolina, surrenders to Gen[eral] Butler, sealing off one o[f the] South's most important p[orts.] This is the first successful i[nva]sion of Confederate terri[tory.]

Below: With the fleet firing on the fort and providing cover, Union forces land at Hatteras

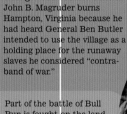

WAR IN THE EAST

Above: John Magruder is a flamboyant character with luxuriant muttonchop whiskers, a taste for fancy uniforms, and a love of amateur theatricals. His excessive lifestyle earns him the nickname "Prince John." (M)

● Aug 7 Confederate General John B. Magruder burns Hampton, Virginia because he had heard General Ben Butler intended to use the village as a holding place for the runaway slaves he considered "contraband of war."

Aug 20 ●
Major General George Brinton McClellan assumes command of the Army of the Potomac.

Aug ?
Unprecedentedly, the Confed[erate] government in Richmon[d pro]motes five full generals: S[amuel] Cooper (the Confederate ad[jutant] general), Albert Sidney John[ston,] Robert E. Lee, Joseph E. Joh[nston] and P.G.T. Beau[regard.]

Left: Confederate spy Rose Greenhow (right of picture). She later goes to Britain to raise money and support for the Confederate cause. (LC)

Part of the battle of Bull Run is fought on the land of Wilmer McLean. Afterwards, McLean moves his family to a place of greater safety, Appomattox Court House.

POLITICS

● Aug 8 The Confederate Government recognizes Kentucky, Missouri, Maryland and Delaware as being part of the Confederacy, even though it doesn't control any of these states. But this means that troops can be raised in these states and mustered into the Confederate army.

● Aug 16 Lincoln formally declares the southern states to be in rebellion.

● Aug 24 Mrs. Rose Greenhow, a prominent leader of Washington soci[ety] is arrested for spying. She had sent coded notes, hid[den] in the hair of a sympathet[ic] girl, which revealed McDowell's movements before Bull Run.

● Aug 24 Confederate P[resident] Davis names James M. M[ason] commissioner to Great Br[itain] and John Slidell as comm[issioner] to France, with the job o[f gaining] recognition and also of p[urchas]ing arms and equipment.

SUNDAY

SEPTEMBER 1861

SUNDAY

SUNDAY

SUNDAY

OCTOBER 1861

SATURDAY

03 04 05 06 07 08 09 10 11 12 13 14 15 16 17 18 19 20 21 22 23 24 25 26 27 28 29 30 01 02 03 04 05 06 07 08 09 10 11 12 13 14 15 16 17 18 19

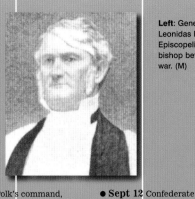

Sept 2 The Confederate government assigns General Leonidas Polk, formerly Episcopalian bishop of Louisiana, command of Arkansas and Missouri.

Left: General Leonidas Polk, an Episcopelian bishop before the war. (M)

● **Sept 22** Kansas Jayhawkers – pro-Union guerrillas – loot and burn the town of Osceola, Missouri.

● **Oct 7** Frémont belatedly leaves St. Louis to begin the chase of Sterling Price, unaware that Lincoln and Secretary of War Simon Cameron are already considering his dismissal.

● **Sept 20** Mulligan capitulates at Lexington after waiting in vain for relief from Frémont. The victory is a big morale booster for the South, but Price doesn't hold onto Lexington for long, instead retreating toward Arkansas.

● **Oct 8** General William Tecumseh Sherman assumes command of the Department of the Cumberland after his predecessor, Robert Anderson (the hero of Fort Sumter) is forced to retire due to ill health.

● **Sept 3** On Polk's command, General Gideon Pillow marches his Confederate troops into Kentucky on his way to Columbus, Kentucky, thus breaking the state's neutrality. Polk claims he has to take Columbus to protect it from Union forces across the Mississippi River.

● **Sept 12** Confederate General Sterling Price lays siege to the Irish Brigade, founded and led by Chicago politician James Mulligan, at Lexington, Missouri.

Right: General Sterling Price. (M)

● **Sept 6** Recognizing that the Confederate occupation of Columbus threatens the Tennessee and Cumberland Rivers, Grant acts by seizing Paducah, Kentucky without a shot being fired.

Right: General Albert Sydney Johnston. (M)

Right: Building a temporary breastwork of hemp bales for cover, Confederate soldiers fire at the Union forces penned up in Lexington. The bales are soaked with water so they will not catch fire in the shooting. (B&L)

CONFEDERATES FIGHTING BEHIND HEMP BALES AT LEXINGTON. SEE PAGE 212.

● **Sept 10** General Albert Sidney Johnston is appointed head of Confederate armies in the west.

● **Oct 4** USS *South Carolina* captures 4,000 to 5,000 stands of arms when it seizes two Confederate blockade runners near the mouth of the Mississippi River.

● **Oct 12** For the first time, the Confederate navy uses a metal-sheathed ram, *Manassas*, accompanied by two other armed steamers, to attack Union ships in the Mississippi delta south of New Orleans. USS *Richmond* and USS *Vincennes* are both forced aground.

Below: A Confederate attempt to re-take Hatteras is repulsed, and the attackers have to withdraw to their boats. (B&L)

● **Sept 17** The Federal navy destroys Confederate defenses at Ocracoke Inlet, North Carolina, closing another port to blockade runners.

● **Oct 12** The Union navy launches its first ironclad, the *St. Louis* on the Mississippi River at Carondelet, Missouri.

● **Sept 17** A landing party from USS *Massachusetts* captures Ship Island, Mississippi, which will become an important refueling base for the blockading squadrons.

Left: Woodsmen from Michigan in the Fourth Michigan Infantry. They wear tasseled caps and short leggings. (M)

● **Sept 10** Union General Rosecrans attacks Confederate lines at Carnifix Ferry in western Virginia. The Confederates withdraw.

● **Sept 15** Lee closes his campaign in western Virginia.

● **Sept 11** In western Virginia, General Lee attempts a complex five-pronged attack on Union forces on Cheat Mountain, but the troops are ill-coordinated, the weather is appalling and the attempt fails.

Oct 9 ●
A Confederate attack on the Union troops in control of Fort Pickens, Florida, is beaten back.

Early Oct Troops North and South start moving into winter quarters.

Below: General Frémont. (M)

● **Sept 10** In a letter hand-delivered to Lincoln by his wife, Frémont declares that he will not rescind the emancipation order except if ordered by the President. Lincoln is displeased with the letter and has a furious row with firebrand Mrs Frémont.

● **Sept 12–17** Maryland legislators suspected of being disloyal to the Union are arrested. The state remains loyal.

● **Oct 6** The Pony Express, the hard-riding mail service that linked the east and west coasts of America, is officially discontinued after a mere 18 months of existence.

Above: Cold canvas in the snow. The Forty-fourth New York's winter quarters. (M)

THE *TRENT* INCIDENT

Above: The Fifth Vermont regiment on review at their 1861 camp near Washington. (M)

Sept 2 Lincoln orders Frémont to rescind his emancipation order in Missouri.

● **Sept 7** The furor over Frémont's high-handed manner, profligacy, and inaction in the face of Confederate General Sterling Price's advance on Lexington prompts Lincoln to dispatch General David Hunter to St. Louis to "assist" Frémont.

● **Sept 25** Secretary of the Navy Gideon Welles instructs that "contrabands," escaped slaves, can be enlisted in naval service.

● **Oct 3** Governor Moore of Louisiana bans the shipment of cotton to New Orleans. This is part of a concerted effort across the South to starve England and France of cotton and so force diplomatic recognition.

● **Oct 12** James Mason, Confederate Commissioner to England, and John Slidell, Commissioner to France, slip through the blockade aboard CSS *Theodora* bound for Cuba.

37

03 04 05 06 07 08 09 10 11 12 13 14 15 16 17 18 19 20 21 22 23 24 25 26 27 28 29 30 01 02 03 04 05 06 07 08 09 10 11 12 13 14 15 16 17 18 19

OCTOBER 1861

NOVEMBER 1861

NOVEMBER 1861

SUNDAY

SUNDAY

20 21 22 23 24 25 26 27 28 29 30 31 01 02 03 04 05 06 07 08 09 10 11 12 13 14 15 16 17 18 19 20 21 22 23 24 25 26 27 28 29 30 01 02 03 04 05 0

● **Oct 24** General R.S. Curtis receives, from Lincoln, the orders that will relieve Frémont from command, though they are not to be delivered if Frémont has just won a battle. Frémont's pursuit of Price, meanwhile, is gallant but far from a victory.

● **Oct 28** Confederate General Albert Sidney Johnston takes over command of the Army of Central Kentucky from General Simon Bolivar Buckner.

Right: General Gideon Pillow, Grant's opponent at the Battle of Belmont. (M)

Oct 29 ●
77 ships, the largest Union fleet assembled to date, sail from Fort Monroe on Hampton Roads, intent on capturing Port Royal, South Carolina.

Below: A sailing ship of the old navy, the *Sabine* is the first blockader in the South Atlantic. (M)

● **Oct 23** In an effort to stamp out Confederate privateers, the officers and men of the CSS *Savannah* are placed on trial in New York and accused of piracy.

● **Oct 21 BATTLE OF BALL'S BLUFF** Union troops under General Charles P. Stone are ferried across the Potomac in inadequate boats, but are unable to establish a bridgehead. On the retreat the boats are swamped, leading to large numbers of Union troops being drowned or captured. Stone is blamed for the debacle, accused of treason, and imprisoned, though he will later be restored to duty.

Right: General Winfield Scott, 75 at the outbreak of the war and so fat and incapacitated with gout that he cannot mount his horse unaided, he remains one of the finest strategic minds in the North until the emergence of Grant. (VMI)

● **Oct 24** Western Union's transcontinental telegraph line is finally completed.

● **Nov 1** The order relieving Frémont of duty has now been delivered by subterfuge, but Frémont has arrested the messenger so news won't get out. He now sets out to pursue Sterling Price, but Price has already retreated beyond reach.

● **Nov 2** Frémont finally accepts the inevitable and leaves his command.

● **Nov 1** The fleet sailing for Port Royal hits a storm off Cape Hatteras. The ships are scattered and one transport is sunk.

● **Oct 25** The keel is laid for the USS *Monitor* at Greenpoint, NY.

● **Nov 4** The Union fleet has now re-grouped and is gathering outside Port Royal Sound while a survey vessel takes readings of the channel.

Nov 9 ●
Union troops from Port Royal capture Beaufort, South Carolina, without a fight, effectively cutting all Confederate communications by water between Charleston and Savannah.

Oct–Nov General George B. McClellan has spent the autumn organizing and training the Army of the Potomac, ensuring food and medical supplies and imposing discipline. He has become a great favorite with his troops, who call him "Little Mac," but despite continuous calls from the administration he has taken no offensive action. During this period he has taken to criticizing Lincoln personally, both in private and in public. Lincoln has taken to asking if he can "borrow" the army for a while.

● **Nov 1** General Winfield Scott, hero of the Mexican War and senior officer in the Union army, retires.

THE SHENANDOAH VALLEY CAMPAIGN

● **Nov 4** "Stonewall" Jackson leaves Fairfax Court House for the Shenandoah Valley.

Nov 8 ●
Confederate Commissioners Mason and Slidell leave Cuba aboard the British ship *Trent*. The *Trent* is stopped in international waters by USS *San Jacinto*, and Mason and Slidell are taken aboard the Union ship.

● **Nov 7** U.S. Grant captures a Confederate position near Belmont, Missouri, but is soon forced to retire when General Polk launches a counterattack.

● **Nov 9** General Henry Halleck is assigned command of the Department of the Missouri, making him the superior officer for both Grant and Sherman.

● **Nov 7** The fleet enters Port Royal Sound, quickly disposes of the small Confederate squadron, and turns its fire on the two forts that guard the bay. The forts are quickly abandoned, giving the Union control of another major Confederate port.

WAR IN THE WEST

Nov 9 William Tecumseh Sherman has been bombarding Secretary of War Cameron with reports about Confederate movements and claiming that at least 200,000 troops will be needed for victory in the Mississippi Valley (a conservative estimate, as it turns out). This, with his usual melancholy, is interpreted as a sign of madness and Sherman is replaced by Don Carlos Buell. Sherman is re-assigned to Halleck's command in Missouri.

THE NAVAL WAR

Below: General Halleck (NA), and **right:** General Buell (M), are supposed to work together in the west.

● **Nov 21** Jefferson Davis names Judah P. Benjamin the Confederate secretary of war.

Nov 18 ●
A convention at Russellville, Kentucky, passes an ordinance of secession from the Union.

POLITICS

● **Nov 20** A convention at Hatteras, North Carolina, repudiates Kentucky's secession and establishes a provisional pro-Union state government. Kentucky now, effectively, has two governments.

Diplomats A.P. Mason (**left**) amd John Slidell (**above right**) are nearly the cause of war between the Federal government and Britain. (M)

● **Nov 15** *San Jacinto* refuels at Hampton Roads, Virginia, and Captain John Wilkes informs the shore authorities that he has Mason and Slidell aboard.

THE *TRENT* INCIDENT

● **Nov 16** Senator Sumner and Montgomery Blair, a member of Lincoln's cabinet, both urge the President to release Mason and Slidell immediately.

● **Nov 24** In the face of five Union ships, Confederates abandon Tybee Island in Savannah Harbor, and the Union takes possession.

● **Nov 25** The first load of armor plate arrives at Norfolk Navy Yard for the transformation of the USS *Merrimack* into the CSS *Virginia*.

● **Nov 24** Mason and Slidell are imprisoned at Fort Warren, Boston, while Captain Wilkes is hailed as a Union hero.

● **Nov 27** The *Trent* arrives in England with news of the seizure of Mason and Slidell in international waters.

Dec 5
General William J. Hardee assumes command of the Confederate Central Army of Kentucky.

Left: The Battle of Belmont (LC)

BEAUREGARD'S MARCH.

CHAS. LENSCHOW.

● **Dec 2** In his firs annual report to th President, Secreta of the Navy Gideo Welles is able to sa that the Union blo ade of the South h already resulted ir the capture of 153 blockade runners.

● **Dec 1** Lincoln, increa ly exasperated with McClellan's inaction, demands to know: "hov long would it require to actually get in motion?"

● **Dec 2** Lincoln authorizes Halle suspend the writ *habeus corpus* w ever he feels it n sary in the Department of Missouri. This is significant exter of his autocratic powers.

● **Nov 30** The British Parliament has been in u about this act of piracy, a the British Foreign Secre Lord Russell, announces boarding the *Trent* const tutes an act of aggression against Britain. He prepa to recall the British Minis in Washington, Lord Lyor

● **Dec 1** Lincoln's Cal split over the incident William H. Seward, th retary of state, thinks war with Britain is lik that it will reunite the try to face a common Lincoln is less certain war at a time," he say in his address to Cong today omits any ment the *Trent*.

Another Confederate agent, J.W. Zacharie, is removed from another F ship, *Eugenia Smith*, by another US vessel, USS *Santiago de Cuba*, in national waters, this time off the mouth of the Rio G.

38

20 21 22 23 24 25 26 27 28 29 30 31 01 02 03 04 05 06 07 08 09 10 11 12 13 14 15 16 17 18 19 20 21 22 23 24 25 26 27 28 29 30 01 02 03 04 05

DECEMBER 1861   SUNDAY   SUNDAY   SUNDAY   # JANUARY 1862   SUNDAY   SATURDAY

10 11 12 13 14 15 16 17 18 19 20 21 22 23 24 25 26 27 28 29 30 31 01 02 03 04 05 06 07 08 09 10 11 12 13 14 15 16 17 18 19 20 21 22 23 24 25

Left: General Hardee resigns from the U.S. Army in January 1861 in order to join the Confederate Army. (LC)

● **Dec 26** Halleck declares martial law in St. Louis and on all railroads through Missouri.

● **Dec 31** Lincoln discovers that his two most senior officers in the West, Buell and Halleck, not only do not, but will not, cooperate on concerted action.

● **Jan 7** Grant gains valuable information about the defenses around Forts Henry and Donelson after the USS *Conestoga* sails up the Tennessee and Cumberland rivers.

● **Jan 19**
THE BATTLE OF MILL SPRINGS (LOGAN'S CROSS ROADS)
Confederate General Felix Zollicoffer, a former journalist, has placed his men in a weak position with the Cumberland River at his back, but refuses to move on the instructions of his superior, General Crittenden. When Union troops under General George H. Thomas approach, Crittenden decides his only option is a surprise flank attack. But a week of continuous heavy rain means all troop movements are slow, and Thomas is not surprised. Zollicoffer, wearing a conspicuous white coat, is killed, and this precipitates a Confederate flight. It is the worst Confederate defeat so far and destroys all Confederate defenses in Kentucky.

Right: From a sketch by A. E. Mathews of the 31st Reg. Ohio Volunteers, of a scene in January 1862. Colonel Schoepf's Union troops are crossing Fishing Creek, Kentucky to join General Thomas before the Battle of Mill Springs. (LC)

Below: General Felix Zollicoffer, killed at Mill Springs. (M)

eet music, ch as for auregard's ", published in eft), and "Our National onfederate em" (**right**), shed in 1862, keep morale igh. (LC)

● **Dec 28–31** A Confederate attempt to isolate the Union troops at Port Royal is defeated in a three-day amphibious operation which entails closer cooperation than ever before between the Union army and navy.

● **Dec 10** The crew of a Union ship takes possession of an abandoned Confederate fort on the Ashepoo River in South Carolina.

Right: The Union's river iron-clad *Essex*, completed in January 1862. Converted from a snagboat by James Eads, the *Essex* is one of the "Mississippi monsters." (M)

● **Jan 9** Flag Officer David Glasgow Farragut is given command of the West Gulf Blockading Squadron, with the primary target of capturing New Orleans.

● **Dec 13** Union and Confederate forces clash at Buffalo Mountain in western Virginia. The two sides sustain about the same number of casualties, and both sides retreat.

Jan 12 ●
General Ambrose Burnside sails from Hampton Roads on an amphibious mission to capture Roanoke Island, which will give the Union control of most of the North Carolina coast.

● **Jan 13–20** Burnside's fleet gathers off Hatteras Inlet, only to be so buffeted by storms it is impossible to do anything. A number of boats are wrecked, and others badly damaged.

● **Jan 18** The USS *Kearsarge* sets out for Cadiz, Spain, to begun the hunt for Confederate raider Raphael Semmes aboard the CSS *Sumter*, a hunt that will take most of the war.

Dec 16 ●
ckson's command, including the newall Brigade, begins its inces-marching through the Valley by leaving camp at Winchester and marching nearly 30 miles via tinsburg to the Chesapeake and Ohio Canal.

THE SHENANDOAH VALLEY CAMPAIGN

● **Dec 17–20** Despite coming under fire from Union troops, the Stonewall Brigade destroys Dam No. 5 on the C&O Canal, making it useless for transporting goods.

Jan 1 ●
The Stonewall Brigade sets out for Romney with the aim of cutting the Baltimore and Ohio Railroad.

● **Jan 6** Though he continues to try to force McClellan in the east and Buell in the west into action, Lincoln resists demands from a group of influential senators that McClellan be removed from office due to his inactivity.

● **Jan 13** Lt. John L. Worden is assigned command of the USS *Monitor*, now being built at New York.

Jan 25 to Feb 3 ●
At Hatteras Inlet the ships of Burnside's fleet are slowly moved across the sandbar into Pamlico Sound ready for the assault on Roanoke Island.

ec 9 Congress estab-es the Joint Committee he Conduct of the War.

● **Dec 21** The Stonewall Brigade leaves the canal to begin a two-day march to their winter camp at Winchester.

Jan 4 ●
Jackson captures the town of Bath. The small Union force there is chased as far as the Potomac.

● **Jan 15** After two weeks on the march, the Stonewall Brigade finally reaches Romney.

● **Dec 10** Kentucky is admitted as the 13th state of the Confederacy. It will be the last state to join the Confederacy.

● **Jan 5** The town of Hancock, Maryland refuses to surrender to Jackson. The Confederates allow time for women and children to leave the town, then start shelling.

● **Jan 18** Jackson finally orders his exhausted troops into winter quarters at Bath. He had twice tried to attack Cumberland, Maryland, but each time had to call off the assault because he had too few troops fit for battle.

● **Dec 11** A fire sweeps through the business district of Charleston, South Carolina, exacerbating shortages already created by the blockade and the needs of the Confederate army.

● **Jan 6** Union reinforcements reach Hancock and Jackson is forced to withdraw, thus abandoning any plans to raid across the Potomac.

● **Dec 14** Prince Albert, the Prince Consort, dies. He had been a staunch advocate of moderation in the British response to the *Trent* affair.

● **Jan 7** After a surprise skirmish at Hanging Rock Pass, Jackson withdraws south as far as Unger's Store.

Left: In February 1862 Julia Ward Howe publishes her lyrics "The Battle Hymn of the Republic," to the tune of "John Brown's Body." She wrote the words after watching a military review in 1861. (M)

Dec 18 ●
Lord Russell drafts an ultimatum demanding the release of Mason and Slidell and an apology or Britain will go to war with America.

● **Dec 25** Lincoln's cabinet meets to discuss the fate of Mason and Slidell. A reply to the British ultimatum is needed the next day.

Above: Often in plain sight of each other, armies maneuver around the Shenandoah Valley. (B&L)

Dec 20 ●
8,000 British troops set sail for Canada to reinforce existing garrisons there.

● **Dec 21** Seward meets Lord Lyons to discuss British demands.

● **Dec 26** The cabinet decides that the seizure of Mason and Slidell was illegal and they should be released. Lord Lyons is informed. The *Trent* Incident is effectively over.

● **Jan 1** Confederate Commissioners Mason and Slidell are quietly released from their prison in Boston and board HMS *Rinaldo* to continue their long-interrupted journey to England.

● **Jan 11** Following charges of corruption in the War Department, Union Secretary of War Simon Cameron resigns.

● **Jan 15** Edwin M. Stanton is confirmed as Cameron's successor as Secretary of War.

JAN 1862 — FEBRUARY 1862 — FEBRUARY 1862 — M...

SUNDAY · SUNDAY · SUNDAY · SUNDAY

26 27 28 29 30 31 01 02 03 04 05 06 07 08 09 10 11 12 13 14 15 16 17 18 19 20 21 22 23 24 25 26 27 28 01 02 03 04 05 06 07 08 09 10 11 12 13

FORTS HENRY AND DONELSON CAMPAIGN

Feb 2 ●
Flag Officer Foote sets out with four gunboats from Cairo. Grant follows with troop transports carrying 23 regiments.

Jan 30 ●
After putting off the decision for several days, General Halleck finally orders General Grant accompanied by gunboats under Flag Officer Andrew Hull Foote to advance up the Cumberland and Tennessee Rivers.

Feb 4 ●
Grant's troops land five miles below Fort Henry. General Tilghman has only 3,000 troops in the garrison at the fort, and the high level of the river due to heavy winter rains means that parts of the fort are flooded.

● **Jan 26** General Beauregard is appointed second-in-command to Albert Sidney Johnston in Tennessee.

Below: The battle outside Fort Donelson. (LC)

● **Feb 6** Fire from Foote's gunboats is enough to convince General Tilghman to surrender. Tilghman knew that the fort could not be defended against assault, so he has already sent most of his garrison overland to Fort Donelson. The capture of Fort Henry means that the entire navigable length of the Tennessee River is now in Union hands. Foote now takes his boats back to Cairo for repairs while Grant prepares to take his still-fresh troops on to Fort Donelson on the Cumberland River.

● **Feb 7** Confederate reinforcements are hurried to Fort Donelson, because the Confederates recognize that if Donelson falls, the road to Nashville will lie open.

● **Feb 7** Union General John A. McClernand renames Fort Henry, "Fort Foote."

● **Feb 7** Three Confederate steamers, one of them loaded with torpedoes, are abandoned and burned on the Tennessee River to prevent them from falling into Union hands.

● **Feb 9** Confederate General Gideon J. Pillow assumes command of Fort Donelson.

Jan 30 ●
USS *Monitor* is launched at Greenpoint, Long Island. Although not the world's first ironclad, she was the most advanced ship in the world at the time, with innovative shape (most of the ship was below the waterline) and design (mounted on a turntable, both guns could be brought to bear all the time).

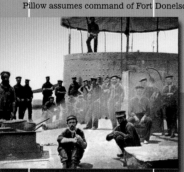

Right: The multi-racial crew aboard the *Monitor*, the most advanced ship in the world at the time. (M)

Left: Flag Officer Andrew Foote. (B&L)

● **Jan 27** Confederate General Wise, in charge of the defenses at Roanoke Island, is ordered to hold it at all costs.

● **Jan 27** Lincoln issues General War Order No. 1, announcing that on February 22 all land and sea forces will attack the rebels. This is a final act of desperation to force McClellan and Buell to move.

● **Feb 7** Confederate troops abandon Romney and move back toward Winchester.

● **Jan 30** Mason and Slidell finally arrive in Southampton.

● **Feb 11** Confederate General Simon Bolivar Buckner arrives at Fort Donelson with reinforcements.

● **Feb 11** Flag Officer Foote sets sail once more to assist Grant in his assault on Fort Donelson. Meanwhile, General McClernand is taking his troops cross-country from Fort Henry, while Grant himself is following the river.

● **Feb 12** Grant establishes a ring around Fort Donelson.

● **Feb 13** General Floyd arrives at Fort Donelson and assumes command. Meanwhile the first Union gunboat to arrive commences bombarding the fort.

● **Feb 14** Grant begins his assault on Fort Donelson with a bombardment by the gunboats, but Confederate fire cripples two of the ships and the attack is broken off.

● **Feb 8** Off Roanoke Island, Union ships enter Albemarle Sound, facing only token resistance from Confederate ships. Burnside's troops, meanwhile, face murderous fire from a battery that can supposedly be approached from only one direction. However, a way is found through what are meant to be impassable swamps, the battery is captured and with it the island falls. The capture of Roanoke not only closes off most of North Carolina's access to the sea, it also opens a back door to Norfolk and the Gosport Navy Yards.

Feb 7–8 ●
BATTLE OF ROANOKE ISLAND

Feb 7 ●
The amphibious assault on Roanoke Island gets under way.

● **Feb 10** Following the victory at Roanoke, USS *Delaware* pursues the retreating Confederate fleet, sinking one ship, capturing another and forcing the Confederates to burn three others to prevent their capture.

● **Feb 3** Washington decrees that the crews of captured Confederate privateers will be considered prisoners of war, not pirates.

Feb 13 ●
CSS *Virginia*, formerly the USS *Merrimack*, is launched at Norfolk Naval Yards. Such are the fears that she will not float, that when she is launched only five men are actually on board.

● **Feb 3** The King of Siam offers Lincoln war elephants, which Lincoln politely refuses.

— **Feb 17** Grant is promoted to major general.

● **Feb 19** Confederates evacuate Clarksville, Tennessee.

● **Feb 20** The government of Tennessee moves from Nashville to Memphis, while Confederate troops leave the city for Murfreesboro.

● **Feb 21** A mountain of food supplies stored in Nashville for the army in Georgia and Virginia is destroyed.

● **Feb 24** Union troops under Buell reach the Cumberland River opposite Nashville.

● **Feb 25** Nashville falls to Union troops.

WAR IN THE WEST

● **Feb 15** General Pillow assaults McClernand's lines and briefly manages to break them, but the advantage is not pursued and Pillow retreats back into the fort. Floyd decides to surrender, then flees the fort, Pillow follows suit, command devolves on General Buckner, an old friend of Grant's.

● **Feb 15–16** During the night, Nathan Bedford Forrest leads his cavalry through a freezing swamp to safety, the only large body of troops to escape.

● **Feb 16** General Buckner asks Grant for surrender terms. Grant replies: "No terms except unconditional and immediate surrender." This response will earn U.S. Grant the nickname "Unconditional Surrender Grant". Buckner accepts and the way to Nashville is open to the Union.

● **Feb 16** Flag Officer Foote sends gunboats upriver to destroy the Tennessee Iron Works at Dover.

● **Feb 20** Farragut arrives at Ship Island, Mississippi, to prepare his assault on New Orleans.

THE NAVAL WAR

● **Feb 22** Union gunboats on the Savannah River, Georgia, isolate Fort Pulaski from other Confederate defenses

Above: The inauguration of President Davis. (ILN)

POLITICS

● **Feb 22** Jefferson Davis inaugurated as the first Confederate president.

● **Feb 20** Lincoln's 12-year-old son, William, dies of typhoid fever.

Feb 23
Lincoln names Andrew Johnson, a native of the state, as military governor of Tennessee.

● **Feb 26** For the first time, paper money is recognized as national currency in the U.S.

Feb 18 ●
The first elected Congress of the Confederate States meets in Richmond.

March 2 ●
General Polk completes the Confederate withdrawal from Columbus, leaving the whole of Kentucky now in Union hands.

● **March 1** As Grant moves his forces along the Tennessee River from Fort Donelson, an advance party lands at Pittsburg Landing to sound out the Confederate forces that Albert Sidney Johnston is concentrating nearby at Corinth.

● **March 3** General Halleck has Grant removed from command for alleged misconduct (the charge is rumored to be drunkenness) and replaced with General C.F. Smith. This is the first of numerous clashes between Grant and Halleck.

● **March 3** Union General John Pope begins an assault on New Madrid, Missouri, which, together with Island Number 10, commands a vital bend in the Mississippi.

● **March 5** The first of Smith's troops arrive at Pittsburg Landing.

● **March 4** Flag Officer Foote sets off to assault a fort on the Columbus bluff above the Mississippi, only to find it already occupied by Union cavalry. The Confederates had mysteriously abandoned the fort some days before.

March 6 ●
Union General Samuel R. Curtis concentrates his forces between Sugar Creek and Pea Ridge in Arkansas, in the face of Confederate troops under Earl Van Dorn.

March 6 ●
USS *Monitor* leaves New York en route to Hampton Roads, Virginia.

March 7–8 ●
Monitor's southward progress is beset by storms and leaks, and at one point it seems she might sink, but she continues to limp on.

March 8–9 ●
BATTLE OF HAMPTON ROADS
March 8 CSS *Virginia*, "like a huge, half-submerged crocodile," sails from Norfolk Naval Yards into the Union fleet in Hampton Roads. The most powerful conventional Union ships are no match for the new ironclad. Shots bounce off her. *Virginia* rams and sinks USS *Cumberland*, sets USS *Congress* afire and drives USS *Minnesota* aground before retiring up the James River for the night.

● **March 3**
A curious engagement in Florida occurs when a Union gunboat fires on and chases a Confederate train.

THE SHENANDOAH VALLEY CAMPAIGN

March 5 ●
Union General Nathaniel Banks begins to move toward Jackson's positions at Winchester.

● **March 7**
Banks's troops skirmish with Jackson's at Winchester.

March 13 ●
Confederate troops evacuate New Madrid, and move to Island Number 10.

Confederate Brigadier General Stand Watie, a Cherokee, commander of Indian troops at Pea Ridge. (B&L)

● **March 7–8**
BATTLE OF PEA RIDGE
Overnight, Van Dorn splits his forces and maneuvers around the Union positions to a two-pronged attack on the rear. The surprise is not complete and Curtis is able to turn his forces to meet the attack. During a day of fierce fighting, initial Confederate success is not exploited and Confederate Generals McCulloch and McIntosh are killed. Next day, Van Dorn is forced to retreat.

March 13 ●
General Burnside moves his troops from Roanoke Island to the North Carolina mainland ready for an assault on New Bern.

March 14 ●
Burnside captures New Bern.

● **March 9** *Monitor*, the "cheesebox on a raft," arrives in Hampton Roads 1:00 a.m. *Virginia* returns to the fray not long after. The two oddly mis-matched ironclads fight each other fiercely for four and a half hours without inflicting noticeable damage on each other. But when *Virginia* draws off, *Monitor* is left the victor.

● **March 11** McClellan is retained as General-in-Chief but retains command of the Army of the Potomac.

● **March 13** McClellan reveals his plans to move his army to the tip of the York Peninsula and advance on Richmond that way.

● **March 13** Jackson withdraws south closely followed by Banks.

40

26 27 28 29 30 31 01 02 03 04 05 06 07 08 09 10 11 12 13 14 15 16 17 18 19 20 21 22 23 24 25 26 27 28 01 02 03 04 05 06 07 08 09 10 11 12 13

862   SUNDAY   SUNDAY   SUNDAY   APRIL 1862   SUNDAY   SUNDAY   MAY

18 19 20 21 22 23 24 25 26 27 28 29 30 31 01 02 03 04 05 06 07 08 09 10 11 12 13 14 15 16 17 18 19 20 21 22 23 24 25 26 27 28 29 30 01 02 03

rch 15 General Sherman and General Hurlbut arrive at ...sburg Landing with their ...sions, and Don Carlos ...ll is ordered to bring his ...ops down from Nashville. ...anwhile, General C.F. Smith ...dentally injures his leg, ... Halleck restores Grant to ...mand to replace him.

● March 24 The last of Albert Sidney Johnston's army arrives at Corinth.

● April 3 Albert Sidney Johnston begins to move his troops from Corinth to attack the Union armies at Pittsburg Landing. Despite numerous delays, sporadic skirmishing does break out around Shiloh Church. Even so, the Union forces remain unaware of the Confederate move.

● April 4 More skirmishing around the edges of the Union position at Pittsburg Landing as Johnston continues to face delays in bringing all his troops up. Nevertheless, Johnston somehow retains the advantage of surprise.

● APRIL 6–7 BATTLE OF SHILOH (SEE PAGE 102)
April 6 Johnston finally gets all his troops together and launches an all-out attack early in the morning. Union troops caught completely by surprise are sent rushing back toward the river. Hurlbut organizes a new line of defense, and at the Hornet's Nest Prentiss and his division hold up the rebel advance for six vital hours. Early in the afternoon Johnston is wounded in the leg and bleeds to death. Command passes to Beauregard. The Confederates have become disorganized, and by the end of the day the Union line has stabilized near the river.

Above: Prentiss defending the Hornets' Nest at the climax of the first day's fighting at Shiloh. His tenacious resistance in the Union center effectively saved the day for Grant. (WP)

: General Wallace, who ...s late at the ...of Shiloh, ...on to write ...ur after the ...ll Grant's ...n command- ... Shiloh – ...ut, ...ernand, ...ss, Sherman, ...Wallace and ... Wallace – ...wyers. (M)

● April 7 Overnight, Buell's troops arrive, and in the morning General Lew Wallace's division also arrives having spent the previous day hopelessly lost. Thus reinforced, Grant is able to counterattack, quickly regaining all the ground lost yesterday. Late in the afternoon, Beauregard decides to break off the engagement and retreat toward Corinth. It has been the bloodiest battle to date, a total of nearly 24,000 killed, wounded or missing.

Below: General Beauregard orders the Confederate withdrawal at Shiloh. (B&L)

...elow: The last hour of the Battle of Pea Ridge, ...e Union forces advancing to retake Elkhorn ...vern. (B&L)

● April 11 General Halleck arrives at Pittsburg Landing to take direct command of the troops there. Grant is again relegated to a subordinate position and even considers resigning.

● April 12 A party of Union volunteers under James J. Andrews seize a Confederate train, The General, at Big Shanty, Georgia. The Confederate train crew immediately gives chase. The hijackers are captured and Andrews and seven others are later executed.

Above: The "Great Locomotive Chase" in Georgia inspired Buster Keaton's film "The General." (B&L)

Above: Gunboats close in on Island Number 10 (NHC)

April 4 ● A canal is cut through swamps near Island Number 10 to enable small boats to move safely past the Confederate emplacements.

● April 7 With Union gunboats now above and below Island Number 10, General Pope launches his assault on the island and on Confederate positions at Tiptonville. After a brief defense, both positions surrender. The Mississippi River is now in Union control as far south as Memphis.

● May 1 Union General Ben Butler assumes control of New Orleans.

● March 20 General Ben Butler assumes command of the troops that will accompany Farragut in his assault on New Orleans.

Left: The epic Battle of Hampton Roads, the first between two ironclads. Hammering away at each other at close range, the *Monitor* and the *Merrimack* are making wooden warships obsolete. (LC)

● April 4 Union troops are landed near the mouth of the Mississippi River and destroy a Confederate camp.

● April 12 Captain Raphael Semmes and his crew abandon the Confederate raider CSS *Sumter* at Gibraltar because of boiler problems that cannot be repaired.

Above: Farragut running the gauntlet of fire to take New Orleans. (B&L)

● April 18 Union ships begin six days of mortar bombardment of the two forts, Jackson and St. Philip, which guard the mouth of the Mississippi. The bombardment has little effect.

● April 24 In the early hours of the morning, Farragut runs his fleet past the forts at the mouth of the Mississippi. The ships come under intense fire, but practically all make it through. The small Confederate fleet awaiting them soon flees upriver.

● April 25 New Orleans surrenders.

March 17 ...e Army of ...e Potomac ...gins board- ... transports ... the move ... the York ...ninsula.

● March 22 Jackson's "foot cavalry" are once again on the move, covering the 26 miles between Mt. Jackson and Strasburg. At Kernstown, Jackson's advance guard clashes with Union troops.

● March 29 A minor skirmish at Middleburg forces a Confederate retreat from the town. This is the first recorded use of a machine gun in battle.

● April 3 Lincoln insists that McDowell's corps be retained to defend Washington instead of moving to join McClellan at Fort Monroe.

● April 10–11 A Union force under Colonel Quincy Adams Gillmore attacks Fort Pulaski which guards the entrance to Savannah Harbor. After a bombardment of some 30 hours, the fort surrenders. Savannah itself is not taken, but the Confederacy has lost one more port for the remainder of the war.

● April 28 Forts Jackson and St. Philip at the mouth of the Mississippi surrender. The lower part of the river is now fully open to Union shipping.

● March 23 BATTLE OF KERNSTOWN
During the morning, Jackson brings the rest of his army up to Kernstown, and immediately goes into battle. His small army (variously reported at 2,700 and 3,500 men) is vastly outnumbered by a Union force of up to 11,000 men under General Shields. Jackson loses, but the battle convinces Washington that many more men are needed in the Shenandoah Valley, draining troops from McClellan's army.

● April 5 At Yorktown near the tip of the York Peninsula, Confederate General John Bankhead Magruder, with 20,000 men, holds McClellan's 100,000-strong army at bay by bluff, marching his men in a huge circle, in and out of woods so that it appears he has a much larger army.

May 3 ●
Having positioned siege guns around the Confederate positions at Yorktown, McClellan finds he doesn't have to use them. The Confederates withdraw. Even so, and although he has almost twice the number of troops opposing him, McClellan still calls for reinforcements as the rebels retreat.

: The new Confederate ...ary of state, Judah ...nin. (M)

● March 24 Jackson starts to move back to Mt. Jackson.

● March 29 General Frémont takes over from General Rosecrans in western Virginia. Frémont's army will be one of three employed in pursuit of Jackson.

● April 3 The U.S. Senate votes to abolish slavery in the District of Columbia.

● April 9 The Confederate government passes its first draft law.

● March 18 Judah Benjamin is named the new Confederate secretary of state, while George W. Randolph replaces him as secretary of war.

April 10 ●
The U.S. Congress passes a joint resolution calling for the gradual emancipation of slaves in all states.

Above: Dummy guns such as these wooden logs are used throughout the war to fool attackers about the strength of defenses. Carefully placed dummies help delay McClellan's march up the Peninsula. (M)

April 30 ●
the song "Dixie" is published.

41

18 19 20 21 22 23 24 25 26 27 28 29 30 31 01 02 03 04 05 06 07 08 09 10 11 12 13 14 15 16 17 18 19 20 21 22 23 24 25 26 27 28 29 30 01 02 03

MAY 1862

SUNDAY | SUNDAY | SUNDAY

04 05 06 07 08 09 10 11 12 13 14 15 16 17 18 19 20 21 22 23 24 25 26 27

MAY

JUNE 1862

SUNDAY | SUNDAY

28 29 30 31 01 02 03 04 05 06 07 08 09 10 11 12 13 14 15 16 17 18 19

● **May 8** A landing party from a Union gunboat captures the Confederate arsenal at Baton Rouge.

May 9 ●
Flag Officer Foote is relieved of command due to injuries received in the attack on Fort Donelson.

May 9 ●
Skirmishers from Halleck's army start to clash with Confederate troops at Corinth.

● **May 10** Union troops occupy Pensacola on the Gulf Coast of Florida, only to find the Confederates have already destroyed the Naval Yards there.

● **May 12** Having sailed up the Mississippi from New Orleans, Farragut takes Natchez.

● **May 10** In New Orleans, Ben Butler seizes $80,000 in gold from the Dutch Consulate.

Below: The naval Battle of Memphis. In the center, the USS *Monarch* is ramming the CSS *Beauregard*. (NHC)

● **May 15** General Butler issues his infamous Order Number 28 in response to reports that the women of New Orleans have been insulting Union troops to the extent of emptying chamber pots over them. The Order states that women who insult Union troops "shall be regarded and held liable to be treated as a woman of the town plying her avocation."

May 11 ●
CSS *Virginia* is blown up by her Confederate crew. After the destruction of the Norfolk Naval Yards she has no harbor, and her draft is too great for the James River, so this is the only alternative to falling into Union hands. Her destruction opens the entire James River to the Union fleet almost as far as Richmond itself.

Right: At Drewry's Bluff, Confederate guns repel the Union fleet approaching Richmond. (NHC)

May 15 ●
The CSS *Alabama* is launched in Liverpool, England.

● **May 4** Union forces enter Yorktown, then continue on toward Williamsburg, where advance units clash with Confederate troops led by Generals Longstreet and D.H. Hill.

● **May 9** Confederates evacuate Norfolk Navy Yard. Union troops move in behind them.

● **May 15** A Union fleet comes within eight miles of Richmond on the James River, but is halted by strong Confederate gun emplacements at Drewry's Bluff. Meanwhile the Confederate army under Joseph E. Johnston has retreated to within three miles of the capital.

● **May 5** Heavy fighting around Williamsburg continues as the main body of the Union army comes up. Longstreet and Hill fight a valiant rearguard action as the Confederate army retreats.

● **May 5** Lincoln travels to Fort Monroe to get a close look at what McClellan is doing.

● **May 6** Union troops occupy Williamsburg.

● **May 20** President Davis announces to the Confederate Congress that Richmond shall be defended at all costs. Meanwhile, despite occasional skirmishing, McClellan's advance has come to a halt.

Left: The fighting at Williamsburg (MARS)

THE SHENANDOAH VALLEY CAMPAIGN

● **May 4** Jackson's troops travel by train from Mechum River to Staunton, where they prepare to counter a Union advance from western Virginia.

Below: Frémont's men are run ragged in turn chasing and being chased by Jackson up and down the Shenandoah Valley. (LC)

● **May 8 BATTLE OF MCDOWELL**
6,000 men of Frémont's command attack Jackson's 10,000-strong army but are beaten back and retreat toward Franklin with Jackson in hot pursuit.

● **May 10** Jackson's advance toward Franklin has effectively stopped Frémont from linking up with the Union army advancing from western Virginia under Robert Huston Milroy.

May 20 ●
Jackson's Brigade is reinforced with fresh troops under General Ewell.

May 21 ●
Using his superior knowledge of the Shenandoah Valley, Jackson avoids Union General Banks by crossing Massanutten Mountain.

● **May 23 BATTLE OF FRONT ROYAL**
Jackson takes Banks by surprise, capturing many of his smaller force.

Above: Pictured in May 1862 near Cumberland Landing, Virginia, McClellan's secret service chief Allan Pinkerton (left, with pipe) was a successful private detective. A friend of McClellan, he leaves the army after McClellan's dismissal in November 1862, but remains in government service throughout the war. (NA)

● **May 20** Lincoln signs the Homestead Act which opens up huge areas of the West to new settlement by guaranteeing 160 acres of public land to anyone who settles and improves it for five years.

June 4 ●
Confederates evacuate Fort Pillow, opening the way to Memphis.

Right: General Joseph Johnston. (NA)

Above: Professor Thaddeus Lowe's Union team preparing his observation balloon *Intrepid* for reconnoitering at Fair Oaks. (M)

WAR IN THE WEST

WAR IN THE EAST

● **June 6 BATTLE OF MEMPHIS**
That rare thing, a naval battle inland, occurs when Union gunboats under Commodore Charles Davis sail down the Mississippi to engage Confederate ships just below the bluffs at Memphis. Citizens of Memphis line the bluffs to watch, confident of a Confederate victory, but in two hours the Union gunboats destroy most of the Confederate ships. The battle is over by 7:30 a.m., at 11:00 a.m. the city is surrendered and the Mississippi is now open to Union shipping as far south as Vicksburg.

● **June 7** Union troops shell Chattanooga.

● **June 7** In New Orleans, General Butler hangs a local man who tried to destroy the Union flag flying over the Mint.

June 18 ●
Union troops under General George W. capture the Cumberland Pass, a vital r the pro-Union counties of East Tenne

June 12 ●
Confederate General Jeb Stuart with 1,200 cavalry sets out from Richmond on a four-day ride that will take him completely around the Union army of George McClellan.

● **May 31–June 1 BATTLE OF FAIR OAKS**
McClellan has made the mistake of splitting his army either side of the Chickahominy. Johnston sees the opportunity and attacks. The Confederate attack is slow and uncoordinated, and is finally halted when Union General Sumner moves into battle without waiting for orders from McClellan. General Johnston, meanwhile, is wounded and has to withdraw, and Robert E. Lee is brought in as Johnston's replacement. Eventually the Confederate troops withdraw to their original lines, and neither side is able to claim the victory.

Left: Nicknamed "Beauty" at West Point (though this is meant ironically), James Ewell Brown Stuart has a love of gaudy uniforms which he designs himself, and likes to be thought of as a dashing cavalier. (Wilson)

● **May 29** More skirmishing at Seven Pines along the Chickahominy River near Richmond.

May 24 Jackson fails to cut Banks off from Winchester, a move which would have allowed him to destroy the Union army piecemeal. Nevertheless Jackson's cavalry, under Turner Ashby, creates such panic among the Union troops that large quantities of food and equipment are abandoned.

May 25 After a brief stand at Winchester, Bank's vastly outnumbered army again breaks and runs for Harpers Ferry, leaving yet more supplies and munitions for the Confederates.

May 25 Separately, armies under Frémont and McDowell move into the southern part of the Shenandoah Valley to cut off Jackson's retreat.

May 26 Jackson continues to pursue Banks toward Harpers Ferry, with a brief skirmish at Loudoun Heights.

● **May 31** In heavy rain, Jackson leads his men on a fast march south and manages to escape before Frémont and McDowell are able to close their trap.

● **June 17 A** army and na expedition ca tures the Confederate teries at St. Charles, Ark giving contro the White Ri the Union.

June 20 ●
Raphael Semmes takes command of t CSS *Alabama* in Liverpool, England, an starts to outfit her for se

● **June 15** Jeb Stua returns to a hero's w come in Richmond. I boosted southern m embarrassed McClel and brought valuabl information about te and dispositions. Bu ride has probably pr little of real value to South and may have ed McClellan to the ness on his flanks.

● **June 16** At Secessionville, So Carolina, Union General Benham ignores orders an assaults Confeder defenses. He suffe severe casualties a forced to retreat.

● **Mid-June** The Army of the Potomac is now within four miles of Richmond, but the army is split on either side of the Chickahominy River. Lee plans to exploit th weakness by weakening his own positions in front of Richmond in order to launch a massive flank attack.

● **June 8 BATTLE OF CROSS KEYS**
Jackson faces two Union columns, one under Frémont and one under Shields. But the two columns (with McDowell's third column inactive on the sidelines) do not coordinate their attack. Frémont begins with an attack on the troops of Richard Ewell, but is fought off and makes a partial retreat.

● **June 9 BATTLE OF PORT REPUBLIC**
Jackson now deals with the second column opposing him. Without Frémont realizing what is happening, Jackson pulls back most of Ewell's troops to rejoin the main body of his army and launch a combined attack against Shields which sends the Union troops into retreat. This is the last battle in the Shenandoah Valley Campaign.

● **June 6** In an otherwise minor skirmish near Harrisonburg, Jackson's cavalry chief, Colonel Turner Ashby, is killed.

● **June 17 G** Beauregard t unofficial sicl and is replace Confederate General Bra Bragg.

● **June 17** General Joh Pope is give command of new Army of Virginia, whi brings toget. one commar the Union ar which have fought in the Shenandoah Valley. Frém resigns in pr and is replac by Franz Sig

● **June 17** Jackson's troops begir leaving the Shenandoah Valley to rei force Lee's troops arou Richmond.

June 19 ●
A new law makes slavery illegal in all the territories of the United States.

May 29 ●
everal days of skirmishing Corinth without any real engagement, Confederate eral Beauregard pulls out.

June 26 ●
Farragut's gunboats gin shelling Vicksburg.

● **June 28** During the night Farragut's gunboats make a daring run past the guns of Vicksburg. Despite heavy enemy fire, all but three of the boats get through.

● **July 1** Union cavalry under Colonel Philip H. Sheridan defeats a Confederate force south of Corinth.

Right: General John Hunt Morgan, who is killed at Greenville on September 4, 1864. (M)

● **July 1** Having gotten past Vicksburg, the fleet of Farragut is united with the fleet of Flag Officer Davis.

July 9 ●
Confederate raiders under John Hunt Morgan capture Tompkinsville, Kentucky.

July 12 ●
Morgan's raiders capture Lebanon, Kentucky.

July 14 ●
Morgan's raiders now reach Cynthiana, Kentucky, causing increasing panic in the southern parts of Ohio and Indiana.

July 15 ●
Farragut again takes his fleet past Vicksburg under heavy fire.

July 13 ●
Nathan Bedford Forrest leads his Confederate cavalry into Murfreesboro, Tennessee, and captures the Union garrison there.

July 17 ●
Grant assumes command of all Union armies in the West.

July 18 ●
Morgan's raiders cross the Ohio River and attack Newburg, Indiana.

● **July 15** A Confederate gunboat, *Arkansas*, attacks two Union ships on the Yazoo River. *Arkansas* partially disables both ships and sails out onto the Mississippi where she has to run through heavy fire from the Union river fleet to reach the safety of Vicksburg.

● **July 19** Morgan's raiders clash with Union troops near Paris, Kentucky.

● **July 22** Morgan reaches Livingston, Tennessee.

July 25 ●
Union troops evacuate Natchez.

CSS *Arkansas*, still not fully repaired, sails south from Vicksburg to assist the attack on Baton Rouge, but her engines fail and when attacked by the Union gunboat *Essex* the *Arkansas* is scuttled.

Below: The frantic struggle at Baton Rouge. (ASKB)

● **July 23** General Braxton Bragg begins to move his Confederate army from Tupelo, Mississippi, to Chattanooga, Tennessee, taking a very round-about route via Mobile and Montgomery because these are the only railways still available to the South.

July 22 ●
Two Union ships attack the CSS *Arkansas* which is lying badly damaged at Vicksburg, but have to withdraw without causing any further damage.

Above: Union artillery nearing Cedar Mountain, shortly before they ride into Jackson's withering fire. (M)

● **July 28** Raphael Semmes slips out of Liverpool aboard the CSS *Alabama* heading for the Azores where he will take on guns, and munitions.

Aug 6 ●
Union General Robert L. McCook, riding in an ambulance while unwell, is attacked and wounded by Confederate guerrillas north of Athens, Alabama. He will later die of his wounds.

● **Aug 6** Confederate General Breckinridge attempts an assault on Union troops north of Baton Rouge in the middle of dense fog, but with the aid of gunboats the Union forces are able to beat them back.

● **Early Aug** While McClellan slowly extricates his troops from Harrison's Landing, Pope's smaller Army of Virginia, divided into three corps under McDowell, Banks and Sigel, is astride the Rappahannock River in northern Virginia, while Burnside has around 12,000 men near Fredericksburg. But Halleck is worried that Lee will use his internal lines of communication to attack the separated Union armies piecemeal.

● **Aug 4** Burnside's troops begin to disembark near Fredericksburg, ready to face an advance by Lee into northern Virginia.

Aug 7 ●
Overnight, Lee brings his army up to Malvern Hill anticipating battle, but dawn reveals that McClellan's troops have abandoned their fortifications. McClellan has completed his withdrawal from the James. Lee is now convinced that the next Union push will be in northern Virginia.

Aug 7 ●
Jackson and A.P. Hill are now at Gordonsville facing Pope's army. Lee writes to Jackson urging an attack before McClellan can arrive. But Jackson is already moving his troops to Orange ready for an advance across the Rapidan River.

Aug 8 ●
Pope moves his headquarters south to Culpepper and orders Banks south to delay Jackson.

Aug 9 ●
BATTLE OF CEDAR MOUNTAIN
Banks comes under fire from rebel infantry on Cedar Mountain, between Culpepper and the Rapidan. Banks attacks, breaking the Confederate line in several places, outflanking them and killing Confederate General Winder. At the last minute Hill arrives, and with greatly superior numbers the Confederates are able to fight off the attackers, but Banks withdraws in good order. Jackson continues the pursuit until long after nightfall.

THE SEVEN DAYS

● **June 24** McClellan captures a deserter from Jackson's Brigade who tells him that Jackson is coming to join Lee's army ready for an all-out attack scheduled for June 28.

● **June 25** Acting decisively for once, McClellan decides to forestall a Confederate attack by sending Heintzelman's corps forward along the Williamsburg Road to sound out the enemy strength. The result is a brief, confused and fierce fight in which Confederates under General Ben Huger stop the Union advance. Despite this action, Lee decides to go ahead with his flank attack. This is the first of the Seven Days.

● **June 26 BATTLE OF MECHANICSVILLE**
Lee starts his movement by sending Longstreet and D.H. Hill on a night march to get into position, then there is a long wait for Jackson's delayed troops to arrive. Eventually, A.P. Hill gives up waiting and launches his attack which drives the Union troops back to prepared positions, while Longstreet and D.H. Hill join the attack. The new Union positions, held by General Fitz John Porter, prove too strong for the Confederates and Jackson has still not appeared to turn the flank.

low: neral niel Harvey . (M)

● **June 27 BATTLE OF GAINES MILL**
The first battle of the Seven Days had been a Union victory, but McClellan chose to pull Porter's men back, while Lee chose to continue his advance. Union troops now occupy an even stronger position than they had yesterday, and when battle is joined, again in mid-afternoon, Confederate attacks are repulsed. Jackson has now arrived on the scene, but only commits his men to the attack late in the day; while Longstreet, on the right flank, prepares an all-out attack. At sundown, Confederate Generals Hood and Law finally break the Union line in the center, but it is too late to exploit the breakthrough and the Union troops are able to complete a planned withdrawal in good order.

● **June 28** By morning, all of Porter's men are south of the Chickahominy and McClellan begins a withdrawal to the base he has established at Harrison's Landing on the James River, where Union naval supremacy ensures his supply lines. Lee, meanwhile, is unable to move until he is sure which direction McClellan has taken.

● **June 29 BATTLE OF SAVAGE STATION**
By now, Lee knows where McClellan is heading and sets out to dog his heels. There are numerous clashes between the Confederate advance and the Union rear guard during the day. Late in the day, at Savage Station, General Magruder is supposed to hold the Union troops while Jackson attacks their flank. But again, Jackson does not appear. Magruder goes in anyway and is soundly beaten.

elow: Professor Lowe serving the fighting in his lloon *Intrepid* for the my of the Potomac. With e shortage of materials in e South, the Confederates ve to make their balloons m silk dresses. (M)

● **June 30 BATTLE OF GLENDALE**
After a series of delays that had kept interfering with his plans to deliver a knock-out blow, Lee tries to get all his commanders moving early so that McClellan can be forced to stand and give battle. But again there are delays, partly caused by trying to move the Confederate armies through White Oak Swamps. Attempts by Longstreet and A.P. Hill to cut the Union column come to nothing, and, inexplicably, Jackson makes no attempt to play his assigned part in the battle, instead falling asleep under a tree. As a result of all this confusion and mismanagement, McClellan is able to withdraw his entire army to the safety of Malvern Hill

● **July 1 BATTLE OF MALVERN HILL**
Once again confusion gets in the way of the Confederate advance, and it is afternoon before Lee has a substantial part of his army facing the strong Union positions on Malvern Hill. The opening artillery duel is a resounding victory for the Union, by 2:30 p.m. not a single Confederate battery remains in action. This leaves the infantry, advancing across open ground against an entrenched enemy in a superior position. By nightfall, after repeated attacks by Huger, Magruder and D.H. Hill, the Confederates have lost 5,590, the Union have lost less than a third of that number. McClellan has won all but one of the battles of the Seven Days, but has retreated steadily from Richmond to the banks of the James River.

● **July 2** McClellan completes his withdrawal to Harrison's Landing, where his army is protected by Union naval guns.

● **July 6** Leaving a garrison behind to hold Roanoke Island and New Bern, Bunside sails to reinforce McClellan's army on the James River.

● **July 7** Lincoln sails to meet McClellan at Harrison's Landing.

● **July 9** Lee tries unsuccessfully to use field artillery against Union gunboats on the James River.

● **July 13** While keeping a force around McClellan, Lee starts moving troops toward northern Virginia to face General Pope's Army of Virginia around Manassas.

Left: Field batteries at work at the Battle of Malvern Hill. (NHC)

● **July 22** The Union and Confederate governments sign an agreement regulating the exchange of prisoners.

● **July 22** Lincoln presents the first draft of his Emancipation Proclamation to his Cabinet. The Cabinet is divided in its response: Stanton and Bates want it issued immediately, others fear it may cost the Republicans the Fall election. Eventually, Lincoln is persuaded not to isse the Proclamation until after a Union victory.

Left: This photograph, taken soon after Cedar Mountain, shows two black men, accompanying the Union army, wearing some form of uniform, even before the 1863 official reception of "Negroes ... into the military ... service." (M)

July 19 ●
A court-martial in Richmond clears Flag Officer Tattnall of any offense in scuttling CSS *Virginia*.

● **July 16** France declines to give recognition to the Confederacy in exchange for cotton.

July 1 ●
ederal income tax is introduced, d Lincoln also approves a bill to provide for railroads being built across the West.

July 11 ●
Henry Halleck is promoted to General-in-Chief of all Union armies, an administrative position which mostly amounts to acting as go-between for Lincoln and the commanders in the field.

July 16 ●
David G. Farragut is promoted to be the first rear admiral in the history of the U.S. navy.

● **July 17** Congress passes an act to provide a lifetime pension for all naval personnel disabled on active service.

● **July 29** Belle Boyd is arrested near Warrenton, Virginia, and accused of being a Confederate spy. She is taken to Old Capitol Prison in Washington.

● **Aug 4** In Indiana, enough volunteers have been found to form two regiments of Negro troops, but when offered to Lincoln he declines and suggests they be used as laborers instead.

10 11 12 13 14 15 16 17 18 19 20 21 22 23 24 25 26 27 28 29 30 31 01 02 03 04 05 06 07 08 09 10 11 12 13 14 15 16 17 18 19 20 21 22 23 24 25

● **Aug 12** John Hunt Morgan, on another raid, captures Gallatin, Tennessee, and the Union garrison there.

● **Aug 10** After the people of Donaldson, south of Baton Rouge, have repeatedly fired on his ships as they pass, Farragut orders his ships to fire on the town and destroys a significant portion of it.

● **Aug 16** General Edward Kirby Smith takes a Confederate army across the Cumberland Mountains into Kentucky.

● **Aug 18** Confederate troops recapture Clarksville, Tennessee, without a fight. The commander of the Union garrison will later be court-martialed for cowardice.

Aug 21 ● Confederate General Bragg moves out of Chattanooga to begin his campaign in Kentucky.

● **Aug 21** Shadowing Bragg, Union General Buell moves his headquarters to Murfreesboro.

Aug 30 ● Confederate General Kirby Smith attacks the Union garrison at Richmond, Kentucky. Out of 6,500 Union troops engaged, 5,353 become casualties. The survivors retreat toward Louisville.

Sept 2 ● General Kirby Smith occupies Lexington, Kentucky.

Sept 2 ● Union General Buell moves to Nashville

● **Aug 10** The two armies hold their ground, but Banks is reinforced by McDowell and Sigel, and further troops are on their way from Burnside. Jackson is now heavily outnumbered.

● **Aug 24** CSS *Alabama*, now at Terceira in the Azores, is officially commissioned into the Confederate navy and begins her career as a commerce raider.

Sept 4 The commerce raider CSS *Florida* manages to evade several Union ships and make it into Mobile Bay, even though many of her crew are ill with yellow fever.

● **Aug 17** Jeb Stuart is surprised by Union cavalry near Clark's Mountain. Stuart loses his plumed hat, silk-lined cape and a haversack which contains Lee's plans.

Enemies in the west. **Below**: General Braxton Bragg. (LC) **Right**: General Don Carlos Buell. (M)

Bragg is a martinet with a talent for alienating everyone who worked with him. Buell, like his friend McClellan, is a cautious general.

● **Aug 18–21** Lee probes along the Rappahannock, but wherever he tries to cross he finds Pope in a strong defensive position.

Aug 31 ● Union troops evacuate Fredericksburg, Virginia.

● **Aug 18** Pope's army, wedged in the V of land between the Rappahannock and Rapidan Rivers, seems to be in a natural trap. But before Lee can close the trap, Pope withdraws across the Rappahannock. Pope, meanwhile, is awaiting reinforcements from McClellan – reinforcements which do not arrive.

● **Aug 22** Swinging wide around the flank of Pope's army, Stuart's cavalry sets out on a raid across the Rappahannock which succeeds in capturing Pope's dispatch book with copies of all his orders.

● **Aug 24** Lee now has Pope's orders, but he also has news that General Porter is on his way to reinforce Pope from McClellan's army. Pope's position is already too strong for Lee to attack. Lee starts looking for a way to maneuver him out of his current defenses.

● **Aug 11** Jackson retires back to Gordonsville, south of the Rapidan once more.

● **Aug 13** Lee sends Longstreet to reinforce Jackson at Gordonsville, and John Bell Hood to Hanover Junction facing Burnside's troops at Fredericksburg.

Aug 25 ● Jackson sets out on a wide flanking move with the aim of attacking Pope's line of communications.

● **Aug 26** After two days' hard marching, Jackson's men arrive at sunset at the Union supply depot at Bristoe Station and wreak havoc.

● **Aug 27** Jackson now moves on to the main Union supply depot at Manassas. Pope turns north to deal with the threat to his rear.

Below right: "Stonewall" Jackson. (M)

Aug 28 ● Pope arrives at Manassas around midday, but is unsure where Jackson might be. Jackson, meanwhile, has taken up positions near the old Bull Run battlefield. Longstreet has left the Rappahannock and is hurrying northward following the same roundabout route as Jackson.

Below: Confederates restoring supplies by pillaging the Union depot at Manassas Junction after the battle of Second Bull Run. (B&L)

● **Aug 16** Most of McClellan's troops have now reached Alexandria on the Potomac.

Aug 29–30 Second Battle of Bull Run (see page 108)

Pope attacks Jackson. The fight lasts all the first day, but though the Confederate troops are so low on ammunition they start throwing rocks at the attacking Union troops, Jackson's line holds. Nevertheless, Pope believes he has won a great victory, and telegraphs Washington to that effect. Unknown to Pope, however, Longstreet and Lee arrive on the battlefield during the afternoon of the first day. Next morning, when Pope launches what he believes will be a mopping-up operation, Longstreet launches a devastating flank attack and the Union Army of Virginia flees the field.

Aug 20 ● Horace Greeley publishes an open letter to Lincoln entitled "The Prayer of Twenty Millions" which calls for a declaration that the war is to end slavery.

● **Aug 22** Lincoln responds to Greeley with a public letter of his own in which he declares: "If I could save the Union without freeing any slave, I would do it; and if I could save it by freeing all the slaves, I would do it; and if I could save it by freeing some and leaving others alone, I would also do that."

Aug 31 ● Two corps from the Army of the Potomac arrive to reinforce Pope, but too late.

Aug 17 ● Sioux Indians, facing starvation on their reservation in Minnesota, begin an uprising that will eventually kill nearly 600 people.

Aug 22 ● Sioux again attack Fort Ridgley and are again driven off.

Aug 20 ● A Sioux attack on Fort Ridgley, Minnesota, fails and the Indians withdraw.

● **Aug 28** The Confederate spy, Belle Boyd, is released from Old Capitol Prison for lack of evidence.

WAR IN THE WEST

● **Sept 3** Kirby Smith's troops occupy Frankfort, the Kentucky state capital.

● **Sept 4** John Hunt Morgan's raiders join Kirby Smith in Lexington.

● **Sept 7** Buell leaves Nashville with five divisions to protect the Union supply depot at Bowling Green. General Thomas remains at Nashville with three divisions.

● **Sept 3** USS *Essex* is fired on from Natchez. *Essex* returns fire, and Natchez surrenders.

● **Sept 13** Bragg reaches Glasgow, Kentucky.

● **Sept 14** Buell reaches Bowling Green, Kentucky.

● **Sept 14** Confederate General Sterling Price moves against Iuka, near Grant's base at Corinth.

● **Sept 14** A Confederate infantry brigade under General James R. Chalmers, operating ahead of Bragg's main army, attacks a Union garrison at Munfordville. The Union garrison resists the attack and Chalmers retires.

● **Sept 20** Thomas joins B at Bowling Green, and the reunited army moves on toward Louisville.

● **Sep** Buell reach Louis

Above: Kearney's charge at the Battle of Chantilly. (LC)

● **Sept 20 Battle of Iuka**

Ord attacks Price from th north, but Rosecrans is d in his approach from the s and Price is able to slip av after losing about 1,500 m

● **Sept 16** Bragg surrounds Munfordville with his entire army. After considering the options, the Union garrison surrenders just af midnight.

● **Sept 17** Grant sets in motion a pincers movement against Price, u troops under Ord and Rosecrans.

THE NAVAL WAR

● **Sept 5** CSS *Alabama* takes her first victim, the *Ocmulgee*, off the Azores.

● **Sept 6–9** CSS *Alabama* captures and burns four more Union ships

● **Sept 13–18** CSS *Alabama* destroys five Union whaling ships off the Azores.

WAR IN THE EAST

Sept 2 Union forces withdraw from Winchester in the Shenandoah Valley, leaving a huge store of ordnance for the Confederates.

Sept 1 Battle of Chantilly

In pursuit of Pope's army, Jackson runs into a Union force under Generals I.I. Stevens and Phil Kearny in the middle of a torrential rainstorm. In the confusing fight that follows, both Stevens and Kearny are killed, but Pope is able to continue his withdrawal.

Sept 2 Pope completes his withdrawal into the entrenchments around Washington. Lee continues to press, and there are skirmishes at Fairfax Court House, Vienna, Falls Church and Flint Hill, but the Union army is now safe. Pope is removed from command and, reluctantly, Lincoln places McClellan in command of all armies in northern Virginia.

● **Sept 4** Lee begins getting his army into position to cross the Potomac and invade the North.

● **Sept 11** Leaving D.H. Hill to defend Turner's Gap near Boonsboro, Longstreet moves on to Hagerstown where there are misleading reports of Union troops.

● **Sept 13** A Confederate force under General W.W. Loring forces the Union garrison to abandon Charleston, western Virginia.

● **Sept 14** McClellan attacks D.H. Hill at Turner's Ga Hill's position is not as strong as it first appears, and army is on the point of being overwhelmed when Longstreet arrives in the late afternoon and manages hold the line until darkness ends the fighting.

● **Sept 14** In the morning, McLaws takes Maryland H overlooking Harpers Ferry, but during the day Union under Franklin attack his rear at Crampton Gap. Mc line breaks, but Franklin does not pursue the advant

● **Sept 15** Jackson captures Harpers Ferry. Leaving A.P. Hill to hold the town, he immediat ly starts moving the main body of his army toward Sharpsburg.

Below: Longstreet, known to his friends as "Old Pete," and referred to by Lee as his "old war horse," is probably the most dependable officer Lee has in his command. (NA)

● **Sept 6** McClellan begins moving his army, trying to keep between Lee and Washington but without any real idea of where Lee is or where he is going.

● **Sept 15** Overnight, Longstreet and Hill repor that Turner's Gap cannot be held past daybrea Lee instructs all his armies to converge on Sharpsburg. Longstreet and Hill begin their wi drawal.

● **Sept 6–7** Lee's army crosses the Potomac into Maryland. They expect a warm welcome from a state supposed to be sympathetic to the South, but find none. Meanwhile Lee, Longstreet and Jackson have all suffered minor injuries, while John Bell Hood and A.P. Hill are both under arrest for petty disputes with their superiors.

● **Sept 16** A long-range artillery duel takes place as the two armies gather in a wide v ley on either side of the Antietam stream.

● **Sept 17 Battle of Antietam**/Sharps (see page 110)

The bloodiest day in American histo dawns misty. The battle begins with McClellan's right flank under Hooke attacking Jackson. The Union troops ly overwhelm Jackson before John B Hood launches a counter-attack. Th Union attack again, and so the battl surges back and forth until it comes indecisive halt. About this time the shifts to the center where wave after of Union troops attacks D.H. Hill wh defends the position that will becom known as Bloody Lane.

● **Sept 9** At Frederick, Maryland, Lee issues Special Order 191, splitting his army into three. Jackson will take Harpers Ferry, McLaws will take the Maryland Heights supported by Walker on Loudon Heights, both commanding Harpers Ferry, and Longstreet will move on to Boonsboro where the other parts of the army will meet up after Harpers Ferry has fallen.

Sept 13 ● At Frederick, Union private Billy W. Mitchell finds three cigars wrapped in a piece of paper. The paper is a copy of Lee's Special Order 191. The order gives McClellan all the information he needs to defeat Lee. With the main body of his army, McClellan would force Turner's Gap and defeat Longstreet and D.H. Hill at Boonsboro; while his left wing, under General William Buel Franklin would attack McLaws at Crampton's Gap to relieve the 12,000 Union troops in Harpers Ferry.

● **Sept 18** A stand-off at Antietar neither side willing to resume the tle, though McClellan still has ov 30,000 fresh troops who so far hav been engaged.

● **Sept 19** Lee begins his retr across the Potomac and bac Virginia. The Union is able tc claim a victory at Antietam, McClellan does not pursue L

POLITICS

● **Sept 6** Pope is given command of the Department of the Northwest and sent to Minnesota to fight the Sioux uprising.

● **Sept 22** Lincoln issues his Emancipati Proclamation. Henceforth, the Federal w is both restoration of the Union and free for the slaves.

10 11 12 13 14 15 16 17 18 19 20 21 22 23 24 25 26 27 28 29 30 31 01 02 03 04 05 06 07 08 09 10 11 12 13 14 15 16 17 18 19 20 21 22 23 24 25

SUNDAY   SUNDAY   a SUNDAY   SUNDAY   SATURDAY

OCTOBER 1862   NOVEMBER 1862

30 01 02 03 04 05 06 07 08 09 10 11 12 13 14 15 16 17 18 19 20 21 22 23 24 25 26 27 28 29 30 31 01 02 03 04 05 06 07 08 09 10 11 12 13 14 15

● **Oct 1** ● ● **Oct 1** The defenses of Vicksburg are put in the hands of General John C. Pemberton, a northerner who had married a Virginia lady and threw in his lot with the South when the Civil War started.

● **Early Oct** A combined Confederate force of cavalry and Indians under General Thomas Hindman crosses the border from Missouri into Arkansas, but is easily defeated by Union troops under General John M. Schofield. Hindman regroups at Van Buren on the Arkansas River.

● **Oct 1** After his their escape from Iuka, Price's Confederates have combined with Van Dorn's troops at Ripley. Now they begin what is intended to be a surprise attack on Rosecrans at Corinth, but immediately run into Union cavalry.

● **Oct 1** Buell and Thomas set out from Louisville toward the armies of Bragg and Kirby Smith, which are congregating at Frankfort.

● **Oct 14** Union General Hurlbut is given command of the military district of Mississippi. His replacement in Grant's army is James B. McPherson.

Below: James McPherson. (NA)

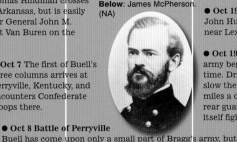

● **Oct 7** The first of Buell's three columns arrives at Perryville, Kentucky, and encounters Confederate troops there.

● **Oct 8 Battle of Perryville**
Buell has come upon only a small part of Bragg's army, but thinks it is the main body. Bragg thinks he is being attacked by only a small part of Buell's force, but it is the main body. These initial errors make for one of the more confusing battles of the war. Union troops under newly-promoted General Philip H. Sheridan attack before dawn and secure the dominant heights, but there is a delay as all Buell's army gathers. In the early afternoon, Polk attack's Buell's left flank. The Confederates have the best of the fighting, but neither side gains an advantage over the other and more than a third of Buell's army is never engaged. After dark, Bragg begins his retreat.

● **Oct 2** Ten miles short of Corinth, Van Dorn's troops encounter Union infantry, and the element of surprise is now clearly lost. Nevertheless, Van Dorn continues his advance.

● **Oct 3–4 Battle of Corinth**
Confederates launch an all-out attack on Rosecrans, who has superior numbers in a well-entrenched position. The Confederate attack forces Rosecrans out of the first line of defenses, but the Union troops are stubborn and do not give ground easily. By the end of the first day, both sides are convinced that another hour of daylight would have given them victory. The second day opens with an artillery duel before dawn, then Van Dorn launches his attack. The Confederates break the Union line, but on this blisteringly hot day (94° in the shade) the Union troops stand firm and by midday the Confederates are in retreat having suffered nearly twice as many casualties as their opponents. Rosecrans does not pursue.

Oct 4 ●   ● **Oct 5** Van Dorn fights a holding action against fresh Union troops at a crossing of the Hatchie river, then retreats south.

● **Oct 10** Confederate General John B. Magruder is assigned to command the District of Texas, Arizona and Mexico.

Below right: The Battle of Corinth. (MARS)

● **Oct 5** A Union fleet steams into Galveston harbor off the coast of Texas and seizes the island.

● **Oct 11** CSS *Alabama* captures the Union ship *Manchester* off the coast of Nova Scotia, and finds on board New York newspapers which give detailed information about the dispositions of Union gunboats.

● **Oct 11** Jeb Stuart leads a cavalry raid to Chambersburg, Pennsylvania, then returns to Emmitsburg, Maryland, without loss.

Left: The 7th Maine attacking during the Battle of Antietam. (NPS)

onfederate line is on the point of ng when McClellan calls off the attack. the battle shifts, now to McClellan's nk where Burnside's men cross a narone bridge. Again the Union is on the of victory when A.P. Hill arrives from 's Ferry, and the day ends with the rs all back more or less where they d. The number killed, wounded or g on both sides is 23,110.

Left: A.P. Hill, known as "Little Powell" to his men, has a taste for picturesque clothes. He often rides into battle wearing a red wool deer-hunter's shirt which his soldiers call his "battle shirt." (NA)

Sept 22 Union oops re-occupy arpers Ferry.

● **Oct 2** Lincoln visits McClellan, who is still at Antietam.

Late Sept In New York, Matthew Brady opens an exhibition of photoraphs called "The Dead of Antietam." creates an immediate sensation.

Sept 29 In Louisville, Kentucky, Union General efferson C. Davis shoots and kills Union General illiam Nelson following a quarrel. It is treated as "matter of honor" and Davis never comes to trial.

● **Oct 22** Confederate troops under General Beauregard defeat an attempt by Union troops to cut the Charleston and Savannah Railroad at Pocotaligo.

Left: Lincoln visiting McClellan at Antietam. Photograph taken on October 8, 1862. (NA)

● **Oct 14** Congressional elections in the midwest produce Democrat victories in most states.

● **Oct 21** Union General John A. McClernand is ordered by Lincoln to raise a force for the assault on Vicksburg. McClernand believes he is to have a free hand on this campaign.

● **Oct 19** Confederate cavalry under John Hunt Morgan defeat Union cavalry near Lexington, Kentucky.

● **Oct 19** At the Cumberland Gap, Bragg's army begins to leave Kentucky for the last time. Driving rain and impassable fords slow the retreat to no more than five miles a day, during which time Bragg's rear guard, under Joseph Wheeler, finds itself fighting 26 skirmishes in two weeks.

● **Oct 24** Don Carlos Buell is removed from command of the Army of the Ohio and replaced by William S. Rosecrans. The army is temporarily renamed the Fourteenth Army Corps.

Right: Joseph Wheeler, an indefatigable cavalry leader. (M)

The aftermath of every battle looks the same. **Left:** after Antietam (LC); **right:** after Corinth. (M)

● **Oct 30** The United States Navy Department offers a reward of $500,000 for the capture of CSS *Alabama*. By now a total of a dozen Union ships are chasing the Confederate raider.

● **Oct 26** In its first significant movement since Antietam, McClellan's Army of the Potomac begins to cross into Virginia once more.

THE VICKSBURG CAMPAIGN

● **Nov 1** Grant starts preparing what will turn out to be one of the longest campaigns of the war when he starts putting his plans together for the assault on Vicksburg.

Left: General Rosecrans. (M)

Below: Seen at the Battle of Perryville is a style of combat which is soon to be out-dated. (LC)

● **Nov 2** Having wreaked havoc among the whaling ships off Nova Scotia, CSS *Alabama* shifts its operations to the seas off Bermuda.

● **Nov 1** Confederate defenders of Plymouth, North Carolina, flee when fired upon by a Union naval task force.

Left: Scouts of the Army of the Potomac. (NA)

● **Nov 6** Confederate Generals James Longstreet and Stonewall Jackson are both promoted to lieutenant general and assigned command of the First and Second Corps of the Army of Northern Virginia respectively.

● **Early Nov** Having retreated from Kentucky, Confederate General Bragg decides to announce the campaign as a success in securing Tennessee for the South. He begins to gather his troops at Murfreesboro where he commands strategic rail lines and river valleys. Meanwhile, his most senior subordinates have all criticized his handling of the Kentucky campaign and he is called to Richmond to explain himself to his old friend Jefferson Davis. He returns with Davis's support, but with all the critical subordinates still in place, a recipe for problems that will plague the Army of Tennessee for most of the next year.

● **Nov 4** The Union task force has moved on from Plymouth to Hamilton, North Carolina, where the Confederates again evacuate allowing Union troops to occupy the town.

● **Nov 5** The task force continues up the Roanoke River toward Tarboro, but withdraws as much due to disease as enemy action.

● **Nov 5** Lincoln issues the order that finally removes McClellan from command of the Army of the Potomac, replacing him with General Ambrose E. Burnside, despite Burnside's protestations that he is not up to the job. At the same time, General Fitz John Porter is replaced by General Joseph Hooker.

● **Nov 7** At nearly midnight, McClellan receives the orders relieving him of command.

Right: Sideburns are named after the luxurious side-whiskers sported by General Burnside. (B&L)

● **Nov 15** Burnside starts moving the Army of the Potomac out of its camp at Warrenton toward Fredericksburg.

● **Nov 8** In New Orleans, Ben Butler orders that all breweries be closed, unaware that this same day Lincoln has appointed General Nathaniel Banks as his replacement with orders to concentrate on opening up the Mississippi.

● **Nov 4** Now that congressional elections are over in the North, Democrats have made considerable gains in many states, but Republicans retain control of the House of Representatives.

45

16 17 18 19 20 21 22 23 24 25 26 27 28 29 30 01 02 03 04 05 06 07 08 09   10 11 12 13 14 15 16 17 18 19 20 21 22 23 24 25 26 27 28 29 30 31 01

WAR IN THE WEST

Below: Nathan Bedford Forrest. He has no formal military training but emerges as a brilliant cavalry leader. He later founds the Ku Klux Klan. (Wilson)

● **Nov 21** Bragg sends Nathan Bedford Forrest to cut the communications of both Grant's and Rosecrans's armies.

Dec 3 ● Confederate General Hindman defies orders to withdraw his troops from Arkansas, and sets out instead to attack the Union force at Fayetteville. Union General James G. Blunt sends for reinforcements, and two divisions under General Francis J. Herron set out on a forced march from Springfield, more than a hundred miles away.

● **Dec 4** General Joseph E. Johnston takes command of the Department of the West.

Above: Thomas C. Hindman becomes commander of the Trans-Mississippi District in 1863. (M)

Dec 6 ● In weather so cold that water freezes in the men's canteens, Hindman moves his army around Blunt ready for a dawn attack. Hearing that Herron's exhausted men are approaching, he decides to attack the Union army can combine.

Dec 7 ● **Battle of Prairie Grove** Hindman attacks Herron, whose men are so tired they are falling asleep even while under fire. Both sides launch attacks that fail, and when Blunt brings up his relatively fresh men they are still unable to break Hindman's lines. Honors are equal when the fighting finally ends after dark, but Hindman then retreats south leaving the field to the Union.

Above: Prairie Grove today. (Author)

Dec 7 ● **Battle of Hartsville** Confederate General John Hunt Morgan leads a cavalry attack on the Union garrison at Hartsville, Tennessee, capturing most of the garrison in the process.

Dec 18 ● Grant re-organizes his army for the advance against Vicksburg. His army is to be divided into four corps led by Sherman, Hurlbut, McPherson and McClernand.

Dec 20 ● Confederate General Van Dorn leads a surprise raid on Grant's base at Holly Springs, Mississippi. The raid is a complete success, capturing 1,800 prisoners and destroying $1.5 million of materiel, and above all forcing Grant to withdraw to LaGrange, Tennessee.

● **Dec 20** The first step in Grant's assault on Vicksburg is launched when Sherman leaves Memphis to attempt an approach through the swamps north of Vicksburg.

Dec 15 ● Nathan Bedford Forrest crosses the Tennessee River on a raid into central Tennessee with four regiments of cavalry.

Dec 18 ● Nathan Bedford Forrest defeats a Union cavalry force near Lexington, Tennessee.

Above: General McClernand. (LC)

Dec 17 ● Plagued by cotton speculators and unscrupulous businessmen, Grant issues his infamous General Order No.11 expelling all "Jews" from the department. The Order will be rescinded by Lincoln, but still follows Grant for the rest of his career.

● **Dec 21** At Davis Mill, an important river crossing twenty miles north of Holly Springs, Van Dorn finds his raiders unable to defeat a force of only 300 Union defenders, and withdraws.

● **Dec 25** After tearing up railroad in southern Tennessee, Van Dorn re[turns] to Mississippi and wins a small ski[rmish] at Ripley.

● **Dec 25** John Hunt Morgan's cavalry raid into Kentucky brings skirmishes at Green's Chapel and Bear Wallow.

● **Dec 29 Battle o[f] Chickasaw Bluffs** Sherman, suppor[ted] by the gunboats [of] Admiral Porter, m[oves] along the Yazoo [River] to attack the blu[ffs] north of Vicksbur[g] but the position [is too] strong to be take[n by] frontal assault an[d] Sherman is force[d to] withdraw.

● **Dec 20** Throwing off his Union pursuers near Jackson, Forrest heads north to begin four days of destroying railroad tracks and capturing more than 1,300 prisoners.

● **Dec 27** After a brief sieg[e] the Union garrison at Elizabethtown surrenders to Morgan's raiders.

Dec 31 ─ For the first and only time in his career, Nathan Bedford Forrest is surprised in battle when his rear is attacked while he is already facing other Union troops at Parker's Crossroads. But Forrest reacts with a charge, then withdraws his troops between the two armies before they can recover.

Jan 1 ● Nathan Bedford Forrest brings his four regiments back across the Tennessee River.

Dec 26 ● Having learned that some of Bragg's troops have been sent to help Pemberton at Vicksburg, Rosecrans begins his advance from Nashville.

● **Dec 28** Union Gene[ral] Schofield sends a ca[valry] attack against Hindman's army at V[an] Buren. Hindman is forced to retreat out [of] Arkansas, losing mos[t of] his supplies and muc[h of] his army in the proce[ss].

Dec 27 ● As Rosecrans's three columns approach Murfreesboro they begin to meet Confederate resistance.

Dec 30 ● Rosecrans puts his three corps in line outside Murfreesboro, ready for battle.

● **Dec 31–Ja[n 2] Battle [of] Stone[s] River [at] Murf[rees]boro page [...]**

Dec 30–31 ● Confederate cavalry under Joseph Wheeler circle Rosecran's army outside Murfreesboro, capturing over a thousand men and destroying four vital supply trains.

Dec 31 ● Not long after midnight, the USS *Monitor* sinks in heavy seas off Cape Hatteras.

WAR IN THE EAST

● **Nov 18** USS *San Jacinto* finally catches up with Captain Semmes and CSS *Alabama* at Martinique. *San Jacinto* blockades the harbor so *Alabama* cannot escape.

● **Nov 19** A bad storm at Martinique allows CSS *Alabama* to slip past the *San Jacinto* and get away.

Nov 30 ● Captain Semmes moves his base of operations yet again, this time to the Leeward Islands.

Right: The CSS *Alabama*, captained by Raphael Semmes, is the South's most successful and notorious commerce raider. 220 feet long with 2 300-hp engines, she carries 144 men and 8 guns. (B&L)

● **Dec 1** Jackson's corps arrives at Fredericksburg.

● **Dec 2** Skirmishing along the Rappahannock near Fredericksburg. Because of a blunder, there are no pontoons to take the Union forces over the river.

● **Dec 10** Pontoon bridges finally arrive at Falmouth to allow Burnside's troops to cross the Rappahannock and attack Fredericksburg.

● **Dec 11** Burnside launches a furious artillery bombardment of Fredericksburg while the pontoon bridges are put in place and a bridgehead is established in the city.

● **Dec 12** Dense fog provides cover for the Union troops crossing the river into Fredericksburg, but does not lift in time to organize an assault, so the two sides settle down for a cold night.

● **Dec 13 Battle of Fredericksburg** (see page 114)
Another dense fog lifts around ten in the morning. Confederate troops are securely entre[nched] along the top of the ridge known as Marye's Heights, with Longstreet on the left flank an[d] Jackson on the right. Burnside's troops can do nothing but attack head-on. Six charges [are] made in all between 11:30 in the morning and 6:00 in the evening, all easily and blood[ily] repulsed. By the time Burnside retreats back across the Rappahannock in the early hou[rs of] the next morning, the Union has lost 1,300 killed and 9,600 wounded, while the South ha[s suf]fered less than 600 killed and 4,100 wounded.

● **Dec 17 Battle of Goldsboro** A Union column destroying railroad lines and bridges near Goldsboro, North Carolina, comes under attack from a Confederate force and is forced to retreat.

Above: Native Americans enlist in both sides. Those pictured here are sharpshooters in the Union army, wounded at Marye's Heights during the Battle of Fredericksburg. (M)

Above: Union troops finally find the means to cross the Rappahannock and face Jackson at Fredericksburg. (LC)

● **Dec 24** A small Union force sent by General Nathaniel Banks arrives at Galveston and starts to fortify the city.

Jan 1 ● The Union fleet blockading Galveston, Texas, is taken by surprise by Confederate gunboats. The Union ships are all rammed, run aground or flee out to sea. Meanwhile, Union troops in the city surrender to a simultaneous assault by General Magruder.

POLITICS

● **Dec 10** The U.S. House of representatives passes a bill creating the new state of West Virginia.

Left: James G. Blunt, commander in Kansas and of the Army of the Frontier. (M)

Dec 17 ● In-fighting in Lincoln's cabinet, mostly resulting from Treasury Secretary Salmon P. Chase's attempt to gain personal and political advantage, comes to a head when Seward offers to resign. Lincoln refuses to accept it.

Dec 19 ● Lincoln cleverly brings the intriguing within his cabinet to an end by engineering a meeting between the full cabinet and the congressmen who have been lobbying on Chase's behalf. Chase has to back down.

Jan 1 ● Lincoln's Emancipation Proclamation goes into effect, declaring that slaves in rebel control are free. It does nothing to free slaves in Union-loyal slave states, but wins popular support for the North in England and France, ensuring that those countries will be unable to recognize the Confederacy.

● **Dec 21** The U.S. Congress authorizes the Medal of Honor to be awarded to naval personnel.

● **Dec 20** Chase offers his resignation, and is greatly put-out when Lincoln accepts it. But Lincoln chooses not to put it into force, so Chase retains his position but has a sword over his head.

● **Nov 19** James A. Seddon is appointed Confederate secretary of war.

Above: Antietam, the bloodiest battle of the war. (LC)

SUNDAY

JANUARY 1863

SUNDAY

SUNDAY

FEBRUARY 1863

SATURDAY

06 07 08 09 10 11 12 13 14 15 16 17 18 19 20 21 22 23 24 25 26 27 28 29 30 31 01 02 03 04 05 06 07 08 09 10 11 12 13 14 15 16 17 18 19 20 21

● **Jan 8** McClernand leaves the Union base at Milliken's Bend for an assault on the Confederate outpost at Arkansas Post. The post is insignificant and the raid a wild goose chase.

● **Jan 9** Having sailed up the White River and Arkansas River, accompanied by Porter's gunboats, McClernand's troops disembark near Fort Hindman outside Arkansas Post.

● **Jan 10** Porter's gunboats pound Fort Hindman.

● **Jan 11** McClernand's troops attack the Confederate lines outside Fort Hindman while the navy continues its bombardment. The Confederates suffer few casualties, but surrender late in the day. A fresh Confederate regiment arriving during the surrender negotiations is among the nearly 5,000 prisoners.

● **Jan 12** Angry at McClernand's actions, Grant receives authorization to relieve McClernand whenever he wants – but is unable to put it into practice so soon after a victory.

● **Jan 11** After savage fighting, Marmaduke's Confederate cavalry destroy another Union supply base at Hartville.

ove:
nn
Allister
hofield.

● **Jan 8** Hindman's cavalry, under General John S. Marmaduke, attack and destroy Schofield's supply base at Springfield.

● **Jan 17** Grant leaves Memphis for Milliken's Bend to take personal charge of the Vicksburg campaign.

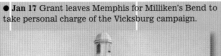

THE
CKSBURG
AMPAIGN

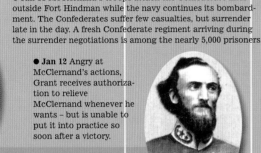

Above: John S. Marmaduke, Confederate leader of cavalry west of the Mississippi. (M)

● **Jan 25** Traveling through snow and sleet, Marmaduke's cavalry cross the White River into safety.

Above: David Dixon Porter wins promotion to rear admiral for his part in the assault on Vicksburg. (M)

● **Jan 30** Grant informs Admiral Porter that he intends to dig a canal cutting off the bend of the Mississippi commanded by Vicksburg, so his troops will be able to take the city from the rear.

Left: The Courthouse at Oxford, Mississippi, which Grant reaches in December 1862, is used to house Confederate prisoners. (M)

● **Early Feb** Engineers under McPherson investigate the chances of cutting a way through to Lake Providence, then on to the headwaters of the Black River. By March it is clear that this route is impassable.

● **Feb 3** Now south of Vicksburg, *Queen of the West* captures three steamers loaded with goods for the Confederate defenders of Port Hudson.

● **Feb 3** A gap is blown in the levee north of Vicksburg to flood Yazoo Pass, in the hope that gunboats will get through to attack Vicksburg from the rear. It doesn't work; the river system it opens into proves too narrow for gunboats.

● **Feb 3** A Confederate force tries to attack Fort Donelson, but comes under fire from Union gunboats and retreats.

Above: Stern-wheel paddle steamers ready to carry soldiers along the rivers. Transporting the troops is a logistical challenge and requires army and navy to work together. (M)

● **Feb 2** USS *Queen of the West*, in broad daylight, sails under the guns of Vicksburg and attacks the Confederate gunboat *City of Vicksburg*. Neither boat is damaged in the exchange.

● **Feb 14** *Queen of the West*, after doing considerable damage to Confederate shipping and shore installations along the Mississippi, comes under fire from a shore battery at Gordon's Landing on the Black River and has to be abandoned.

Rosecrans and Bragg have the same plan for the battle, an k on the left flank, but Bragg gets his blow in first just after , forcing the Union line to give way. But a stout defense by ral Sheridan gives Rosecrans time to reinforce his line, and g the afternoon repeated Confederate attacks on the Union rove futile. Nevertheless, the Union troops have been thrown from their original positions all along the line, and Bragg nes that Rosecrans will retreat overnight. But Rosecrans ns in the field. The next day there is no fighting, neither side in a fit state to resume the attack. Rosecrans takes the rtunity to improve his position, prompting Bragg to order er attack on the afternoon of the third day. The attack is sed, and the battle comes to an end, with heavier casualties at Fredericksburg, a total of 24,988 on both sides.

● **Jan 10** The Union Navy returns to Galveston and bombards the city.

3 In atrocious weath-
ragg pulls his army
from Murfreesboro
establishes new posi-
around Manchester
valley of the Duck
r.

w: The Battle of
ericksburg. (ILN)

● **Jan 11** CSS *Alabama* attacks and sinks the Union warship USS *Hatteras* off Galveston, then escapes before the rest of the Union fleet can react.

● **Jan 19** Contemplating another assault across the Rappahannock, Burnside prepares to move troops a dozen miles upriver to United States Ford.

● **Jan 20–22 The Mud March**
It takes several hours for the men to leave their camp, and by mid afternoon it starts to rain. It rains heavily throughout the night and the next day, and the dirt roads are transformed into mud so deep that cannon sink until only their muzzles are visible, and huge mule teams find it virtually impossible to keep wagons moving. When conditions do not improve the next morning, Burnside gives up the movement and the men return to camp. Desertions and illness are at an all-time high.

● **Jan 24** Burnside presents Lincoln with an extraordinary document demanding that several senior officers be dismissed from the army.

● **Jan 25** Having contemplated Burnside's demands overnight, Lincoln decides instead to relieve Burnside of command and replace him with General Joseph Hooker.

Above: The Battle of Stones River. Union troops move forward to strengthen the line near the Nashville Pike. (LC).

● **Jan 31** Two ships in the Union fleet blockading Charleston Harbor are sunk by Confederate rams.

Below: A Wind rifle on the site of the battle at Stones River. (Author)

Left: Amidst the firing from shore batteries, ironclads clash in Charleston Harbor. (ILN)

Below: A train-load of wounded Union soldiers. This is the first war in which railroads play such a major part. (M)

Right:
es such
as this
ure that
-owning
es could
look to
ort from
northern
pe. (LC)

● **Feb 16** The U.S. Senate passes the first Conscription Act in the North.

● **Feb 20** Mass rallies in Liverpool and Carlisle prove the depth of popular support in England for the Emancipation Proclamation.

47

FEB 1863

SUNDAY

MARCH 1863

SUNDAY

MARCH 1863

SUNDAY

22 23 24 25 26 27 28 01 02 03 04 05 06 07 08 09 10 11 12 13 14 15 16 17   18 19 20 21 22 23 24 25 26 27 28 29 30 31 01 02 03 04 05 06 07 08 09

● **Feb 24** Having raised *Queen of the West*, the Confederates use her to lead the chase of another Union ironclad that has slipped past Vicksburg, USS *Indianola*. *Indianola* is finally caught late in the night and grounded.

March 11 ●
The Union expedition that is approaching Vicksburg by way of Yazoo Pass has now spent more than a month making its way along narrow streams, many of them blocked with trees cut down by slaves from the plantations along the way. At Fort Pemberton outside Greenwood on the Tallahatchie River, barely half way to their destination, they encounter Confederate troops for the first time. The Union ships are repulsed.

March 16–22 ●
The Steele's Bayou expedition is another attempt to find a way around Vicksburg, this time involving Sherman's troops and Porter's gunboats, but the way again proves impassable, the gunboats come under fire, and eventually the expedition retreats.

● **March 13** Union ironclads make another attempt on Fort Pemberton, and are again repulsed.

THE VICKSBURG CAMPAIGN

March 16 ● A third attempt to attack Fort Pemberton is beaten back once more.

Left: Railroads begin to prove vital for the war effort on both sides. And, both North and South devote efforts to destroying track and bridges to hinder the enemy. Engineers can build wooden bridges such as this in just a few hours, but raiders can destroy them even more quickly. (M)

March 5 ●
Battle of Thompson's Station In the relative quiet after Murfreesboro, Union Colonel John Coburn takes a brigade south from Franklin. At Thompson's Station, Tennessee, he attacks a Confederate force but is repelled. General Van Dorn then counter-attacks. Coburn is surrounded and forced to surrender.

● **Feb 25** The capture of a British blockade runner, *Peterhoff*, off the Virgin Islands almost provokes an international incident, until the mail that had been aboard the *Peterhoff* is returned unopened.

● **March 3** In preparation for his proposed attack on Charleston, Union Admiral Du Pont sends three ironclads to fire on Fort McAllister, Georgia. The fort is bombarded for eight hours but little damage is done and the ships retire.

● **March 15** In San Francisco USS *Cyane* seizes the schooner *J.P. Chapman* which its Confederate crew had planned to turn into a commerce raider.

Left: John Mosby, one of the many daring raiders of the war. (NA)

March 14 ●
During the night, Admiral Farragut attempts to take four ocean-going warships and three gunboats past the guns of Port Hudson. There are heavy casualties and only two ships make it past Port Hudson, but Farragut now has ships to oppose Confederate gunboats on the Mississippi between Vicksburg and Port Hudson.

March 9 ●
Leading 29 partisans, the Confederate Captain John Singleton Mosby rides into Fairfax Court House, Virginia, and captures Union General Edwin H. Stoughton, two other officers, 30 men and 58 horses. Embarrassingly, Stoughton is supposed to be leading a Union effort to capture Mosby.

March 14 ●
Confederates launch a surprise night attack on Fort Anderson on the Neuse River, North Carolina, but are beaten back by Union naval gunfire.

Above: Edwin Stoughton, a hunter caught by his prey. (M)

● **Feb 24** The U.S. Congress creates Arizona Territory out of New Mexico Territory.

Above: Raiders such as Mosby not only capture men and provisions, but also wreak destruction on the essential infrastructure of the enemy. (M)

● **March 13** The Confederate States Laboratory on Brown's Island, Richmond, explodes, killing 45 women and children

March 17 The decision is made to abandon the Yazoo Pass expedition.

● **March 19** The flotilla retreating from Fort Pemberton meets reinforcements under General Isaac Quimby and decides to turn around and resume the advance once more.

THE VICKSBURG CAMPAIGN

● **March 20 Battle of Vaught's Hill** A Union brigade under Colonel Albert S. Hill runs into Confederate General John Hunt Morgan's cavalry. Morgan attacks and Hill is forced back into a defensive position, but Morgan fails to break the Union line and when he hears reinforcements are approaching he retires.

WAR IN THE WEST

● **March 25** Confederate cavalry under Nathan Bedford Forrest capture the Union troops protecting the railroad at Brentwood, and do considerable damage to the track.

● **March 18** Confederate commerce raider *Georgiana* is sunk trying to run the Union blockade at Charleston.

Below: Vicksburg under fire, seen from the Union position on the western shore of the Mississippi. (M)

● **March 26** The Union navy buys a French-designed boat that sails partially submerged and is powered by a hand-operated screw propeller. Called the *Alligator*, it is to be used as a reconnaissance craft.

March 17 Union cavalry under General. W.W. Averell cross the Rappahannock at Kelly's Ford. At Brooks Farm they repulse Confederate cavalry under Averell's West Point classmate, Fitzhugh Lee, then clash again at Carter's Run, before the two sides retire.

● **March 20** Texan troops under John Bell Hood, passing through Richmond on their way to join Lee, stop to have a snowball fight in 8-inch deep snow.

● **March 29** Union troops evacuate Jacksonville, Florida.

Below: A less lethal fight in the Confederate camp. (B&L)

WAR IN THE EAST

POLITICS

● **March 29** Grant orders McClernand to begin moving his troops overland from Milliken's Bend to New Carthage, passing Vicksburg on the other side of the Mississippi.

Below: Nicknamed "Whistling Dick," this 18-pounder is part of the formidable Confederate defenses set up by Pemberton at Vicksburg. (M)

● **April 1** Grant, Sherman and Admiral Porter reconnoiter Haynes Bluff, but decide it cannot be assaulted.

April 9 ● Union General Banks launches an expedition up Bayou Teche in western Louisiana.

Apri[l] In a curiously inconclusive encounter, Confederate General Van and Union General Granger clash near Franklin. Both sides ar tative. Union cavalry under General Stanley successfully attac Dorn's rear, but are then driven off by Nathan Bedford F Nevertheless, Van Dorn decides to

● **April 4** Off the coast of Brazil, CSS *Alabama* cap the *Louisa* which turns o be loaded with coal. Capt Semmes decides to take Louisa with him to suppl ment his own supplies.

April 6 ● A Union fleet of nine ironclads, under the command of Admiral Samuel Du Pont, sails into Charleston harbor. The weather is hazy, visibility poor, so Du Pont decides not to attack.

● **April 7 Ba Charleston** This is a bat Pont does n want, after McAllister h not believe ironclads ca destroy the that guard t bor, but und sure from th Department reluctantly ing orders. clads bomba Sumter wit doing any a ble damage, the warship Keokuk is h than 90 tim will sink nex Troops und General Da Hunter emb transports never used. Du Pont ret

● **March 30** Confederate General A.P. Hill lays siege to the Union garrison at Washington, North Carolina.

April 1 ● On the Ware River, Virginia, a Union landing party is attacked by Confederate cavalry, but the Confederates are routed.

April 4 ● Lincoln visits General Hooker at Fredericksburg.

● **April 5** After a 12 reconnaissance, Ge Quimby decides th the Yazoo Pass exp tion is a waste of ti after all, and the fi withdrawal begins.

● **April 11** Confederat General Longstreet la siege to Union troops Suffolk, Virginia, and the opportunity to ro supplies from the regi

● **April 2** Women, protesting the rising cost of food, march through the streets of Richmond calling fo bread. The mayor reads the Riot Act to them, but they ignore him and start looting shops. Finally they disperse after President Dav threatens to order the militia to fire upon them.

● **April 3** In a significant case censorship, the Confederate pa make no mention of the Bread

48

PRIL 1863   SUNDAY   SUNDAY   SUNDAY   SUNDAY   **MAY 1863**   SUNDAY   SATURDAY

14 15 16 17 18 19 20 21 22 23 24 25 26 27 28 29 30 01 02 03 04 05 06 07 08 09 10 11 12 13 14 15 16 17 18 19 20 21 22 23 24 25 26 27 28 29 30

THE VICKSBURG CAMPAIGN

April 16–17 ● During the night Union transport ships and coal ges run past the ns of Vicksburg. ly one transport nk, the rest are position to sup-y Grant's troops the crossing at Grand Gulf.

● April 19 Grierson's cavalry is engaged in skirmishing near Pontotoc, Mississippi.

● April 21 To confuse the chasing Confederates, Grierson detaches one of his three regiments under Colonel Edward Hatch and sends them back north. Hatch fights a delaying action that allows Grierson to get away.

● April 29 Admiral Porter's ironclads attack Confederate fortifications at Grand Gulf to prepare the way for Grant's troops to cross the Mississippi. The batteries at Fort Wade are silenced, but those at Fort Cobun remain active. However, after dark Grant simply marches his men below Grand Gulf and crosses the river unopposed at Bruinsburg.

● April 29 To distract Confederate troops from the crossing at Grand Gulf, Union General Francis Blair takes his troops up the Yazoo River to the mouth of Chickasaw Bayou.

● May 12 BATTLE OF RAYMOND Confederates under General John Gregg attempt to stop the Union XVII Corps under General James B. McPherson from crossing Fourteen Mile Creek. Initial artillery fire causes heavy Union casualties, but McPherson is reinforced and after heavy fighting is able to force the Confederates out of their position.

April 17 ● Union Colonel Benjamin H. erson leads 1,700 cavalry out of LaGrange, nessee, on a raid o Mississippi and ouisiana that will eventually last 16 ays and cover 600 miles.

GRIERSON'S RAID

April 24 ● Grierson reaches Newton Station, wrecking two loco-motives and several miles of track and trestle bridges on the main railroad supply line into Vicksburg.

April 26 ● After a final skirmish which has drawn most local Confederate forces away from Grierson, Hatch arrives back at LaGrange.

April 27 ● At Hazlehurst, Grierson causes more damage, this time to the Jackson and Great Northern Railroad.

April 29 ● Warned of an ambush, Grierson turns away from his intended destination of Grand Gulf and heads south for Baton Rouge, a further 100 miles away.

● April 30 Blair's troops, backed by seven gunboats, engage the Confederate battery at Drumgould's Bluff.

● April 30 Having landed at Bruinsburg and started toward Port Gibson, Grant's troops run into Confederate skirmishers around midnight. Skirmishing lasts into the early hours of May 1.

● May 1 Blair's troops continue their engagement at Drumgould's Bluff, but after dark return to the mouth of the Yazoo.

● May 1 BATTLE OF PORT GIBSON Shortly after dawn Confederate troops try to halt Grant's advance, but the Confederates are repeatedly driven back from one defensive position to another until finally forced to withdraw in the early evening.

● May 9 Confederate General Joseph E. Johnston is ordered to take command of Confederate forces in the field.

● May 13 Johnston arrives at Jackson and learns two Union army corps are advancing on the city. He orders the evacuation of the city.

● May 14 Battle of Jackson Advancing Union troops under Sherman and McPherson engage the Confederate rear guard under Gregg. Union troops push the Confederates steadily backwards until mid-afternoon, when Johnston announces the evacuation is complete and orders Gregg to disengage. The Mississippi state capital falls to Grant.

● May 16 Battle of Champion Hill General Pemberton's Confederate troops from Vicksburg are attacked by Grant at Champion Hill. There is fierce fighting all day, but Pemberton cannot stand up to Grant's superior numbers and by midnight the Confederates are in full flight for Vicksburg.

il 12 Banks's troops reach s. At the same time, sends a third division to ept any Confederate t from Bisland.

pril 13 Union troops attack federate lines at Fort Bisland. e fighting continues throughout day, with gunboats joining in on sides. During the night federate General Richard Taylor ns of the Union troops in his rear begins to evacuate the fort.

● April 14 Banks finds Fort Bisland deserted.

● April 14 At Nerson's Woods Confederate troops sent out from Fort Bisland clash with the troops Banks has sent to cut off their retreat. Despite a bombardment by the Confederate gunboat *Diana*, the Union troops prevail.

● April 21 To relieve pressure on other Confederate troops and dis-rupt Union operations, Confederate General John S. Marmaduke leads a cavalry raid into Missouri.

● April 25 Marmaduke encounters Union troops in a fortified position at Cape Girardeau.

● April 26 Marmaduke attacks the Union force at Cape Girardeau, and is repulsed.

● May 1 At Wall's Bridge across the Tickfaw River Grierson encoun-ters his first serious opposition, three companies of Confederates from Port Hudson, but a charge puts the Confederates to flight.

● May 2 Grierson's men ride into Baton Rouge, having killed or wounded about 100 Confederates, captured over 500 prisoners, destroyed 50–60 miles of railroad and tele-graph, and distracted a huge body of Confederates for the cost of barely two dozen casualties.

● May 1–2 BATTLE OF CHALK BLUFF Attempting to cross the St. Francis River at the end of his raid into Missouri, Confederate General Marmaduke comes under heavy attack from pursuing Union troops under General William Vandever. Marmaduke eventually gets away, but suffers heavy casualties.

● May 3 A Union raid into northern Alabama comes to an end when Colonel Streight's raiders are forced to surrender to Nathan Bedford Forrest.

● May 17 Pursuing the Confederates, Union troops under General McClernand encounter a sizeable Confederate rear guard defending the bridges over Big Black River. Union troops drive the Confederates from their breastworks, capturing 1,700 men and 18 guns, but the Confederates manage to get across the river and burn the bridges after them, delaying Union pursuit.

● May 18 Grant's troops finally converge on Vicksburg and settle down to a siege.

May 19 Grant attempts an assault upon the Confederate lines around Vicksburg but is repulsed.

Left: Leading the Sixth and Seventh Illinois Cavalry, Colonel Grierson parades triumphantly through Baton Rouge on May 2, 1863. (LC)

● May 22 Another attack on the Confederate line results in heavy Union losses.

● April 17 Dogging the heels of the retreating Confederates, Banks clashes with Taylor again at Vermillion Bayou. Following an artillery duel, the Confederates retreat to Opelousas after dark.

w: Lee and on in one ir final ultations, on ght of May 3. (B&L)

May 6 ● Admiral Porter takes a fleet of gunboats up the Red River and captures Alexandria, Louisiana.

● May 7 Confederate General Earl Van Dorn is shot and killed by Dr. George B. Peters, who claimed Van Dorn was having an affair with his wife.

● May 21 BATTLE OF PLAINS STORE Union troops from Baton Rouge encounter Confederate forces near Plains Store. The Confederates are forced to retreat, but a fresh Confederate column arrives and counterattacks. Eventually these troops too are forced to retreat.

● April 20 Four Union ships attack Fort Burton at Butte a la Rose, Louisiana. The fort surrenders.

● April 27 General Hooker attempts to turn the Confederate flank by leading three corps across the Rappahannock and Rapidan Rivers above Fredericksburg.

● May 8 Union ships begin bombarding Port Hudson, the last Confederate stronghold on the Mississippi other than Vicksburg.

● April 29 Lee orders Longstreet to disen-gage from Suffolk and rejoin the main body of the Army of Northern Virginia.

● May 12 The first all-black unit in the Union army, the 54th Massachusetts, is raised by Colonel Robert Shaw.

May 27 ● General Banks makes his long awaited assault on Port Hudson, but the attack is poorly co-ordinated and fails.

April 19–20 ● a surprise night attack, ion troops capture Fort ; along with all the guns i men in the place. They the fort for the whole of next day, then return to own lines along with all their captives.

Below: Unaware that Jackson's men are marching to outflank them, III Corps of the Army of the Potomac turns out for review on May 2 near Chancellorsville. (M)

● April 24 In a reconnaissance in force, Union General Michael Corcoran engages with the right flank of Confederate General George Pickett, and is easily repulsed.

● April 30 Hooker's army concentrates at Chancellorsville.

● May 1 Lee leaves his positions at Fredericksburg and begins to move toward Hooker on his left flank at Chancellorsville.

● May 2–3 Battle of Chancellorsville (see page 118) Rather than advance against Lee's rear, Hooker has taken a defensive position at Chancellorsville. Lee splits his army, sending Jackson on a march around the Union flank. Jackson manages to maintain surprise and attacks late in the afternoon. The Union XI Corps is crushed, but other Union troops rally and begin to coun-terattack, until darkness ends the fighting. In the darkness, Jackson rides ahead of his lines and is shot by his own troops when he returns. Next day Lee attacks again all along his line. A shell hits Hooker's headquarters, temporarily disabling him. Hooker's defenses are broken and he retreats to a position by United States Ford.

● May 30 Lee re-organ-izes the Army of Northern Virginia into three corps under Longstreet, A.P. Hill and Richard Ewell.

April 16 ● onfederate ops occupy Fort Huger ear Suffolk.

● April 16 While keep-ing Union troops penned in Washington, North Carolina, A.P. Hill has been assiduously scouring the country-side for supplies to send on to Lee's army. Now, having removed most supplies from the area, Hill aban-dons the siege.

● May 3 The Union VI and II Corps under Generals Sedgwick and Gibbon attack Confederate General Jubal A. Early's division holding Marye's Heights at Fredericksburg. Early is forced to retire. Sedgwick sets out to reunite with Hooker at Chancellorsville.

● May 3–4 Battle of Salem Church In the afternoon Early regroups at Salem Church and delays Sedgwick's advance. Overnight, Lee sends two fresh divisions from Chancellorsville to reinforce Early. Next day, Sedgwick holds his position against fierce attacks. After dark he withdraws back across the Rappahannock under Confederate artillery fire.

● May 5–6 Overnight, after hearing of Sedgwick's defeat, Hooker finally withdraws across the Rappahannock.

● May 6 General A.P. Hill is assigned command of Jackson's old corps.

● May 10 General Stonewall Jackson dies of his wounds. His last words are: "Let us cross over the river and rest under the shade of the trees."

May 5 ● Clement L. Vallandigham, leader of the pro-Confederate Copperheads in Ohio, is arrested by General Ambrose Burnside and jailed.

● May 6 Vallandigham is tried for treason by a military court and sentenced to two years in a military prison.

● May 19 Lincoln commutes the sen-tence on Vallandigham to banishment to the Confederacy.

49

SUNDAY   SUNDAY   **JUNE 1863**   **JUNE 1863**   SUNDAY   SUNDAY   **JULY 1**

31 01 02 03 04 05 06 07 08 09 10 11 12 13 14 15 16 17 18 19 20 21 22 23 24 25 26 27 28 29 30 01 02 03 04 05 06 07 08 09 10 11 12 13 14 15 16

Early June After the Battle of Murfreesboro, Rosecrans and Bragg have held their respective positions for five and a half months. By early June, however, Rosecrans's superiors fear Bragg will detach troops to break the siege at Vicksburg and urge Rosecrans to act.

Above: Confederates charge at Logan's division during the Battle of Raymond. (Harper's)

June 6 ●
On a reconnaissance toward Richmond, Louisiana, Colonel Herman Lieb's African Brigade encounter Confederate troops. They beat them off, but retreat to Milliken's Bend.

June 7 ●
Jefferson Davis's plantation at Brierfield is burned by Union troops.

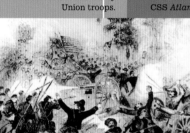

Left: The Battle of Champion Hill. (Harper's)

June 2 CSS *Alabama* chases the Union commercial ship *Amazonian* for eight hours before capturing and burning it off the coast of Montevideo.

June 4–5 ●
A joint army and navy operation destroys a foundry at Walterton, Virginia, on the Mattaponi River where Confederate ordnance is being made.

June 5 Lee's victorious army is congregating at Culpepper, while Jeb Stuart's cavalry holds the line of the Rappahannock at Brandy Station.

June 9
BATTLE OF BRANDY STATION
Union cavalry under General Alfred Pleasonton launch a surprise dawn attack on Stuart's camp at Brandy Station. The fighting lasts all day before Pleasonton retires. It is the largest cavalry battle of the war, and the point from which Union cavalry begin to gain the initiative.

Right: Union General Howard tries to rally his XI Corps at the Battle of Chancellorsville. (B&L)

June 1 General Burnside closes the Chicago *Times* for publishing disloyal statements.

June 4 Lincoln orders that Burnside's closure of the Chicago *Times* be revoked.

THE VICKSBURG CAMPAIGN

June 18 Grant finally gets the chance to relieve General McClernand of command after McClernand issues a message to his troops calling in question the bravery of other units.

TENNESSEE CAMPAIGN

June 23
Rosecrans feints toward Bragg's left wing at Shelbyville, while massing his army against Bragg's right flank.

June 7 Around 3:00 a.m. a large Confederate force under General Henry E. McCulloch attacks Lieb's line at Milliken's Bend. The Confederates are close to victory when two Union gunboats arrive and help to drive them off.

June 14 Banks renews his attack on Port Hudson but is beaten off. The siege continues.

June 20–21 ●
BATTLE OF LAFOURCHE CROSSING
In an attempt to force a Union withdrawal from Port Hudson a Confederate force under Colonel James P. Major has been causing disruption in the Union rear. Late in the afternoon of the 20th they encounter Union troops under Colonel Albert Stickney at LaFourche Crossing. They are driven back. Next day they attack again, and again are driven back.

June 15 ●
A new Confederate ironclad, CSS *Atlanta*, sets out from Wilmington.

June 17 CSS *Atlanta* attacks two Union warships in Wassaw Sound, Georgia, but *Atlanta* first runs aground then damages her rudder and eventually has to be surrendered.

June 12 At last aware that Lee's army is on the move, Hooker starts to move out of his camp at Falmouth.

June 21 ●
Lee's infantry begins crossing the Potomac into Maryland.

June 13 Charged with clearing the Shenandoah Valley, Ewell's corps attacks the Union garrison at Winchester commanded by General Robert Milroy.

June 14 At Winchester, Ewell captures West Fort. After dark, Milroy abandons his entrenchments in an attempt to reach Charles Town.

June 15 An overnight flanking march allows Confederates to cut off Milroy's retreat. More than 2,400 Union troops surrender.

THE GETTYSBURG CAMPAIGN

June 10 Confederate prisoners being transported to a Union prison camp aboard the steamer *Maple Leaf* overpower their guards and escape.

June 17 At Aldie in the Blue Ridge Mountains, Union cavalry under General Judson Kilpatrick clashes with Colonel Thomas Munford's Confederate cavalry, after four hours Munford retires toward Middleburg.

June 17 After the clash at Aldie, Munford goes on to rout a brigade of cavalry under Colonel Alfred Duffié at Middleburg.

June 19 Stuart's cavalry at Middleburg is attacked by Union cavalry under General David M. Gregg. Stuart is driven back, but continues to cover the approaches to the Blue Ridge Mountains.

June 11 Despite his exile, the Peace Democrats in Ohio nominate Vallandigham as governor.

June 20 ●
The new state of West Virginia is officially admitted into the Union.

July 3 ●
After six weeks of siege, and constant bombardment by Union artillery and ironclads, white flags appear on the defenses of Vicksburg. Grant and Pemberton meet to discuss surrender.

June 24–26 BATTLE OF HOOVER'S GAP
Rosecrans's main army, under General George H. Thomas, sweeps aside Bragg's right flank in Hoover's Gap, but runs into a Confederate division under General Alexander P. Stewart. Fighting continues until midday on the 26th, when Stewart is forced to retreat. Bragg falls back on Tullahoma.

TENNESSEE CAMPAIGN

June 28 Thomas continues to move around Bragg's right flank, moving not toward Tullahoma as Bragg expects but toward Hillsboro. Meanwhile Granger and McCook occupy Shelbyville and Wartrace.

June 28–30 Thomas sends a brigade under General John Thomas Wilder to cut railroad lines in Bragg's rear.

WAR IN THE WEST

July 1 ●
Bragg withdraws from Tullahoma.

July 3 Skirmishing between Union cavalry and Bragg's rear guard near Cowan.

July 4 Bragg reaches Chattanooga, abandoning Middle Tennessee.

June 28 ●
Confederate troops attack Fort Butler at Donaldsonville on the Mississippi. Gunboats come to the aid of the Union defenders, and the Confederates are forced to retire.

July 4 In an attempt to relieve pressure on Vicksburg, Confederates under General. Theophilus Holmes attack Helena, Arkansas, but are driven off.

June 29 ●
A Confederate raid from Arkansas under Colonel William H. Parsons, which aims to recapture slaves and destroy crops from Louisiana plantations now being operated for the Union, reaches Lake Providence, where the Union garrison surrenders.

June 30 ●
U.S. Marines under General Alfred Ellet reach Goodrich's Landing in pursuit of Parsons. Parsons is attacked and forced to fall back.

THE GETTYSBURG CAMPAIGN

June 26 General Jubal Early, in the advance of Lee's army, passes through Gettysburg on his way to York.

June 28 Lee starts to concentrate his army west of Gettysburg.

June 29 Meade's army moves south of Gettysburg to stay in a position between Lee and Washington, D.C. Meanwhile Union cavalry under General Buford is already in Gettysburg scouting for Lee's army.

June 21 At Middleburg and at Upperville Union cavalry make a determined effort to break Stuart's screen. Stuart is driven back, but establishes a strong defensive position at Ashby Gap.

WAR IN THE EAST

June 25 Stuart takes his cavalry on a ride around the Union army, an exploit that will deprive Lee of his "eyes" until the middle of the battle of Gettysburg.

June 30 ●
Stuart attacks a Union cavalry regiment at Hanover, but in a counterattack Stuart himself is nearly captured. Stuart attacks once more but is unable to break the Union line. He is eventually forced to withdraw east and north, delaying his efforts to rejoin Lee's army.

June 28 ●
Tired of constant squabbles with Halleck, General Hooker resigns his command. He is replaced by General George Meade.

July 4 Vicksburg surrenders.

July 2 Confederate General John Hunt Morgan sets out with 2,500 men to disrupt supplies and communications in the rear of Rosecrans's army.

MORGAN'S RAID

July 5 Morgan captures the Union garrison at Lebanon, Kentucky.

July 8 Despite orders to remain in Kentucky, Morgan crosses into Indiana.

July 9 At Corydon, Indiana, Morgan captures some 400 Home Guards.

July 1–2 A Union supply train to Fort Gibson, Oklahoma (then Indian Territory) is attacked by Confederates under Colonel Stand Watie, a Cherokee Indian, at Cabin Creek. The Confederates are driven off, and supplies necessary for upcoming operations are delivered.

July 1–3 BATTLE OF GETTYSBURG (SEE PAGE 120)
The two armies arrive piecemeal at Gettysburg for the greatest battle of the war in the East, beginning around dawn on July 1. Outnumbered, the Union forces, are pushed back through the town onto Cemetery Ridge. The Confederates take position on Seminary Ridge paralleling it. On July 2 Lee attacks both flanks of the Union line, but the Confederate troops are pushed back. On July 3

July 4–5 Overnight, Lee begins to move his battered army south.

July 6 Cautiously, Meade begins his pursuit.

Below: Lancers in the 6th Pennsylvania Cavalry. (B&L)

July 7 Buford's cavalry almost capture Confederate trains at Williamsport, but are driven off by Imboden's cavalry. Meanwhile, Kilpatrick drives two Confederate brigades back through Hagerstown until Stuart arrives to stop him.

July 8 Pleasonton's cavalry clashes with Stuart's men holding the South Mountain passes at Boonsboro, Maryland.

July 11
Sherman surrounds the city of Jackson, where General Joseph Johnston has his Confederate army.

July 13 Morgan crosses into O... pursued by Un... cavalry under General Edwa... Hobson.

July 13 A Un... foraging exped... at Kocks's Plantation nea... Donaldsonville attacked by a s... er Confederate... and forced to r... to Donaldsonv...

July 9 After hearing... the fall of Vicksburg... after a siege of 48 d... the defenders of Po... Hudson finally surr... The Mississippi is n... Union hands along... entire length.

July 10 Under cover of a bom... bardment by Union artillery an... Admiral John Dahlgren's ironcl... troops under General George C... Strong land on Morris Island ne... Charleston, South Carolina, an... approach Fort Wagner.

July 11 Strong attacks For... Wagner, but is thrown back.

Action Wagne...

July 11 Lee entrenche... protect the river cross... Williamsport, but can... cross because the pon... have been destroyed a... the river is flooded.

July 12 Meade arriv... there are skirmishes a... along Lee's line. Mean... Lee's men are building... new bridge.

July 13 After da... Lee manages to c... his army back ac... the Potomac.

July 14 Un... cavalry unde... Buford and... Kilpatrick a... Lee's rear gu... and take ove... prisoners.

July 13–15
Opposition to... Draft results i... ing in New Yo... black churche... orphanages ar... homes the ma... get of the mob... Eventually, tro... fresh from Ge... have to be bro... to control the...

50

31 01 02 03 04 05 06 07 08 09 10 11 12 13 14 15 16 17 18 19 20 21 22 23 24 25 26 27 28 29 30 01 02 03 04 05 06 07 08 09 10 11 12 13 14 15 16

) 21 22 23 24 25 26 27 28 29 30 31 01 02 03 04 05 06 07 08 09 10 11 12 13 14 15 16 17 18 19 20 21 22 23 24 25 26 27 28 29 30 31 01 02 03 04 05

y 16 After dark, Johnston anages to slip quietly out of ckson. Sherman pursues as as Brandon.

ly 19 Union troops rcle Morgan at ngton Island. gan himself, with t 400 followers, ages to escape but est of his command nders.

● July 26 Morgan, with his few surviving followers, is cut off at Salineville, Ohio, and surrenders.

Early Aug After its success at Vicksburg, Grant's army is being broken up for service as occupation troops.

CHICKAMAUGA CAMPAIGN

● Aug 16 General Rosecrans launches his campaign to take Chattanooga.

● Aug 16 General Burnside leaves Louisville for East Tennessee in a move designed to complement Rosecrans's campaign.

● Aug 21–Sept 8 Union troops under Colonel John T. Wilder take up a prominent position to the north-east of Chattanooga and begin shelling the town. Convinced the attack is due from this direction, Bragg fails to notice that Rosecrans is moving the bulk of his army into position west and south of Chattanooga.

Right: Under relentless pressure, such as this mine exploding under their fortifications, the Confederate forces at Vicksburg have to surrender. (Harper's)

Above: Veterans, even though most of them have still not yet learnt to stand at attention. (M)

15 Anticipating a federate attack on Fort son in Indian Territory, on General James G. nt crosses the Arkansas er for a pre-emptive strike he Confederate base at ey Springs.

uly 17 BATTLE OF HONEY PRINGS
unt attacks the Confederate troops f General Douglas H. Cooper early the morning and by mid-afternoon full-scale battle is in progress. espite counterattacks, the onfederates are soundly beaten and ee. Some of the heaviest fighting is ndertaken by the black troops of e 1st Kansas.

ly 18 The attack on Fort Wagner is sumed, with the assault spearheaded y the black troops of the 54th assachusetts. They scale the ramparts t after fierce fighting are driven back ith heavy casualties, including the eath of Colonel Robert Gould Shaw he Union settles down to a siege.

Below: A typical temporary field hospital consisting of log shacks and mud. It was originally a rough winter camp for Confederate troops outside Petersburg before falling into Union hands. (M)

● Aug 21 In supposed response to a Union raid on Osceola, Mississippi, Colonel William C. Quantrill leads a force of partisans into Lawrence, Kansas. His men hold the town for several hours, killing about 150 unarmed men and boys, before withdrawing.

Sept 4 ●
In New Orleans, U.S. Grant is injured when his horse falls on him. He will be on crutches for several weeks.

Sept 1 ●
Having been chased out of Indian Territory, Confederate General Cabell ambushes his pursuers at Devil's Backbone, Arkansas, but the Union forces regroup, counterattack and put the Confederates to flight again.

Sept 2 ●
General Burnside captures Knoxville, the starting point for his East Tennessee expedition.

Above: The siege of Port Hudson. (WP)

● Aug 1 Brandy Station is again the scene of a cavalry skirmish.

● Aug 5 A cheering crowd at Table Bay, Cape of Good Hope, watch Confederate raider CSS *Alabama* capture the *Sea Bride* with her load of provisions.

● Aug 15 The Confederate submarine *H.L. Hunley* arrives at Charleston.

● Aug 24 The submarine *Hunley* tries to blow up USS *New Ironsides* by towing a torpedo (mine) underneath her, but the water isn't deep enough.

● Aug 29 The *Hunley* is accidentally sunk in Charleston Harbor when the steamer she is moored beside pulls away unexpectedly. Five members of her crew are drowned.

● Aug 6 Confederate cavalry under John Singleton Mosby capture a Union wagon train at Fairfax Court House.

Left: Awarded the Congressional Medal of honor after distinguishing himself in 1864, Christian Abraham Fleetwood is one of the many black soldiers who fight for the Union. After the war he writes *The Negro as a Soldier*. (LC)

● Aug 26 Union troops finally manage to capture the rifle pits directly outside Fort Wagner.

Right: The "Marshal Ney of Gettysburg," General George Pickett leads a famous but hopeless charge on the Union line at Cemetery Ridge. (M)

● Aug 8 In the wake of his defeat at Gettysburg and possibly suffering from a heart attack, Robert E. Lee offers to resign. Jefferson Davis rejects the offer.

● Aug 17–23 While siege operations continue against Fort Wagner, Union batteries on Morris Island bombard Fort Sumter and the defenses of Charleston Harbor, but to no significant effect.

ly 16 At the fords across the otomac at Shepherdstown nion cavalry under David regg clashes with onfederate cavalry under tzhugh Lee and J.R. ambliss, but neither side ins an advantage.

● July 23
Union troops under General William H. French attempt to force their way through Manassas Gap in order to capture Front Royal and cut off Lee's retreat. Confederate troops successfully resist the attack.

Below: John Burns, a local Gettysburg man, becomes a folk hero during the battle. In his seventies, he takes his rifle and joins the Union forces trying to force the Confederates from his area. Wounded three times, he needs crutches afterwards. (M)

Left: Steuart's brigade at Culp's Hill, Battle of Gettysburg. (LC)

Above: The field of Gettysburg, the battle considered by many to be the turning point of the war. An 1863 perspective drawing by John B. Bachelder. (LC)

Sept 5 ●
A patrol from Sully's camp is attacked by a larger band of Sioux and forced to flee.

● July 24 Union troops move into Front Royal, but Lee is now safely past.

● Aug 1 The Confederate spy Belle Boyd is arrested yet again and imprisoned in Old Capitol Prison, Washington.

o 100 people lled or ded. where, there nti-draft riots ston, mouth, New oshire, nd, Vermont, er, Ohio, and New York.

● July 24 The Santee Sioux who started an uprising in August 1862 have now joined forces with the Teton Sioux, and they attack General Henry Hastings Sibley who is pursuing them at Big Mound, North Dakota. Sibley counterattacks, and the Sioux scatter across the prairie.

● July 26 The Sioux offer battle again at Dead Buffalo Lake, but are again defeated.

● July 28 A large body of Sioux attack Sibley again at Stony Lake, but unable to find any weak point in the Union defenses, they ride off again, too fast for pursuit.

Sept 3 ●
In England, British shipbuilders have been making ships for the Confederacy, but the Union has claimed this violates neutrality. The matter is settled when Lord Russell, British Foreign Secretary, orders that two ironclads currently under construction in Birkenhead be kept in port.

Sept 3 ●
After their defeat by Sibley, the Sioux have simply waited for Sibley to leave the area and returned to their old hunting grounds. Now Union troops have come after them again, under General Alfred Sully. At Whitestone Hill Sully attacks a Sioux camp and the Indians flee.

● Aug 22 A postal strike in Richmond means no mail is being delivered, even if it is vital to the war effort.

Sept 16 Rosecrans starts to concentrate his forces around Lee and Gordon's Mills on Chickamauga Creek, 12 miles south of Chattanooga.

Sept 8 When he finally discovers where the bulk of Rosecrans's army is, Bragg abandons Chattanooga.

Sept 17 Bragg halts his retreat from Chattanooga and turns north again, intending to defeat a portion of Rosecrans's army so he can re-occupy the city.

Sept 18 The first skirmishes between elements of the two armies.

CHICKAMAUGA CAMPAIGN

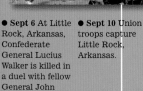

Above: The Battle of Chickamauga. (LC)

Sept 19–20 BATTLE OF CHICKAMAUGA (See page 122)
The only major Confederate victory in the West begins with the two armies hammering against each other, but without either side making any significant impact. The first of Longstreet's troops finally arrive on Sept 19. When fighting resumes the next day, Rosecrans is erroneously informed of a gap in his line, and in moving troops to correct it he creates a real gap which is quickly exploited by Longstreet. The Union line is split and most of the army retreats. Only General George Thomas stands firm, fighting a rearguard action which earns him the name "The Rock of Chickamauga" and allows the Union army to retire safely into Chattanooga. Bragg takes up positions on the heights above the city and begins a siege.

Sept 6 At Little Rock, Arkansas, Confederate General Lucius Walker is killed in a duel with fellow General John Marmaduke.

Sept 10 Union troops capture Little Rock, Arkansas.

Sept 8 A Union flotilla of four gunboats and seven troop transports sails up the Sabine River in an attempt to seize Fort Griffin, Texas. The garrison at Fort Griffin consists of just 44 men, but their artillery fire proves to be so accurate that the Union expedition is forced to withdraw.

Sept 22 General Ambrose Burnside begins his expedition into East Tennessee by attacking the Confederate forces at Blountsville. The Confederates are forced to withdraw.

Mid–Sept Following the defeat at Fort Griffin, Union General Banks decides to make another attack on Texas, sending a force overland from Bayou Teche to the Atchafalaya River.

Sept 28–9 BATTLE OF FORDOCHE BRIDGE
Overnight, Confederate forces under General Tom Green cross the Atchafalaya River to attack Union troops under General Napoleon J.T. Dana who have now reached Fordache Bridge. Skirmishing begins at dawn and the battle proper is joined by midday, resulting in a rapid Confederate victory, with many of the Union troops captured and only the cavalry able to get away.

Sept 6–7 Overnight, Confederates finally abandon Fort Wagner and withdraw from Morris Island.

Sept 8 A party of Union marines attempts to storm Fort Sumter, but is repulsed.

Sept 8 Longstreet and his corps are detached from Lee's Army of Northern Virginia and sent West to reinforce Bragg at Chattanooga. Because Union successes have so disrupted Confederate railroads, this will entail a roundabout journey of nearly 1,000 miles.

Sept 19 H.L. Hunley, the inventor of the submarine that bears his name, is given command of the boat that has just been raised, and arrives in Charleston from Mobile with his own crew.

Below: Battles between cavalry units often become single-combat duels. (M)

Left: Amphibious soldiers of the U.S. Marine Corps. On the left is an officer; the other two are privates. (M)

Sept 25 The Union 11th and 12th Corps, commanded by Joseph Hooker, begin to travel west to reinforce Rosecrans at Chattanooga.

Sept 13 Lee pulls back from Culpeper Court House, and the town is immediately occupied by Meade.

Right: Union cavalry line up to move out. (M)

Sept 30–Oct 17 Confederate General Joseph Wheeler sets out on a cavalry raid in Rosecrans's rear that will cause considerable disruption to supplies and communications to the Union troops in Chattanooga.

Oct 2 Hooker's 20,000 men arrive at Bridgeport, having traveled 1,159 miles in seven days. The only route open between Bridgeport and Chattanooga is a difficult mountain trail.

Oct 6 Quantrill's raiders attack a Union post at Baxter Springs, Kansas, but are fought off. However, by chance the raiders encounter a column escorting General James G. Blunt. Many in the column are killed, including the band, though Blunt manages to escape.

Oct 10 Jefferson Davis arrives at Bragg's headquarters in an attempt to quell the open dissent among all of Bragg's senior officers.

THE SIEGE OF CHATTANOOGA

Right: General Thomas, the "Rock of Chickamauga."

Oct 18 Davis leaves Bragg's headquarters having signally failed [to] restore anyone's faith [in] the general.

Oct 16 A new Union Militar[y] Division of the Mississippi is created, uniting all the old Western commands. Grant is put in change.

Oct 17 Grant meets Secretary of War Stanto[n] [at] Indianapolis. Stanton gi[ves] him a choice of two orde[rs:] one will retain Rosecran[s in] command of the Army o[f the] Cumberland, the other w[ill] relieve Rosecrans of com[mand] and replace him with Th[omas]. Grant chooses to give com[mand] to Thomas.

Oct 2[?] Grant arrives [at] Chattanoo[ga].

Oct 10 BATTLE OF BLUE SPRINGS
Having regrouped his forces, Carter attacks Williams's cavalry in force. The Confederates suffer heavy casualties and are forced to retire into Virginia.

Left: Using the trees for cover, Confederate soldiers hold their line in the woods at the Battle of Chickamauga. (B&L)

Oc[t] Sherman as[sumes] command [of the] Army [of the] Tennessee [on its] cession to [Grant].

Oct 15 The submarine *Hunley* sinks again in Charleston Harbor with the loss of all crew.

Oct 18 The *Hunley* [is] located in nine fatho[ms] of water, and efforts begin to raise her aga[in].

Oct 16–18 Starting on Oct [?], two Union ships bombard Fo[rt] Brooke near Tampa, Florida, [but] this is only a diversion while a landing party marches 14 mil[es] across country to the Hillsborough River where the[y] capture two blockade runner[s] and cause the Confederates [to] scupper a third.

WAR IN THE WEST

Oct 7 A landing party from USS *Osage* travels overland from the Mississippi to the Red River where they manage to capture and destroy two Confederate steamers.

Oct 5 In Charleston Harbor the CSS *David* tries to destroy the USS *New Ironsides* by ramming it with a 60-pound torpedo fixed on a ten-foot spar. When the torpedo explodes it sends up a column of water that puts out the boilers on the *David*, but an engineer manages to relight the fires before the ship can be captured. *New Ironsides* is not seriously damaged.

Oct 13 Stuart's cavalry skirmishes with Union forces near Auburn. Stuart is almost cut off from the Confederate army, but nimbly escapes again.

Oct 14 At Auburn, two brigades of the Union army fight a rearguard action against Stuart's cavalry.

Oct 14 BATTLE OF BRISTOE STATION
A.P. Hill's corps encounters two corps of the Union army and attacks without proper reconnaissance. The Union force turns out to be stronger than Hill thinks, and the attack costs him dearly. After this, Meade is able to complete his retreat to Centreville unmolested.

THE NAVAL WAR

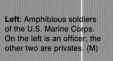

Oct 9 Lee begins an offensive movement around Meade's flank to threaten Washington and force the Union army to withdraw. Meade is not caught by surprise and manages to cover his flank.

Above: A Louisiana "Tiger." (B&L)

WAR IN THE EAST

Oct 19 BUCKLAND RACES
While shielding Lee's withdrawal from Manassas Junction, Stuart's cavalry is pursued by Union cavalry under Kilpatrick. Stuart lures Kilpatrick into an ambush near Buckland Mills where the Union cavalry is routed then chased for five miles in what becomes known as the "Buckland Races."

Right: The "dashing cavalier" Jeb Stuart. (ILN)

Oct 20 Stu[art] takes the las[t of] his cavalry b[ack] across the Rappahanno[ck] bringing to a [close] a brief camp[aign] in which neit[her] side was abl[e to] outmaneuve[r the] other, or will[ing to] bring on a m[ajor] engagement.

NOVEMBER 1863
DECEMBER 1863

SUNDAY   SUNDAY   SUNDAY   SUNDAY   SATURDAY

27 28 29 30 31 01 02 03 04 05 06 07 08 09 10 11 12 13 14 15 16 17 18 19 20 21 22 23 24 25 26 27 28 29 30 01 02 03 04 05 06 07 08 09 10 11 12

ct 25 Grant initiates the
cker Line", a plan originally
sed by Rosecrans to bring sup-
into the beleaguered city.

● **Oct 27** In the early hours
of the morning, portions of
General William B. Hazen's
brigade float on pontoons
around Moccasin Bend to
Brown's Ferry. Here they
establish a bridgehead on
the Confederate-held bank,
then position a pontoon
bridge across the river. This
is the first stage in the
"Cracker Line".

● **Oct 28** General Hooker brings his
divisions through Lookout Valley to
link up with the bridgehead at
Brown's Ferry. As he does so, he
detaches troops under General John
W, Geary to secure Wauhatchie
Station on the Nashville and
Chattanooga Railroad.

● **Oct 29 BATTLE OF
WAUHATCHIE STATION**
In a rare night engagement, Confederates
launch a surprise attack on Wauhatchie
Station at midnight. Hearing the din of
battle, Hooker sends more and more troops
along Lookout Valley to reinforce Geary's
division. The Confederates are forced to
retreat to Lookout Mountain, and the
"Cracker Line" is open.

t 25 A Union cavalry com-
runs into a Confederate
under General
naduke. The Union troop-
ithdraw slowly into Pine
, Arkansas, where an
try company has con-
ted a makeshift defense of
n bales. The Confederates
k but are unable to break
Jnion defenses and are
d to retire.

w: A typical raid by Stuart's cavalry.

● **Oct 28** Confederate commerce raider CSS *Georgia*
arrives in Cherbourg, France,
for major repairs.

e: A target the hungry
and his men can not
The massive Union
train, belonging to
th Corps of the Army
Potomac, is heavily
ted. (M)

● **Nov 3** Confederate
cavalry attack
Collierville, Tennessee,
but find the place more
strongly defended than
expected, and when
Union reinforcements
arrive the Confederates
withdraw back to
Mississippi.

Right: Cleburne's
repulse of
Sherman at
Missionary Ridge.
(LC)

● **Nov 2** Preparing for
another advance upon
Texas, General Banks
begins landing troops at
Brazos Santiago, Texas.

● **Nov 4** Bragg sends
Longstreet against
Burnside in East
Tennessee.

● **Nov 4** Banks's troops
occupy Brownsville,
securing the Mexican
border area.

● **Nov 6** In West Virginia Union troops
under General W.W. Averell defeat a
Confederate brigade at Droop Mountain,
spelling the end of Confederate resistance
in West Virginia.

● **Nov 7** General Averell unites
with General Alfred Napoleon
Alexander Dufflé to capture
Lewisburg, West Virginia.

● **Nov 7** Union troops force a
crossing of the Rappahannock
at Rappahannock Station capturing more than 1,600 men of
Jubal Early's division. At the
same time, another Union
force seizes the crossing at
Kelly's Ford. On the point of
going into winter quarters,
Lee's army is suddenly forced
to retreat beyond the Rapidan.

● **Nov 2** Lincoln
receives and accepts
a last-minute invita-
tion to speak at the
dedication of the
new National
Cemetery at
Gettysburg.

Nov 16 ●
Banks occupies Corpus Christi, Texas.

Below: A spy photo. A.D. Lytle, the
local photographer taking pictures
of the Union garrison occupying
Baton Rouge, is passing his photographs on to the Confederate Secret
Service. Details of regiments, such
as these units of the First Indiana
Heavy Artillery, as well as numbers
of Union guns and ships, are soon
in the hands of the enemy. (M)

● **Nov 16 BATTLE OF
CAMPBELL'S STATION**
In East Tennessee, Burnside and Longstreet
are moving on parallel roads. Burnside reaches
the crossroad at Campbell's Station just 15
minutes before Longstreet. Longstreet attacks
both flanks of Burnside's line, but the Union
troops hold firm. Burnside is able to stage an
orderly movement back into his defenses at
Knoxville. If Longstreet had won the race to
the crossroad, it might have changed the outcome of the entire East Tennessee campaign.
Longstreet begins a siege of Knoxville.

● **Nov 17** Union troops defeat the
Confederates defending Mustang
Island, Aransas Pass, Texas.

● **Nov 9** One of the most
successful blockade runners,
the *Robert E. Lee*, is finally
captured off the coast of
North Carolina. The *Robert
E. Lee* had run the blockade
21 times, carrying merchan-
dise worth several million
dollars.

Nov 27 ●
Meade attempts to move around Lee's right
flank. In fighting between General William
French's III Corps and Jubal Early's division, the
Confederates are scattered. After dark, Lee with-
draws to defensive positions along Mine Run.

● **Nov 8** Lincoln
goes to the the-
ater to see a per-
formance of
Marble Heart
starring John
Wilkes Booth.

● **Nov 12** Pro-Union
delegates in
Arkansas meet to
discuss how to rejoin
the Union.

Right: "Lone Star"
soldiers. Texans with
the Army of Northern
Virginia. (NA)

Left: The
assault on
Fort
Sanders.
(MARS)

● **Nov 19 THE GETTYSBURG ADDRESS**
The dedication of the National Cemetery at
Gettysburg opens with a speech by the noted
orator, Edward Everett, that lasts two hours.
Lincoln follows with his few appropriate remarks
that last just two minutes. His speech is over so
quickly that no photographer present has time to
record the scene. Initial response to the
Gettysburg Address is decidedly mixed, and
Lincoln is convinced the speech is a failure.

● **Nov 23-5 BATTLE OF CHATTANOOGA** (See page 124)
One of the most extraordinary Union victories of the war begins with
Sheridan's seizure of Orchard Knob in front of the Confederate lines
along Missionary Ridge, while Sherman begins moving men across the
Tennessee River ready to attack Bragg's right flank. On Nov 24 Hooker
storms Lookout Mountain on the extreme left of the Confederate line in
what becomes known as the "Battle Above the Clouds". Meanwhile, on
the other flank, Sherman moves against Confederate positions but finds
a ravine separating him from Missionary Ridge. On Nov 25 Sherman's
advance has ground to a halt when Thomas sends his men forward in a
diversionary attack against Confederate positions at the foot of
Missionary Ridge, but the troops don't stop and charge up the ridge,
which is so steep the Confederates on the summit cannot depress their
guns enough to fire on the attackers. When Thomas's men reach the
summit the Confederate lines break and run.

● **Nov 27** Confederate General Patrick Cleburne, protecting Bragg's rear on the retreat to Dalton, Georgia,
holds Ringgold Gap against Hooker throughout five
hours of heavy fighting.

● **Nov 30**
Bragg resigns from command
of the Army of Tennessee, and
is temporarily replaced by
General William Joseph
Hardee.

Left: Major General
John G. Foster. (M)

● **Nov 27** John Hunt Morgan
and some of his officers
escape from the Union
prison at Columbus, Ohio.

● **Nov 29** Amid snow and
ice, Longstreet attempts
to force an end to the
siege of Knoxville by
launching an assault
upon Fort Sanders, but
the Union positions prove
too strong and the
assault fizzles out after
only 20 minutes.

● **Nov 28** Meade
approaches
Lee's lines at
Mine Run, but
though there is
skirmishing, no
battle develops.

● **Dec 4** Longstreet abandons the siege of
Knoxville and begins to
retreat to the northeast.

Dec 9 ●
Pursued by Union
cavalry under
General James
Murrell Shackelford,
Longstreet reaches
Rogersville.

● **Dec 6** Sherman
arrives at Knoxville to
relieve Burnside.

Dec 9 ●
Burnside is
replaced as com-
mander of the
Department of
the Ohio by
General John G.
Foster.

Dec 7 ●
A party of 17 Confederate sympa-
thizers take over the steamer
Chesapeake as it sails between New
York and Portland. They take the
boat to the Bay of Fundy, Nova
Scotia.

● **Dec 1-2** After con-
cluding that Lee's posi-
tion along Mine Run is
too strong to attack,
Meade withdraws dur-
ing the night.

● **Dec 8**
In West Virginia
General Averell
sends out cavalry
raids to destroy
railroads.

Right:
Society
lady and
secret
agent Belle
Boyd. (M)

● **Dec 1** Confederate spy Belle Boyd,
ill with typhoid, is released from
prison in Washington and sent to
Richmond.

● **Dec 28** Union General Samuel D. Sturgis receives a report that a portion of Longstreet's cavalry is at Dandridge, and orders most of his troops out of their camp at Mossy Creek to attack the enemy.

● **Dec 29 BATTLE OF MOSSY CREEK**
Once Sturgis's troops have left Mossy Creek, Confederate cavalry under General William T. Martin attack the troops remaining in the camp. The Union forces are pushed steadily backwards until Sturgis manages to get the rest of his army back from Dandridge. Then the situation is reversed and the Confederates are forced to retreat.

Above: General "Fighting Joe" Hooker (standing, center), on the ground where he directed the "Battle Above the Clouds" at Chattanooga. In the same class at West Point as Braxton Bragg and Jubal Early, Hooker is so well-known for his patronage of prostitutes that his name becomes a synonym for them. (M)

● **Jan 16** Union cavalry under General Samuel D. Sturgis encounter Confederate troops near Kimbrough's Crossroads and start forcing them back, but as they reach the Crossroads they find a larger Confederate force waiting and Sturgis is forced to retire to Dandridge.

Left: Women's war work does not only mean raising funds and support for their cause. Mary Tippee is a sutler with Collis Zouaves (114th Pennsylvania), who over-winter at Brandy Station in 1863.

● **Jan 15** Longstreet brings in additional forces to start threatening the Union base at New Market.

● **Jan 26** A Confederate cavalry force about 600 attacks the Union garris at Athens, Alabama. Th Union troop number only about 100, b though grea outnumbere they fight of attack.

● **Jan 25** Long sends out cava stop Union cav forces that are rupting his sup lines.

WAR IN THE WEST

● **Dec 13** Longstreet decides to turn about and attack his pursuer.

● **Dec 16** General Joseph E. Johnston replaces General Hardee in command of the Army of Tennessee.

● **Dec 14 BATTLE OF BEAN'S STATION**
Skirmishing between Longstreet's troops and Shackelford's pickets begins as early as 2:00 a.m. Longstreet launches a series of flanking attacks, but the Union line holds until Confederate reinforcements arrive. After dark the Union troops withdraw through Bean's Gap to Blain's Cross Roads.

● **Dec 15** Longstreet finds Shackelford too well entrenched at Blain's Cross Roads to try another attack. He retires into winter quarters at Russellville.

Artillery plays a crucial role in the war. **Above**: A battery line drawn up ready for action. (LC)
Below: Slow and ponderous when moving, gun carriages make easy targets for fast-movin cavalry attacks. (B&L)

Above: Heavily guarded and a desirable target for raiders: the ammo train. (M)

Jan 14 ●
Union forces advance on Dandridge, East Tennessee, forcing Longstreet to fall back.

● **Jan 17 BATTLE OF DANDRIDGE**
Late in the afternoon, Longstreet attacks the Union lines at Dandridge. The fighting continues after dark, when the Union forces pull back to New Market. The Confederates are in no position to pursue.

● **Jan 26** Th are several mishes bet Longstreet cavalry and troops of General St who learns Longstreet forces are c centrating around Fa Garden.

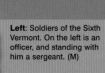

Left: General Longstreet (B&L) and **right**: General Shackelford (M), who chase each other throughout early December.

Dec 17 ●
The U.S. Navy catches up with the *Chesapeake*, but though the ship is returned to its rightful owners, the Confederates who seized it escape.

Left: Soldiers of the Sixth Vermont. On the left is an officer, and standing with him a sergeant. (M)

Below: A soldier's life cannot consist solely of fighting. A common "entertainment" when relaxing in camp is cock-fighting. (M)

● **Dec 16** Union General John Buford, whose cavalry opened the Battle of Gettysburg, dies of typhoid.

Above and left: Bomb shelters and bunkers vary widely. (LC, M, B&L)

● **Jan 22** While reconnoitering Andrew's Bay, Florida, Ensign. J. Russell from USS *Restless* a companions happen to encou the captain of blockade runner *William A. Kain*. They immedia capture him and force him to t them out to the schooner, whic they also capture.

● **Jan 20** Lincoln proposes an immediate election in Arkansas so the state can return to the Union.

THE NAVAL WAR

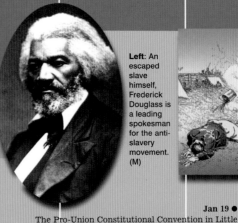

Left: An escaped slave himself, Frederick Douglass is a leading spokesman for the anti-slavery movement. (M)

Above: The devasting result of being o a shelter when a shell hits. (B&L)

Jan 19 ●
The Pro-Union Constitutional Convention in Little Rock, Arkansas, passes an anti-slavery measure that could qualify the state for return to the Union.

● **Jan 21** A Pro-Union convention Nashville, Tennessee, also propos an anti-slavery resolution.

● **Jan 11** Senator John B. Henderson of Missouri proposes the resolution that will become the 13th Amendment, abolishing slavery.

● **Jan 22** Pro-Union Isaac Murphy is inaugurated as provisional governor of Arkansas.

POLITICS

54

FEBRUARY 1864

MARCH 1864

01 02 03 04 05 06 07 08 09 10 11 12 13 14 15 16 17 18 19 20 21 22 23 24 25 26 27 28 29 01 02 03 04 05 06 07 08 09 10 11 12 13 14 15 16 17 18 19

● **Feb 1** Union General William Sooy Smith is ordered to lead a cavalry expedition out of Memphis with the aim of meeting up with Sherman at Meridian.

● **Feb 3** Sherman leaves Vicksburg with 20,000 men en route for the railroad center at Meridian.

Jan 27–8 BATTLE OF FAIR GARDEN
In dense fog, Sturgis attacks Confederate forces under General William T. Martin. By the end of the day, the Confederates are routed. Next day Sturgis sets out in pursuit, but when the weary Union forces learn of the approach of fresh Confederate troops they withdraw.

● **Feb 11** Against orders, General W.S. Smith has waited for reinforcements, and only now leaves Memphis.

Feb 13 ●
On an expedition to clear Confederate forces out of Indian Territory, the biggest of numerous small conflicts is today at Middle Boggy Depot in what is now Atoka County, Oklahoma.

Below: General William S. Smith. (M)

● **Feb 14** Confederate General Leonidas Polk realizes he cannot defend Meridian against Sherman and evacuates the town. Sherman's men enter the town the same day and begin destroying track and equipment.

Feb 10 ●
After a long refit in Brest, commerce raider CSS *Florida* slips out of harbor in atrocious weather and avoids USS *Kearsarge* which has been standing guard outside the harbor.

● **Feb 1** At Batchelder's Creek, Confederate forces under General George Pickett attack Union troops in a move to regain New Bern. Union troops move into prepared positions and Pickett withdraws.

● **Feb 6** Meade forces several crossings of the Rapidan River. The crossings are resisted by Ewell's corps.

● **Feb 7** The Union advance across the Rapidan stalls, and during the night troops withdraw back across the Rapidan.

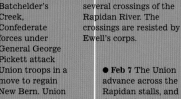

Above: Libby Prison. (NA)

Feb 1 Congress revives the rank of lieutenant general (a rank the South has used throughout the war). There is only one possible candidate for this new rank: Grant.

● **Feb 9** 109 Union prisoners tunnel out of Libby Prison in Richmond. Eventually, 59 will make it back to Union lines.

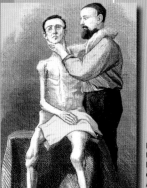

Left: The chaos of battle. (B&L)

Below: General William S. Smith. (M)

● **Feb 20** Smith has not shown up at Meridian as planned, so Sherman leaves the town and heads west looking for him.

● **Feb 20** 10 days after his supposed rendezvous with Sherman, Smith nears West Point, 90 miles north of Meridian. He skirmishes with Confederate cavalry at Prairie Station and Aberdeen.

● **Feb 21** Confederate cavalry engage Smith, then withdraw, gradually drawing Smith into a swamp west of the Tombigbee River where more Confederates join the attack. Convinced he has walked into a trap, Smith retreats, leaving a rear guard who hold off the Confederates for two hours before withdrawing in good order.

● **Feb 22** Confederates, now commanded by Nathan Bedford Forrest, continue their attack on Smith. Smith's line is broken and he retreats again, there is then a running battle for a distance of eleven miles, with both sides attacking and counterattacking. Smith eventually gets away, but his men are harassed by state militia all the way to the Tennessee state line.

Feb 22 ●
Union General Thomas probes Johnston's line to see if it has been weakened by detaching troops to Polk at Meridian.

● **Feb 17** Off Charleston, the submarine *H.L. Hunley* rams a torpedo into the side of USS *Housatonic*, which sinks immediately, the first ship ever sunk by a submarine in warfare. However, the *Hunley* also sinks in the attack.

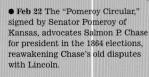

Above: The Battle of Olustee. (MARS)

● **Feb 14** Union troops under General Truman Seymour capture Gainesville, Florida.

● **Feb 20 BATTLE OF OLUSTEE**
The Union expedition in Florida under General Truman Seymour encounters Confederates entrenched at Olustee. Union forces attack but are repulsed, then when Confederate commander General Joseph Finegan commits the last of his reserves the Union line breaks. But the Confederates are too exhausted to exploit the victory.

● **Feb 22** Seymour's troops reach the safety of Jacksonville.

Feb 22 ●
"Qualified" votes in Louisiana elect pro-Union Michael Hahn as governor.

● **Feb 22** The "Pomeroy Circular," signed by Senator Pomeroy of Kansas, advocates Salmon P. Chase for president in the 1864 elections, reawakening Chase's old disputes with Lincoln.

● **Feb 24** Jefferson Davis appoints General Braxton Bragg as Chief of Staff of the Confederate armies.

Left: One of the Union prisoners who barely survive incarceration in Andersonville prison. (LC)

● **Feb 27** The first Union prisoners arrive at Camp Sumter, near Americus, Georgia. The new prison camp will eventually become known as Andersonville.

● **Feb 26** Smith's cavalry finally limp into Collierville near Memphis.

● **March 1** In preparation for the Red River expedition, Admiral Porter sends a reconnaissance expedition up the Black and Ouachita rivers.

● **March 3** The reconnaissance returns from the Black and Ouachita rivers having encountered little opposition.

● **March 5** A Confederate attack on Yazoo City is beaten off by Union gunboats.

● **March 1** At Funchal, Madeira, USS *St Louis* fails in an attempt to capture CSS *Florida*.

● **Feb 28** While General George A. Custer creates a diversion in Albemarle County, Virginia, General Judson Kilpatrick and Colonel Ulric Dahlgren lead a Union cavalry raid designed to free Union prisoners at Belle Isle in Richmond.

● **Feb 29** Dahlgren leaves Kilpatrick to approach Richmond from the rear.

● **March 1** Kilpatrick reaches the outskirts of Richmond and skirmishes with the city defenses. Dahlgren does not make the rendezvous and Kilpatrick has to withdraw.

● **March 2** Confederate cavalry under General Wade Hampton attacks Kilpatrick, but Kilpatrick manages to reach Union lines at New Kent Court House.

● **March 2** Dahlgren is ambushed and killed. Papers found on his body order the assassination of Jefferson Davis. Kilpatrick, Meade and Lincoln all disavow any knowledge of these orders.

● **March 2** The Senate confirms the appointment of Ulysses S. Grant to the rank of lieutenant general.

March 12 ●
General Banks sends an expedition against Confederate General Kirby Smith's Trans-Mississippi Department. Admiral Porter's fleet supported by troops under General A.J. Smith set off up the Red River, while Banks himself goes by way of Berwick Bay and Bayou Teche.

● **March 13** Smith's troops approach Fort DeRussy, chasing away an enemy brigade as they do s

THE RED RIVER EXPEDITION

Below: A placid scene, but everything afloat is pressed into military service. (M)

Below: Shooting through a gap in the wall. (B&L)

Right: A zouave, wearing one of the more unusual uniforms seen in the war. The uniform is based on the French model, originating with a body of French infantry composed of Algerian recruits. (B&L)

● **March 8** U.S. Grant arrives in Washington. Still in his normal, dusty uniform he attends the White House in the evening unaware that it is a formal reception.

Above: Truman Seymour. (M)

● **March 9** Grant officially receives his commission as lieutenant general.

● **March 12**
At his own request, Halleck is relieved as General-in-Chief. Grant assumes command of all the Union armies, and Halleck becomes his Chief of Staff. Meanwhile, Sherman steps into Grant's shoes in the West.

Above: Sherman and his staff posing for the camera. (M)

● **Feb 25** At Crow Valley Thomas almost succeeds in turning Johnston's flank, but the Confederate line holds.

● **Feb 27** Realizing that Johnston has not been weakened, Thomas returns to Dalton.

55

02 03 04 05 06 07 08 09 10 11 12 13 14 15 16 17 18 19 20 21 22 23 24 25 26 27 28 29 01 02 03 04 05 06 07 08 09 10 11 12 13 14 15 16 17 18 19

THE RED RIVER EXPEDITION

● **March 25** Banks joins up with Porter and Smith at Alexandria.

● **March 28** Banks's expedition starts on its way to Shreveport.

Below: Union engineers bridging the Tennessee near Chatanooga in March 1864. (NA)

Below: Even bales of hay are better than no protection for General Berdan's Union sharpshooters. (B&L)

● **March 25** Nathan Bedford Forrest leads his men into Paducah, Kentucky. The small Union garrison, vastly outnumbered, withdraws into Fort Anderson. While most of Forrest's men are rounding up supplies and destroying anything that is unwanted, a portion of his force attacks Fort Anderson. They are repulsed with heavy losses. By the end of the day, Forrest withdraws.

Below: Launched in April 1864 with workmen still on board finishing her armor, the powerful CSS ram *Albemarle* sees action on its second day afloat, sinking the *Southfield* on the Roanoke River. In the same action the Union gunboat *Miami* (**above**) manages to escape. (M)

● **April 8**
BATTLE OF MANSFIELD
Confederate General Richard Taylor establishes a defensive position at Sabine Cross Roads near Mansfield. Banks probes the line but does not attack. Then in the afternoon, though outnumbered, Taylor turns the tables and attacks. He pushes back both of Banks's flanks, until a third Union division manages to halt him after dark. Banks withdraws.

● **April 3** Union forces under General Frederick Steele move south from Arkansas as both support and diversion for Banks's Red River expedition. Confederates under General Marmaduke try to stop them as they cross the Little Missouri River at Elkin's Ferry, but fail.

● **April 9**
BATTLE OF PLEASANT HILL
Though still outnumbered, Taylor organizes an audacious attack which succeeds in routing Banks's left flank. But the Union center holds firm, and Taylor is forced to retreat. Nevertheless, Banks starts to withdraw toward Alexandria.

● **April 10–11**
BATTLE OF PRAIRIE D'ANE
Steele finds Confederate troops under General Sterling Price in line of battle at Prairie d'Ane, near Moscow, Arkansas. Steele attacks and drives the Confederates back, but late in the day his advance is halted. Skirmishing continues throughout the next day, until Steele diverts his line of march.

● **April 4** Grant appoints General Philip Sheridan head of the cavalry of the Army of the Potomac.

● **April 7** General Longstreet is ordered to leave Tennessee and rejoin Lee's Army of Northern Virginia.

● **April 9** Throughout the war, Lincoln has been urging his commanders to concentrate on defeating Lee's army rather than securing territory, but successive generals have ignored or misinterpreted him. Now the character of the war changes with Grant's order to Meade: "Wherever Lee goes, there you will go also."

Above: The massacre at Fort Pillow. (MARS)

● **April 8** The U.S. Senate passes a joint resolution approving the 13th Amendment, which will abolish slavery.

April 12 Confederate cavalry under General Tom Green attack Union transports and supply boats that have been grounded at Pleasant Hill Landing, but the attackers are repelled with heavy losses. Green is among those killed.

THE RED RIVER EXPEDITION

● **April 13** The convoy, afloat again, comes under more Confederate fire, but delivers its supplies to Banks.

● **April 13** Price returns to Prairie d'Ane to attack Steele's rear guard. After heavy fighting for four hours, Price withdraws.

● **April 18** Confederates under General Marmaduke attack a Union party gathering forage for Steele, who is running short of supplies in Camden.

WAR IN THE WEST

April 12 MASSACRE AT FORT PILLOW
Nathan Bedford Forrest attacks the small Union garrison at Fort Pillow, about 40 miles above Memphis. Almost 50% of the garrison consists of colored troops. Forrest's attack is successful and he demands unconditional surrender. When the demand is refused, he renews the attack. Forrest's men over-run the fort and kill 200 of the 262 black soldiers who defend the fort, many after they have surrendered. Forrest then moves on, but the Fort Pillow Massacre becomes a rallying cry in the North.

● **April 17** Confederate forces under General R.F. Hoke attack the Union garrison at Plymouth, North Carolina.

● **April 20** The Union garrison at Plymouth surrenders.

WAR IN THE EAST

● **April 19** The newly launched Confederate ironclad, *Albemarle*, arrives off Plymouth, ramming two Union ships and driving off the others that have been supporting the Plymouth garrison. Without naval support, the garrison is driven out of Fort Comfort.

Above: 1864 – "the bloodiest year." (LC)

● **April 17** Grant forbids all future prisoner exchanges until the Confederates agree to exchange on a one-for-one basis and treat all prisoners, white and black, without distinction. Although this hurts the South more than the North, it also leads to the severe overcrowding experienced at prisons like Andersonville.

● **April 23** Banks's advance encounters Confederate cavalry under General Hamilton P. Bee who are blocking the crossing of the river at Monett's Ferry. A Union brigade finds another crossing of the river and attacks Bee's flanks. The Confederates have to retreat.

● **April 25** At Marks' Mills, Arkansas, another supply train is captured by Confederates before it can reach Steele in Camden. Steele's first priority now is working out how to save his army.

April 29 ●
On the retreat from Camden, Steele's force reaches the Saline River at Jenkins' Ferry and begins to cross.

April 30–May 3 ●
At Sand Mountain, Alabama, a Union brigade led by Colonel Abel D. Streight runs into the brigade of Nathan Bedford Forrest. Although Forrest is repulsed, he keeps up the attack and there is a series of short, sharp engagements before the exhausted Union troops are finally forced to surrender near Rome, Georgia on May 3.

● **May 2–13** At Alexandria, the level of the Red River is so low that the Union flotilla cannot continue. Colonel Joseph Ba[...] has his men build [a] dam to raise the ri[ver] level. On May 10 p[...] the dam bursts, cr[...]ing a chute of wate[r] that allows several ships to sail safely [through] the rapids. On Ma[...] the dam is finally [com]plete, creating a h[igh] enough river level [for] the rest of the flee[t to] pass the rapids.

May 5 ●
Confederate troops attack t[he] Union ships near Dunn's Ba[you]. All three ships are badly da[m]aged and forced to surrende[r].

● **April 30** Confederate forc[es] attack Steele as he is tryin[g to] cross the swollen river. Stee[le] repulses the attack and ma[n]ages to regroup across the [river] at Little Rock.

May 5 ●
To support Grant's Overland Campaign, Union General Ben [F.] Butler lands at Bermuda Hundred with the Army of the James.

May 6 ●
Butler's advance on the Richmond– Petersburg Railroad [is] halted by Confederate troops at Port Walthall Junctio[n.]

Ma[...]
A Union division drives away the Confederate troo[ps] Port Walthall Junction and cuts the rai[l]

Ma[...]
On a raid into southwestern Virginia, Union t[roops] under General George Crook inflict a heavy defe[at] Confederate troops at Cloyd's Mountain. Immed[iately] after the victory, Crook moves on to destroy a se[ction] of the Virginia and Tennessee Railroad at D[...]

May 5 ●
At the mouth of the Roanoke River the Confederate ram CSS *Albemarle* fights seven Union blockade ships.

May 4 ●
Grant moves the Army o[f the] Potomac across the Rap[pahannock] River to begin his new offe[nsive]

THE OVERLAND CAMPAIGN

● **M[...]**
BATTLE OF THE WILDERNESS (see pag[...])
Grant's sustained campaign against Lee opens with [an] attack through the Wilderness, the woodland that wa[s] the setting for the Battle of Chancellorsville. Dur[ing the] first day the fighting is intense but incon[clusive.] Overnight, as both sides rush reinforcements forwa[rd, the] dry forest catches fire and wounded men between th[em] are burned to death. On the second day both side[s fight] each other to a standstill, but on May 7 Grant, rathe[r than] retreating, moves his army to t[...]

Union troops reach Spotsylvania Court House, b[ut find] that Lee has just gotten there ahead of [...]

Confederate General A.P. Hill falls ill [and is] temporarily replaced by Juba[l Early]

Union cavalry under General [...] Sheridan sets out on a raid in Lee['s...]

As Sheridan's cavalry reach wi[thin...] miles of Richmond, Jeb Stuart tak[es...] position at Yellow T[avern]

In a report to Halleck, Grant declares: "I prop[ose to] fight it out on this line if it takes all sum[mer."]

● **April 30** Jefferson Davis's [...]year-old son Joe is killed in [a fall] at the Confederate White H[ouse]

Left: Desperate hand-to-hand fighting at the Battle of Spotsylvania. (B&L)

MAY 1864   JUNE 1864

SUNDAY SUNDAY SUNDAY SUNDAY SATURDAY

9 10 11 12 13 14 15 16 17 18 19 20 21 22 23 24 25 26 27 28 29 30 31 01 02 03 04 05 06 07 08 09 10 11 12 13 14 15 16 17 18 19 20 21 22 23 24 25

THE ATLANTA CAMPAIGN

● **ay 7** In a move coordinated with Grant's ımpaign, Sherman starts to advance gainst Johnston's army. Johnston is ıtrenched on Rocky Face Ridge in a posi- on too strong to take by frontal assault. ıerman demonstrates against Johnston's osition with the armies of Thomas and hofield, while McPherson leads a flank tack through Snake Creek Gap.

● **May 9** McPherson finds Confederate roops entrenched at Resaca.

● **May 10** Sherman moves the rest of his army to join McPherson.

● **May 12** Johnston pulls back to Resaca.

● **May 13** Sherman tries to find weak points in Johnston's line at Resaca.

● **May 14–15 BATTLE OF RESACA** Sherman attacks but is repulsed all along the line except on the Confederate right flank, but fails to take advantage of this. The battle continues the next day with no advantage to either side until Sherman begins to threaten Johnston's supply line, and Johnston is forced to retire.

● **May 16** Johnston retreats toward Adairsville. Confederate cavalry fight a rearguard action.

● **May 17** Toward evening, Howard's Union troops encounter Hardee's entrenched infantry just north of Adairsville. There is stiff fighting, but darkness prevents a full battle. Sherman concentrates his troops for a battle next day; Johnston quietly withdraws.

● **May 19–20** Johnston retreats to Allatoona Pass. Sherman realizes that the Confederate position is too strong for a frontal assault and tries a flanking maneuver to bring him around into Johnston's rear.

May 25–6 ● **BATTLE OF NEW HOPE CHURCH** The Union suffers heavy casualties and next day both sides entrench with skirmishing continuing throughout the day.

● **May 27 BATTLE OF PICKETT'S MILLS** Johnston repulses a flank attack.

● **May 28 BATTLE OF DALLAS** General Hardee's Confederates probe the Union entrenchments near Dallas and heavy fighting breaks out. The Confederates are repulsed.

June 1 ● Sherman's cavalry occupy Allatoona Pass, giving him a supply line by rail to Chattanooga.

June 5 ● Sherman's infantry abandons the lines at Dallas and moves toward the railhead at Allatoona Pass, Johnston is forced to follow.

● **June 9–18** Sherman finds Johnston entrenched in the Marietta area. As the armies jockey for position, Sherman gradually extends his forces beyond the Confederate line, threatening a flank movement and forcing Johnston to withdraw.

● **June 18–19** Overnight, Johnston moves to prepared positions in an arc around Kennesaw Mountain, protecting his supply line, the Western and Atlantic Railroad.

● **June 20** Sherman begins extending his right wing to threaten the Confederate flank and the railroad.

June 22 ● Johnston counters by moving General John Bell Hood to his right flank. Hood attacks without orders, but is driven back with heavy casualties.

● **June 1** Union General Samuel Sturgis sets out from Memphis on the hunt for Nathan Bedford Forrest.

● **June 10 BATTLE OF BRICE'S CROSS ROADS** In a brilliant victory against long odds, Forrest's small cavalry corps of about 2,000 defeats a much larger Union force of over 8,000 infantry and cavalry under Sturgis.

● **June 14** Confederate General Polk is killed by a Union cannonball.

● **June 13** Harried by Forrest, Sturgis arrives back in Tennessee.

May 16 Banks's retreating forces encounter Confederate forces ıder General Richard Taylor at Mansura. There is a four-hour ıllery duel, but as the large Union force ses, Taylor falls back.

May 17 ● ıanks's army reaches the Atchafalaya ver. Beyond the river they will be free of Confederate harassment, but they have to wait while bridges are built.

● **May 18 BATTLE OF YELLOW BAYOU** Banks detaches a force under General Joseph A. Mower to hold off Taylor's Confederates while his army waits to cross the river. Mower attacks and drives back the Confederates, who then counterattack. The battle see-saws for several hours until the ground cover is set alight and both sides are forced to retire.

● **May 20** Banks finally gets his army across the Atchafalaya River on a bridge of boats.

● **June 6** Union troops occupy Lake Village, Arkansas, after overcoming Confederate resistance at Red Leaf and Ditch Bayou.

June 7 The troops from Lake Village rejoin the Union flotilla at Columbia on the Mississippi.

● **June 11** At Cynthiana, Kentucky, John Hunt Morgan, with 1,200 men, captures a Union garrison of about 300, as well as trapping and capturing Union reinforcements at nearby Keller's Bridge.

● **June 12** Overnight a Union force comes up and attacks Morgan at dawn. Morgan escapes though many of his men are killed or captured.

● **June 8** John Hunt Morgan captures the Union garrison at Mount Sterling, Kentucky. During the raid, the town bank is robbed of $18,000.

June 19 ● **BATTLE OF CHERBOURG** Captain Raphael Semmes decides to take the CSS *Alabama* out of Cherbourg to battle the USS *Kearsarge*. The two ships are evenly matched, and for over an hour circle each other firing broadsides. But *Alabama*'s ammunition is old and the *Kearsarge* is well protected by chains hung over the side. In the end *Alabama* is holed and sinks. Semmes and 13 of his crew get away, the rest are captured.

June 11 ● After nearly two years at sea, having captured and sunk 55 U.S. ships, the CSS *Alabama* puts in to Cherbourg, France, for repairs. Almost immediately, the news reaches Captain Winslow of USS *Kearsarge* in England.

June 13 ● USS *Kearsarge* sails from Dover to blockade the CSS *Alabama* in Cherbourg.

● **May 9** Butler defeats a Confederate division under General ushrod Johnson at Swift Creek, ut does not follow up.

● **May 10** Union cavalry under General Averell, riding to support Crook, are attacked by Confederates under John Hunt Morgan at Crockett's Cove near Wytheville. Only darkness allows Averell the chance to get away.

● **May 20** Confederates under General Beauregard attack Butler at Ware Bottom Church. Butler is driven back and bottled up in Bermuda Hundred.

● **May 10** Crook burns the New River Bridge on the Virginia & Tennessee Railroad then heads toward Lewisburg in West Virginia.

● **May 10** Confederates attack a portion of Butler's army at Chester Station, and the Union troops retire to their Bermuda Hundred lines.

● **May 12** Butler advances against Confederate positions at Drewry's Bluff.

● **May 13** Butler attacks the Confederate flank at Drewry's Bluff, but his attack is cautious and Confederate General Beauregard is able to repel the attack.

● **May 16** Confederates attack Butler's right flank. In the fog, the attack quickly becomes disorganized, nevertheless the Union troops are demoralized and after severe fighting withdraw to the Bermuda Hundred again.

June 9 ● Butler's infantry demonstrate outside Petersburg while his cavalry attempts to enter the city from the south. They are repulsed by the Home Guard.

SIEGE OF PETERSBURG

June 21 ● Two Union Corps try to cut the Weldon Railroad, a main supply route into Petersburg.

● **June 22** At White House, Sheridan captures a Confederate supply train of 900 wagons.

● **June 22** Cavalry under Generals James Wilson and August Kautz set out to disrupt Confederate rail communications into Petersburg. In the evening they cut the South Side Railroad.

● **June 22** A.P. Hill counterattacks, forcing the Union troops back from the railroad to positions along the Jerusalem Plank Road, though this has extended the Union line further to the west.

SHENANDOAH VALLEY CAMPAIGN

May 14 ● Confederate General John Cabell ıreckinridge heads north through the enandoah Valley with a makeshift force a bid to counter Sigel's slow advance.

May 15 ● ATTLE OF NEW MARKET General Franz Sigel's Union army of 10,000 men is attacked by a Confederate orce of just over 4,000 under eneral John C. Breckinridge. gallant Confederate charge ollapses the Union line, and Sigel retreats to Strasburg.

May 26 ● Union General David Hunter, who has replaced Sigel, begins to move south from Strasburg.

● **June 5 BATTLE OF PIEDMONT** General Hunter attacks a Confederate force under General William E. "Grumble" Jones just north of Piedmont. Hunter manages to turn the Confederate flank. Jones is killed in the confusion, and the retreat becomes a rout.

June 6 ● Hunter occupies Staunton.

● **June 11** Hunter captures Lexington, Virginia.

June 17 ● Hunter reaches Lynchburg at the southern end of the Shenandoah Valley, but his attack is defeated by the timely arrival of Early.

● **June 18** After sporadic fighting, shortage of supplies persuades Hunter to withdraw from Lynchburg toward West Virginia, opening the Shenandoah Valley to the Confederates once more.

May 23–6 ● **BATTLE OF NORTH ANNA** Grant's armies find Lee once more across their route at North Anna. On May 23 A.P. Hill's division attacks the Union V Corps at Jericho Mill. The battle rages back and forth but is indecisive. Next day a Union attack is repulsed, but Grant has more luck on the Confederate right flank. Eventually Grant withdraws his army back across the North Anna and prepares for another move to the left.

● **May 28 BATTLE OF ENON CHURCH** As Grant's army crosses the Pamunkey River and moves toward Totopotomoy Creek, Confederate cavalry under Fitzhugh Lee attacks the Union cavalry under General David M. Gregg that is covering the movement. The two cavalry forces fight each other to a standstill while the infantry of both sides start to arrive in the area.

● **May 29–30 BATTLE OF BETHESDA CHURCH** The Union attacks Confederate positions along Totopotomoy Creek. A Union flanking move bogs down in swampy ground next morning, but the right wing manages to drive the Confederates back, while at the same time General Early on the Confederate right drives the Union left wing back.

● **June 11–12 BATTLE OF TREVILIAN STATION** Sheridan's cavalry attack the Confederate cavalry divisions of Wade Hampton and Fitzhugh Lee. Sheridan drives a wedge between the Confederate divisions, throwing them into confusion. Next day Hampton and Lee set up a defensive line across the Virginia Central Railroad and beat back several assaults. Eventually Sheridan retires to rejoin Grant.

● **May 10–13 BATTLE OF SPOTSYLVANIA** (see page 128) On May 10 the Union launches an attack upon Confederate positions at the "mule shoe" (which soon becomes the Bloody Angle). This attack is renewed on May 12. A Confederate counterattack leads to nearly 20 hours of the worst fighting of the war. On May 13 Grant moves his army to the left again.

● **May 24** Confederate cavalry under Fitzhugh Lee attack the Union supply depot at Wilson's Wharf, but are repulsed.

● **May 30** In an attempt to break the stalemate at Bethesda Church, Union cavalry under General Alfred Torbert defeat a Confederate cavalry brigade and open the road to Old Cold Harbor.

● **June 12** In one of the best-executed maneuvers of the war, Grant leaves Warren's corps in the lines at Cold Harbor to hold Lee in place while the rest of the army begins a race toward Petersburg.

● **June 2** Both armies have now congregated, forming a seven-mile line that stretches from Bethesda Church to the Chickahominy River.

● **May 25** Sheridan's cavalry rejoin the Army of the Potomac.

June 14 ● Transports are in place to ferry Grant's II Corps across the James River.

● **June 15** The rest of the army now cross the James over pontoons at Weyanoke.

● **June 15–18 BATTLE OF PETERSBURG** (see page 136) On June 15 W.F. Smith's corps attacks and drives Beauregard's men from the first line of defenses at Petersburg. Overnight the leading divisions of Grant's army come up and capture more of the Confederate lines over the next two days, while Lee desperately rushes reinforcements into the city. By June 18 the city is heavily defended and a big Union attack is repulsed with heavy casualties. The siege of Petersburg begins.

May 11 ● ATTLE OF LOW TAVERN uart attacks ıidan at Yellow Tavern. The ıfederates are ted, and Stuart ıtally wounded.

May 12 ● . Stuart dies.

● **May 14–21** The two armies continue to face each other at Spotsylvania, probing each other for a weakness. On May 14 Grant moves Warren's corps from his right flank to his left for a surprise attack that doesn't come off. A couple of days later he reverses this, moving troops back to his right for another attack that fails. The pattern is interrupted on May 19 when Ewell's Confederates attempt to turn the Union right flank at Harris Farm. But this attack too is beaten back with heavy losses. On May 20, Grant starts his whole army moving to the left once more. On May 21 Lee responds, shifting his troops to Hanover Junction near the North Anna River.

● **May 27** Cavalry skirmishes along the Pamunkey River.

May 31 ● Sheridan's cavalry seize the vital crossroads at Old Cold Harbor.

June 1 ● Sheridan's cavalry repulse an attack by Confederate infantry.

● **June 3–12 BATTLE OF COLD HARBOR** The battle opens at dawn with a Union attack all along the line. Within an hour the Union have lost 7,000 dead and wounded, the costliest fighting of the entire war. Later, Grant will write that this is one of two charges he ever regretted ordering. After the initial bloodbath, the battle settles down to skirmishing and artillery duels.

June 15 ● Arlington House, Lee's home, is designated a military cemetery.

● **June 8** Lincoln is nominated as the Republican Presidential candidate, with Andrew Johnson of Tennessee as his running mate.

57

10 11 12 13 14 15 16 17 18 19 20 21 22 23 24 25 26 27 28 29 30 31 01 02 03 04 05 06 07 08 09 10 11 12 13 14 15 16 17 18 19 20 21 22 23 24 25

SUNDAY JUNE SUNDAY JULY 1864 SUNDAY | JULY 1864 SUNDAY AUGUST 1864

26 27 28 29 30 01 02 03 04 05 06 07 08 09 10 11 12 13 14 15 16 17 18 19 | 20 21 22 23 24 25 26 27 28 29 30 31 01 02 03 04 05 06 07 08 09 10 11

THE ATLANTA CAMPAIGN

● **June 27 Battle of Kennesaw Mountain** Convinced that Johnston has spread his line too thin, Sherman launches a frontal assault, but is beaten off with heavy casualties.

● **July 2** Johnston pulls his troops back from Kennesaw Mountain to escape being outflanked by Sherman.

● **July 3** Sherman moves forward to Johnston's new line at Nickajack Creek.

● **July 4** Johnston pulls back yet again, to prepared positions on the Chattahoochee River.

● **July 9** General Schofield crosses Chattahoochee River and turns Johnston's flank. Johnston withdraws to Peachtree Creek.

● **July 9** Outflanked again, Johnston retreats into Atlanta.

July 17 ● General Joseph E. Johnston is relieved of command of the Army of Tennessee. His replacement is General John Bell Hood.

● **July 11** Laying waste to the countryside as he passes, Smith arrives in Pontotoc, Mississippi. Forrest, meanwhile, is nearby in Okolona, waiting reinforcements from General Stephen D. Lee.

June 23 After fighting off Confederate cavalry at Burke Station, Wilson and Kautz destroy about 30 miles of railroad.

● **July 2** Union troops occupy James Island in Charleston Harbor.

● **July 3** In Charleston Harbor a Union assault on Fort Johnson is repulsed.

● **July 5** Union General A.J. Smith leaves LaGrange, Tennessee with 14,000 men to stop Nathan Bedford Forrest from threatening Sherman's supply line.

July 13 ● Fearing an ambush, Smith moves east to Tupelo.

● **July 14 BATTLE OF TUPELO** The combined Confederate forces of Forrest and Stephen D. Lee attack Smith at 7:30 in the morning, but the attacks are uncoordinated and are beaten back with high casualties. Lee withdraws.

June 24 Kautz skirmishes around Burkeville while Wilson begins cutting the Richmond and Danville Railroad.

SHENANDOAH VALLEY CAMPAIGN

● **July 9 BATTLE OF MONOCACY** In an attempt to stop Early's advance, Union General Lew Wallace faces him with a makeshift force along the Monocacy River. Despite stout resistance, Wallace is outflanked and defeated, but he has delayed Early long enough for extra Union troops to bolster the defenses of Washington.

● **July 15** Having succeeded in keeping Forrest away from the supply line, Smith starts back toward Memphis.

June 24 Confederate General Wade Hampton tries to cut off Sheridan with his captured supply train. Sheridan fights a delaying action but keeps the train.

June 30 Jubal Early moves his army from Staunton to New Market, threatening Winchester and Washington.

● **July 5–6** Sidestepping the Union garrison at Harpers Ferry, Early crosses the Potomac at Shepherdstown

June 25 Confederate cavalry under General William H.F. "Rooney" Lee close in on Wilson and Kautz and cause them to abandon their attempt to destroy the Staunton River Bridge.

● **July 6** Early captures Hagerstown, Maryland, and demands $20,000 in reparations for General Hunter's activities in the Shenandoah.

Right: General Wade Hampton. (M)

● **June 26** Sheridan and his captured supply train finally reach Union lines.

● **July 11** Early reaches the outskirts of Washington, just as the last divisions of VI Corps reach Washington from Petersburg.

● **June 28** Pursued by "Rooney" Lee, Wilson and Kautz head north to Stony Creek Depot on the Weldon Railroad, where they are attacked by Wade Hampton's cavalry. Later, Lee joins Hampton and the Union troops are heavily pressed. During the night, Wilson and Kautz disengage and slip away.

● **July 12** With Washington now well defended, Early withdrasw. In the evening Union troops under General Horatio Wright engage his rear guard, with Lincoln watching the action.

● **June 29** Wilson and Kautz reach Ream's Station, supposed to be in Union hands, but find themselves facing Confederate infantry. Almost surrounded, the Union cavalry abandon their wagons and artillery and cut their way out. Kautz reaches Union lines at Petersburg after dark, while Wilson turns south and east.

● **July 13** On Grant's express orders, Wright sets out in pursuit of Early.

● **July 14** Early crosses the Potomac back into Virginia.

SIEGE OF PETERSBURG

● **July 2** General James Wilson finally reaches Union lines at Light House Point.

Right: The CSA charge at the Battle of Trevilian Station. (LC)

● **July 17** At Berryville, Early learns that Union Generals Hunter and Crook are waiting ahead of him.

June 30 ● The Fugitive Slave Act, originally passed in 1850 to enable slaveowners to easily reclaim runaways, is repealed.

● **July 1** General Irvin McDowell, the unfortunate Union commander at the first Battle of Bull Run, is given command of the Department of the Pacific in San Francisco, as far from the fighting as it is possible to get.

● **July 5** Horace Greeley, editor of the New York *Tribune*, learns that Confederate emissaries in Canada have authority to negotiate peace. He passes the news to Lincoln.

June 30 ● Treasury Secretary, Salmon P. Chase, resigns from the cabinet yet again, and is astonished when this time Lincoln accepts the resignation.

● **July 1** Lincoln appoints Senator William Pitt Fessenden of Maine as secretary of the Treasury.

● **July 7** General Sully, freshly reinforced by troops from Minnesota, establishes Fort Rice at the mouth of Cannonball River, Dakota, at the start of a new campaign against the Sioux.

July 18 ● Lincoln's terms for peace are a restoration of the Union. Having met the Confederate emissaries at Niagara Falls, Greeley discovers they are only interested in peace with independence. Lincoln dismisses the effort.

WAR IN THE WEST

● **July 20 BATTLE OF PEACHTREE CREEK** Hood attacks George Thomas's Army of the Cumberland as it crosses Peachtree Creek, but Thomas holds firm and the Confederates retreat.

● **July 27** A change in command for the Army of the Tennessee. After McPherson's death command passed to General Logan, but now General Otis Oliver Howard is given the command. General Hooker, who feels he should have gotten the job, resigns.

● **Aug 4** In another attempt to cut t railroad west of Atlanta, Union Gen John M. Schofield's Army of the Oh crosses Utoy Creek.

● **Aug 5** Schofield's initial adva against Confederate positions i successful, but when he pauses regroup, it gives the Confederat time to secure their position.

● **July 22 BATTLE OF ATLANTA** Following his defeat at Peachtree Creek, Hood turns his attention to McPherson's Army of the Tennessee. General Hardee is sent on a 15-mile march to attack the Union rear east of the city. Hardee launches his attack in the afternoon but is repulsed by McPherson's reserve. McPherson is killed, but the Union forces hold until General John Logan launches a counterattack that restores the Union line and Hood retires with high casualties.

● **July 28 BATTLE OF EZRA CHURCH** Sherman sends General O.O. Howard west of the city to cut Hood's last railroad supply line. Confederate troops under Generals Stephen D. Lee and Alexander P. Stewart attack Howard at Ezra Church. But Howard has anticipated the attack and has troops entrenched and ready. The Confederates are beaten off with heavy casualties, but Howard fails to cut the railroad.

● **Aug 6** Schofield's renew attack is repulsed with heavy losses.

Aug 10 ● Confederate General Jose Wheeler sets out on a month- cavalry raid into northern Ge and eastern Tennessee.

● **Aug 8** Fort Gaines surrenders.

● **Aug 9** Farra begins a bombardment of t one remaining Confederate f at Mobile Bay Fort Morgan.

Aug 2 ● Admiral Farragut begins a combined army and navy operation to close Mobile Bay to blockade runners.

● **Aug 3** Union troops land on Dauphin Island in Mobile Bay and lay siege to Fort Gaines.

THE NAVAL WAR

July 25 ● At Mobile Bay, boats from the blockading squadron begin entering the harbor at night to dismantle the torpedoes (mines) that the Confederates have laid there.

● **July 27** In a daring daylight raid, Lieutenant J.C. Watson leads a Union boat crew into Mobile Bay to take soundings and mark the limits of the torpedo field.

● **Aug 5 BATTLE OF MOBILE BAY** At dawn, Admiral Farragut aboard US *Hartford* leads 18 warships into Mobile They are met by heavy fire from Forts Ga and Morgan, and from four Confederate ships in the Bay. The monitor *Tecumse* strikes a torpedo and sinks in seconds lo 90 of her crew. Lashed to the rigging of t *Hartford*, Farragut cries: "Damn the tor does! Full speed ahead." The Union fleet c the torpedoes and by 10:00 a.m. all th Confederate ships have either run agrou sunk or surrendered. Later, Confederates uate Fort Powell.

● **Aug 2** Reading in a Confederate newspap of a meeting to organize a coast guard at McIntosh Court House, Georgia, Union Commander George M. Colvocoresses slips ashore with a party of 115 men and arrests everyone who attends the meeting.

WAR IN THE EAST

July 18 As Crook attempts to cross the Shenandoah River, he is attacked by Confederate troops under General Robert Emmet Rodes. The attack is held off until nightfall, when the Union troops withdraw. The pursuit of Early has been seriously delayed.

● **July 26** Crook crosses the Potomac River, leaving the Shenandoah Valley to Early.

● **July 29** Early crosses the Potomac once more, into Maryland and Pennsylvania.

● **July 20** At Rutherford's Farm, the Union division of General Averell launches a surprise attack on the Confederate troops of General Stephen Dodson Ramseur. Ramseur retreats in confusion to Winchester, and Early starts to withdraw his army further south.

● **July 30** Early enters Chambersburg, Pennsylvania and demands $500,000 ransom. When the money is not paid, he burns the town.

● **July 31** Averell's cavalry attack Confederate cavalry under General John McCausland near Hancock, Maryland. McCausland flees.

● **Aug 7** Returning to Shenandoah Valley fro Cumberland, Confede cavalry under Genera John McCausland are prised by General Ave cavalry and routed at Moorefield.

SHENANDOAH VALLEY CAMPAIGN

● **July 22** Wright leaves to rejoin Grant at Petersburg, Crook takes over the pursuit of Early.

● **Aug 1** General Philip Sheridan is appointed commander of the Army of the Shenandoah.

● A Ear beg mov Win to C Cre

● **July 24** Early turns back north and attacks Crook at Kernstown near Winchester. The Union line collapses and Crook retreats to the Potomac River.

● **Aug 1** Pursued by Averell, Confederate cavalry rides toward Cumberland, Maryland, to attack the B&O Railroad. But Union General Benjamin Kelly hurriedly organizes a small force of soldiers and civilians who ambush the Confederates. After skirmishing for several hours, the Confederates withdraw.

July 26–7 ● During the night, General Winfield Scott Hancock crosses to the north side of the James River round New Market Heights to threaten Richmond and divert Confederate troops from the upcoming attack on Petersburg.

● **July 28** Hancock finds the Confederate lines have been reinforced, and when the Confederates counterattack, he withdraws.

● **Aug 2** McCausland's Confederate cavalry skirmishes with Averell's Union cavalry near Hancock.

● **July 29** Hancock recrosses the James and returns to his original position.

● **Aug 9** Two Confederates braz carry a bomb past Union tries at City Point and us blow up an ammunition b

SIEGE OF PETERSBURG

Aug 1 Duri night, G Hancock cross James near Bot th Rich

POLITICS

July 28 ● **BATTLE OF KILLDEER MOUNTAIN** Sully arrives near a strongly held Sioux position on the banks of the Little Missouri River. After initial negotiations get nowhere, Sully attacks. Superior firepower wins the day, the Sioux start to retreat, this turns into flight, and soon there is a running battle that continues for nearly nine miles. This battle breaks the back of Sioux resistance.

● **July 30 THE CRATER** After weeks of preparation by Union soldiers from mining communities, a bomb is exploded under the Confederate defenses at Pegram's Salient. Unfortunately the follow-up attack is ill-prepared and ill-coordinated. Many Union soldiers charge into the Crater, then find they have no way out. The Confederate defenders under General William Mahone recover quickly, counterattack, and the Union suffers high casualties. General Ambrose Burnside is relieved of command as a result.

58

26 27 28 29 30 01 02 03 04 05 06 07 08 09 10 11 12 13 14 15 16 17 18 19 | 20 21 22 23 24 25 26 27 28 29 30 31 01 02 03 04 05 06 07 08 09 10 11

5 16 17 18 19 20 21 22 23 24 25 26 27 28 29 30 31 01 02 03 04 05 06 07 08 09 10 11 12 13 14 15 16 17 18 19 20 21 22 23 24 25 26 27 28 29 30 01

THE ATLANTA CAMPAIGN

● **Aug 18** Sherman sends General Judson Kilpatrick on a cavalry raid to cut Confederate supply lines. Kilpatrick begins by destroying part of the Atlanta and West Point Railroad.

● **Aug 25** In an effort to cut all Confederate supply lines into Atlanta, Sherman begins to move six of his seven infantry corps out of their lines. Not realizing Sherman is moving in force, Hood counters by sending two corps under General Hardee.

● **Sept 1** Union troops break through Hardee's line. Hardee retreats to Lovejoy's Station.

● **Sept 7** Sherman orders Atlanta to be evacuated.

● **Sept 28** By now, the civilian evacuation of Atlanta is complete.

THE MISSOURI CAMPAIGN

● **Sept 28** Price continues his advance toward St. Louis.

g **14–15 BATTLE ALTON**
ral Wheeler
nds the surren-
f Union forces at
n. Union Colonel
ard Laibolt refus-
d withdraws his
ly outnumbered
into fortifica-
outside town.
eler continues
king until after
ight, but the
troops hold
Next morning a
relief column
General James
eedman forces
er to withdraw.

● **Aug 19** Kilpatrick's raid destroys a store of Confederate supplies at Jonesborough.

● **Aug 20** As Kilpatrick is destroying parts of the Macon and Western Railroad at Lovejoy's Station he is attacked by Confederate infantry under General Cleburne. After fighting into the night, Kilpatrick retreats to escape encirclement.

● **Aug 21** In dense dawn fog, Nathan Bedford Forrest stages a surprise attack upon Memphis, Tennessee. Union generals posted there manage to evade capture, and an attempt to free Confederate prisoners at Irving Block Prison is stalled, so after two hours Forrest withdraws.

● **Sept 1–2** Overnight, Hood evacuates Atlanta.

● **Sept 2** Sherman sends his famous message to Lincoln: "Atlanta is ours, and fairly won!" It gives Lincoln the victory he needs to ensure his election victory in November.

● **Aug 31 – Sept 1** Hardee attacks Sherman near Jonesborough and is easily repulsed.

Sept 3 ●
Hearing reports of Confederate cavalry around Greenville, Tennessee, a Union cavalry regiment sets out to investigate.

● **Sept 4** Attacking at daybreak, Union cavalry take the Confederates in Greenville completely by surprise. Most of the Confederates are killed or captured, and in the process General John Hunt Morgan is killed.

● **Sept 16** Nathan Bedford Forrest rides out of Verona, Mississippi, at the start of another raid behind Sherman's lines.

● **Sept 19** Confederate General Sterling Price leads yet another raid into Missouri. His target, this time, is to capture St. Louis.

Sept 27 ●
General Price attacks the Union garrison at Fort Davidson, Missouri. Price assaults the fort repeatedly with high casualties but fails to capture it. During the night, the Union garrison slips away.

Sept 24 ●
Price attacks Fayette, Missouri.

● **Sept 21** Forrest threatens the Union garrison at Athens, Tennessee.

Sept 29 ●
Forrest's cavalry skirmish with Union forces near Lynchburg, Tennessee.

Sept 27 ●
Confederate guerrillas under "Bloody Bill" Anderson kill 24 unarmed soldiers at Centralia, Missouri, then ambush union troops coming to reinforce the town.

2 Confederate raider CSS
hassee captures six ships
andy Hook, New Jersey.

● **Aug 23** After two weeks of naval bombardment, Fort Morgan surrenders.

g **13** CSS *Tallahassee* cap-
res and burns two more
ips off New York.

● **Aug 25** CSS *Tallahassee* slips past the blockading ship into the safety of Wilmington, North Carolina.

Above: The fighting at Opequon Creek. (B&L)

Sept 28 ●
After Admiral Farragut has taken sick leave, Admiral David Dixon Porter assumes command of the Union blockading squadron, while Admiral S.P. Lee takes his place in command of the Mississippi Squadron.

Aug 15 CSS *Tallahassee* captures
six more ships off New England.

● **Aug 16** CSS *Tallahassee* captures and burns five more merchantmen off New England.

● **Aug 17** Heading toward Nova Scotia to resupply with coal, CSS *Tallahassee* captures three more ships.

Left: Having dared the torpedoes to do their worst, Farragut relaxes after the Battle of Mobile Bay. (M)

Sept 29 ●
A party of Confederates violate the neutrality of Cuba in order to seize U.S. steamship *Roanoke* bound for New York.

● **Sept 19 BATTLE OF OPEQUON CREEK**
Sheridan's advance on Winchester is delayed long enough for Early to concentrate all his forces. Nevertheless, Early's line is driven back with high casualties, and when Crook turns the Confederate left flank Early orders a retreat. Confederate General Rodes is one of those killed.

13 Fighting occurs at Berryville.
eridan moves toward Cedar
k in pursuit of Early.

● **Aug 26** After a stand-off at Halltown, Early sets out for Maryland again.

● **Sept 3** In response to calls from Lee, Early detaches General R.H. Anderson's corps to reinforce the diminishing army around Petersburg. En route, Anderson encounters Sheridan's army as it is going into camp around Berryville. Anderson attacks the corps of General George Crook, but to no effect.

● **Sept 16** Grant and Sheridan meet at Charles Town to discuss the situation in the Valley.

● **Sept 20** Sheridan harries Early's retreating troops through Middletown, until Early takes up a strong defensive position at Fisher's Hill.

Aug 15 Having problems with his supply lines,
heridan withdraws from Cedar Creek.

● **Aug 16** Union cavalry under General Wesley Merritt surprise a Confederate column as it is crossing the Shenandoah River near Front Royal, capturing 300. The Confederates rally and counterattack, driving Merritt back to Cedarville. After dark he withdraws to Ninevah.

● **Aug 28** Sheridan starts out from Halltown toward Charles Town.

● **Sept 4** Overnight, Early brings his whole army up, but in the morning finds that Sheridan is too strongly entrenched to attack, and withdraws beyond Opequon Creek.

Sept 17 ●
Early starts moving down the valley to attack the Baltimore and Ohio Railroad at Martinsburg.

● **Sept 21–2 BATTLE OF FISHER'S HILL**
Sheridan's advance pushes back the Confederate picket line and seizes the high ground. Next day, Crook again outflanks Early, and the Confederate line collapses. Early withdraws to Rockfish Gap and the Shenandoah Valley is opened to Sheridan.

● **Aug 21** In a two-pronged attack, Early converges on Sheridan near Charles Town. Sheridan fights an effective delaying action.

● **Aug 29** Two Confederate infantry divisions cross Opequon Creek at Smithfield and force back Merritt's Union cavalry, but Union infantry arrives to stop the Confederate advance.

Sept 18 ●
Early's force is widely separated, a part of it having a run-in with Union cavalry at Bunker Hill. Sheridan starts moving behind him.

Sept 24 ●
As Sheridan slowly advances along the Valley after Early he takes to burning crops, barns and anything else that might be of use to the Confederacy.

● **Sept 25** Early is forced to withdraw to Brown's Pass in the Blue Ridge Mountains.

● **Aug 16** Hancock attacks Confederate lines at Fussell's Mill. At first Hancock captures some of the Confederate positions, but a counterattack drives him back out again.

● **Aug 22** Sheridan withdraws toward Halltown.

Below: The Battle of Mobile Bay. (NHC)

Sept 29 ●
Sheridan and Early skirmish near Waynesboro.

Sept 29–30 ●
BATTLE OF NEW MARKET HEIGHTS
Overnight, General Benjamin Butler moves his army across the James River and attacks the Richmond defenses at dawn. After initial success, the Confederates are able to rally and contain the breakthrough. Next day Lee counterattacks, but Butler's men are well-entrenched and hold him off. Lee is forced to move troops to defend Richmond and weaken his lines at Petersburg.

Aug 18 ●
Union General Gouverneur Kemble Warren drives back
federate pick-
ion railroad at
obe Tavern. In
the afternoon,
Confederate
General Henry
Heth counter-
attacks.

● **Aug 20** Hancock returns across the James River, but retains a bridgehead at Deep Bottom.

● **Aug 20** Warren extends his defensive line from Globe Tavern to the main Union lines at Jerusalem Plank Road.

● **Aug 21** Confederates under General A.P. Hill attack Warren's lines but find no weakness, Warren has succeeded in cutting Petersburg's rail link with Wilmington, North Carolina.

● **Sept 16** General Wade Hampton attacks a small force herding cattle for the Union army, and gets away with over 2,000 cows and about 300 prisoners.

Sept 30–Oct 2 ●
As Butler attacks north of Richmond, Grant extends his line southwest of Petersburg. The initial Union advance seizes Fort Archer and outflanks the Confederate line on Squirrel Level Road. Confederate reinforcements slow the advance, but A.P. Hill's counterattack on Oct 1 is repulsed and on Oct 2 the Union troops resume their advance and seize Fort MacRae.

Aug 19 ●
Five Confederate
nfantry brigades
under General
m Mahone drive
Warren out of his
renchments, but
ren is reinforced
recaptures most
of his positions.

● **Aug 25** Confederate General Henry Heth overruns General Winfield Scott Hancock's position at Reams's Station, capturing 9 guns, 12 colors, and many prisoners.

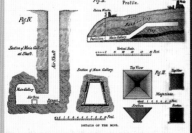
Left: How to create a crater – the plans for the mine underneath the Confederate defenses at Petersburg. (B&L)

● **Sept 2** Grant continues to extend his line along the Weldon Railroad, tearing up track and cutting off supplies to the Confederates.

● **Sept 19** Confederate agent John Yates Beall and 19 companions seize the steamer *Philo Parsons* en route from Detroit to Sandusky on the Great Lakes. The plan is to free Confederate prisoners held at Johnson's Island in Sandusky Bay, but another agent in the conspiracy is arrested and a vital signal is not given, so Beall takes the *Phil Parsons* on to Canada instead.

Sept 17 ●
General John C. Frémont, who had been running for president as a Radical Republican, withdraws his name from the ballot.

Oct 1 ●
Confederate spy Rose Greenhow is drowned when the blockade runner aboard which she is trying to return from Europe to New Inlet, North Carolina, is run aground. Carrying gold and dispatches, she leaves the stricken ship by boat, but it overturns in the surf and she is killed.

● **Aug 31** At the Democratic Convention in Chicago George B. McClellan is formally nominated as the Presidential candidate.

16 17 18 19 20 21 22 23 24 25 26 27 28 29 30 31 01 02 03 04 05 06 07 08 09 10 11 12 13 14 15 16 17 18 19 20 21 22 23 24 25 26 27 28 29 30 01

OCTOBER 1864
SUNDAY
02 03 04 05 06 07 08 09 10 11 12 13 14 15 16 17 18 19 20 21 22 23 24 25

OCT 1864
SUNDAY

NOVEMBER 1
26 27 28 29 30 31 01 02 03 04 05 06 07 08 09 10 11 12 13 14 15 16 17

● **Oct 2** General P.G.T. Beauregard is given overall command of Confederate armies in the west, on condition he does not interfere with tactical operations.

● **Oct 4** Having come within 50 miles of St. Louis, Price gives up his idea of capturing that city and turns toward Independence.

● **Oct 2–4** After the fall of Atlanta, General John B. Hood tries to distract Sherman by launching a campaign into Tennessee. He begins by moving north to threaten Sherman's supply line, the Western and Atlantic Railroad. Sherman sends reinforcements under General John M. Corse to Allatoona.

● **Oct 3** Sherman sends General Thomas to Nashville in case Hood heads in that direction.

● **Oct 5** At sunrise a Confederate division under General Samuel G. French reaches Allatoona. When the garrison refuses to surrender, French attacks. The outer line of Union defenses withstands a sustained attack of two-and-a-half hours before pulling back into a fort at Allatoona Pass. Despite repeated attacks the fort holds out, and French eventually withdraws because of shortage of ammunition.

THE MISSOURI CAMPAIGN

● **Oct 15** A detachment from Sterling Price's army attacks Glasgow, Missouri, in search of weapons and supplies. Union troops under Colonel Chester Harding fall back through the town to Hereford Hill, but unable to sustain another attack, Harding surrenders.

● **Oct 19** A small Union force under General James G. Blunt opposes Price at Lexington. The Union troops are driven back through the town and pursued until nightfall, but Price has been delayed.

● **Oct 20** Blunt takes up a strong defensive position on the Little Blue River east of Independence. Under orders from General Samuel Curtis, Blunt then takes most of his troops on into Independence.

● **Oct 11** Sherman begins to concentrate his forces at Rome, Georgia.

Oct 12 ● Sherman and Hood clash near Resaca.

THE NASHVILLE CAMPAIGN

● **Oct 17** Hood moves away from Sherman's supply lines, heading for Gadsden, Alabama. After this, Sherman will give up the chase, leaving Hood for Thomas to deal with.

Oct 7 ● At 3:00 a.m USS *Wachusett* sails into Bahia harbor, Brazil, and attacks the commerce raider CSS *Florida* which is there for provisions. The *Florida* is rammed and after a brief exchange of cannon fire, surrenders. *Wachusett* then takes her under tow and leaves the harbor under fire from Brazilian defenses. *Wachusett* will eventually tow *Florida* all the way back to Hampton Roads.

Oct 21 ●
BATTLE OF LITTLE BLUE RIVER
Price attacks the Union troops left at Little Blue and forces them out of their defensive positions. Blunt then returns with the rest of his army and counterattacks, forcing the Confederates to give ground. But numerical superiority takes its toll over the five-hour battle and Blunt retreats into Independence.

Oct 22 ●
While Pleasonton's cavalry presses his rear, ahead of Price is General Curtis's Army of the Border at Westport. Price forces a crossing of the Big Blue River at Byram's Ford, and decides to attack Curtis before Pleasonton can come up.

Oct 22–3 ●
As Price continues westward toward Kansas City, his rear guard is attacked by Union cavalry under General Alfred Pleasonton. A Confederate division under General Marmaduke then attacks Pleasonton's cavalry west of Independence, holding them at bay until the morning of the 23rd.

Oct 19 ●
Forrest leads his cavalry from Corinth, Missouri toward Jackson, Tennessee, in a move to support Hood's advance on Tennessee.

Oct 23 ●
BATTLE OF WESTPORT
For four hours the Confederates hurl themselves against the strong defensive lines Curtis has established at Westport, but cannot break through. Meanwhile, Pleasonton has pursued Marmaduke across the Big Blue. Price breaks off the battle and begins to retreat south.

Above: Sergeant Berry Benson, one of nine Confederate prisoners who tunnel out of Elmira Prison on October 7, 1864. (M)

Oct 6 ●
Having burned or destroyed everything that might be of use to the Confederates, Sheridan begins to withdraw from the Valley. Confederate cavalry under General Thomas Rosser attack Union cavalry under George Armstrong Custer.

Oct 7 ●
Lee tries to turn Grant's right flank. Union cavalry along Darbytown Road is routed, but Union infantry positions along New Market Road are too strong to take and Lee is repulsed. During the fighting Confederate General John Gregg is killed.

SHENANDOAH VALLEY CAMPAIGN

● **Oct 9** At Tom's Brook, Union cavalry turn on their pursuers and deliver an overwhelming defeat.

● **Oct 10** Sheridan moves into positions near Cedar Creek.

Below: The fighting at Allatoona Pass. (LC)

Left: General Philip Sheridan. (LC)

● **Oct 13** Confederates begin to probe Union positions around Cedar Creek.

● **Oct 13** Union troops start to feel out the new Confederate defensive line in front of Richmond, but suffer heavy casualties and withdraw to their New Market Road lines.

● **Oct 19 BATTLE OF CEDAR CREEK**
Early launches a surprise dawn attack on the Union army at Cedar Creek and sends them fleeing from the field. Sheridan is away from the army at the time, but hearing of the battle he makes an epic ride from Winchester, rallies his troops and delivers a decisive counterattack.

● **Oct 19** A small group of Confederate raiders from Canada rob three banks in St. Albans, Vermont, getting away with over $200,000.

● **Oct 1** A Union raid into southwest Virginia runs into Confederate troops near Saltville. After day-long fighting, the Union troops are forced to retire.

Oct 12 ●
Chief Justice of the Supreme Court Roger Taney dies at the age of 89. His most notorious decision was in the Dred Scott case in 1857 which exacerbated tensions between slave states and free states.

● **Oct 13** Confederate partisan John Singleton Mosby holds up a Union payroll train near Harpers Ferry and gets away with $173,000.

● **Oct 13** Maryland adopts a new state constitution abolishing slavery.

● **Oct 20** Lincoln proclaims that the last Thursday in November will be a new national holiday, Thanksgiving Day.

● **Oct 26–9** Hood tries to take his army across the Tennessee River at Decatur, but a much smaller Union force under General Robert S. Granger opposes the crossing and successfully prevents Hood from getting the greater part of his army across.

NASHVILLE

THE MISSOURI CAMPAIGN

● **Oct 28** Union troops under General Blunt surprise Price's army at Newtonia. A determined rearguard action by General Joe Shelby holds up Blunt while the bulk of Price's army escapes into Indian Territory, but Union reinforcements force Shelby to retreat.

● **Oct 25** Pleasonton's cavalry overtakes part of Price's army as it struggles to cross Mine Creek. Although outnumbered, the Union cavalry soon surrounds the Confederates, capturing General Marmaduke, another Confederate general, and around 600 troops.

Oct 25 Later the same day, another division of Pleasonton's cavalry catches up with more of Price's army at Marmiton River. Price hurriedly forms a defensive line and, unaware that many of the men facing him are unarmed, Union General John S. McNeil refrains from an all-out attack. Price continues his retreat.

Oct 25 BATTLE OF MARAIS DES CYGNES
Around 4:00 a.m., Pleasonton begins to bombard Price, following it up with an all-out attack. Although heavily outnumbered, the Union cavalry break the Confederate line and force Price to retreat.

● **Oct 26** The Confederate bushwhacker "Bloody Bill" Anderson, is killed in an ambush near Richmond, Missouri.

WAR IN THE WEST

Right: Commander of cavalry General Alfred Pleasonton. (M)

THE NAVAL WAR

● **Oct 27** In a daring night-time raid Naval Lieutenant William B. Cushing with 14 men sails up the Roanoke and, despite determined opposition, sinks the Confederate ironclad *Albemarle*. Only Cushing and one other get away after this exploit.

● **Oct 27** A move by Union troops under Warren and Hancock to capture the South Side Railroad comes to a standstill when they run into determined Confederate opposition from Heth and Mahone.

SIEGE OF PETERSBURG

● **Oct 27–8** General Benjamin Butler attacks the Richmond defenses along the Darbytown Road, but the Union attack is easily repulsed, and a Confederate counterattack nets some 600 prisoners.

WAR IN THE EAST

Nov 16 ●
Nov 18 ● Hood final crosse th Tennesse River a Florenc Alabam

Nov 16 ● Having c communi tions wit North, an without a supply tr Sherman out from Atlanta o March to Sea.

Forrest and Hood have now joined forces, and Hood is on the point of entering Tennessee.

● **Nov 4–5** Toward the end of his raid through Tennessee, Nathan Bedford Forrest positions his artillery across the Tennessee River from the Union supply base at Johnsonville. Union artillery and gunboats are unable to hinder the Confederate works, but Forrest's artillery disables some of the gunboats. The Union forces then burn the boats to stop them from falling into enemy hands, but the fire spreads to the warehouses and under Confederate artillery fire the Union forces are unable to put out the blaze. When Forrest withdraws next morning, he leaves behind over $2million of damage.

● **Nov 11** In Atlanta, preparing to begin his March to the Sea, Sherman orders all the railroads to be destroyed.

Below: Sherman's last telegram is sent North before he cuts the wires. On his March to the Sea he destroys everything behind him which could help the enemy. (B&L)

● **Nov 5** Forrest sets out to rejoin Hood.

Above: Union destruction of railroads is conducted with the precision of a military operation. (B&L)

● **Nov 11–13 BATTLE OF BU GAP**
Breckinridge attacks on the m ing of Nov 11 but is repulsed. day both sides resume the ba and fighting continues throug the day without anyone gainin advantage. After sporadic figh on Nov 13 the Union troops w draw just before the Confede can launch a flank attack.

Nov 10 ● Confederate General Breckinridge advances into East Tennessee from Virginia, Union forces pull back before him and gather at Bull's Gap.

Left: Burnt by Un General Hunter in the wrecked Virgi Military Institute t the destruction in Virginia. (M)

● **Nov 14** Brecki pursues the Uni forces but they a reinforced, and face of appalling weather conditio Breckinridge pu back into Virgin

SHENANDOAH VALLEY

Nov 10 ●
Despite the fact that his army has been largely destroyed, Early makes another effort to challenge Sheridan, moving north from New Market.

● **Nov 2** Secretary of State Seward notifies the mayor of New York that there is a Confederate plot to burn New York on election day.

● **Nov 8** Election day passes without New Y being burned.

● **Nov 8** Lincoln is re-elected president, with Andrew Johnson of Tennessee as vice president.

● **Nov 12** There is skirmishing at Middletown and Cedar Creek.

● **Nov 14** After t defeat in the Presidential ele McClellan resig commission as general.

SUNDAY SUNDAY SUNDAY SUNDAY SUNDAY SATURDAY

DECEMBER 1864

JAN 1865

22 23 24 25 26 27 28 29 30 01 02 03 04 05 06 07 08 09 10 11 12 13 14 15 16 17 18 19 20 21 22 23 24 25 26 27 28 29 30 31 01 02 03 04 05 06 07

● **Nov 22** With Hood threatening to get between General John Schofield's advance guard at Pulaski and General George Thomas's main force at Nashville, Schofield pulls out of Pulaski and heads for Columbia.

● **Nov 30 BATTLE OF FRANKLIN**
Schofield reaches Franklin around dawn and quickly forms a defensive line. Hood's approach is delayed, but in the afternoon he launches a frontal assault. The Union line is broken but eventually holds. By the end of the day Hood has suffered frightful casualties, including six Confederate generals dead, but continues his advance on Nashville.

● **Dec 15–16 BATTLE OF NASHVILLE** (see page 134)
Thomas's left flank attacks before dawn in freezing mist and pins down an entire Confederate corps for the rest of the day. After noon Thomas launches a charge on his right flank which successfully drives the Confederates back and unleashes further attacks upon the Confederate left. During the night Hood throws up further fieldworks, but come morning Thomas attacks again on Hood's right flank and after the two strongest points on the Confederate line are captured, the rest of Hood's army flees.

TO THE SEA

● **Nov 24** General Schofield reaches Columbia, Tennessee, and quickly builds two earthworks outside the town, all the time skirmishing with elements of Forrest's cavalry.

● **Dec 1–14** All the elements of General George Thomas's army are now concentrated in Nashville. During the first two weeks of December he makes careful preparations for a battle in which he intends to destroy Hood's army. The weather is atrocious, freezing rain and storms, so despite repeated pressure from Grant and Washington, it is not until the evening of Dec 14 that Thomas informs Halleck he will attack next day.

THE NASHVILLE CAMPAIGN

● **Nov 22** Sherman's left wing, under General Slocum, enters the Georgia state capital, Milledgeville.

● **Nov 26** Hood's infantry reach Columbia, where he demonstrates against Schofield's defenses while the bulk of his army moves along the Duck River to find a crossing at Davis Ford.

● **Dec 2** Hood detaches an infantry division under General William B. Bate to destroy railroad lines between Nashville and Murfreesboro.

● **Dec 2** Hood reaches Nashville and occupies positions parallel to the Union lines.

Left: The Battle of Nashville – a Union charge on a Confederate redoubt, December 15, the first day of battle. (LC)

● **Nov 22** Union General Charles Walcutt runs into Confederate cavalry under General Joseph Wheeler and drives them back beyond Griswoldville. He is then attacked by Confederate infantry but withstands repeated assaults until he is reinforced.

● **Nov 28** Hampered by foul weather, Schofield spots Hood's flanking maneuver and pulls his army north of the river, leaving Columbia to the Confederates.

● **Dec 4** Bate attacks Blockhouse No.7 at Overall Creek, but the Union defenders fight him off.

● **Dec 5** Nathan Bedford Forrest with two cavalry divisions joins Bate to attack Blockhouse No.4 and the fort at La Vergne. Both Union garrisons surrender. Forrest continues on to Murfreesboro. Union forces withdraw into Fortress Rosecrans.

● **Dec 16–26** For ten days Thomas pursues and harries the remnants of Hood's army which is disintegrating due to desertion and capture. Eventually, Hood reaches Tupelo and resigns, by which time he has no army worth the name.

● **Nov 24** General Judson Kilpatrick's cavalry leave Sherman to feign an attack on Atlanta and destroy railroad lines. General Wheeler is fooled and concentrates his forces around Atlanta.

● **Nov 29** Hood's army converges on Spring Hill to cut Schofield's line of retreat, but the Union force already there is able to hold off piecemeal Confederate attacks. During the night Schofield is able to move all his army from Columbia through Spring Hill to Franklin.

● **Dec 6** There is sporadic fighting outside Murfreesboro during the morning, but it settles down to an uneasy calm during the afternoon. Forrest is reinforced by more infantry divisions.

● **Dec 7** Union General Lovell Rousseau sends two brigades to feel out the Confederate line. Fighting breaks out again and some of Forrest's troops run away, forcing Forrest to make an orderly withdrawal with the rest of his army.

● **Dec 2** Sherman liberates the Union prisoners held at Millen, the first sight of the conditions in which Union prisoners are held.

Above: When the supplies run out, soldiers on both sides are reduced to "foraging" for whatever food they can find. (B&L)

...eeler catches up with Kilpatrick, attacking two Union regiments.

● **Nov 28** Wheeler almost catches Kilpatrick at Buck Head Creek, but a rear guard action causes high Confederate casualties and Wheeler is eventually forced to retire.

● **Dec 4 BATTLE OF WAYNESBORO**
As Sherman's infantry continue to meet no resistance, his cavalry under General Judson Kilpatrick sets out to defeat the Confederate cavalry of General Joseph Wheeler. Advancing on Waynesboro, they overcome successive lines of barricades until Wheeler's cavalry finally flee.

● **Dec 13** Union troops under General William B. Hazen attack and capture Fort McAllister on the coast of Georgia south of Savannah, opening up a base for supply ships to reach Sherman.

Left: One of Sherman's wagon trains. (M)

MARCH TO THE SEA

...: In the ... of a battle, ...ounded ...le to the ...hile the ...nition ...s go ...d. (B&L)

Nov 30 ●
Sherman gets his army across the Ogeechee River without serious opposition.

Dec 10 ●
Confederate Flag Officer Hunter attempts to run three gunboats past Union batteries on the Savannah River to join the city defenses, but is beaten back.

● **Dec 10** Sherman reaches Savannah and his cavalry start probing the city defenses. Confederate General Hardee has flooded the rice fields so few roads are open.

● **Dec 20** With less than 10,000 men to face Sherman's army of more than 62,000, Hardee slips out of Savannah taking a route previously thought impassable.

● **Dec 21** Sherman captures Savannah at the end of his March to the Sea.

● **Dec 7** General Benjamin Butler is relieved of command of the Army of the James, and assigned to command an amphibious assault on Fort Fisher guarding the entrance to Wilmington.

● **Dec 13** Lee learns that Butler's troops have embarked for Wilmington and detaches Hoke's division to protect Fort Fisher.

● **Dec 22** Sherman sends a telegram to Lincoln: "I beg to present you as a Christmas gift, the city of Savannah, with one hundred and fifty heavy guns and plenty of ammunition, also about twenty-five thousand bales of cotton".

Above: Porter (l) and Meade (r) meet to discuss their plans for the expedition against Fort Fisher. (M)

● **Jan 1** A canal that General Benjamin Butler has been digging across Trent's Reach, bypassing Confederate batteries that command the James River, is finally to be opened by blowing up the last earth wall. The explosion blows up the earth, but it falls back in exactly the same place and the canal remains closed.

Nov 28 ●
A combined Union naval and military force lands at Boyd's Landing on the Broad River intending to cut the ...rleston-Savannah Railroad.

● **Nov 30 BATTLE OF HONEY HILL**
The naval and military force encounters Confederate troops and despite repeated attacks is unable to capture their entrenchments. After dark the Union force retires.

● **Dec 8–9** Though the troops on both sides have settled into their entrenchments for the winter, there is occasional skirmishing at Hatcher's Run.

● **Dec 17** Union General George Stoneman leads an expedition through the Cumberland Gap into eastern Virginia. At Marion he defeats a makeshift force under General John C. Breckinridge.

● **Dec 24** Admiral Porter's fleet arrives off Fort Fisher and begins shelling while the first of Butler's troops are landed. Hoke arrives after the assault on the fort has already begun, and discourages further action.

● **Jan 3** Grant assigns General Alfred H. Terry to command a renewed expedition against Fort Fisher.

Nov 24–5 ●
...e delayed arson ...ck on New York ...ally takes place, ...ires being set in ...al hotels and at ...num's Museum. ...es are badly set ...d no significant ...age is done. The ...ists flee toward Canada.

● **Nov 27** The steamer *Greyhound*, which General Butler uses as his headquarters, is blown up with Butler, General Schenck and Admiral Porter on board, though none are seriously injured.

SIEGE OF PETERSBURG

● **Dec 10** Union troops probe along the Weldon Road.

● **Dec 6** Lincoln nominates former Treasury Secretary, Salmon P. Chase, to be Chief Justice of the Supreme Court.

● **Dec 18** Stoneman destroys the leadworks and mines around Marion.

● **Dec 20–1** Stoneman moves on to Saltville to destroy the salt works there.

● **Dec 27** Butler gives up the attack on Fort Fisher and withdraws to Fort Monroe.

● **Jan 7** Lincoln finally accedes to Grant's request, and removes General Butler from command.

● **Nov 29 SAND CREEK MASSACRE**
Colonel John Chivington, who advocates exterminating the Indians, marches his Colorado Regiment to Sand Creek, Colorado, where Black Kettle's Cheyenne have established a winter camp. The Indians believe they are at peace, but despite white flags and American flags flying over the camp Chivington attacks, killing and mutilating over 200, most of them women and children.

● **Dec 23** A new naval rank of vice admiral (the equivalent of lieutenant general in the army) is created and awarded to Admiral Farragut.

61

Jan 13 ● General John Bell Hood resigns and is replaced by General Richard Taylor.

Below: Union cavalry. (M)

● **Jan 16** General John M. Schofield begins to move his Twenty-Third Army Corps from Clifton Tennessee to Wilmington, North Carolina, where he will re-unite with Sherman.

Below: Confederate officers at rest. (M)

Below: Potentially the most formidable fighting ship of the war, the ironclad ram *Stonewall* was only acquired by the South in January 1865, too late for her to see action. (M)

Below: The below-decks view of a naval battle. (B&L)

● **Jan 11** On a raid into West Virginia Confederate General Thomas L. Rosser captures nearly 600 prisoners and, more importantly, several tons of rations.

Jan 13 ● In the renewed attack upon Fort Fisher, Admiral Porter's fleet of nearly 60 ships resumes bombarding the fort while Terry's infantry force is landed.

Jan 14 ● The naval bombardment is pouring 100 shells per minute into Fort Fisher, with only one gun in the fort left in useable condition.

Jan 15 ● An assault on Fort Fisher by marines and sailors is repulsed with heavy casualties, but while this is happening Terry's infantry capture the fort from the rear and the garrison surrenders. The last remaining port in the Confederacy is now closed.

● **Jan 20** Unaware that Fort Fisher has fallen, two blockade runners sail into Wilmington, and are immediately captured.

Above: The assault on Fort Fisher. (Nav.Ac.)

● **Jan 23** In a daring attack on Grant's headquarters at City Point, a Confederate fleet of three ironclads, a gunboat and a torpedo boat sail down the James River. Union defensive ships withdraw before the Confederate fleet, but all bar one of the Confederate ships run aground and are brought under fire by Union batteries.

SIEGE OF PETERSBURG

Above: Admiral Porter's fleet attack Fort Fisher on January 15. (NA)

THE MARCH THROUGH THE CAROLINAS

● **Jan 19** Sherman sets out from Savannah marching north to come upon Lee from the rear.

● **Jan 24** The Confederate ships that survive or can be refloated withdraw back up the James River, bringing to an end the last Civil War battle between ironclads.

Left: An unexpected encounter between scouts and outriders. (B&L)

● **Jan 11** Missouri officially abolishes slavery within the state.

● **Jan 16** Francis Preston Blair, Sr. delivers a letter to Jefferson Davis calling for peace negotiations "between the two nations". Lincoln rejects it.

● **Jan 16** Robert E. Lee is given command of all Confederate armies.

Feb 1 Illinois is the first state to ratify the Thirteenth Amendment.

Feb 1 Three Confederate peace commissioners arrive at Hampton Roads.

Jan 31 ● The House of Representatives passes the Thirteenth Amendment abolishing slavery.

62

● **Early Feb** General John Schofield's corps arrives at Wilmington and Schofield takes command of the forces there.

● **Feb 2** In freezing weather, the Union has to send ships up the James River to break the ice.

Above: Piles of shells in Charleston in 1865. (NA)

● **Feb 16** Admiral Porter's gunboa begin bombarding the remaining Confederate fort at Wilmington, Anderson, while Union troops are ferried across to face the fort.

● **Feb 17–18** After a wide flank march, a Union division close on Fort Anderson from the re

● **Feb 18–19** Seeing the t about to close, Confeder abandon Fort Anderson take up new lines at Tov Creek.

● **Feb 10** Captain Raphael Semmes takes command of the Confederate James River Squadron.

Below: Contemplating the beginning of the end – Grant watches his army crossing the James River. (Author)

● **Feb 20** Confed lines at Town C collapse under ' attack.

WAR IN THE EAST

● **Feb 5** Union cavalry under General David Gregg sets out to intercept Confederate supply trains.

● **Feb 5** General Gouverneur K. Warren extends his line across Hatcher's Run to the Vaughan Road to cover Gregg's operation. Confederate General John B. Gordon attacks Warren's flank but is repulsed.

SIEGE OF PETERSBURG

● **Feb 6** Gregg's raid is unsuccessful and he returns to Union lines.

● **Feb 6** Warren is attacked by Confederates under General John Pegram and General William Mahone. Pegram is killed, and the Confederates are unable to dislodge Warren from his new positions.

● **Feb 2** At Hickory Hill Sherman finds the crossing of the Salkehatchie River held by Confederates under McLaws. Sherman's troops begin building bridges across the swamp to bypass the roadblock.

● **Feb 11** With Sherman now between Confederate forces in Charleston and those at Augusta, Jefferson Davis is ordering that Confederate forces be concentrated at Charleston while Beauregard is suggesting the evacuation of the city.

● **Feb 21–2** During the r Confederate uate Wilming

● **Feb** Gener Joseph Johns assign mand Confed forces South Caroli Georg Florid Tenne and N Caroli

● **Feb 3** Two Union brigades cross the swamp and attack McLaws on the right flank. McLaws retreats toward Branchville.

Above: Ducking for cover as the skirmish-line falls back. (B&L)

● **Feb 13** Confederate General Hardee withdraws his troops from Charleston into North Carolina, while the Confederate naval ships in Charleston are scuttled.

A gunbo

Geor

Car est
li
Sh
Fort V
the e
to th
aba

THE MA THROUG CAROLI

THE MARCH THROUGH THE CAROLINAS

● **Feb 4** Concerned at the speed of Sherman's advance upon Columbia, Jefferson Davis places Beauregard in command of defending the Carolinas.

● **Feb 10** Ohio and Missouri ratify the Thirteenth Amendment.

● **Feb 7** Maine and Kansas ratify the Thirteenth Amendment, but it fails to pass the Delaware legislature.

● **Feb 15** Despite skirmishes at Lexing and several other points, Sherman's a making rapid progress and is now wit reach of Columbia. Confederate caval under Wade Hampton make a flambo charge which achieves nothing, but Hampton claims to have repulsed She

● **Feb 16** Union artillery shell Columbia.

● **Feb 17** Columbia surrende Sherman. The city is burned though it remains controvers whether the fire is started by troops or by Hampton's cava ting fire to cotton to keep it Union hands.

● **Feb 2** Lincoln travels to Hampton Roads to meet the peace commissioners.

● **Feb 2** Michigan and Rhode Island ratify the Thirteenth Amendment.

Below: A Confederate sharpshooter. (B&L)

POLITICS

● **Feb 3** Lincoln meets the peace commissioners aboard the steamer *River Queen* at Fort Monroe. No terms can be agreed on because Lincoln will not accept anything less than the Confederate states rejoining the Union.

● **Feb 3** Maryland, New York and West Virginia ratify the Thirteenth Amendment.

● **Feb 6** Confederate Secretary of War James A. Seddon resigns. General John C. Breckinridge is his replacement.

● **Feb 8** Massachusetts and Pennsylvania ratify the Thirteenth Amendment.

● **Feb 17** Union troops land Charleston in a diversionary to keep Confederate troops from Sherman. Confederate around the city are abandon

● **Feb 18** Charleston sur to Union troops under (Alexander Schimmelfen

● **Feb 19** Sherman begins to move on (Columbia toward Fayetteville.

Feb 22 Kentucky rejects the Thirteenth Amendment.

THE NAVAL WAR

● **March 1** Admiral Dahlgren's flagship hits a torpedo and sinks as she sets sail from Georgetown for Charleston. Only one life is lost, but the Admiral is left with just the uniform he was wearing.

March 6 ●
A Union force trying to clear [Confed]erates from around St. Marks [Flor]ida comes under fire as it tries [to] cross the St. Marks River at [l] Bridge. Fighting lasts all day, [the] Union troops are unable to take the bridge and withdraw.

March 7 ●
[a] troops under General Jacob Cox [ad]vancing from New Berne to unite [with] Sherman run into Confederate [tro]ops under General Braxton Bragg at Kinston, North Carolina.

March 8 ●
Bragg attacks Cox's flank, but after initial success the attack stalls.

March 2 ●
[H]e suggests a military [con]vention to [. . .] Grant to [r]esolve the ["unhappy dif]iculties", but this would implicitly [reso]lve recognizing the [Co]nfederacy so Grant rejects it.

Below: Some of the defenses around Petersburg. (Author)

March 9 ●
Cox is reinforced.

THE SHENANDOAH CAMPAIGN VALLEY

● **March 2** Confederate General Early's Shenandoah Valley Campaign comes to an end at Waynesboro when Sheridan, with two cavalry divisions, attacks the remnants of Early's army. Although Early escapes, more than 1,500 Confederates surrender. Sheridan starts to move his forces to unite with Grant at Petersburg.

March 10 ●
[Con]federate cavalry under General Wade Hampton [surp]rise Kilpatrick's Union cavalry in their camp at [Mo]nroe's Cross Roads, North Carolina. At first the [U]nion troops are driven back in confusion, losing [suppl]ies and artillery, but they regroup and counter[atta]ck, recovering most of what was lost. Hampton withdraws.

March 22 ●
General James H. Wilson sets out on an expedition against Nathan Bedford Forrest who is at Selma, Alabama.

Left: Signallers on this Union signal tower at Cobb's Hill can see Petersburg as well as large sections of railroad and the James and Appomattox Rivers. Although frequently fired on, it is used to send signals – by flags, torches or lights – from June 1864 until the fall of Petersburg. (M)

● **March** [. . .]
Genera[l . . .]
Goldsb[oro . . .]
unite hi[s . . .]
Sherma[n . . .]

● **March 10** Bragg resumes his attack but is beaten back after heavy fighting. Eventually, Bragg is forced to withdraw across the Neuse River.

● **March 14** Cox captures Kinston without a struggle.

BATTLE OF FOR[T STEDMAN]
In an attempt to [break the] siege, Lee mas[ses] his army for an a[ssault on Fort] Stedman led by [General John] B. Gordon. [The] assault is very [successful at] first, but Unio[n] counterattacks c[ap]ture m[any] Confederates. Me[anwhile] Union troo[ps . . .] Confederate li[nes . . .] been weakened b[y . . .] and capture a la[rge . . .] en[. . .]

● **March 13** Sheridan's cavalry, en route to Petersburg, are involved in skirmishes at Beaver Dam Station just outside Richmond.

R[. . .]
narrowly fail[. . .]
Sheridan's att[. . .]
Ewell's corps s[. . .]
Saylor's Cree[k . . .]

● **March 11**
Sherman captures Fayetteville, North Carolina, taking over the Confederate arsenal there.

Sheridan's [. . .]
Shenandoah Val[ley . . .]
forces with[. . .]
Potomac [. . .]

March 12 ●
Boats from Wilmington reach Sherman at Fayetteville, opening communication and supply routes between Sherman and the sea.

March 4 ●
[Sherm]an's army starts to [move in]to North Carolina.

March 15 ●
Sherman starts moving on from Fayetteville, his destination Goldsborough.

March 16 ●
Sherman's left wing under General Henry Slocum attacks Confederates under Hardee at Averasborough. Hardee's flank is turned and he withdraws.

Above left: Civilians cower together as Richmond is shelled. (B&L)

Above: The fall of Richmond. (LC)

Grant [. . .]
an[. . .]
House [. . .]
out of h[. . .]
fight fo[. . .]
do[. . .]

Confede[rate . . .]
back Sh[. . .]
Dinwi[ddie . . .]
Unior [. . .]

March 19 ●
BATTLE OF BENTONVILLE
Slocum finds Johnston's army entrenched at Bentonville, North Carolina. Johnston attacks with devastating effect, but desperate fighting and reinforcements manage to hold the Union line.

March 20 ●
Johnston withdraws into a strong defensive line. Though Slocum is heavily reinforced, there is only sporadic fighting.

● [. . .]
dra[. . .]
ligh[. . .]
Har[. . .]

● **March 1** The Thirteenth Amendment is passed by Wisconsin, but rejected by New Jersey.

March 9 ●
Vermont ratifies the Thirteenth Amendment.

March 21 ●
Union troops under General Joseph Mower move around Johnston's rear, but Johnston counterattacks and forces Mower to withdraw.

● **March 9** Secretary of the Interior John P. Usher resigns.

● **March 13** The Confederate Congre[ss . . .] the use of Negro troops in the Confe[derate army]

March 3 ●
[T]he Freedman's [Bureau] which will look [after] freed slaves, is established.

● **March 4 THE SECOND INAUGURAL**
Lincoln is inaugurated as President for a second term. In his address he concludes: "[. . . the right as God gives us to] see the right, let us strive on to finish the work we are in, to bind up the nation's wou[nds . . .] all which may achieve and cherish a just and lasting peace among ourselves and with [all nations]"

WAR'S END

Left: The last formal photograph of Abraham Lincoln, taken the day Robert E. Lee surrendered at Appomatox on April 9, 1865. Five days later he was dead, and the task of rebuilding the Union after four years of war was to fall to other hands, perhaps less capable than his. (M)

Above: The ex-president of the Confederacy. Jefferson Davis in the riding dress he wore when he was captured on May 10 by Lieutenant Colonel B. D. Pritchard and men of the 4th Michigan Cavalry in dense pine woods near Irwinville, Georgia. He had left Richmond on the night of April 2d, warned by Lee of the capital's impending fall. (M)

Above: Presidential podium for the Grand Review of the Army, May 23–24, 1865 – but without the president, assassinated the previous month.

Right: Some 200,000 troops marched down the main thoroughfare of Washington to the sound of military bands, flags flying, watched by huge crowds. (M)

Left: Robert E. Lee's mansion, Arlington House, Virginia, was occupied by the Union in 1861 and the grounds became a national cemetery. This picture was taken in June 1864, Union troops posing before the magnificent Doric columns. (M)

Above: Veterans at the dedication of the Bull Run Monument, June 10, 1865. Made of chocolate-colored sandstone, it is topped by a 100-pound shell, and bears the inscription: "TO THE MEMORY OF THE PATRIOTS WHO FELL AT BULL RUN, JULY 21, 1861." (M)

JOHN WILKES BOOTH

Born Maryland, 1838, son of the actor Junius Brutus Booth and brother of actor Edwin Booth. He achieved some success as an actor. A member of a Virginia militia company before the war, he did not continue with the army after secession, believing himself a coward (though he apparently planned to kidnap Lincoln before his inauguration in 1861). A Southern sympathizer, he continued acting in the North throughout the war (the three Booths were acting together for the only time in their careers in one of the New York theaters fire-bombed by Confederates, Nov 1864). With other malcontents he began plotting against the Union, and with the fall of Richmond he assassinated Lincoln (April 14, 1865). Shot near Bowling Green, Virginia, April 26, 1865. Photo: NA

● **May 13** At Palmetto Ranch near the Rio Grande in Texas a skirmish between Union and Confederate forces is the last military action of the Civil War. It is a Confederate victory.

Above: Possibly the last Confederate war photo. These officers are from the Trans-Mississippi Department which does not surrender until May 26. They gather for a commemorative photo in June. (M)

● **May 10** William Quantrill is killed near Taylorsville, Kentucky.

● **May 10** Jefferson Davis is captured near Irwinville, Georgia.

● **May 11** Confederate General Thompson surrenders all Confederate forces in Arkansas.

● **May 11** The Confederate raider CSS *Stonewall* surrenders in Cuba.

Right: Triumphant soldiers celebrate. (ASKB)

May 9 The trial begins of those accused of conspiring with Booth.

Above: The funeral procession as Lincoln's body is taken to the railway station in Washington to be returned to his home in Springfield, Illinois. (M)

● **May 10** President Johnson officially declares that armed resistance to the Government is over.

Above: A war-ruin in Richmond. (M

Left: Har of war in Wildernes

Confe raide *Shena* unav the end war, b un whalin off

Above: With the end of the war, families and friends can reunited. However, there are many unexpected meetings friends during the war. Photographed after the Battle of Oaks are Confederate Lieutenant James B. Washington, aide to General Joe Johnston, and his West Point classn Union Lieutenant George Custer. Taking a message from Johnston calling for Longstreet to send three brigades t battle, Washington was taken prisoner. He goes on to be a railroad president, while Custer goes on to the Battle Little Big Horn. (LC)

The execution c Powell, Atzerodt, David and Mary Sur their involvemen assassination of I

D The Thi Amendment is fina fied, abolishing

N Captain Hen superinter Andersonville P ex

Unable to bel Confederacy nc exists, the Ca the Conf raic *Shenandoa* surrender British at Li

● **May 29** Presic Johnson grants general amnest a few exceptior everyone involv "the existing re

● **May 23–4 THE GRAND REVIEW** For two days the Union armies parade th Washington, Grant's Army of the Potoma 23 and Sherman's army on May 24.

● **May 26** In New Orleans, Ge Simon Bolivar Buckner surre the last Confederate army.

THE ARMY OF NORTHERN VIRGINIA

● R. Lee 06/01/62

LONGSTREET'S COMMAND
During the Seven Days Battles

Divisions: J. Longstreet; A. Hill; T. Holmes

Reorganized prior to Second Bull Run Campaign
into **"Right Wing"**

Divisions: R. Anderson; D. Jones; C. Wilcox; J. Hood;
J. Kemper

Reorganized prior to Antietam Campaign into
"Longstreet's Command"

Divisions: L. McLaws; R. Anderson; D. Jones; J.
Walker; J. Hood

I CORPS
Organized 11/6/62

- ● J. Longstreet
- ● R. Anderson 05/06/64
- ● J. Longstreet 10/19/64

Divisions: L. McLaws; R. Anderson; G. Pickett; J.
Hood; R. Ransom

Reorganized following Jackson's Death in May 1863

Divisions: L. McLaws; G. Pickett; J. Hood

JACKSON'S COMMAND
During the Seven Days Battles

Divisions: T. Jackson; R. Ewell; D. Hill; W. Whiting

Reorganized prior to Second Bull Run Campaign
into "Left Wing"

Divisions: C. Winder; A. Hill; R. Ewell

Reorganized prior to Antietam Campaign

Divisions: R. Ewell; A. Hill; J. Jones; D. Hill

II CORPS
Organized 11/6/62

- ● T. Jackson
- ● A. Hill 05/02/63
- ● J. Stuart 05/03/63
- ● R. Ewell 05/23/63
- ● J. Early 05/29/64
- ● J. Gordon (effectively in
command when corps returned to
Petersburg in December 1864)

Divisions: W. Taliaferro; D. Hill. A. Hill, R. Ewell

Reorganized after Jackson's Death in May 1863

Divisions: J. Early; E. Johnson; R. Rodes

III CORPS
Organized 05/30/63

- ● A. Hill until his death on 04/02/65
at which point troops merged into I Corps

Divisions: R. Anderson; H. Heth; D. Pender

IV CORPS
Organized late in 1864 after Longstreet's return to
army on 10/19/64

- ● R. Anderson

Divisions: R. Hoke; B. Johnson

CAVALRY CORPS
Organized after Chancellorsville,
May 1863

- ● J. Stuart
- ● W. Hampton
(after Stuart's mortal wound at Yellow Tavern
05/11/64)
- ● F. Lee 01/65

CHRONOLOGY

■ **June 2** Confederate dispositions: General Beauregard takes command of the Alexandria line at Manassas, protecting Richmond from Union attack; to the west General J. E. Johnston guards another route into Virginia through the Shenandoah Valley at Harpers Ferry, watched by Union General Patterson.

■ **July 16** Union General Irvin McDowell moves from Arlington, Virginia toward Manassas. Beauregard, aware of this movement through an excellent espionage system, requests Johnston to join him by railroad, the first time railroads are used for this purpose.

■ **July 18** Brigadier General Daniel Tyler [Union] attacks and takes Centreville, advances on Blackburn's Ford; disregarding McDowell's orders he becomes heavily engaged with Brigadier General James Longstreet's force (Battle of Blackburn's Ford). Following a direct personal order from McDowell, Tyler disengages at about 1 p.m. and withdraws to Centreville; Patterson reassures McDowell that Johnston is tied down at Winchester.

■ **July 19/20** Confederate reinforcements, including Johnston, arrive by rail. Union troops at Centreville are augmented by large numbers of civilian sightseers from Washington.

SUNDAY JULY 21

■ **2.00 a.m.** Union troops start night march to outflank Confederates. Due to Tyler's slowness, it falls badly behind schedule.

■ **5:30 a.m.** Union forces demonstrate at the Stone Bridge.

■ **8.00 a.m.** Colonel Nathan G. Evans [Confederate] realizes the Union forces in his front are no danger. Warned there is a flanking movement in progress, he marches most of his force away, seizes high ground north of Young's Branch on Matthews Hill and forms a line blocking Brigadier General David Hunter's advance. Hunter is wounded

■ **9:30 a.m.** Colonel Ambrose E. Burnside, taking over from Hunter, attacks

UNION	CONFEDERATES
Commanders	
Brigadier General Irvin McDowell	Brig. Gen. Beauregard Brig. Gen. Johnston
of the Potomac	of the Potomac of the Shenandoah
Strength	
18,572, infantry, guns	18,053 infantry, cavalry, guns
Casualties	
460 dead, 1,124 wounded, 1,312 missing	387 dead, 1,582 wounded, 13 missing
Perspective	
Opportunities missed due to officers not obeying orders. Green troops fought harder than anyone had a right to expect	Beauregard was too ambitious, lost sight of of the main battle and was fortunate in having Johnston's experience to back him up

Evans who repulses and then pursues the Union troops. Brigadier General Barnard E. Bee and Colonel Francis Barlow join Evans, and the battle becomes a confused melee, with casualties especially heavy among officers. The Union advantage in numbers begins to tell and the Confederates start to retreat back up Matthews Hill.

■ **11.00 a.m.** Tyler fails to press the attack at the Stone Bridge; Colonel William T. Sherman advances across Bull Run by an unguarded ford above the Stone Bridge, reports to McDowell then joins in the pursuit of Bee's force.

■ Jackson moves his men up the reverse slope of Henry Hill and conceals them.

■ **About 11:15 a.m.** McDowell arrives at the point of action. Burnside requests permission to withdraw his men to regroup and fill cartridge boxes: McDowell consents. Burnside's men march off and take no further part in the action. McDowell becomes involved in the battle at a regimental level.

■ **11:30 a.m.** Evans and Bee are driven back in disarray to Bee's original position and attempt to re-form. Bee remarks that Jackson and his Virginians are standing "like a stone wall."

■ McDowell assaults the Henry house plateau and takes the northern portion, establishing batteries near the Henry house. The battle ebbs and flows as both sides throw in their reserves. The Union forces are holding their own due to their excellent regular artillery when a regiment of infantry erupts from woods to the right of the artillery. Mistaken for Union troops, they are Confederates and virtually annihilate the gunners. The Union forces are driven back down the slope.

■ Again McDowell advances up the slope, takes possession of the Henry and Robinson houses and the lost batteries, but has no gunners to man the guns nor horses to move them. Supporting infantry, arriving late, receive a shattering volley from

Left: Burnside's Brigade (1st and 2d Rhode Island and 71st New York Regiments) at Bull Run after the contemporary drawing by A. R. Waud. (LC)

Left: Rallying the Confederate troops of Bee, Barlow and Evans behind the Robinson House.

Jackson's troops and a flank charge from Stuart's cavalry.

■ **3:30 p.m.** Beauregard extends his left to envelop McDowell's disconnected line.

■ **4:30 p.m.** Union troops quietly walk off despite frantic efforts by McDowell and his officers to stop them. The half-hearted Confederate pursuit is stopped by artillery fire.

■ Initially the retreat is orderly, but when shells from Confederate guns fall among Union troops and a bridge over Cub Run is blocked by an overturned wagon, all restraint is lost: panic sets in among soldiers and civilians alike.

Above: Two houses at the centre of the First Bull Run battlefield. Top: The Robinson House. Below it are the ruins of the Henry House. (M)

Confederates
1 Ewell
2 Holmes
3 Jones
4 Longstreet
5 Bonham
6 Early, Jackson, Bee, Barlow
7 Cooke
8 Evans (moves to Matthews Hill)
9 Bee + Barlow followed by Jackson
10 Evans, Bee + Barlow (1st position)
11 2nd Confederate position rallying on Henry Hill
12 Kirby Smith arriving

First Bull Run
Approach and Battle for Matthews Hill

Union
A Initial Union location
B Action of 18th at Blackburn's Ford
C Richardson
D Hunter + Heintzelmann

E Sherman crosses by unguarded ford
F Porter
G Burnside
H Heintzelmann

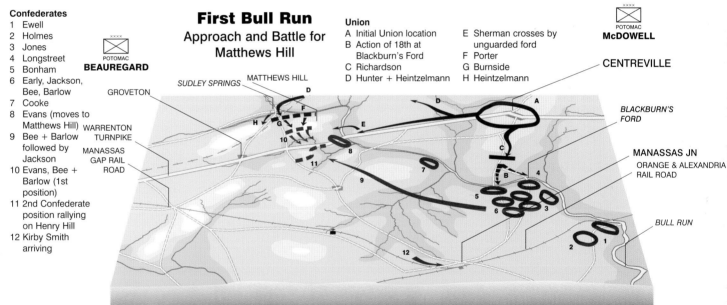

GROVETON
SUDLEY SPRINGS
MATTHEWS HILL
WARRENTON TURNPIKE
MANASSAS GAP RAIL ROAD
BEAUREGARD POTOMAC
McDOWELL POTOMAC
CENTREVILLE
BLACKBURN'S FORD
MANASSAS JN
ORANGE & ALEXANDRIA RAIL ROAD
BULL RUN

First Bull Run
Battle for Henry Hill

Union
A Richardson
B Schenck
C Burnside regrouping

D Bdes of Franklin, Porter, Willcox, Sherman + Howard intermingled

Confederates
1 Jones
2 Longstreet
3 Bonham
4 Bdes of Jackson, Bee, Barlow, Evans + Cooke intermingled
5 Elzey (replacing Kirby Smith, wounded)
6 Early
7 Stuart

BEAUREGARD POTOMAC
JOHNSTON SHENANDOAH
HENRY HILL
McDOWELL POTOMAC
CENTREVILLE
MANASSAS JN
N

CHRONOLOGY

- **September 12 1861** Flag Officer Andrew Foote arrives at Cairo, Illinois and takes command of the station from Commander John Rodgers.
- **October 12** *St Louis* (*De Kalb*) launched at Carondelet (six other ironclad gunboats of similar design are to follow: *Cincinnati, Carondelet, Louisville, Mound City, Cairo* and *Pittsburgh*).
- **Winter 1861/62** Generals McClernand and Grant together with Flag Officer Foote plan an attack on Fort Henry.

FORT HENRY

- **February 2 1862** Foote leaves Cairo, Illinois with *Cincinnati* (Flagship), *St Louis* (Lieutenant Commander L. Paulding), *Carondelet* (Commander H. Walke), *Conestoga* (Lieutenant Commander S. L. Phelps), *Tyler* (Lieutenant Commander William Gwin), *Lexington* (Lieutenant Commander J. W. Shirk) and *Essex* (Commander W. D. Porter).
- **February 5** At a nighttime council of war in Fort Henry, General Tilghman decides that the fort cannot be held in the face of the overwhelming Union forces approaching coupled with the fact that the fort is partially flooded. Plans are made for evacuation of most of the poorly-armed garrison to Fort Donelson.

THURSDAY FEBRUARY 6

- **10:20 a.m.** Foote signals his fleet to prepare for action.
- **10:50 a.m.** Flotilla ordered to steam up to Panther Island two miles below Fort Henry.

FORT HENRY	
UNION	CONFEDERATES
Commanders	
General U. S. Grant/Flag Officer A. H. Foote	General Lloyd Tilghman
Armies	
USSs *Cincinnati, Essex, Carondelet, St Louis, Lexington, Conestoga* and *Tyler* The U.S. army took no part in the action	Part of Company B, 1st Tennessee Artillery Majority of the garrison (estimated at less than 4,000) had left for Fort Donelson before the action commenced

- **11:35** Flotilla forms into line four abreast.
- **Before noon** *Cincinnati* fires the first round followed by the rest of the flotilla. The fort immediately replies.
- **About 12:45 p.m.** *Essex* is badly hit, the boiler being pierced, Captain Porter seriously injured and several members of the crew killed and injured. She then falls out of the action.
- **About 1 p.m.** A rifled gun in the fort explodes and shortly after a Columbiad is disabled by a faulty priming wire. Noting the decrease of fire from the fort, the gunboats close the range with consequent increase in accuracy.
- **About 1:50 p.m.** The fort strikes its colors.
- **Later** The formal surrender of Fort Henry is accepted by Lieutenant Commander Phelps.

FORT DONELSON

- **February 9** Brigadier General Gideon J. Pillow assumes command of Fort Donelson.
- **February 11** Foote's flotilla sets out for Fort Donelson; General McClernand marches from Fort Henry, Grant approaches from downriver.
- **February 13 early** Union skirmishers and sharpshooters are in action; at about 11 a.m. USS *Carondelet* (Commander Walke) exchanges fire with the fort; General John B. Floyd [Confederate] arrives at Fort Donelson and assumes command from General Pillow.

FRIDAY FEBRUARY 14

- **Morning** Union investment of Fort Donelson is now complete. Skirmishers, sharpshooters and artillery of both sides are in continuous action.
- **Late morning** An unsupported infantry assault on three Confederate batteries is repulsed with heavy loss. Dry leaves on the ground ignite and many wounded are burned to death. Following this abortive attack, the Confederates plan to break out and reopen communications with Nashville.
- **After noon** Pillow abandons the Nashville plan.

- **3 p.m.** The Union gunboat flotilla *Louisville, St Louis, Pittsburgh* and *Carondelet* close on Fort Donelson to within 400 yards.
- **Later** *St Louis* and *Louisville*, both disabled and out of control, drift downstream covered by the hulls of *Carondelet* and *Pittsburgh*. The gunboats have been less successful than at Fort Henry due to Fort Donelson being on high ground.
- **Night** At another conference in Fort Donelson the breakout plan is resurrected.

SATURDAY FEBRUARY 15

- **Dawn** Confederates crash through the besiegers' lines on the Union right.
- **11 a.m.** The road to Nashville is open. Pillow, believing he has defeated

FORT DONELSON		
UNION		CONFEDERATES
Commanders		
General U. S. Grant/Flag Officer A. H. Foote		Brigadier General G. J. Pillow, Brigadier General J. B. Floyd, Brigadier General S. B. Buckner
Strengths		
February 12 15,000, 14th reinforcement of 10,000 plus USN vessels, total all arms 25,000 plus four ironclads and two gunboats		About 15,000 infantry, cavalry, artillery
Casualties		
510 dead, 2,152 wounded, 224 missing/prisoners (figures include both U.S. army and U.S. navy personnel)		About 2,000 killed and wounded, about 9,000 captured
Perspectives		
Following the capture of these two forts the Union has freedom of movement on the Tennessee and Cumberland rivers, thus opening Tennessee to invasion		Bad command decisions and vacillation led to a greater loss than was necessary

Below: The Union attack force had to bivouac in the snow outside Fort Donelson. (B&L)

Below right: Henry Walke captained the *Carondelet* and also draw many excellent sketches of war-time action. (B&L)

Bottom: The view from the water battery, Fort Donelson. (Author)

Above left: A gun explodes on the gunboat *Carondelet* during the attack on the forts. From a sketch by the ship's captain, Henry Walke. (B&L)

Above right: The fighting outside Fort Donelson raged to-and-fro before the Confederate breakout attempt was contained. (MARS)

Grant's whole force, orders Buckner to pursue the retreating Union troops.

■ **2 p.m.** A crushing counterattack led by General C. F. Smith drives the Confederates back to their works.

■ **Later** Further attempts by Buckner to break out are met with failure.

■ **Evening** Pillow and Floyd (prime captures for the Union) decide to leave for Nashville by steamboat. Buckner decides to stay to seek terms from his old friend Grant. Forrest and his cavalry escape through an icy swamp under cover of darkness.

■ **Pre-dawn** Floyd and Pillow embark on two steamboats, Pillow taking his brigade with him.

■ **Early** Buckner accepts Grant's terms of "immediate and unconditional surrender."

The Kentucky–Tennessee Border
Strategy of Henry and Donelson Campaign and movements culminating at Shiloh

	KEY						
1	Cairo	6	Fort Randolph	11	Paris	16	Clarksville	21	Lebanon
2	Columbus	7	Corinth	12	Fort Henry	17	Franklin	22	Columbia
3	New Madrid	8	Shiloh	13	Fort Donelson	18	Murfreesboro	23	Somerset
4	Island No.10	9	Savannah	14	Calhoun	19	Carthage	24	Cumberland Gap
5	Fort Pillow	10	Jackson	15	Hopkinsville	20	Bowling Green		

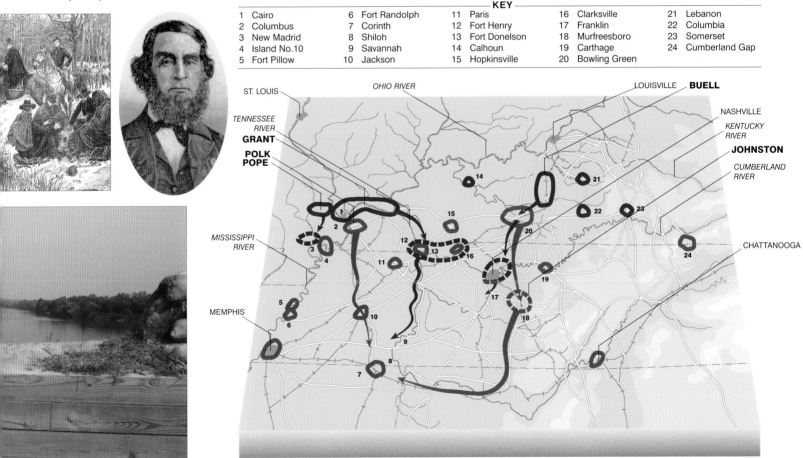

SHILOH

Western Theater of Operations, April 6–7, 1862
Location west bank of Tennessee River near Savannah, Tennessee and the Tennessee/Mississippi border

CHRONOLOGY

■ **March** Grant's army (temporarily commanded by Smith) is sent by Halleck to destroy Confederate railroads at Corinth. The army is halted at Pittsburg Landing on the Tennessee River by order of Halleck. Johnston and Beauregard plan to destroy Grant's army before Buell can join with him.

■ **April 4** Following delays on the march, the Confederates arrive on the day chosen for the attack, which is postponed first to the 5th then the 6th. Due to the delay Beauregard wishes to abandon the attack. Despite skirmishes, Grant and Sherman refuse to believe there is a large Confederate force nearby. The Union encampments are laid out for convenience not defense.

SUNDAY APRIL 6

■ **5.00 a.m.** Confederate forces start to move forward.

■ **5:15 a.m.** Prentiss's outposts come under fire.

■ **6:00 a.m.** Prentiss's entire division under fire.

■ **7:30 a.m.** Polk and Breckinridge dispatched to support Confederate left and right wings respectively.

■ One of Sherman's divisions is swept away and scattered; the other two form up on strong ground behind a stream.

■ Grant, alerted by heavy firing, leaves Savannah.

■ **8 a.m.** Grant arrives at Pittsburg Landing, orders W. H. L. Wallace to secure Snake Creek bridge, and sends Captain Baxter to order Lew Wallace to join him from Crump's Landing by the road nearest the river. Nelson, van of Buell's army, is ordered to close on the Tennessee ready to cross. Grant urges haste on Buell.

■ **9 a.m.** Prentiss's entire line is driven back to sunken road (Hornets' Nest), later joined by Wallace.

■ **10:30–11:30 a.m.** Sherman's troops are almost routed but rally as McClernand comes up. The Union left and right are forced back, but at the Hornets' Nest Prentiss resists succes-sive fierce Confederate attacks over a five-hour period.

■ **2–3 p.m.** Sherman and McClernand retreat across Tillman's Hollow, driving off pursuing cavalry, and form a new line on a ridge along the river road.

■ **2 p.m.** Johnston shot in the back of the knee; dies from loss of blood about 2.30; Beauregard assumes command of Confederate forces.*

■ **About 3.00 p.m.** Stuart's brigade disappears towards the landing;

UNION	CONFEDERATES
Commanders	
Brig Gen U. S. Grant	Gen A. S. Johnston (k)
Maj Gen D. C. Buell	Gen Beauregard
Armies	
of the Tennessee	of the Mississippi
of the Ohio	
Strengths	
1st day	1st day
37,331 infantry, cavalry,	40,335 infantry,
guns plus 2 gunboats	cavalry, guns
Reinforcements	**Reinforcements**
2d day	2d day
5,000 (III Div Tenn)	550
20,000 Army of the	(47th Tenn Regiment)
Ohio (II, IV, V, VI Divs)	
Casualties	
1,754 dead	1,723 dead
8,408 wounded	8,012 wounded,
2,885 missing/prisoners	959 missing/prisoners
Perspectives	
A battle almost lost	An inherently flawed
due to poor intelligence	battle-plan made
and over-confidence,	even worse by a
saved by Prentiss	dilatory advance and
(1st day) and rapid	lack of will to win on
reinforcement by Buell	the first day

Withers, Cheatham and Breckinridge combine against Hurlbut's left.

■ **After 4 p.m.** Hurlbut falls back on Pittsburg Landing, leaving Prentiss's left flank exposed.

■ **5 p.m.** At the Hornets' Nest Prentiss, surrounded, surrenders with his remaining 2,200 men, his flanks having been turned.

■ Meanwhile on the Union left artillery is concentrated north of Dill's Branch to secure Pittsburg Landing. Here two Union gunboats, *Lexington* and *Taylor*, shell the Confederate right, but with effectiveness limited by the height of the riverside bluffs.

* It is not known when Johnston was actually hit but probably while leading the charge. He passed out from blood loss some time later while in the rear.

■ **After 6 p.m.** The Confederate attack, without reserves to commit, runs out of steam. Bragg's final assault on the Union left meets heavy artillery fire. Beauregard has meanwhile ordered suspension of the attack by his exhausted army, and combat ebbs. Beauregard has been told that Buell is marching towards Decatur, Alabama, and he expects an easy victory on the morrow.

■ The stabilized Union line has been reinforced on the right by Lew Wallace, on the left by Nelson.

■ The opposing forces remain on the battlefield, during a stormy night, and the remainder of Buell's army (25,000 men) arrives. The gunboats maintain fire on the Confederate positions, causing a withdrawal by the Confederate right beyond the Hamburg–Savannah road.

MONDAY APRIL 7

■ **5:20 a.m.** With no consultation between Buell and Grant, Union forces advance from Pittsburg Landing. There is heavy fighting: attack is followed by counter-attack.

■ **1 p.m.** Beauregard orders captured arms taken to the rear.

The 14th Wisconsin Volunteers charging and recapturing a Confederate battery during the second day of the battle. (LC)

Right: The Union attack on the morning of the second day, gunboats supporting the assault. The contemporary artist has, however, reversed the direction of attack – see map. (MARS)

■ **3:30 p.m.** Having led a counter-attack in person, Beauregard gives the order to retreat, ordering Breckinridge to cover. During the withdrawal the Confederate artillery fights some brilliant delaying actions.

■ **After 5 p.m.** The battle winds down, and the Union troops are back where they were on Sunday morning.

The Union is now firmly established in Tennessee with considerable numerical advantage and begins a slow advance. Despite sharp criticism by Buell, Grant emerges a hero. On the Confederate side, Johnston is dead and Beauregard is beginning to lose the prestige he gained from Fort Sumter and First Manassas.

Above: Union artillery where they stood atop the bluff by Pittsburg Landing, overlooking a deep ravine that opens into the Tennessee River. (B&L)

Left: W. H. L. Wallace's line in the Hornet's Nest: a painting after the Cyclorama in Chicago. (B&L)

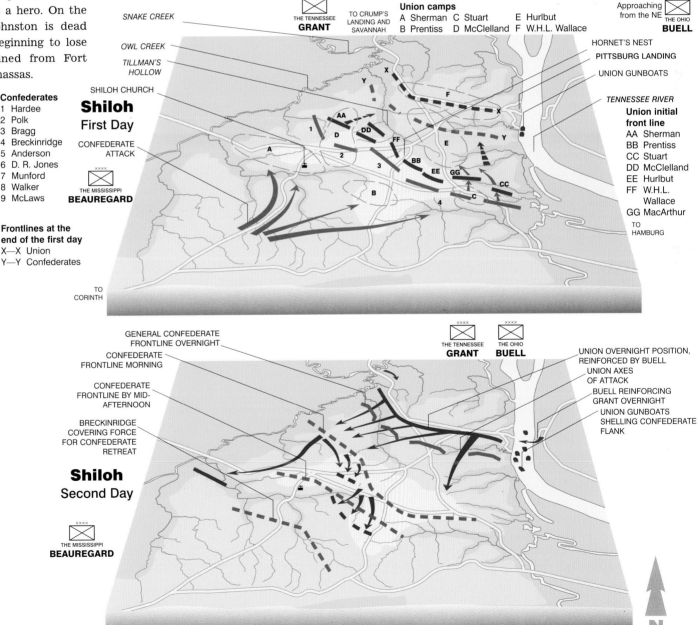

SNAKE CREEK

THE TENNESSEE
GRANT

TO CRUMP'S
LANDING AND
SAVANNAH

Union camps
A Sherman C Stuart   E Hurlbut
B Prentiss D McClelland F W.H.L. Wallace

Approaching
from the NE

THE OHIO
BUELL

OWL CREEK

TILLMAN'S
HOLLOW

SHILOH CHURCH

HORNET'S NEST

PITTSBURG LANDING

UNION GUNBOATS

TENNESSEE RIVER

**Union initial
front line**
AA Sherman
BB Prentiss
CC Stuart
DD McClelland
EE Hurlbut
FF W.H.L.
Wallace
GG MacArthur

TO
HAMBURG

Shiloh
First Day

Confederates
1 Hardee
2 Polk
3 Bragg
4 Breckinridge
5 Anderson
6 D. R. Jones
7 Munford
8 Walker
9 McLaws

CONFEDERATE
ATTACK

THE MISSISSIPPI
BEAUREGARD

**Frontlines at the
end of the first day**
X—X Union
Y—Y Confederates

TO
CORINTH

GENERAL CONFEDERATE
FRONTLINE OVERNIGHT

CONFEDERATE
FRONTLINE MORNING

THE TENNESSEE
GRANT

THE OHIO
BUELL

UNION OVERNIGHT POSITION,
REINFORCED BY BUELL

UNION AXES
OF ATTACK

BUELL REINFORCING
GRANT OVERNIGHT

CONFEDERATE
FRONTLINE BY MID-
AFTERNOON

BRECKINRIDGE
COVERING FORCE
FOR CONFEDERATE
RETREAT

UNION GUNBOATS
SHELLING CONFEDERATE
FLANK

Shiloh
Second Day

THE MISSISSIPPI
BEAUREGARD

N

CHRONOLOGY

In the aftermath of First Bull Run, Jackson, one of the few officers to emerge with enhanced credit, is promoted to major general and on October 28, 1861 appointed to command the Valley District of Virginia. The following month he is reinforced to about 10,000 men all arms. In December Jackson sets out on his first foray. Covering his movements by demonstrations, he attackes Union communications in the vicinity of the Potomac, destroying a dam on the Chesapeake & Ohio Canal. Following another expedition he occupies the towns of Bath (January 4) and Romney (January 10). He then goes into winter quarters.

In March 1862, General J. E. Johnston marches to the York Peninsula to confront McClellan's army advancing on Richmond. Jackson, heavily outnumbered, withdraws up the Valley. Following the withdrawal of Union troops to reinforce McClellan, Jackson sets about scotching this movement.

KERNSTOWN, SUNDAY MARCH 23

■ **Daylight** Firing on both sides commences.

■ **8 a.m.** Union troops drive Confederates from their positions.

■ Union troops forced back. Kimball holds original position despite instructions from Shields to advance.

■ **2 p.m.** Confederates move forward, forcing back Union skirmishers. Attack is followed by counter-attack through the afternoon.

■ **Dusk** Jackson withdraws in good order to the vicinity of Swift Run Gap. Although Jackson has been repulsed, the battle has been a victory insofar as Shields reports to Washington that Jackson has been reinforced.

Following this engagement Jackson is reinforced so that by May 1 his force numbers 13–15,000. Opposing him are about 80,000 Union troops under the command of Frémont, Banks and McDowell. Early in May, Jackson "disappears", leaving only his cavalry under Ashby in detachments observing the Union forces' every move.

KERNSTOWN, MARCH 23	
UNION	**CONFEDERATES**
Commanders	
Brig. Gen. James Shieldsand Col. Nathan Kimball	Maj. Gen. Thomas J (Stonewall) Jackson
Strengths	
7,000 infantry, cavalry, guns	3,087 infantry, cavalry, guns
Casualties	
118 dead, 450 wounded, 22 missing	80 dead, 375 wounded, 263 missing

McDOWELL, MAY 8	
UNION	**CONFEDERATES**
Commanders	
Brig. Gen. Robert C. Schenck	Maj. Gen. Thomas J (Stonewall) Jackson
Strengths	
2,268 infantry, cavalry, guns	Estimated at about 6,000
Casualties	
26 dead, 227 wounded, 3 missing	75 dead, 424 wounded

McDOWELL, THURSDAY MAY 8

■ Following a secret move by railroad from Mechum's River Station, Jackson arrives at Bull Pasture Mountain.

■ Schenck, in a disadvantageous position, decides his only course is to withdraw.

■ **Morning** Desultory shelling by Union troops and skirmishing by both sides.

■ **3 p.m.** Union forces attack to prevent Confederates establishing a battery on the mountain above them. There is intense fighting, for some hours.

■ **Following morning** Schenck and Milroy withdraw toward Franklin, their flanks protected by the steep sides of the valley.

Once again Jackson disappears behind a dense veil of secrecy. Cavalry patrols block all roads and arrest all travelers.

FRONT ROYAL, FRIDAY MAY 23

■ **2 p.m.** Jackson surprises Colonel John R. Kenly. Following an ineffective resistance lasting almost three hours, Kenly retires, making a stand at a crossroads at which point he is overrun and many of his men are captured. Jackson now threatens Banks's rear.

■ **May 24** At Fredericksburg, McDowell is ordered by Lincoln to send a large force into the Valley to capture or destroy Jackson; Frémont is ordered to cut off Jackson's retreat.

NEWTOWN, SATURDAY MAY 24 1862

■ Banks, apprised of Kenly's defeat at Front Royal, abandons his works at Strasburg and sets out for Winchester. At Newtown, Jackson strikes his flank, inflicting heavy casualties and capturing much *materiél* and many

FRONT ROYAL, MAY 23	
UNION	**CONFEDERATES**
Commanders	
Colonel John R. Kenly	Maj. Gen. Thomas J (Stonewall) Jackson
Strengths	
1,000	16,000
Casualties	
900	50

FIRST BATTLE OF WINCHESTER, MAY 25	
UNION	**CONFEDERATES**
Commanders	
Brig. Gen. Nathaniel P. Banks	Maj. Gen. Thomas J (Stonewall) Jackson
Strengths	
	Total force estimated at 16–17,000
Casualties	
62 dead, 243 wounded, 1,714 captured or missing (these figures include Battle of Newtown and skirmishes)	

Below: The death of Confederate Brigadier General Turner Ashby during the rearguard action at Harrisonburg two days before the Battle of Cross Keys. (B&L)

prisoners. Jackson continues the pursuit as far as Winchester.

FIRST BATTLE OF WINCHESTER, SUNDAY MAY 25

■ Banks makes a stand, but following some sharp fighting with Ewell's div-

Below: "Stonewall" Jackson praying before battle. A pious man, he did not smoke or drink and abhorred profane language. (LC)

ision flees to the Potomac and crosses the river into Maryland.

HARPERS FERRY, THURSDAY MAY 29

■ Jackson marches to Harpers Ferry and draws the Union troops' attention there long enough to move his booty from Winchester to Staunton. Jackson then returns to Winchester.

CROSS KEYS, SUNDAY JUNE 8

■ Frémont attacks Jackson in a day-long engagement with heavy casualties on both sides. Frémont withdraws at dusk. Leaving Ewell to contain Frémont should he return, Jackson marches off toward Port Republic.

PORT REPUBLIC, MONDAY JUNE 9

■ **Early hours** Jackson arrives, and his troops drive a Union picket from the Shenandoah bridge.
■ **Daybreak** Brigadier General Winder crosses the bridge and attacks Shields' division two miles downstream.
■ **9 a.m.** Union troops put up a very stubborn resistance and the Confederates are stalled. Jackson crosses the Shenandoah and personally leads his own "Stonewall" brigade forward. A

flank attack on the Union left by Colonel Scott followed shortly by an attack on the right by Ewell puts the issue beyond doubt.
■ **Later** Hearing the sound of battle, Frémont hurries from Harrisonburg to assist Shields. He is delayed by Ewell and arrives when the battle is over. Jackson has burned the bridge thus leaving Frémont impotent on the wrong side of the river. Allegations that Union soldiers fire on ambulances collecting the wounded are denied.

■ **Midnight** Jackson is safe at Brown's Gap while a vast amount of booty is moved on to Richmond in wagons two and three abreast.

JACKSON'S VALLEY CAMPAIGN	
UNION	**CONFEDERATES**
Perspectives	
For the Union this campaign was a dismal example of the disadvantages of a divided command and poor intelligence	For upwards of a century Jackson's Valley Campaign has been hailed as a supreme example of a lesser force dominating a greater

Above: The Battle of Cross Keys as seen from the Union position, an illustration based upon an eyewitness sketch. The beauty of the Valley was generally lost on the Union troops who had to fight there, contending with bad roads and the fear of sudden attack. (B&L)

--- **KEY** ---

1	Cumberland	7	Romney	12	Strasburg	17	Groveton	22	New Market	27	West View
2	Bath	8	Winchester	13	Front Royal	18	Manassas	23	Franklin	28	Staunton
3	Williamsport		and Kernstown	14	Upperville		Junction	24	McDowell	29	Charlottesville
4	Harpers Ferry	9	Perryville	15	Chantilly	19	Woodstock	25	Harrisonburg	30	Gordonsville
5	Frederick	10	Moorefield	16	Fairfax Court	20	Mount Jackson	26	Port Republic	31	Chancellorsville
6	Leesboro	11	Newtown		House	21	Warrenton		and Cross Keys		

● GENERAL LINE OF UNION ARMIES APPROACHING THE VALLEY TO TRAP JACKSON

The Shenandoah Valley
To illustrate Jackson's Campaign, 1862

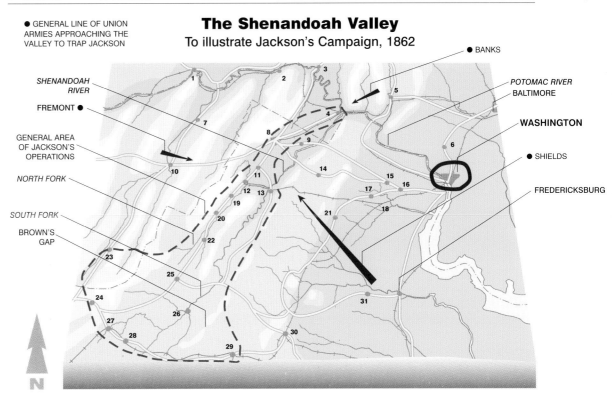

CHRONOLOGY

■ **June** Following the indecisive and confused fighting at Seven Pines, Lee strengthens the fortifications surrounding Richmond to free Confederate troops with which to drive McClellan out of the Peninsula. McClellan demands more troops from Washington in addition to the 105,000 he already has. Lincoln, in fear of Jackson in the Shenandoah Valley, too close to Washington for comfort, refuses.

■ Jackson has been summoned from the Valley and expects to be near Mechanicsville on the 25th, initiating the attack on Porter at dawn on the 26th. After an arduous march and an appalling train journey, Jackson and his Army of the Valley halt six miles short at Ashland Church, camp and rest.

■ **June 25** Lee concentrates his army west of Mechanicsville.

MECHANICSVILLE, THURSDAY JUNE 26

■ **Dawn** Jackson is detailed to attack the Union's exposed flank. A message to Lee in the late morning saying he is running late is all that is heard from him.

■ **3 p.m.** A. P. Hill, ordered to attack at the sound of Jackson's guns, hearing no firing attacks on his own. There is a skirmish in the village; the Union forces fall back on prepared positions on the far bank of Beaver Dam Creek. A Confederate regiment follows across the creek but is driven back with heavy casualties.

■ **5 p.m.** Jackson, hearing the battle raging, but unsure of his position due to poor maps and scant knowledge of the area, halts and bivouacs for the night

■ **Late afternoon** Extra Confederate artillery is sent forward to silence the Union guns.

■ **Dusk** A final attack on the Union position is made by Pender above Ellerson's Mill, he advances into a tempest of artillery and musketry.

■ **Late that night** McClellan concedes defeat and evacuates the position at Beaver Dam Creek.

■ McClellan now abandons his plan to besiege Richmond. He changes his supply route from the York River to

the James River, which means he will be unable to bring his siege guns to Richmond. Lee has won a major strategic victory.

GAINES MILL, FRIDAY JUNE 27

■ **3 a.m.** Porter begins to withdraw his troops from Beaver Dam Creek, moving to a new position four miles away at Gaines Mill. His left is anchored on the Chickahominy at the confluence with Powhite Creek, with a swamp to his front. The front stretches four miles to Old Cold Harbor and covers a bridge over the river.

■ D. H. Hill is in position, but Jackson is again late. The situation is worsened by Porter's flank being some distance from where it was reported to be. Instead of a flank attack, Hill is faced with a frontal assault. Jackson appears disoriented and stops. Porter has the benefit of fresh brigades; Hill's men have been moving since early morning and are outnumbered almost two to one.

■ **3 p.m.** Again A. P. Hill's division leads the attack, charges past Gaines Mill and attacks Porter's right center.

■ **4 p.m.** Porter begins to gain the upper hand. The Confederates' attack is in danger of stalling.

■ **6 p.m.** Jackson finally joins the action, with Longstreet adding his weight on the right. Porter is now outnumbered and resistance slackens.

■ **7 p.m.** An attack across the whole front begins. Hood's Texans burst across the creek and the Union first line gives way. Reinforced by fresh troops from McClellan, the Union forces gradually withdraw to the bridges, crossing the Chickahominy after dark.

■ During the last two days McClellan has been mesmerized by Magruder marching and counter-marching troops, lighting large numbers of campfires and making threatening demonstrations. McClellan is convinced he is heavily outnumbered. "Little Mac" then withdraws toward the James River.

SATURDAY JUNE 28

■ Lee closely pursues McClellan but cannot bring him to battle. Lee's troops are tired, the ground is waterlogged and the few maps are deficient.

SAVAGE'S STATION, SUNDAY JUNE 29

■ **10 a.m.** Lee catches up with McClellan. The Confederate attack is in disarray: Jackson, ordered to attack the Union left is late; Huger, ordered to attack on Magruder's right, is also late; Longstreet and A. P. Hill have become lost and are also late.

■ **3 p.m.** The ever-combative Magruder attacks virtually unaided. It is a half-hearted affair and the Union withdrawal goes on unhindered.

■ Union troops spend the rest of the day destroying munitions, locomotives and railroad cars they cannot take with them. They leave 2,500 wounded behind.

WHITE OAK/GLENDALE, MONDAY JUNE 30

■ **10 a.m.** The last Union troops (Richardson's corps) cross White Oak Swamp bridge and destroy it.

■ **About 10:30 a.m.** A fierce artillery duel erupts which lasts about 30 minutes then dies away. Few casualties result.

Above left: A painting by William Trego showing the charge of the 5th U.S. Cavalry during the Battle of Gaines Mill. (NA)

UNION
Commanders
Maj. Gen. George B. McClellan
Armies
of the Potomac
Strengths
105,445 infantry, cavalry, engineers, guns (As of June 20)
Casualties
1,734 dead, 8,062 wounded, 6,053 missing/prisoners
Perspectives
McClellan's timidity and consistent over-estimation of the forces ranged against him lost the campaign and Lincoln's confidence. He was saved from disaster by Lee's mistakes

The Seven Days
Battles of Mechanicsville, Gaines Mill and Frayser's Farm

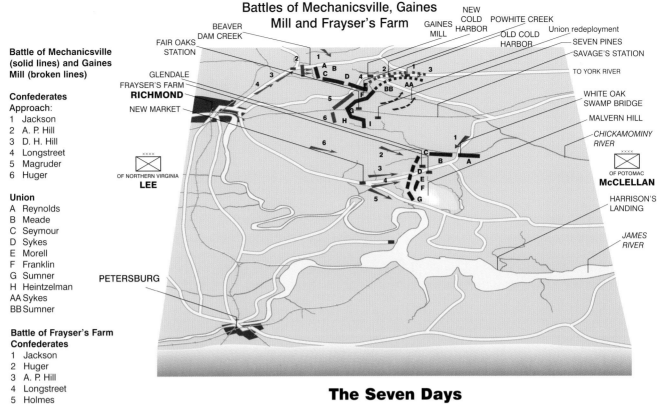

Battle of Mechanicsville (solid lines) and Gaines Mill (broken lines)

Confederates
Approach:
1 Jackson
2 A. P. Hill
3 D. H. Hill
4 Longstreet
5 Magruder
6 Huger

Union
A Reynolds
B Meade
C Seymour
D Sykes
E Morell
F Franklin
G Sumner
H Heintzelman
AA Sykes
BB Sumner

Battle of Frayser's Farm
Confederates
1 Jackson
2 Huger
3 A. P. Hill
4 Longstreet
5 Holmes
6 Mugruger

Union
A Richardson
B Smith
C Slocum
D Sedgwick
E McCall
F Heintzelman
G Porter

The Seven Days
Battle of Malvern Hill

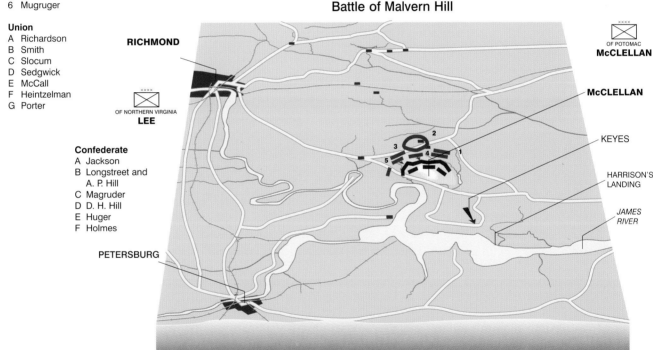

Confederate
A Jackson
B Longstreet and A. P. Hill
C Magruder
D D. H. Hill
E Huger
F Holmes

Above: The Union retreat from the Chickahominy on June 29. Below: The 16th New York at Frayser's Farm. (B&L)

CONFEDERATES
Commanders
General
Robert E. Lee
Armies
of Northern Virginia
of the Valley
Strengths
80–90,000
infantry, cavalry, guns
Casualties
3,286 dead, 15,909 wounded, 940 missing/prisoners
Perspectives
Lee's performance was far below what he would later achieve; Jackson showed none of his brilliance

■ **Afternoon** Longstreet and A. P. Hill launch a series of sharp attacks on Union troops, driving them back and inflicting heavy casualties.

MALVERN HILL, TUESDAY JULY 1

■ The Union forces establish themselves around the summit with eight divisions and 200 guns. The Confederates have 60 artillery pieces with which to counter the guns.

■ Lee's plan of attack is vague: "Batteries have been established to act upon the enemy's line. If it is broken, as is probable, Armistead, who can witness the effect of the fire, has been ordered to charge with a yell. Do the same."

■ The Confederate artillery, deployed one battery at a time, is destroyed by the superior Union guns. The line is not broken.

■ Union sharpshooters advance to harry the Confederates' first line. Armistead advances to repulse them. Magruder sees this advance and contacts Lee who orders Magruder to follow Armistead. The Confederates are mown down by the Union artillery and musketry.

■ **5 p.m.** D. H. Hill hears the firing and yelling, and obeys Lee's original order. He advances, followed by Huger. Lee sends more and more brigades into the attack and only darkness halts the slaughter.

■ Following this disaster Lee decides to allow McClellan to withdraw in peace.

■ During The Seven Days, D.H. Hill captured his old tent-mate General John F Reynolds.

CHRONOLOGY

■ **June 27** Pope, against his wishes, assumes command of the newly formed Union Army of Virginia (the army corps of McDowell, Frémont and Banks).

■ **June 28** Frémont resigns in protest (Pope is his junior in rank).

■ **June 29** Sigel takes command of Frémont's corps.

■ **July 11** Halleck is appointed as General-in-Chief in place of McClellan.

■ **July 19** Jackson concentrates his forces at Gordonsville.

■ **August 9** Banks is defeated at the Battle of Cedar Mountain.

■ **August 23** Halleck assures Pope he will be reinforced from the Army of the Potomac within two days.

■ **August 26** Not having been reinforced, Pope falls back from Rappahannock Station to Warrenton and Gainesville; Fitzhugh Lee (Confederate) falls on Manassas Station, cutting communications and capturing tons of supplies and destroying what his troops cannot carry off.

■ **August 27** Pope again falls back along the line of the Orange & Alexander Railroad; there is a sharp engagement between Hooker (Union) and Ewell (Confederate) near Bristoe Station (Kettle Run).

■ **August 28, late afternoon** McDowell, moving toward Centreville, collides with Jackson near Groveton. A fierce battle

UNION	CONFEDERATES
Commanders	
Maj. Gen. John Pope	General Robert E. Lee
Armies	
of Virginia, of the Potomac	of Northern Virginia
Strengths	
about 63,000 all arms (or 70,000)	about 54,000 all arms (or 47,000)
Casualties	
1,747 dead, 8,452 wounded, 4,262 captured or missing (figures approximate: include Cedar Ridge and Kettle Run)	1,553 dead, 7,812 wounded, 109 captured or missing
Perspectives	
Poor intelligence and personality clashes with Porter and McClellan led to this crushing defeat. The Union had again surrendered the initiative	Again Jackson proved that leadership means more than numbers or material resources

Left: Confederate defenses at Manassas. Key points in the area were fortified after the First Battle of Bull Run – Manassas is less than thirty miles from the Union's capital. (M) Center: Second Bull Run as depicted in a colorful contemporary print, showing Union troops pouring fire into the advancing lines of Confederates. (ASKB) Bottom: Union infantry retreat gloomily but in good order over the Stone Bridge toward Centreville on August 30. (B&L)

begins, continuing until dark with heavy casualties on both sides.

FRIDAY AUGUST 29

■ **Dawn** Pope orders McDowell and Porter to move toward Gainesville and attack Jackson; Jackson, under attack from Sigel, takes up a position along and behind a railroad embankment.

■ **Noon** Pope arrives from Centreville.

■ **Early afternoon** Longstreet has connected with Jackson. Urged by Lee to attack, he demurs, stating that there is a Union force of unknown size in the woods (Porter and McDowell). Thus Longstreet and Porter neutralize each other, neither taking an active part in the day's fighting.

■ **1:30 to 4 p.m.** Fierce fighting rages all along the line of the embankment.

■ **About 2 p.m.** Pope hears a discharge of artillery which he believes, wrongly, is Porter attacking Jackson's right flank.

■ **4:30 p.m.** Pope sends a sharp order to Porter to advance from Dawkins's Branch to assault Jackson's right and rear.

■ **5:30 p.m.** Pope orders an attack on Jackson's left. Following an hour's bloody fighting, Kearny turns the Confederate left. Fierce fighting continues all along the line until dark. Some Confederate brigades pull back.

■ **After dark** A moonlight skirmish takes place between some of McDowell's regiments and Longstreet

■ **Night** Pope sends a victory telegram to Washington; Halleck from Washington urges McClellan to reinforce Pope, McClellan "tries his best" but fails to reinforce Pope.

■ For his inactivity on this day Porter is later court-martialed and cashiered. He spends much of the remainder of his life trying to clear his name.

SATURDAY AUGUST 30

■ **Daylight** Pope receives a note from McClellan via Franklin that rations and forage are available at Alexandria if Pope sends cavalry to escort the trains. His cavalry is unfit for service, so Pope decides to renew the engagement which he believes he is winning.

■ **12 noon to 2 p.m.** Porter's corps is advanced to attack Longstreet along the Warrenton Pike, unaware that his flank is

turned.

■ **Later** Following severe fighting, Porter's corps retires. They halt and reform being subjected to repeated ferocious attacks.

■ **Late afternoon** Franklin's corps arrives at Centreville.

■ **Dark** Union left has been forced back about three-quarters of a mile almost to the Henry house.

■ **8 p.m.** Pope gives the order for a gradual retirement on Centreville, which is accomplished in an orderly manner.

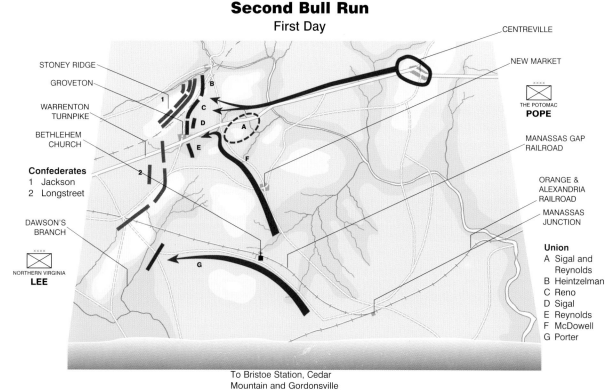

Second Bull Run
First Day

Confederates
1 Jackson
2 Longstreet

Union
A Sigal and Reynolds
B Heintzelman
C Reno
D Sigal
E Reynolds
F McDowell
G Porter

To Bristoe Station, Cedar Mountain and Gordonsville

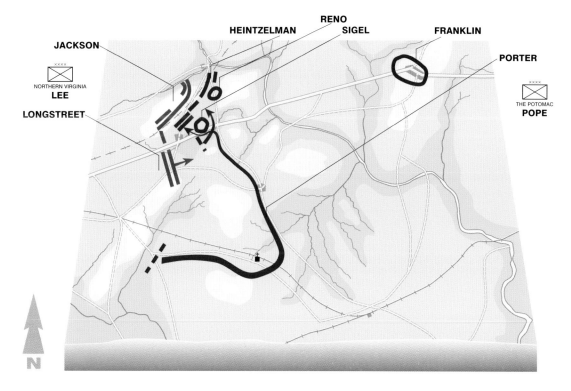

Right: The rolling countryside of the north of the ba[ttle]
field, looking toward the Roulette Farm, which [was]
attacked by Sumner's II Corps. Lines of Union troops [can]
be seen advancing from the right. (N[...])

CHRONOLOGY

■ **September 3** Following his defeat of Pope at Second Manassas, Lee writes to President Davis suggesting taking the war to the North – into Maryland and beyond.

■ **September 5** Army of Northern Virginia crosses the Potomac into Maryland. Lee expects Marylanders to welcome the Confederates as liberators and join them but meets both veiled and open hostility.

■ **September 9** Lee reveals his plan to divide his force, sending Jackson and 26 brigades to Harpers Ferry while the balance marches on toward Pennsylvania.

■ **September 13** A copy of Lee's campaign plan (Special Orders No. 191) falls into the hands of McClellan, reinstated as commander of the Union Army of the Potomac. As usual McClellan procrastinates. Lee meanwhile becomes aware of McClellan's possession of his plan of campaign and starts to withdraw.

■ **September 14** Battle of South Mountain. After bitter fighting the Union troops drive the Confederates off.

■ **September 16** Lee deploys his army around Sharpsburg, a superb natural defensive position.

WEDNESDAY SEPTEMBER 17

■ **6 a.m.** After intermittent skirmishing through the night Hooker begins his advance. His left flank comes under artillery fire and is held up.

■ Gibbon's brigade engages a Confederate brigade in a cornfield, but despite repeated attempts cannot drive them out. Both sides throw in reinforcements and the fighting surges to and fro with heavy losses on both sides.

■ **7:30–9 a.m.** Mansfield's repeated advances on the Dunker Church are driven back with heavy casualties.

■ **9 a.m.** Confederates driven from the cornfield by sheer weight of numbers.

■ Hooker, wounded in the foot, leaves the field believing the battle to be won.

■ **9:30 a.m. to 1 p.m.** Repeated attacks by Sumner's II Corps on D. H. Hill's position in a sunken lane (Bloody Lane) are driven off with huge loss. The raging fight draws in other units until a Confederate mistake allows the Union troops to flank the position and pour in enfilade fire. The lane becomes a slaughter pen.

Above: Union troops charge at Antietam. (WP)

Rohrbach's bridge, on the right flank of the Confederate line, was finally crossed by Burnside's troops at 1 p.m., shown below in James Hope's painting (NPS).

UNION	CONFEDERATES
Commanders	
Maj. Gen. George B. McClellan	General Robert E. Lee
Armies	
of the Potomac	of Northern Virginia
Strengths	
87,164 infantry, cavalry, guns	Less than 40,000 (Lee's figure)
Casualties	
2,108 dead, 9,549 wounded, 753 missing/prisoners	1,512 dead, 7,816 wounded, 1,844 missing/prisoners
McClellan's timidity and inflexibility threw away the advantage of knowing Lee's plans	Lee's flexibility and ability to think on his feet saved him from almost certain defeat

■ **After 10 a.m.** Burnside's first advance on the Rohrbach Bridge gets lost and then pinned down by artillery and musketry.

■ **After 11 a.m.** Burnside's second advance on the Rohrbach Bridge (subsequently known as Burnside Bridge) is decimated by artillery and rifle fire.

■ **1 p.m.** Union troops who have advanced through Bloody Lane are halted at an orchard and driven back by Longstreet's artillery fire; Union troops finally cross Rohrbach Bridge.

■ **3 p.m.** After wasting precious time, Burnside continues his advance toward Sharpsburg, heavily engaged.

■ **About 3 p.m.** A. P. Hill's Light Division crosses the Potomac at Boteler's Ford.

■ **After 4 p.m.** Hill's division arrives from Harpers Ferry in time to crash into Burnside's exposed flank and drive him back almost to Rohrbach Bridge.

■ **Dusk** Fighting gradually dies away although there is sporadic gunfire through the night.

THURSDAY SEPTEMBER 18

Lee, in defiance of McClellan who still has unblooded brigades, gathers up his wounded and only then starts his march back into Virginia.

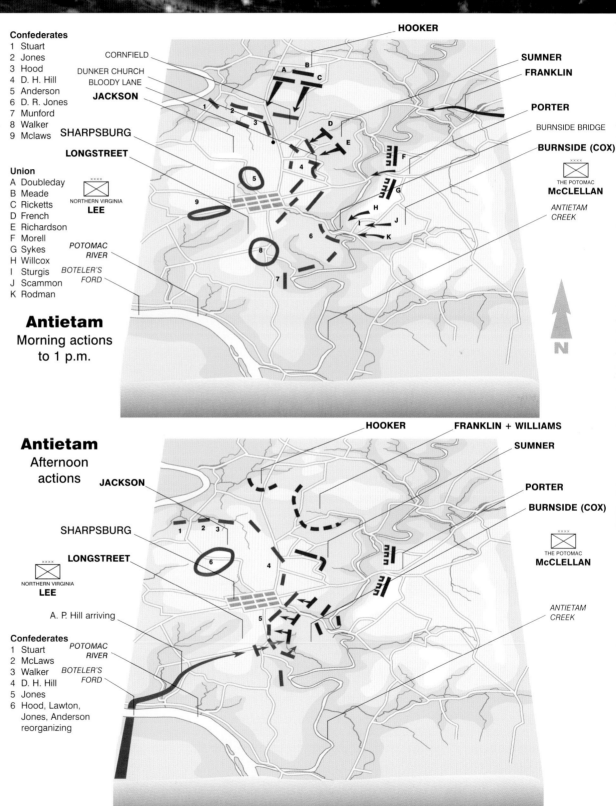

Confederates
1 Stuart
2 Jones
3 Hood
4 D. H. Hill
5 Anderson
6 D. R. Jones
7 Munford
8 Walker
9 Mclaws

Union
A Doubleday
B Meade
C Ricketts
D French
E Richardson
F Morell
G Sykes
H Willcox
I Sturgis
J Scammon
K Rodman

Antietam
Morning actions
to 1 p.m.

CORNFIELD
DUNKER CHURCH
BLOODY LANE
JACKSON
SHARPSBURG
LONGSTREET

HOOKER
SUMNER
FRANKLIN
PORTER
BURNSIDE BRIDGE
BURNSIDE (COX)
THE POTOMAC
McCLELLAN
ANTIETAM CREEK

NORTHERN VIRGINIA
LEE
POTOMAC RIVER
BOTELER'S FORD

N

Antietam
Afternoon actions

JACKSON
SHARPSBURG
LONGSTREET
NORTHERN VIRGINIA
LEE
A. P. Hill arriving

HOOKER   **FRANKLIN + WILLIAMS**
SUMNER
PORTER
BURNSIDE (COX)
THE POTOMAC
McCLELLAN
ANTIETAM CREEK
POTOMAC RIVER
BOTELER'S FORD

Confederates
1 Stuart
2 McLaws
3 Walker
4 D. H. Hill
5 Jones
6 Hood, Lawton, Jones, Anderson reorganizing

CHRONOLOGY

1862

■ **July** Grant takes over as commander of the Army of the Tennessee following Hallecks's departure for Washington.

■ **November** Grant marches south to Grand Junction. He then sets up a huge supply depot at Holly Springs, where he is joined by Sherman.

■ **December 8** Sherman is detached to return to Memphis, organize a wing of some 32,000 then travel downriver and attack Vicksburg, while Pemberton's attention is diverted by Grant's overland approach.

■ **December 20** Confederate cavalry under Earl Van Dorn swoops down on Grant's depot at Holly Springs, overcomes the 15,000-man garrison and puts all Grant's stockpiled supplies to the torch. At about the same time Nathan Forrest tears up 60 miles of rail road in western Tennessee that connects Grant with his source of supply in Columbus, Kentucky. Grant's overland attack is thus halted. Sherman, already on his way, cannot be warned.

■ **December 26** Sherman lands his force on the banks of the Yazoo north of Vicksburg: two days later he attacks and is repulsed from Chickasaw Bluffs with the loss of 1776 men. He then abandons the campaign.

1863

■ **January** A political general, Maj Gen John W. McClernand, is imposed on Grant. He outranks Sherman and Porter, taking credit for their success against Fort Hindman. Sherman and Porter find it increasingly difficult to work with McClernand, and at their request Grant takes command at Young's Point a few miles north of Vicksburg on the opposite bank.

■ **Dawn, February 2** Grant sends the *Queen of the West* past Vicksburg's batteries: although fired on, she receives few hits and sustains little damage.

■ **March 31** McClernand's and McPherson's divisions make an amphibious march to Bruinsburg where they will cross the Mississippi.

■ **April 16/17** Under cover of darkness Porter steams his gunboats and some transports past the batteries, losing one transport. Six nights later the remaining transports follow, losing one vessel.

■ **April 30/May 1** McClernand and McPherson cross the river at Bruinsburg almost unopposed; Grant marches on Port Gibson forcing the evacuation of the Grand Gulf garrison.

■ **May 12** Grant's army (now including Sherman) defeats a scratch force at Raymond.

■ **May 14** Sherman and McPherson take Jackson, destroying the industrial area.

■ **May 16** Pemberton engages Grant at Champion Hill and is heavily defeated, losing 3,800 out of 23,000 plus the loss of a routed division which later joins Johnston. The following day there is a brief action at Big Black Bridge. Pemberton withdraws to Vicksburg.

MONDAY MAY 18

■ Grant invests Vicksburg.

TUESDAY MAY 19

■ **2 p.m.** Grant's first assault, fighting is general, in places the Federals reach the outer parapet but are driven off. A bombardment both from the land and Porter's gunboats begins.

FRIDAY MAY 22

■ **10 a.m.** Second assault meets spirited resistance. Only McClernand has any success, gaining a toehold on the Railroad Redoubt; he is driven off by a counter-attack in the evening. The day has cost Grant 3,200 casualties, he

now opts for a siege which he thinks will take a week.

SATURDAY MAY 23 ONWARD

■ **Early** Almost incessant bombardment; garrison and townspeople live a troglodyte existence. As food grows scarce, horses, mules, dogs and cats are eaten – eventually rats and mice feature on the menu.

EARLY JUNE

■ J. E. Johnston approaches with a relieving force, and Grant dispatches

Above: Union pontoon bridge across the Big Black River. (Old Courthouse Museum, Vicksburg)

Right: The fight in the crater at Fort Hill after the explosion of a mine on 25 June. But tunneling, mining and assaults were not decisive: Pemberton was starved out. (ASKB)

Confederates
Initial dispositions:
1 Forney
2 Smith
3 Stevenson
4 Loring
5 Garrison, inadequately reinforced, evacuated

6 Johnston arrives May 13; retreats NE after attack by Grant May 14
7 May 71 skirmish at Big Black Bridge

Union
A Dec 28, 1862 Sherman repulsed at Chickasaw Bluffs
B Jan 1863 Grant assumes command at Young's Point
C March 31McCleland and McPherson's divisions reach Bruinsburg
D (not shown) Porter's fleet passes the Vicksburg batteries April 16/17 to ferry the troops across at Bruinsburg

E April 30/May 1 crossing of the Mississippi
F May 12 Grant, now reinforced by Sherman, defeats Confederates at Raymond
G May 14 Grant storms Jackson
H May 16 Grant defeats Pemberton at Champion Hill
J May 18 Grant invests Vicksburg

Left: Porter's Union fleet makes the hazardous passage of the Mississippi past the Confederate defenses of Vicksburg by night. (NavAc)

Below left: The Battle of Champion Hill. Most of the fighting on the Union side was done by McPherson's division. (MARS)

Below: Preparing for an assault at Vicksburg, as seen from behind the Union lines. (LC)

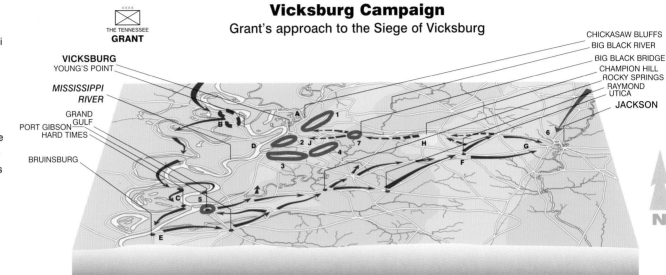

Vicksburg Campaign
Grant's approach to the Siege of Vicksburg

date of the surrender. As a sop to Pemberton's honor, the garrison is to be paroled and allowed to march from the city before the Union troops march in.

SATURDAY JULY 4

■ Vicksburg changes ownership. The Confederates march out, the Union marches in. Grant pays tribute to the role of Admiral Porter and the US Navy.

UNION	CONFEDERATES
Commanders	
Major General Ulysses S. Grant	Lieutenant General John C. Pemberton
Armies	
of the Tennessee	Garrison
Strength	
From 43,000 to 75,000	Over 40,000 Effectives at beginning of siege 28,000
Casualties	
Assault May 19: 157 dead, 777 wounded, 8 captured/missing	From May 1 to July 3 1260 dead, 3572 wounded,
Assault May 22: 502 dead. 2,550 wounded 147 captured/missing	4227 captured/missing.
Siege operations: 104 dead, 419 wounded, 7 captured/missing	
Totals: 763 dead, 3746 wounded, 162 captured/missing	
Perspective	
An example of Grant's single-mindedness and will to win	Pemberton received no help from anyone, not even Johnston who was as usual indecisive

Sherman with more than 30,000 men to hold him.

LATE JUNE

■ Grant's engineers tunnel under the defenses. The city is ripe for assault. Still Pemberton holds out.

FRIDAY JULY 3

■ Pemberton seeks a truce to meet with Grant and discuss surrender , only Grant's magnanimous terms keeping the talks in progress. One thing Grant will not negotiate is the

CHRONOLOGY

■ **November 7** McClellan is relieved of command of the Army of the Potomac; the reluctant Burnside is appointed in his place.

■ Burnside plans to march on Richmond via Fredericksburg and along the tracks of the Richmond, Fredericksburg & Potomac Railroad (thus having both river and rail transport).

■ **November 18** Sumner arrives at Falmouth with the Right Grand Division of the Army of the Potomac. He sends word to Burnside that he can ford the river and take the virtually undefended city. Burnside tells him to wait for the pontoons.

■ **November 21 late** Longstreet arrives in Fredericksburg with his division of the Army of Northern Virginia and begins to dig his forces in.

■ **November 24** Pontoons begin arriving at Falmouth.

■ **December 10** Burnside issues ambiguous final orders to his commanders; late in the day the engineers move the pontoons close to the river.

■ **December 11 pre-dawn** Union engineers begin building the bridges under cover of dark and fog; later the sun dissipates the fog leaving them exposed to fire from Confederate sharpshooters in buildings along the waterfront. Subsequently a fierce bombardment is directed at the city from the Union artillery on Stafford Heights, but to little effect.

■ **12:30 p.m.** Crossing established south of the city.

■ **2:30 p.m.** The 7th Michigan paddle pontoons across the Rappahannock and start to clear the Confederate snipers from the city. Union troops continue to cross during the remainder of the afternoon.

■ **3:20 p.m. onwards** The first bridge is completed opposite the town itself, enabling more Union troops to cross. There is fierce house-to-house fighting during the remainder of the afternoon and early evening.

■ **7 p.m.** Confederate withdrawal from the city completed.

■ **December 12** The day is wasted due to confusion on the Union side. Some Northern troops indulge in looting.

SATURDAY DECEMBER 13

■ **About 8 a.m.** An attack by Meade on the Confederate right is held up by the fire of two guns (later one) commanded by Major John Pelham who continually shifts position, only withdrawing when he runs out of ammunition.

■ **Morning** Confederate artillery shells the city, causing casualties from falling masonry.

■ **11 a.m.** Meade continues his advance.

■ **Noon** The first of six frontal assaults on the Confederate line on Marye's Heights is launched. Assailed on the flanks by artillery fire, Kimball's brigade receives one shattering volley and halts; a second volley breaks them. Andrews' brigade following suffers the same fate as does that of Palmer. None get within 200 feet of the wall. As the shattered remnant make their way back, the Union artillery shells the Confederate position furiously. General Thomas R. Cobb is struck by a piece of shrapnel and mortally wounded; he is replaced by General Cooke, who is also wounded and replaced by General Kershaw.

Above: Strategically placed on Marye's Heights, the New Orleans Washington Artillery fire upon Union troops forming up for the assault. (B&L)

Below: Protected by a stone wall overlooking Telegraph Road, men from Kershaw's and Cobb's brigades repulse six Union charges, leaving the ground before the wall heaped with bodies. (B&L)

UNION	CONFEDERATES
Commanders	
Maj. Gen.	General
Ambrose E. Burnside	Robert E. Lee
Armies	
of the Potomac	of Northern Virginia
Strengths	
116,683 infantry,	58,500 infantry,
cavalry, artillery	cavalry, artillery
Casualties	
1,284 dead, 9,600	608 dead, 4,116
wounded, 1,769	wounded, 653
missing/prisoners	missing/prisoners
Perspectives	
A sound plan that may	Burnside's chances of
well have been	success were fading
successful had it not	when Longstreet
been subject to so	arrived at
much delay. Burnside's	Fredericksburg. With
inflexibility contributed	the arrival of Lee he
greatly to the appalling	stood no chance of
casualties	success

■ **Noon** Meade's advance is halted by Confederate artillery fire.

■ **1 p.m.** Second assault on Marye's Heights goes in. As Colonel Samuel Zook's brigade advances, the Union artillery ceases fire. The Confederates hold their fire until the Union troops are close, then shatter them with one murderous volley. Meagher's Irish Brigade follow: as they leave the shelter of the city Confederate artillery pours in shells, and as they advance they are raked on the flanks by canister and in front by ferocious musketry. They fall in rows.

■ **1 p.m.** On the Confederate right Meade advances over ground thought to be impassable and thus unguarded. He crosses and falls upon Gregg's division. Gregg, believing the soldiers to be Confederates, orders his men to hold their fire. During the fight he is shot and mortally wounded.

■ **2 p.m.** Unsupported, Meade is forced to fall back. (Franklin has 20,000 Union troops standing idle).

■ **2 p.m.** Third assault. Sturgis' and Howard's divisions, ordered to attack from right and left, have hardly left the city when they are enfiladed by artillery fire, the left wing breaking first.

■ **Hooker**, having seen the disastrous results of the day, rides back to Burnside and urges him to cease the attacks. Burnside is adamant: the heights must be taken that day.

■ **3 p.m.** Griffin's assault is even less successful than the previous ones. The troops now have an additional obstacle in the thousands of dead, wounded and survivors hugging the earth in front of the wall.

Left: Again and again Union troops charged up Telegraph Road (on right) towards Marye's Heights only to run into devastating fire. (M)
Below left: Willis Hill, just south of Marye's Heights, became a National Cemetery after the war. (M)

■ **5 p.m.** Humphreys orders his men to fix bayonets and charge the wall. Hindered by the mass of dead and wounded, they are stopped after only 50 yards. In the gathering dusk, Getty's brigade makes the final assault of the day, getting to within 50 yards of the wall.

■ **After dark** Burnside plans to renew the attack on Marye's Heights the following day, leading the assault in person. He is gradually talked out of this action.

SUNDAY DECEMBER 14

Morning Confederate Sergeant Richard Kirkland goes into the no-man's land in front of the wall to give water to wounded Union soldiers. His mission of mercy lasts over 90 minutes.

POSTSCRIPT

Following the disaster of Fredericksburg, Burnside is relieved of command of the Army of the Potomac at his own request. Hooker, whom Burnside had attempted to have dismissed from the service, replaces him.

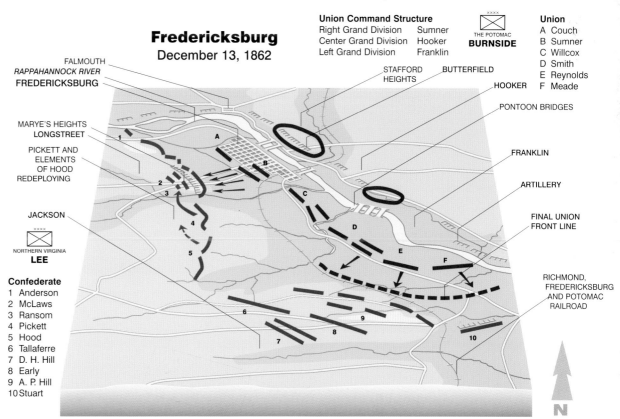

Fredericksburg
December 13, 1862

FALMOUTH
RAPPAHANNOCK RIVER
FREDERICKSBURG

MARYE'S HEIGHTS
LONGSTREET

PICKETT AND
ELEMENTS
OF HOOD
REDEPLOYING

JACKSON

NORTHERN VIRGINIA
LEE

Confederate
1 Anderson
2 McLaws
3 Ransom
4 Pickett
5 Hood
6 Tallaferre
7 D. H. Hill
8 Early
9 A. P. Hill
10 Stuart

Union Command Structure
Right Grand Division — Sumner
Center Grand Division — Hooker
Left Grand Division — Franklin

THE POTOMAC
BURNSIDE

STAFFORD
HEIGHTS
BUTTERFIELD

HOOKER

PONTOON BRIDGES

FRANKLIN

ARTILLERY

FINAL UNION
FRONT LINE

RICHMOND,
FREDERICKSBURG
AND POTOMAC
RAILROAD

Union
A Couch
B Sumner
C Willcox
D Smith
E Reynolds
F Meade

N

CHRONOLOGY

■ **October 30** Buell replaced by Rosecrans as head of the Army of the Ohio, which is renamed XVI Corps and later Army of the Cumberland.

■ **December** Following his failure in Kentucky, General Braxton Bragg has laid the blame on everyone but himself, especially on General Breckinridge, who had not even been there. Already unpopular among his officers, he orders a private soldier executed for desertion on December 26, bringing some of the Kentucky units close to mutiny.

■ Rosecrans, who has recently replaced Buell, is under pressure to achieve something. He decides to drive Bragg from Murfreesboro, a road and rail junction that gives Bragg attack options against the Union in both east and west.

■ **December 26** Rosecrans, his army divided into three unequal parts (Major Generals Alexander M. McCook, George H. Thomas and Thomas Crittenden) leaves Nashville, his divisions moving in different directions in an attempt to confuse Bragg.

■ **December 28** Despite bad weather and early fog, McCook takes Triune without a fight.

■ **December 29 Late afternoon** Union forces cross Stones River and are driven back by Breckinridge's Kentuckians.

■ **December 30 Afternoon** Thomas and McCook arrive to complete Rosecrans' army. Both Bragg and Rosecrans have planned to attack the other's right wing: the advantage will go to the one who attacks first.

WEDNESDAY DECEMBER 31, 1862

■ **6:10 a.m.** Confederates move to within 200 yards of the Union line before being detected. The Union right begins to crumple; but the rapid Union collapse causes the Confederate line to fragment and lengthen, losing its impetus.

■ **Later** Alerted by the sound of firing, Post is able to organize his troops to resist the Confederate pressure before he, too, gives way.

UNION	CONFEDERATES
Commanders	
Maj. Gen. William S. Rosecrans	General Braxton Bragg
Armies	
of the Cumberland	of Tennessee
Strengths	
43,400 (December 31 1862)	37,712
Casualties	
1,730 dead, 7,802 wounded, 3,717 missing/prisoners	1,294 dead, 7,945 wounded, 1,027 missing/prisoners
Perspectives	
A defeat that made the Confederates' position in Tennessee even more untenable	Bragg not only mismanaged the battle, he alienated many of the officers and men of his army

■ **7:30 a.m.** The Union right stabilizes and holds for a short while before it is again broken. Wharton's Confederate cavalry are about to complete the rout and capture McCook's reserve ammunition when Union cavalry drive them off.

■ **8 a.m.** Polk's attack slows as he encounters Sheridan. Cheatham's division is almost an hour late into action. Sending his brigades in singly, he allows Sheridan to defeat them in detail. Palmer sends Hazen's brigade into the Round Forest where they construct barricades from fallen timber, and from this concealed position they slaughter Chalmers' brigade, the firefight lasting 30 minutes.

■ **10 a.m.** Sheridan finds himself in a salient fighting on three sides and is forced to withdraw rapidly, followed by the newly arrived Rousseau. But the Confederates begin to fade, exhausted and short of ammunition.

■ **Later** General Hascall arrives in the Round Forest and takes command. Polk's brigades make repeated unsuc-

cessful assaults until almost noon. The Round Forest exerts an almost magnetic attraction, and fighting there reaches a terrible intensity. The level of noise causes soldiers to stuff their ears with cotton from the plants around their feet.

■ **1 p.m.** Bragg orders Breckinridge to send in two brigades to reinforce Polk. But Polk again sends them in singly, achieving nothing but losses. Breckinridge arrives with a further two brigades and makes a small advance.

■ The furious fighting at the Round Forest continues. Rousseau has been pushed back and the Confederates are close to victory. Some Union soldiers become so short of ammunition they resort to the bayonet, rocks and rifle butts. Dusk is now thickening and the fighting dies down. Bragg is so certain of victory that he sends a telegram announcing a victory to Richmond.

THURSDAY, JANUARY 1, 1863

■ Bragg allows his men a day of rest to watch the Union forces digging in.

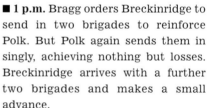

Above: General William Carlin and staff, and a bird's-nest-like regimental bandstand. Although outnumbered, Carlin's brigade managed to hold firm at Stones River. (M)

Below: Rosecrans' ability to cobble together a defensive line after his army had absorbed a punishing surprise attack was key to the Union victory at Stones River. (MARS)

Left: The sweeping rebel assault at Stones River threatened to destroy Rosecrans' army. (LC)

x—x Union frontline c.10:00
y—y Final Confederate position late Dec 31
z—z Final Union position late Dec 31

Rosecrans correctly guesses Bragg's next move and makes his arrangements accordingly.

FRIDAY, JANUARY 2, 1863

■ Bragg is confident that the Union will have evacuated its positions, his cavalry having reported large numbers of Union troops moving toward Nashville.

■ Crittenden has occupied high ground opposite Breckinridge, who has returned to the east bank and whose own reconnaissance has made him aware of the Union strength in this area.

■ **After noon** Bragg orders Breckinridge to drive the Union troops from his front. Hardee and Polk disagree, claiming that there is no threat from Crittenden but that the threat comes from the Union forces on the west bank. Bragg insists on the attack.

■ When Breckinridge returns to give his brigade commanders their orders for the attack they come near to mutiny.

■ **4 p.m.** Following a brief bombardment, the Confederates drive the Union troops back across the river. The Confederates then come under the concentrated fire of over fifty guns and their attack is halted.

■ **4:30 p.m.** In the deepening gloom of dusk, sleet begins to fall. A Union division falls back across the river: the Confederates follow and again come under murderous artillery fire.

■ **5 p.m.** The battle is over. In the deepening darkness, Breckinridge rides along his reforming lines in tears. He never forgives Bragg for the slaughter of his Kentuckians.

SATURDAY JANUARY 3

■ Bragg withdraws from Murfreesboro overnight, moving to new positions at Duck River. Rosecrans has achieved his victory and with it Lincoln's gratitude.

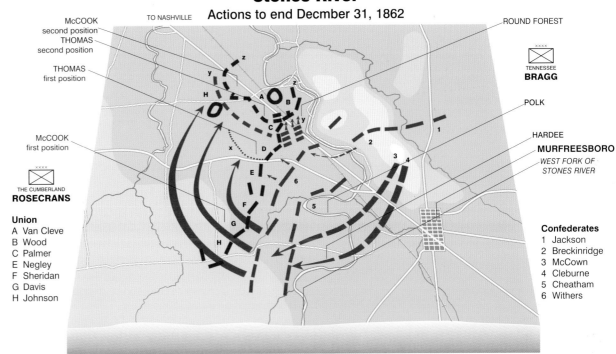

Stones River
Actions to end Decmber 31, 1862

TO NASHVILLE

McCOOK second position
THOMAS second position
THOMAS first position
McCOOK first position

THE CUMBERLAND
ROSECRANS

Union
A Van Cleve
B Wood
C Palmer
E Negley
F Sheridan
G Davis
H Johnson

ROUND FOREST

TENNESSEE
BRAGG

POLK

HARDEE
MURFREESBORO
WEST FORK OF STONES RIVER

Confederates
1 Jackson
2 Breckinridge
3 McCown
4 Cleburne
5 Cheatham
6 Withers

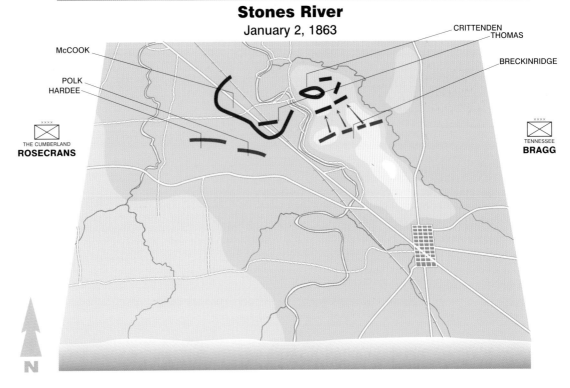

Stones River
January 2, 1863

McCOOK

POLK
HARDEE

THE CUMBERLAND
ROSECRANS

CRITTENDEN
THOMAS

BRECKINRIDGE

TENNESSEE
BRAGG

N

CHRONOLOGY

■ **Early April** Following his appointment as chief of the Army of the Potomac (for which he has intrigued tirelessly) Hooker plans to cross the Rappahannock, advance on Lee, held in Fredericksburg by demonstrations, cut him off from Richmond and destroy him.

■ **April 13** Stoneman with Hooker's cavalry heads north and then west. Progress is slow, being hampered by heavy rain and an apparent lack of urgency.

■ **April 27** Hooker's infantry begin to march, moving upriver to cross the Rappahannock at Kelley's Ford. The crossing is unopposed, and Confederate videttes are taken prisoner, preserving security.

■ **April 28, evening** Following a minor cavalry skirmish near Wilderness Tavern, a prisoner warns the Confederates to flee: Lee is now aware that a major force is on the march.

■ **April 29** Lee dispatches Anderson to hold the Orange Plank Road and Orange Turnpike. Anderson holds the roads four miles east of Chancellorsville near the Zoar and Tabernacle churches.

■ **April 30, 2 p.m.** Hooker now has a substantial force behind Lee. Hooker's plan is to ocupy a position where Lee must attack, so, instead of pressing on he orders his force to halt, consolidate and form a defensive cordon, handing Lee the initiative.

■ **April 30/May 1** Leaving the minimum force under Early to hold Fredericksburg, Lee marches to Chancellorsville.

FRIDAY MAY 1

■ **Before noon** Firing starts. Confederate forces are still joining Lee.

■ **2 p.m.** Hooker ceases offensive action and waits for Lee to attack him.

■ **Later** Hooker orders his army to fall back on the previous night's positions and improve the defenses.

SATURDAY MAY 2

■ **4 a.m.** Jackson begins to move his divisions by a hidden route towards Howard's position on the Union right.

UNION	CONFEDERATES
Commanders	
Maj. Gen. Joseph Hooker	General Robert E. Lee
Armies	
of the Potomac	of Northern Virginia
Strengths	
130,576 infantry, cavalry, guns	60,000 infantry, cavalry, guns
Casualties	
1,606 dead, 9,762 wounded, 5,929 missing/prisoners	1,649 dead, 9,106 wounded, 1,708 missing/prisoners
Perspectives	
A brilliant start which went wrong when Hooker yielded the initiative	Outnumbered, Lee's flexibility enabled him to utterly defeat a superior foe, but the death of Jackson was an irreplaceable loss

■ **Later** Throughout the day Lee holds Hooker's attention with feint attacks and sporadic artillery fire. Hooker and Howard disregard reports of Confederate movements.

■ **Mid-afternoon** Jackson has reached his destination and silently deploys his troops in three ranks on a two-mile front ready to crush Howard's flank.

■ **5 p.m.** Howard's troops are cooking their suppers when from out of the setting sun, yelling and shooting, the Confederates fall upon them. They instantly dissolve.

■ **5:30** Due to a temperature inversion Hooker cannot hear the small arms fire on his right. He becomes aware of the disaster only when he sees the masses of fugitives running towards him.

■ **7 p.m.** Hooker is in a desperate plight: his army has collapsed in on itself and is now in a roughly circular formation being squeezed by Jackson and Lee. Jackson's force has become disorganized, and its advance ceases.

■ **9:15 p.m.** Jackson is shot by a nervous Confederate picket and hit three times; two wounds are superficial, but one smashes his left arm, severing an artery. Stuart takes command. The rest of the night is spent in feverish activity.

SUNDAY MAY 3

■ **Around 9 a.m.** Stuart drives in to within a quarter-mile of Chancellorsville. About this time Hooker is concussed when a shell hits a post he is leaning against, and Couch takes command.

■ **9 a.m.** Sedgwick launches a full-scale attack on Fredericksburg, making two unsuccessful assaults on Marye's Heights. Early has denuded his defenses to reinforce Lee.

■ **10 a.m.** During a truce to remove wounded, the Union troops see how thin the Confederate defenses are.

■ **10:25 a.m.** A third wave of Union troops assaults Marye's Heights, moving at the double. The defenders are overcome at the point of the bayonet.

Above: Lee at Chancellorsville. (LC)

Below: An illustration based on a contemporary sketch of Union artillery, athwart the Plank Road, resisting Jackson's advance on the evening of May 2. (B&L)

Far right: A popular depiction of Jackson's death. In fact, he received his mortal wound from friendly fire while scouting in front of the rebel lines. (LC)

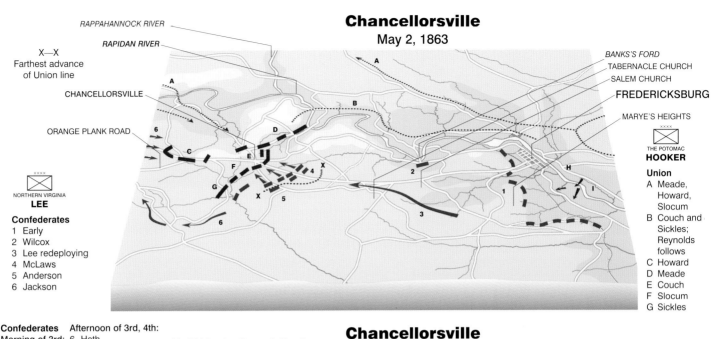

Chancellorsville
May 2, 1863

RAPPAHANNOCK RIVER
RAPIDAN RIVER
X—X
Farthest advance
of Union line
CHANCELLORSVILLE
ORANGE PLANK ROAD

BANKS'S FORD
TABERNACLE CHURCH
SALEM CHURCH
FREDERICKSBURG
MARYE'S HEIGHTS

NORTHERN VIRGINIA
LEE
Confederates
1 Early
2 Wilcox
3 Lee redeploying
4 McLaws
5 Anderson
6 Jackson

THE POTOMAC
HOOKER
Union
A Meade,
  Howard,
  Slocum
B Couch and
  Sickles;
  Reynolds
  follows
C Howard
D Meade
E Couch
F Slocum
G Sickles

Confederates	Afternoon of 3rd, 4th:
Morning of 3rd:	6 Heth
1 Rodes	7 Rodes
2 Colston	8 Colston
3 Heth	9 McLaws
4 Anderson	10 Anderson
5 McLaws	11 Early

Chancellorsville
May 3 and 4, 1863

X—X Union frontline early May 3

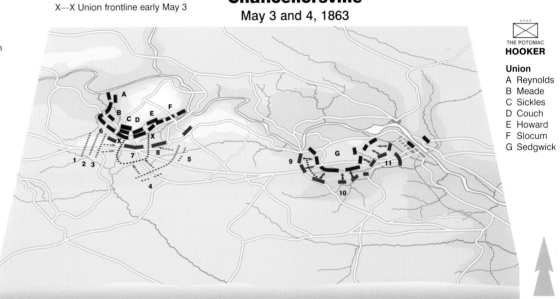

THE POTOMAC
HOOKER
Union
A Reynolds
B Meade
C Sickles
D Couch
E Howard
F Slocum
G Sedgwick

N

■ **Late morning** At Chancellorsville fighting continues. The Union yields dominant high ground, allowing the rebel artillery to enfilade Union lines. The Union begins to retreat.

■ **10:45 a.m.** Sedgwick starts to pursue Early along the Orange Road but is continually harassed by Wilcox on his front and flanks.

■ **3 p.m.** Sedgwick halts near Salem Church to await reinforcements; the Confederates in the churchyard also await reinforcements.

■ Lee has again split his force: leaving a fraction to contain Hooker he marches to Salem Church.

■ **5:30 p.m.** Dusk approaches. Sedgwick can wait no longer and attacks. A fierce fight in the churchyard ensues until nightfall.

MONDAY MAY 4

■ **Morning** Early easily drives the Union troops from Marye's Heights and out of Fredericksburg.

■ **Later** Early marches to Salem Church to combine with Lee and crush Sedgwick.

■ **Noon** Lee arrives at Salem Church; but the day is wasted in maneuvering.

■ **6 p.m.** Confederate attack on Sedgwick is half-hearted. Nightfall and fog put an end to fighting. Sedgwick withdraws and crosses the Rappahannock at Banks' Ford.

■ **Late** Hooker, still suffering from concussion, orders a withdrawal north of the Rappahannock to safety.

The 20th Maine at Gettysburg, July 2. National Guard Heritage Painting by H. Charles McBarron.

CHRONOLOGY

■ **May 26** Lee gets Davis's approval for a secret march through the Shenandoah Valley, across the Potomac River and into Maryland.

■ **June 9** Pleasonton and Stuart fight an inconclusive cavalry action at Brandy Station, Va.

■ **June 15** Lee crosses the Potomac into Maryland.

■ **June 27** Hooker resigns from command of the Army of the Potomac.

■ **June 28** Lincoln, without consultation, replaces Hooker with Meade.

■ **June 30** Heth approaches Gettysburg seeking supplies and shoes, then-withdraws when confronted by Federal cavalry.

WEDNESDAY JULY 1

■ **Dawn** Heth again approaches Gettysburg and clashes with Buford's Union cavalry.

■ **10 a.m.** Gen. Reynolds reaches Gettysburg and orders Buford to hold until his troops arrive.

■ **Noon** Reynolds is shot and killed while personally placing troops; Doubleday assumes command.

■ **12:15 p.m.** Howard arrives at Gettysburg, assumes command and establishes his HQ on Cemetery Hill.

■ **2 p.m.** Lee arrives on the field.

■ **3 p.m.** Union troops are engaged on a semi-circular front by numerically superior Confederate forces.

■ **4 p.m.** Union are driven back through Gettysburg and consolidate on Cemetery Hill and Ridge; Gen. Winfield Scott Hancock arrives to take overall command.

■ **Later** Union forces have consolidated their line, losing about 8,500 men. Reinforcements, including General Meade, continue to arrive through the night.

THURSDAY JULY 2

■ **Morning and early afternoon** Meade inspects his position, making changes here and there.

■ **About 4 p.m.** Meade finds that Sickles has disobeyed orders and advanced his line on to low ground that he perceives dominates his position. Sickles' line extends from a peach orchard, across a wheatfield to a rocky outcrop (Devil's Den) near the base of Little Round Top.

■ **Just after 4 p.m.** Longstreet's corps attacks Sickles' left and is met with dogged resistance.

■ **6:30 p.m.** Ewell makes a full attack on Culp's Hill in a badly mis-managed engagement.

■ **Later** Warren discovers that Little Round Top is virtually unguarded. Union forces just beat the Confederates in occupying this decisive feature, holding it only after desperate fighting.

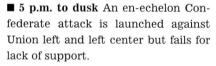

■ **5 p.m. to dusk** An en-echelon Confederate attack is launched against Union left and left center but fails for lack of support.

■ **Midnight** Firing ceases.

FRIDAY JULY 3

■ **Dawn** Lee has planned a reprise of yesterday's actions: concerted assaults on the right and left of the Union line. Longstreet, however, seeing the strength of the Union line, attempts a flanking maneuver.

■ **6 a.m.** Lee discovers Longstreet's move and halts it; Ewell is already engaged at Culp's Hill.

■ **Later** Lee orders Longstreet to make a frontal assault on the Union center; Longstreet demurs, Lee insists.

■ **Before noon** Ewell's attack on Culp's Hill is driven off with heavy casualties, enabling Meade to reinforce Hancock's center.

Above center: The steep, heavily wooded, boulder-strewn slopes of Culp's Hill made it a natural fortress. (LC)

Above: Union reinforcements counterattack during the fighting on July 2 in front of Cemetery Ridge. (WP)

Left: Hancock at Gettysburg, by Thure de Thulstrup. Hancock personally directs artillery as the Confederate lines of "Pickett's charge" approach. (LC)

UNION	CONFEDERATES
Commanders	
July 1	General
Maj. Gen. John Hancock	Robert E. Lee
July 2	
Maj. Gen. G. G. Meade	
Armies	
of the Potomac	of Northern Virginia
Strengths	
1st day	At least 70,000
I Corps and XI Corps	all arms
19,982	
2nd day	
I, II, III, V, VI, XI, XII	
Corps, Artillery Reserve	
plus Cavalry Corps	
101,679 all arms	
Casualties	
3,072 dead,	2,592 dead,
14,497 wounded, 5,434	12,709 wounded,
missing/prisoners	5,150 missing/prisoners
Perspectives	
A victory gained at enormous cost and not followed up. The loss of senior officers has obscured Meade's part in the battle	Arguably Lee's worst-fought battle: having no prior knowledge of the terrain he ran out of ideas and fell back on the frontal attack

■ **1 p.m.** Confederate artillery commences a furious bombardment on the Union center.

■ **2:55 p.m.** Union artillery fire diminishes (Hancock is conserving ammunition) and the Confederates believe they have silenced the enemy guns.

■ **3 p.m.** Longstreet reluctantly gives Pickett the nod to start the assault. Pickett's line, over a mile wide, begins to move; they have to cross 1,400 yards of open ground to reach the Union line.

■ **3:10 p.m.** As soon as Pickett's brigades come within range of the Union artillery, fire is opened with redoubled fury both from Cemetery Ridge and from Little Round Top.

■ **Later** Gen. Armistead places his hat on his sword-point and leads perhaps 150 men over the wall front of the Union line. He puts his hand on a Union gun and then is mortally wounded.

■ **Later still** The Confederates begin to retreat, again suffering an unmerciful hammering from the Federal artillery.

■ **Dusk** Fighting dies away.

SATURDAY JULY 4

■ **Morning** Both sides have taken such a beating that all they do is stare balefully at each other.

■ **Afternoon** Heavy rain sets in, and after dark Lee withdraws, heading back to Virginia. Meade lets him depart in peace.

Confederates
Approach to 2:30 p.m. July 1:
1 Pender
2 Heth
3 Rodes
4 Early

Situation 3:30 p.m., July 2
5 Pender
6 Anderson
7 McLaws
8 Hood

NORTHERN VIRGINIA
LEE

THE POTOMAC
MEADE

Union
Initial forward deployment
A Rowley
B Wadsworth
C Robinson
D Schurz

Situation 3:30 p.m., July 2
E Slocum
F Howard
G Newton
H Hancock
I Sykes
J Barnes
K Sickles
L Sedgwick

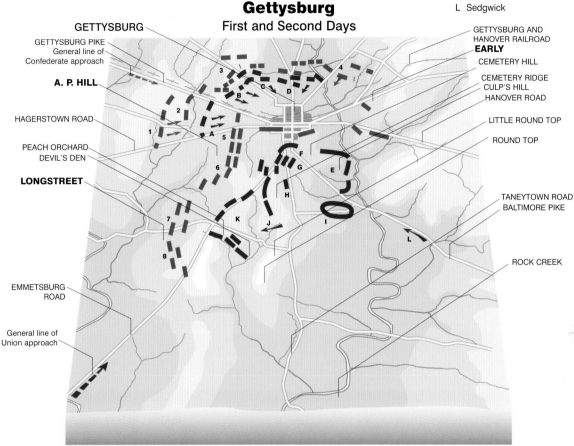

Gettysburg
First and Second Days

GETTYSBURG
GETTYSBURG PIKE
General line of Confederate approach
A. P. HILL
HAGERSTOWN ROAD
PEACH ORCHARD
DEVIL'S DEN
LONGSTREET
EMMETSBURG ROAD
General line of Union approach
GETTYSBURG AND HANOVER RAILROAD
EARLY
CEMETERY HILL
CEMETERY RIDGE
CULP'S HILL
HANOVER ROAD
LITTLE ROUND TOP
ROUND TOP
TANEYTOWN ROAD
BALTIMORE PIKE
ROCK CREEK

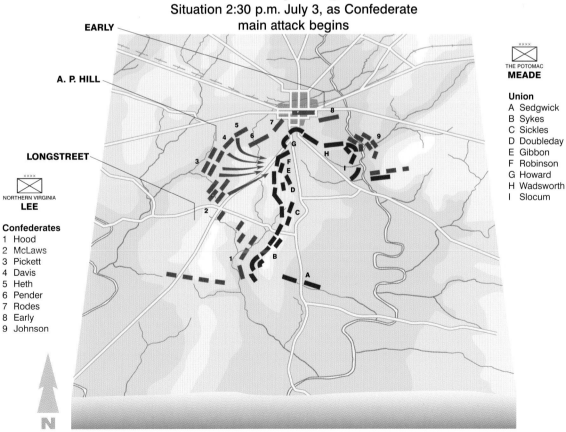

Gettysburg
Situation 2:30 p.m. July 3, as Confederate main attack begins

EARLY
A. P. HILL
LONGSTREET

NORTHERN VIRGINIA
LEE

Confederates
1 Hood
2 McLaws
3 Pickett
4 Davis
5 Heth
6 Pender
7 Rodes
8 Early
9 Johnson

THE POTOMAC
MEADE

Union
A Sedgwick
B Sykes
C Sickles
D Doubleday
E Gibbon
F Robinson
G Howard
H Wadsworth
I Slocum

N

CHRONOLOGY

■ **Sept 9** Rosecrans marches into Chattanooga after having maneuvered Bragg out in a brilliant campaign.

■ **Sept 10** Leaving Crittenden in Chattanooga, Rosecrans splits his forces. Negley stumbles upon Bragg's army in McLemore's Cove, and only confusion between Hill, Cleburne and Bragg on the opposing side, reinforcements from Thomas and the onset of darkness save him from destruction.

■ **Sept 11** Hindman allows Negley to slip out of McLemore's Cove (Hindman is later arrested for disobedience of orders).

■ **Sept 12** This evening Rosecrans realizes that he is faced by Bragg's entire force, not just a rearguard. He orders Crittenden and McCook to hasten to Thomas.

■ **Sept 17** Bragg plans to cross Chickamauga Creek on the 18th, cut Rosecrans off from Chattanooga, occupy the city himself and force Rosecrans to either retake the city or retreat to Nashville.

■ **Sept 18** Bragg's corps are prevented from crossing Chickamauga Creek by Union cavalry. Rosecrans spends the day disposing his forces to make best use of the terrain.

THURSDAY SEPTEMBER 19

■ **Early morning** Thomas sends two brigades to destroy what he believes to be a single Confederate brigade west of the creek.

■ **Around 9 a.m.** Instead of a single brigade the Union forces encounter Bragg's reserve corps with Forrest in support.

■ **Later** Reinforcements from both sides are drawn in. The fighting has now escaped the control of either Bragg or Rosecrans: due to the broken nature of the ground formal lines cannot be established.

■ **After 11 a.m.** On the Union side an ad hoc command system has developed with Thomas in command on the left, Crittenden in the center and McCook on the right.

■ **Noon** A wide gap has opened in the Union front.

UNION	CONFEDERATES
Commanders	
Maj. Gen. William S. Rosecrans	General Braxton Bragg
Armies	
of the Cumberland	of Tennessee (plus Longstreet's Corps from the Army of Northern Virginia)
Strengths	
56,965 infantry, cavalry, guns	71,551 infantry, cavalry, guns
Casualties	
1,656 dead, 9,749 wounded, 4,774 missing/prisoners	2,312 dead, 14,674 wounded, 1,486 missing/prisoners
Perspectives	
A shattering defeat. Thomas, though gaining the sobriquet 'Rock of Chickamauga' possibly caused the gap in the Union front by his calls for reinforcements	Bragg won a great victory then frittered away the advantage of it. Shortly after a cabal of officers tried unsuccessfully to have him removed

■ **1 p.m.** Van Cleve's brigade is driven back, creating a bulge. Reynolds' division straightens the front.

■ **3 p.m.** Hood, of Longstreet's corps, arrives and piles straight into Rosecrans' right.

■ **After 5 p.m.** Erupting from the shadows of the trees, Cleburn slams into Thomas: a furious firefight begins

that continues until after fall of dark.

■ **11 p.m.** Bragg reorganizes his army into two wings, Longstreet on the left, Polk on the right.

FRIDAY SEPTEMBER 20

■ **8 a.m.** Polk, ordered to attack at daylight (6 a.m.), begins to move.

■ **9:30 a.m.** Breckinridge launches a shattering attack on the Union left flank.

■ **10 a.m.** The pressure on Thomas increases as Cleburne and Cheatham throw their weight behind Breckin-

Right: The second day of fighting at Chickamauga saw futile rebel charges against well-positioned defenders until a Union staff blunder opened a hole in the Union line. (LC)

Below: Many of the Union troops shouted "Chickamauga! Chickamauga!" as they charged up Missionary Ridge. (LC)

Bottom: On September 19, fighting at Chickamauga raged around the Kelly Field, one of the few open areas on the heavily wooded battlefield. (LC)

ridge's attack. Thomas calls on Rosecrans for reinforcements.

■ **10:45 a.m.** Rosecrans' attention is focused on Thomas to the exclusion of all else. A poorly worded order, obeyed to the letter, opens a wide gap in the front.

■ **11 a.m.** A probing Confederate attack finds the gap.

■ **11:30 a.m.** Longstreet with almost 20,000 men attacks furiously, and Sheridan, taken in flank, collapses.

■ **Noon** The Army of the Cumberland is split in two.

■ **1 p.m.** The Union right dissolves in panic, Rosecrans, Sheridan, McCook and Davis joining the precipitate flight. Thomas stands alone, inflicting heavy casualties on his attackers. Longstreet realigns his forces for the final push.

■ **2 p.m.** Longstreet attacks Horseshoe Ridge, held by remnants of shattered regiments. Many acts of personal valor take place, inspired by Thomas's example.

■ **2:30 p.m.** A concerted double attack by Hindman and B. R. Johnson reaches the crest of the ridge only to be shattered and driven off.

■ **Later** Granger marches his reserve corps on to Horseshoe Ridge in time to drive off a Confederate battery that would have enfiladed Thomas's rear.

■ **4 p.m.** Longstreet makes a final effort, but his troops have had more than enough and break.

■ **5–5:30 p.m.** Thomas makes an orderly withdrawal towards Chattanooga.

■ **Later** Bragg declines to pursue the beaten Union forces, to the intense disgust of Forrest, who has been sorely harassing them.

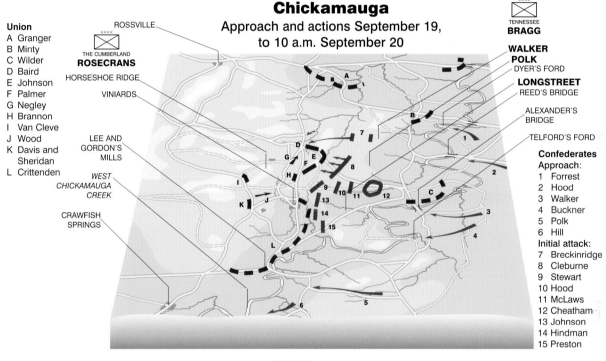

Chickamauga
Approach and actions September 19, to 10 a.m. September 20

Union
A Granger
B Minty
C Wilder
D Baird
E Johnson
F Palmer
G Negley
H Brannon
I Van Cleve
J Wood
K Davis and Sheridan
L Crittenden

ROSSVILLE
THE CUMBERLAND
ROSECRANS
HORSESHOE RIDGE
VINIARDS
LEE AND GORDON'S MILLS
WEST CHICKAMAUGA CREEK
CRAWFISH SPRINGS

TENNESSEE
BRAGG
WALKER
POLK
DYER'S FORD
LONGSTREET
REED'S BRIDGE
ALEXANDER'S BRIDGE
TELFORD'S FORD

Confederates
Approach:
1 Forrest
2 Hood
3 Walker
4 Buckner
5 Polk
6 Hill
Initial attack:
7 Breckinridge
8 Cleburne
9 Stewart
10 Hood
11 McLaws
12 Cheatham
13 Johnson
14 Hindman
15 Preston

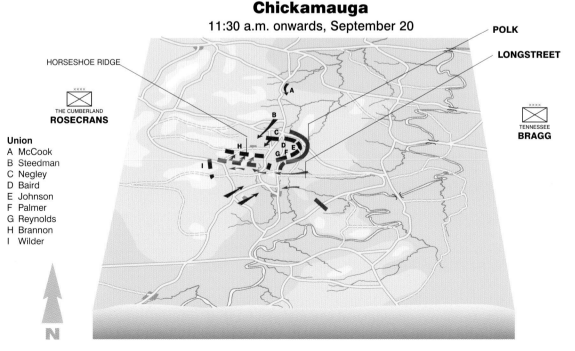

Chickamauga
11:30 a.m. onwards, September 20

HORSESHOE RIDGE
THE CUMBERLAND
ROSECRANS

Union
A McCook
B Steedman
C Negley
D Baird
E Johnson
F Palmer
G Reynolds
H Brannon
I Wilder

POLK
LONGSTREET
TENNESSEE
BRAGG

N

CHRONOLOGY

■ **September 20** Rosecrans withdraws to Chattanooga following his disastrous defeat at Chickamauga.

■ **September 24** Rosecrans abandons his positions on Lookout Mountain and Missionary Ridge allowing Bragg to dominate the city and interdict his railroad supply line.

■ **October** President Davis travels to Chattanooga in answer to a petition to remove Bragg; Polk is replaced by Hardee.

■ **October 23** Grant, now in command of the newly-formed Military Division of the Mississippi, arrives in Chattanooga. Thomas replaces Rosecrans.

■ **October 26** Hooker with reinforcements from the Army of the Potomac crosses the Tennessee at Bridgeport.

■ **October 28** The "cracker line" allowing reinforcements and rations to reach the Union troops in Chattanooga is opened.

■ **October 28/29** Confederate attempt to cut the "cracker line" at Wauhatchie fails.

■ **November 4** Longstreet, at his own request, leaves Chattanooga to take Knoxville from Burnside.

■ **November 15** Sherman arrives at Chattanooga, confers with Grant and leaves for Bridgeport on the 16th.

■ **November 20** Union attack delayed due to heavy and persistent rain.

■ **November 22** Bragg sends more of his forces to strengthen Longstreet at Knoxville.

UNION	CONFEDERATES
Commanders	
Major General Ulysses S. Grant	General Braxton Bragg
Armies	
of the Cumberland with the addition of units from the Army of the Potomac	of Tennessee with the addition of Longstreet's division from the Army of Northern Virginia) (detached before the battle commenced).
Strengths	
c.70,000 infantry, cavalry, guns	c.50,000 infantry, cavalry, guns
Casualties	
752 dead, 4,713 wounded, 350 missing/prisoners	361 dead, 2.180 wounded, 4,146 missing/prisoners
Perspectives	
An overwhelming victory from what seemed an impossible situation	From a position of overwhelming advantage to a shattering defeat, the one bright point was that this marked Bragg's last field command

■ **Early** An opposed crossing of Lookout Creek by Grose attracts Confederate attention, allowing Hooker to advance on Lookout Mountain.

■ **8 a.m.** Hooker easily pushes Stevenson back on Lookout Mountain (the "Battle Above the Clouds"). Hooker gradually encircles the base of the mountain. Despite the presence of Breckinridge, the heavily outnumbered defenders can do little but hold on until night covers their withdrawal to Missionary Ridge.

MONDAY NOVEMBER 23

■ **2 p.m.** Thomas advances and carries the Confederate forward position at Orchard Knob, turning and strengthening the fortifications.

■ **Later** Grant shifts his headquarters to Orchard Knob.

TUESDAY NOVEMBER 24

■ **2 a.m.** Union troops cross the Tennessee River, surprising and capturing the Confederate outposts. Sherman's infantry then cross in pontoons, the pontoons then being used to build a bridge to take artillery and cavalry across.

WEDNESDAY NOVEMBER 25

■ **Dawn** Sherman advances on Tunnel Hill and runs into Cleburne. A ding-dong battle commences which lasts for some hours, neither side gaining an advantage.

■ **3:30 p.m.** Thomas' division is ordered to advance on the foot of the ridge, capture the rifle pits there and re-form.

■ **Later** The rifle pits are easily taken, the occupants fleeing up the ridge, not stopping at the crest and disrupting the defenses there.

■ **Later** The Union forces are now being fired at from the top of the ridge, and, having no shelter, go the only way they can – up.

■ Unable to depress their guns sufficiently to fire on the ascending Union troops, the Confederate gunners light the fuses of shells and roll them down the slope.

■ **Later** Sheridan and Wood reach the crest more or less simultaneously. Captured Confederate guns are turned on their previous owners, after some sharp rearguard actions the Confederates are driven from the ridge.

THURSDAY NOVEMBER 26

■ **Early hours** Sheridan, in hot pursuit of the retreating Confederates, catches up with their rear guard crossing Chickamauga Creek, capturing many prisoners and much *matériel*.

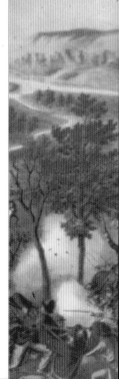

Chattanooga
November 24

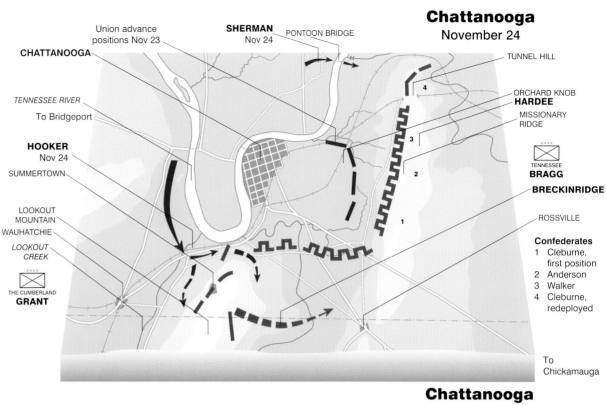

CHATTANOOGA

Union advance positions Nov 23

SHERMAN Nov 24

PONTOON BRIDGE

TUNNEL HILL

4

ORCHARD KNOB

HARDEE

MISSIONARY RIDGE

3

2

TENNESSEE RIVER

To Bridgeport

HOOKER Nov 24

SUMMERTOWN

LOOKOUT MOUNTAIN

WAUHATCHIE

LOOKOUT CREEK

THE CUMBERLAND
GRANT

TENNESSEE
BRAGG

BRECKINRIDGE

ROSSVILLE

Confederates
1 Cleburne, first position
2 Anderson
3 Walker
4 Cleburne, redeployed

To Chickamauga

Above: Hooker's men attack up the rugged slopes of Lookout Mountain. (MARS)
Left: Troops of Baird's division take Confederate artillery on Missionary Ridge. (LC)
Below: The battle for Missionary Ridge. The craggy terrain made assaulting the ridge a daunting prospect. (MARS)
Below right: Thure de Thulstrup's *Grant at Missionary Ridge*. He is at left, watching from Orchard Knob. (LC)

Chattanooga
November 25

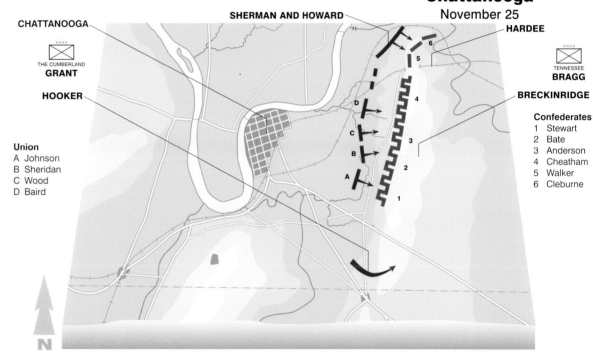

CHATTANOOGA

THE CUMBERLAND
GRANT

HOOKER

Union
A Johnson
B Sheridan
C Wood
D Baird

SHERMAN AND HOWARD

HARDEE

6

5

4

3

2

1

D

C

B

A

TENNESSEE
BRAGG

BRECKINRIDGE

Confederates
1 Stewart
2 Bate
3 Anderson
4 Cheatham
5 Walker
6 Cleburne

N

CHRONOLOGY

■ Following Chattanooga, Grant is appointed General-in-Chief. His grand strategy for 1864 is to be a 60,000-man amphibious assault on North Carolina, cutting Lee off from the more southern states of the Confederacy. Lincoln, however, vetoes this proposal on the grounds that it will weaken the defenses of Washington.

■ Grant then falls back on the tried and tested crossing of the Rapidan to confront Lee on his home ground. The key to Grant's strategy is rapidity of movement, to get through the tangled Wilderness before Lee can react to stop him.

■ **First minutes of May 4** Grant's army starts to move south toward Germanna and Ely's Fords.

■ **6 p.m.** Union troops hold the intersection at Wilderness Tavern. The Union cavalry meanwhile fail to detect Lee's countermoves: Ewell is within four miles of the Orange Turnpike with Hill and Longstreet under orders to move north.

THURSDAY MAY 5

■ In effect the fighting on this day consists of two separate battles: on the Orange Turnpike (Ewell) and the Orange Plank Road (A. P. Hill).

■ **5 a.m.** Union advance continues.

■ **6 a.m.** Griffin reports Confederate troops (Ewell) moving toward him.

■ **7:15 a.m.** Meade arrives at Griffin's position and orders him to attack, at the same time halting Hancock. Lee has stopped Grant without firing a shot.

■ **Later** During the time it takes to deploy the Union infantry in line of battle, reports come in from Wilson's cavalry that another force of Confederates (Hill's vanguard) is approaching.

■ **About 9:30 a.m.** Grant arrives at the rear of Griffin and decides to abandon the attempt to march through the Wilderness. He decides instead to fight it out where he is, trusting in his numerical superiority (70,0000 against 40,000).

■ **About 10 a.m.** A furious Union attack is launched against Johnson's division.

UNION	CONFEDERATES
Commanders	
Lieutenant General Ulysses S. Grant	General Robert E. Lee
Armies	
of the Potomac	of Northern Virginia
Strengths	
118,000 infantry, cavalry, artillery (about 70,000 engaged on first day)	About 61,000 infantry, cavalry, guns
Casualties	
2,246 dead, 12,037 wounded, 3,383 missing/prisoners	About 8,700
Perspectives	
A drawn battle that proved nothing except that there was to be no quick end to the war	Unlike his predecessors, Grant would not give up on his task. Lee would have to destroyed

■ **Around 1 p.m.** Johnson's division begins to waver. Bartlett's brigade breaks through the center of Johnson's line and runs into a Confederate counterattack. Union troops are driven back over ground they have only just advanced over.

■ **Later** Muzzle flashes set dry leaves and undergrowth on fire. The fire reaches the cartridge boxes of dead and wounded, detonating the gunpowder and blowing living and dead to pieces. Following this horror both sides resume fighting

■ **3 p.m.** Grant's efforts to achieve a concerted assault are thwarted by the difficult terrain.

■ **After 4 p.m.** Hancock attacks and is badly mauled by Heth's division, and by 5 p.m. the assault has stalled.

■ **6:30 p.m.** Hancock again attacks and a race ensues between Lee trying to reinforce Heth and Hancock attempting to flank him. Lee wins by a whisker.

■ On the Union right there is a similar story, Sedgwick's assault on Ewell's flank being halted and driven back.

■ **9 p.m.** The fighting dies down to mere skirmishing with both sides being equally exhausted.

FRIDAY MAY 6

■ **1 a.m.** Longstreet begins his march from Gordonsville.

■ **4:30 a.m.** Ewell sends in a modest attack that catches Union forces flat-footed; Sedgwick and Warren regain

most of the lost ground, but assaults on Johnson's breastworks are severely punished.

■ **5 a.m.** Hancock's attack goes in. Grant's all-out battle has begun. However, from the start things go awry. Hancock, heavily engaged, is making good headway against Hill's right, but Burnside is not only 90 minutes late getting started but brings only half his troops. A gap between Ewell and Hill goes unexploited.

■ **6 a.m.** Hill's corps, hit front, left and right, collapses, the rout being witnessed by Hill and Lee.

■ **Later** As Hill's troops flee along the Plank Road they encounter the vanguard of Longstreet's corps. The fugitives reform and, stiffened by Kershaw's and Field's men, slam into the Union troops stopping them dead. Lee attempts to lead the Confederates forward but is stopped by cries of "General Lee to the rear." His horse's bridle is gently but firmly grasped and horse and rider are led to the rear.

■ **8 a.m.** The Union attack has come to a grinding halt, due in part to the timidity of Gibbon and Burnside.

■ **After 9 a.m.** Longstreet begins to extend his line in an endeavor to envelop Hancock's left.

Above: A later, romanticised depiction by Currier & Ives of the Wilderness battle. (LC)

Above: With the defenses on fire, the Confederates capture a part of the Union breastworks on the Brock Road. (B&L)

Left: Officers at Grant's headquarters observe the train of events. The fire on May 5 further obscured visibility that was already severely hindered by the nature of the wooded terrain. (Author)

The Wilderness
May 5

RAPIDAN RIVER

GERMANNA FORD

BURNSIDE   GERMANNA PLANK ROAD   SEDGWICK

WILDERNESS TAVERN

WARREN

ELY'S FORD

POTOMAC
MEADE

Confederates
1 Early
2 Johnson
3 Rodes
4 Wilcox
5 Heth

NORTHERN VIRGINIA
LEE

EWELL

ORANGE CH TURNPIKE

ORANGE PLANK ROAD

A. P. HILL

Union
A Ricketts
B Wright
C Griffin
D Robinson
E Wadsworth
F Crawford
G Getty
H Birney
I Mott
J Gibbon
K Barlow

HANCOCK

To Chancellorsville and Fredericksburg

BROCK ROAD

To Gordonsville

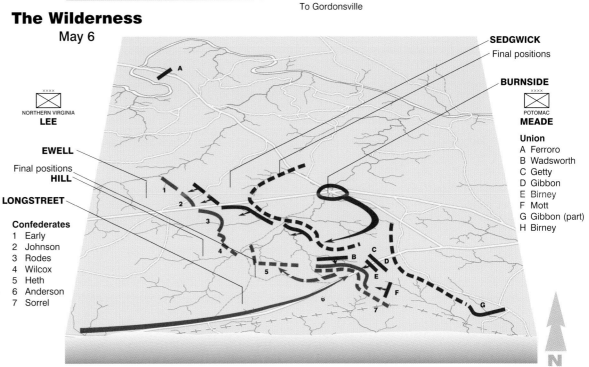

The Wilderness
May 6

SEDGWICK
Final positions

BURNSIDE

POTOMAC
MEADE

NORTHERN VIRGINIA
LEE

EWELL
Final positions
HILL

LONGSTREET

Confederates
1 Early
2 Johnson
3 Rodes
4 Wilcox
5 Heth
6 Anderson
7 Sorrel

Union
A Ferroro
B Wadsworth
C Getty
D Gibbon
E Birney
F Mott
G Gibbon (part)
H Birney

N

- **10 a.m.** Grant abandons his attacking battle and orders Sedgwick and Warren to start building defenses.
- **Later** Longstreet moves three brigades to the Union left under cover of dense woods, attacks them in flank and rear and rolls them up in confusion.
- **Later** Following a momentary lull in the firing, General Jenkins is killed outright and the ubiquitous Longstreet is badly injured in a friendly fire incident.
- **4 p.m.** An attack on the Union lines on the Brock Road comes to nothing: parts of the breastworks are aflame and neither side can cross. Burnside attacks and drives the Confederates back but is in turn forced back.
- **Late afternoon** Ewell makes an assault on the Union right. Surprised, the Union troops are driven from their positions with the loss of 600 prisoners plus two general officers, Seymour and Shaler.
- **Darkness** The battle ends.

CHRONOLOGY

■ **May 7** Following the indecisive Wilderness battle, Grant moves south. This time there woill be no retreat across the Rapidan: Grant is south to stay.

■ **Night of May 7/8** Both armies move south almost parallel to each other in what amounts to a race.

SUNDAY MAY 8

■ **8 a.m.** Union artillery and cavalry driven from Spotsylvania Court House without offering much resistance.

■ **Later** Troops of both sides arrive during the rest of the day and entrench themselves. They will remain in these positions for the next ten days with minor adjustments.

■ **Afternoon** An attack by Sedgwick's and Warren's corps against Anderson and Ewell is repulsed with heavy loss to the Union forces.

MONDAY MAY 9

■ No fighting of note occurs. Hill's corps (under command of Early due to Hill's illness) arrives in the morning; General Sedgwick (Union) is killed by a sharpshooter moments after claiming: "They couldn't hit an elephant at that distance."

TUESDAY MAY 10

■ **Early morning** Hancock's corps has crossed the Po River and is threatening the Confederate rear. Early attacks Hancock in the rear and drives him back across the river with heavy loss.

■ **3:45 p.m.** General Warren (Union) leads an attack on the Confederate left which is driven back with heavy loss.

■ **5 p.m.** Union Colonel Emory Upton attacks the left of the salient in four waves advancing at the run. The first Confederate line is taken easily, and following furious hand-to-hand fighting the second line also falls with 1,200 prisoners. Upton is forced to retreat due to Mott's failure to support him.

■ **7 p.m.** Another Union assault is repulsed with heavy loss.

WEDNESDAY MAY 11

■ The day is spent in deploying troops for a massive assault on the salient on the morrow. Lee, hearing the sound of the movement, suspects that Grant is going to try to flank him. He moves 22 guns from the salient to make them available on the threatened flank.

THURSDAY MAY 12

■ **Dawn** Hancock's corps comes rushing out of the dawn mist driving back the Confederates and capturing the guns which had only just been reinstated, plus 3,000 troops and Generals Johnson and Steuart. Lee's army is split.

■ **Later** Lee prepares to lead his reserves in person. As at the Wilderness, he is politely led to the rear.

■ **Later** The Confederate counterattack drives the Union forces out of the works, but they refuse to retreat farther. At this opportune moment a section of Battery C 5th U.S. Artillery (Lieutenant Richard Metcalf) arrives and from point-blank range pours rounds of canister into the Confederates. The gunners are soon shot down and a hand-to-hand struggle develops that is unequaled for ferocity and duration.

■ **Later** Gun and mortar fire from a less advanced position aid the Union troops in their struggle. At close range the bayonet is used with lethal effect, some

Union units' rifles being so fouled that it is impossible to load them.

■ **Later** A kind of berserk frenzy overcomes troops on both sides. Soldiers climb on to the top of the breastwork, discharge their muskets and then throw the weapons with fixed bayonets down like spears, repeating the action until they are bayoneted or shot down.

■ So intense is the firing that oak trees with a diameter of almost two feet are cut down by bullet strikes; many Union troops expend more than 400 cartridges in the engagement.

Above: The vicious hand-to-hand struggle at "Bloody Angle" as portrayed in an 1887 chromolithograph by L. Prang & Co. The image is, as so often, somewhat romanticised. (LC)

Left: Lee's army refuses to let him lead them from the front. (LC)

Right: Taken after the Battle of Spotsylvania, this picture shows the temporary camp for Confederate prisoners near Falmouth on the Rappahannock. (M)

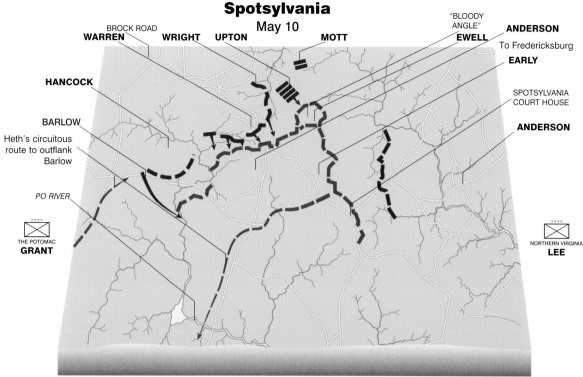

Spotsylvania
May 10

BROCK ROAD
WARREN WRIGHT UPTON MOTT
"BLOODY ANGLE"
EWELL ANDERSON
To Fredericksburg
EARLY

HANCOCK

SPOTSYLVANIA COURT HOUSE

BARLOW
ANDERSON

Heth's circuitous route to outflank Barlow

PO RIVER

THE POTOMAC
GRANT

NORTHERN VIRGINIA
LEE

UNION	CONFEDERATES
Commanders	
Major General Ulysses S. Grant	General Robert E. Lee
Armies	
of the Potomac	of Northern Virginia
Strengths	
About 100,000 infantry, cavalry, guns	About 52,300 infantry, cavalry, guns
Casualties	
2,725 dead, 13,416 wounded, 2,258 missing/prisoners	Estimated 4,000 dead, wounded, missing/prisoners
Perspectives	
Grant again showed that he would not be beaten; that he was south of the Rapidan and would stay if it "takes all summer"	The Army of Northern Virginia yet again showed that though vastly outnumbered, by skillful use of fieldworks it could still hold the Army of the Potomac. Lee's movement of his limited forces from May 13–18 was brilliant

■ A group of Confederates 20 or 30 strong who clamber on top of the breastwork in an effort to surrender are shot down by a volley from their comrades.

■ **About midnight** Lee withdraws and the fighting ends for the day.

FRIDAY MAY 13
■ **Early** Union volunteers are called for to bury the Confederate dead in the Bloody Angle. The Confederate corpses lie feet deep in the waterlogged trenches. In some instances the Union troops merely shovel the trenches in to cover what lies within them.

MAY 13–18
■ A war of move and countermove takes place. In the end Grant entices Lee from behind his works by a move to the North Anna River.

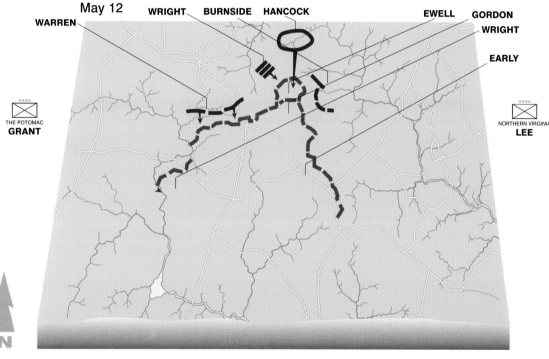

Spotsylvania
May 12

WARREN WRIGHT BURNSIDE HANCOCK EWELL GORDON WRIGHT EARLY

THE POTOMAC
GRANT

NORTHERN VIRGINIA
LEE

N

CHRONOLOGY

■ **May 5–16** Butler fails in his assault on Petersburg and is bottled up in Bermuda Hundred by Beauregard.

■ **May 15** Sigel is defeated by Breckenridge at the battle of New Market (Breckenridge's force includes cadets from the Virginia Military Institute).

■ **June 17–18** Hunter, after skirmishing with Early at Lynchburg, withdraws west due to shortage of ammunition.

■ **July 6** Early crosses the Potomac.

■ **July 9** Early defeats General Lew Wallace at the Battle of the Monocacy and continues his march on Washington.

UNION	CONFEDERATES
Commanders	
Major General Philip H. Sheridan	Lieutenant General Jubal A. Early
Armies	
of the Shenandoah	Early's Corps of the Army of Northern Virginia
Strengths	
About 56,000 infantry, cavalry, artillery (inc. garrisons at Harpers Ferry, Martinsburg and guards on the Baltimore & Ohio Railroad)	About 20,000 infantry, cavalry, artillery
Casualties	
Opequon Creek	
697 dead, 3,983 wounded, 338 captured or missing	total of 3,611 dead, wounded, captured or missing
Fisher's Hill	
52 dead, 457 wounded, 19 captured or missing	30 dead, 210 wounded 995 captured or missing
Cedar Creek	
644 dead, 3,430 wounded, 1,591 captured or missing	700 or 800 dead and wounded (General Early gave figures for Cedar Creek as 1,860 dead and wounded and 1,000 prisoners)
	Union figures for prisoners captured August 1, 1864 to March 1, 1865 13,000
Campaign loss 1,938 dead, 11,893 wounded, 3,121 captured or missing	(Early claimed many of these were not from his corps)
Perspectives	
A brilliantly successful campaign which left a legacy of great bitterness. The Union cavalry was now greatly superior to that of the Confederates	A succession of shattering defeats, particularly at Cedar Creek where a brilliant victory became a humiliating defeat in the course of a day

■ **July 11** Early is before the Washington defenses.

■ **July 12** Lincoln is an interested spectator of the skirmishing before Fort Stevens which covers Early's withdrawal at about 10 p.m.

■ **July 14** Early is back across the Potomac after raising hell on his retreat from Washington.

■ **July 23–30** Early again moves north, defeating General Crook's Army of West Virginia at Kernstown and Winchester and burning Chambersburg before again moving south.

■ **August 7** Army of the Shenandoah formed with Major General Philip H. Sheridan in command with orders to "follow Early to the death" and to so despoil the Shenandoah Valley that even crows flying over will have to "carry their own provender."

BATTLE OF CEDARVILLE TUESDAY AUGUST 16 1864

■ **About 2 p.m.** Confederate cavalry under Fitzhugh Lee engages Union cavalry, driving in the skirmishers before being repulsed. A brigade of Confederate infantry approach and are driven off after a sharp engagement with the dismounted Union cavalry.

■ The Union force then withdraws, driving off livestock and burning grain both standing and in barns.

BATTLE OF OPEQUON CREEK (THIRD BATTLE OF WINCHESTER) MONDAY SEPTEMBER 19 1864

■ **2 a.m.** Army of the Shenandoah is astir early to attack Early.

■ **Daybreak** Union cavalry cross the Opequon and carry Confederate earth-

works. There they wait for the Union infantry to come up.

■ **11:30 a.m.** Union forces advance to collide with Early. A furious battle rages for some hours. When the Union troops break through, they are assailed by Confederate artillery firing canister at short range, the Union center is driven back, the Confederates are struck in flank and the situation stabilizes. There follows a lull, which both leaders use to reform their lines.

■ **Later** Merritt leads the Union cavalry in an attack on the Confederate rear. Early changes face to repel Merritt and a confused fight ensues with the Union infantry advancing to join in. The Confederates withdraw in confusion under cover of darkness to Fisher's Hill.

■ **September 21** Sheridan plans to turn Early's strong position by moving on Little North Mountain. After a sharp struggle, high ground to the north of Tumbling Run is secured.

■ **Night of September 21/22** Sheridan conceals Crook's command in dense woodland north of Cedar Creek.

BATTLE OF FISHER'S HILL THURSDAY SEPTEMBER 22 1864

■ **Morning** Crook marches to woodland near Little North Mountain and masses there (still undetected by Early).

■ **Just before sundown** Crook's infantry strikes the Confederates' left and rear, breaking their line and causing them to flee in complete rout.

■ **September–October** Union cavalry under Torbert, dispatched on a mission of destruction, badly damage Virginia Central Railway and destroy a

Above left: Fort Stevens, north of Washington, where Early's forces penetrated on July 12, 1864. Like many other non-combatants, Lincoln himself stood on the ramparts to watch, until a bystander next to him was wounded. The fort was hastily strengthened after Early's withdrawal and Sheridan was given the task of ensuring the Confederacy could no longer advance so far north. (M)

Above center: "Sheridan's Ride." Sheridan gallops from Winchester to rally the Union forces at the Battle of Cedar Creek. (ASKB)

Above right: The Confederate flanking column, on the right, takes the Union by surprise at Cedar Creek, forcing a withdrawal to the outer side of the rifle-pits. (B&L)

large quantity of military stores at Staunton; under threat from Early's force Torbert retires to Winchester.

■ **October 9** All-day cavalry action: Confederates are quickly broken and the rest of the day is spent by the Union troops in pursuit, the Confederates losing their entire train and all their guns but one. General Lomax [Confederate] is for a time a prisoner but overpowers his captor and escapes.

■ **October 15** Sheridan leaves Cedar Creek for Washington.

BATTLE OF CEDAR CREEK WEDNESDAY OCTOBER 19

■ **Early dawn** Union forces are taken completely by surprise. Crook and Emory are taken in flank and rear, the rudely awakened troops flee, their situation not helped by being fired on by artillery of both sides.

■ **Later** The stunning Confederate attack has captured almost all the Union artillery. Many Confederates now begin to plunder the Union camps.

■ **6 a.m.** Sheridan, at Winchester on his return from Washington, is told of artillery fire at Cedar Creek.

■ **10 a.m.** Confederate advance is held by dismounted Union cavalry firing from behind stone walls.

■ **Later** On the way from Winchester Sheridan encounters large numbers of fugitives. Hurrying onward he single-handedly (and profanely) rallies his troops.

■ **Later** Union cavalry on the left charges into the Confederates in their front scattering them. Union infantry move forward at the double and the Confederates crumple.

■ **End of the day** Early has lost all his wagons and most of his artillery plus what he captured from the Union at dawn.

■ **January 1865** Most of Sheridan's infantry is redeployed, notably around Petersburg.

■ **March 2** General G. A. Custer with 5,000 Union cavalry charges into Early at Waynesboro. The Confederates collapse after very poor resistance, Early and a few of his generals flee to escape capture. Early's force has now ceased to exist.

■ Following Waynesboro, Sheridan's cavalry again goes on a rampage of destruction, a prime target again being the Virginia Central Railroad with a detachment wrecking the James River Canal.

The Shenandoah Valley
To illustrate Sheridan's Campaign, 1865 and events from May 1864

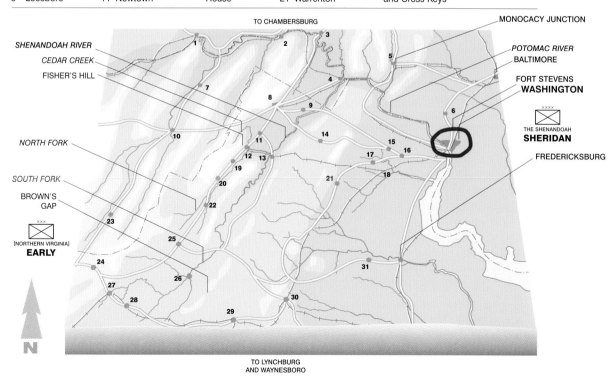

KEY

1 Cumberland	7 Romney	12 Strasburg	17 Groveton	22 New Market	27 West View
2 Bath	8 Winchester	13 Front Royal	18 Manassas	23 Franklin	28 Staunton
3 Williamsport	and Kernstown	14 Upperville	Junction	24 McDowell	29 Charlottesville
4 Harpers Ferry	9 Perryville	15 Chantilly	19 Woodstock	25 Harrisonburg	30 Gordonsville
5 Frederick	10 Moorefield	16 Fairfax Court	20 Mount Jackson	26 Port Republic	31 Chancellorsville
6 Leesboro	11 Newtown	House	21 Warrenton	and Cross Keys	

CHRONOLOGY

■ **March 18** Sherman takes command of the western armies – the Army of the Ohio, General John M. Schofield;, the Army of the Cumberland, Major General George H. Thomas (the "Rock of Chickamauga"); and the Army of the Tennessee, General James B. McPherson

SHERMAN'S MARCH TO ATLANTA

■ **May 9** Sherman maneuvers General Joe Johnston out of Dalton, by a feint on Johnston's front and a wide turning movement on his left. Johnston falls back in good order toward Resaca, destroying the track of the Western & Atlantic Railroad as he goes. Sherman rebuilds the track as he pursues Johnston

■ McPherson moves through unguarded Snake Creek Pass but fails to take lightly-held Resaca. Sherman tells him he has missed the opportunity of a lifetime.

■ **May 12/13** Johnston's army moves into the works at Resaca.

■ **May 14–16** Sherman probes Johnston's works, fighting being confined to skirmishing and long-range sharpshooting. Sherman, finding no weakness, decides the works are too strong for a frontal attack, so again moves to Johnston's left, marching toward Cassville.

■ **May 15 night** Johnston, fearful of his railroad link being cut, abandons Resaca in another masterly withdrawal toward Cassville.

■ **May 19** At Cassville Johnston resolves to fight, concentrating his troops on his right under Hood and Polk, with orders to attack Schofield and Hooker. Hood, alarmed that Union forces have gotten in his rear, goes on the defensive and informs Johnston who falls back on prepared positions at Allatoona Pass.

■ **May 20–23** Sherman rests his troops and repairs the railroad up to Kingston.

■ **May 24** Sherman marches past Johnston's position at Allatoona Pass; Johnston hurriedly marches to Marietta.

■ **May 25–8 Battle of New Hope Church** A series of savage skirmishes in which neither side gains the advantage and both sides lose heavily.

■ **June 10** In an abortive attempt to destroy Nathan Forrest whose cavalry is a danger to Sherman's communications, General Samuel D. Sturgis marches from Memphis. At Brice's Crossroads, Mississippi he suffers a humiliating defeat at Forrest's hands.

■ **June 27 Battle of Kennesaw Mountain** After days of heavy skirmishing, during which General Leonidas Polk is hit by an artillery shell and killed instantly, Johnston shortens his line. Sherman orders a frontal attack but after three hours calls a halt, the heavy losses being almost four to one in favor of the Confederates.

■ **June 30** Johnston, again outflanked on his left (McPherson), leaves his positions at Kennesaw Mountain and falls back on strong entrenchments on the Chattahoochee River. He claims he can hold Sherman north of the river for two months.

■ **July 9** Schofield crosses the Chattahoochee several miles upstream from Johnston's positions; at one point Union troopers make novel use of their superior firearms technology by wading through neck-deep water reloading their Spencer carbines (waterproof metallic cartridges) under water, surfacing to aim and fire then submerging to reload.

■ **July 5** A second expedition against Forrest moves out from La Grange under General A. J. Smith.

■ **July 10** Johnston pulls back to works behind Peachtree Creek four miles from Atlanta. General Braxton Bragg, on a trouble-shooting mission to Georgia, urges Davis to replace Johnston with Hood.

■ **July 14** Smith defeats the numerically inferior Forrest with heavy casualties at Tupelo, Mississippi. Forrest himself is wounded. Sherman's lifeline is safe for a while.

■ **July 16** Davis telegraphs Johnston requesting his plan of operations. He receives a reply with a hint that Atlanta may be abandoned.

■ **July 17** Johnston is replaced by Hood

UNION	CONFEDERATES
Commanders and Armies	
Maj. Gen. William T. Sherman, Army of the Tennessee; Gen. James B. McPherson/ Gen. Oliver O. Howard, Army of the Ohio; Gen. John B. Schofield, Army of the Cumberland; Maj. Gen. George B. Thomas	General Joseph E. Johnston/General John B. Hood Army of Tennessee
Strengths	
Maximum strength 112,819 all arms (as Sherman marched toward Atlanta his forces were diminished by the large numbers detached to secure his railroad supply line against the depredations of Nathan Forrest). On September 1 Sherman's force numbered 81,758 infantry, cavalry and artillery	42,856 infantry, cavalry, artillery (as Johnston retreated toward Atlanta his force increased as it took in detachments left to guard his railroad)
Casualties	
4,423 dead, 22,822 wounded, 4,442 missing/prisoners	3,044 dead, 18,952 wounded, 12,983 prisoners (including deserters)
Perspectives	
Sherman conducted a brilliant campaign, the only failure being the assault on Kennesaw Mountain. The capture of Atlanta assured Lincoln's victory in the November election leading to the continued prosecution of the war	Johnston had conducted an admirable fighting retreat. His replacement by Hood led only to heavy losses in men and the fall of Atlanta sooner rather than later

– a poor decision for the Confederacy but one which pleases Sherman.

■ **July 20 Battle of Peachtree Creek** Hood attacks as Thomas crosses Peachtree Creek. The attack is late and Union forces have already crossed. Though surprised they rally and inflict heavy casualties on the Confederates.

■ **July 21** Hood retreats behind the powerful defenses of Atlanta.

■ **July 22 Battle of Atlanta** Following an all-night march McPherson's open left flank is fiercely assaulted by Hardee's corps plus cavalry. McPherson recovers and inflicts a stinging repulse on the Confederates. McPherson is later shot and killed after blundering into a Confederate line (Oliver O. Howard takes over the Army of the Tennessee).

■ **July 28 Battle of Ezra Church** Sherman sends Howard around the Confederate left in an attempt to cut Atlanta's railroad links. Hood sends a

Above: When Polk's Corps reinforced Johnston's Army of Tennessee, Johnston elected to defend a strong position at Resaca. Sherman's threatened envelopment forced Johnston to retreat. (LC)

Below: Bringing men up to fill a gap in the Union line, Major General James McPherson is killed. (LC)

corps against them but the Confederates are badly mauled and entrench instead of continuing to attack. However, the railroad is saved.

■ **July 28 to August 22** Sherman launches a series of cavalry raids on both sides of Atlanta, the main aim of which again is to sever the railroad links. An attempt is made to liberate Union prisoners from Andersonville. Major General George Stoneman and 600 of his troopers reach the prison – as captives.

■ **August 26** Sherman sends the majority of his army south to cut off Atlanta.

■ **August 31 to September 1 Battle of Jonesboro** Hardee's attack, delivered at 2 p.m. on the 30th, is too late as the Union forces have had time to entrench; a portion of the Union entrenchments are, however, taken.

The following day Sherman sends in a counterattack and severely punishes the Confederates.

■ **September 1 Evacuation of Atlanta** To avoid being bottled up in Atlanta with no lines of supply, Hood destroys all military supplies and evacuates the city.

■ **September 2** Sherman telegraphs Washington: "Atlanta is ours, and fairly won."

■ **September 7** Sherman orders the evacuation of all non-military personnel from Atlanta, another step in his campaign to make him Georgia's least welcome visitor ever.

Above: Kennesaw Mountain: Sherman's belief that his men had grown over-cautious about assaulting fieldworks led him to order a doomed charge. (LC)

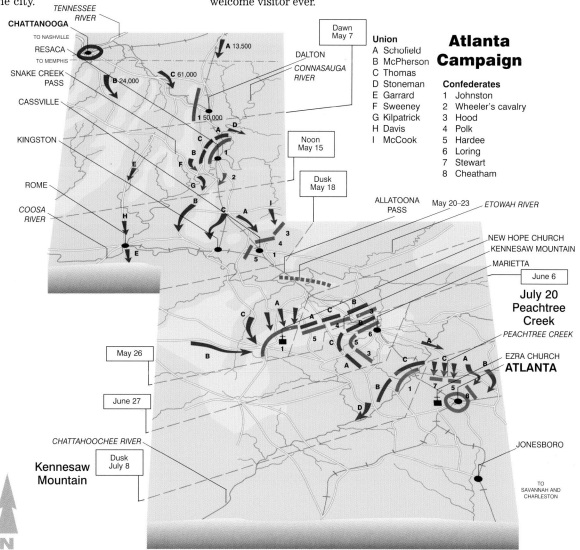

Atlanta Campaign

Union
A Schofield
B McPherson
C Thomas
D Stoneman
E Garrard
F Sweeney
G Kilpatrick
H Davis
I McCook

Confederates
1 Johnston
2 Wheeler's cavalry
3 Hood
4 Polk
5 Hardee
6 Loring
7 Stewart
8 Cheatham

Kennesaw Mountain

N

CHRONOLOGY

■ **October 2** General Hood's Army of Tennessee attacks Sherman's rail link at Big Shanty, Georgia, destroying the track of the Western & Atlantic Railroad.

■ **October 4** Sherman marches toward Big Shanty, Georgia to safeguard his rail supply line. There is skirmishing at Ackworth, Georgia.

■ **October 5** Major General S. G. French attacks the Union garrison at Allatoona Pass, Georgia. Brigadier General John M. Corse refuses to surrender. For a minor battle the casualties are heavy. French withdraws after receiving false reports of a Union force marching to relieve Corse.

■ **October 11** Sherman begins to concentrate his army at Rome, Georgia, to settle with Hood.

■ **October 12** Sherman and Hood clash around Resaca and Rome, Georgia.

■ **October 17** Hood leaves the line of the Western & Atlantic Railroad, moving westward in the direction of Gadsden, Alabama.

■ **October 26** Hood demonstrates against the Union garrison at Decatur, Alabama, but finding it too strong moves on west.

■ **October 28** Sherman turns his armies about, heading back to Atlanta. Union gunboats on the Tennessee River harass Hood's army and keep Thomas informed of Hood's whereabouts.

■ **October 30** Near Fort Henry, Forrest's cavalry capture the Union gunboat *Undine* after she has run out of ammunition and is disabled. Two transports are also captured.

■ **October 31** Hood arrives at Tuscumbia, Alabama, where he waits twenty days for supplies.

■ **November 24** Schofield's XXIII Corps crosses the Duck River at Columbia just ahead of Hood. Schofield then entrenches.

■ **November 27** Schofield's entrenchments being too strong to attack, Hood heads for Spring Hill.

■ **November 29** Due to appalling confusion and a lack of coordination, Schofield's force is allowed to escape from Spring Hill unmolested.

BATTLE OF FRANKLIN NOVEMBER 30

■ **3 p.m.** Furious fighting erupts lasting until after darkness has fallen, the Confederates losing five generals due to their recklessness in leading from the front. Casualties among the other ranks are also very heavy, 6,300 out of 27,000.

■ **December 1** Schofield reaches Nashville closely pursued by Hood who builds entrenchments.

■ **December 4** Thomas is urged to attack Hood by Grant and Lincoln.

■ **December 6** Grant orders Thomas to attack Hood.

■ **December 9** Grant orders Thomas to hand over command to Schofield. Nashville has been struck by heavy freezing rain, which makes movement impossible. Grant relents and cancels the order.

■ **December 11** Grant orders Thomas to attack, ice notwithstanding.

■ **December 12** Grant sends Major General John A. Logan to Nashville under orders to take command if Thomas has not attacked.

■ **December 14** Thomas meets with his generals and outlines his plans for the morrow. Demonstrations across the entire front are to tie down the Confederate infantry, Smith and Wood are to attack Hood's left while Wilson's cavalry attacks as the opportunity offers. Steedman is to attack Hood's right.

THURSDAY, DECEMBER 15, 1864

■ **Pre-dawn** Union forces begin to form up and move to their positions.

■ **8 a.m.** Steedman's attack on the Confederate right makes good progress at first but is then stalled by earthworks and spirited resistance. He draws back.

■ **10 a.m.** Smith's corps, delayed by the fog, pivots on Wood, swings to its left and crushes the hopelessly outnumbered Confederate force covering a three-mile gap between Stewart and the river.

■ **Later** A series of Confederate

redoubts (Nos 5, 4, 3, 2, 1) are dealt with by furious artillery bombardments followed by infantry charges.

■ **Later** Schofield marches his division to the right of the Union army to intensify the pressure on the Confederate left. This frees Wilson's cavalry to move south, circle around and assault Hood's rear.

■ Walthall's division, sheltered by a stone wall, are heavily shelled then driven out by infantry assault. Stewart and Lee barely have time to move their divisions out before the Confederate left collapses entirely.

■ Only darkness halts the complete collapse of Hood's army.

■ During the night Hood shortens his line, reinforces his shattered left and hurriedly constructs defenses.

FRIDAY, DECEMBER 16, 1864

■ **6 a.m.** Wood and Steedman advance and occupy the works abandoned by Hood to hold his attention while Schofield, Smith and Wilson again swing around the Confederate left.

■ **Early afternoon** Thomas inspects his line ensuring all is as planned.

■ Feint attacks against Hood's right, followed by a serious attack, cause Lee to call for reinforcements.

■ **2 p.m.** Hood transfers a division of Cheatham's troops to assist Lee. By

UNION	CONFEDERATES
Command	
Major General George H. Thomas	General John Bell Hood
Armies	
Fourth Army Corps, the Army of the Tennessee, XXIII Army Corps plus odds and ends	of Tennessee
Strengths	
At least 55,000 infantry, cavalry, guns	About 27,000, infantry, cavalry, guns
Casualties	
387 dead, 2,558 wounded, 112 missing/prisoners	No exact figures are available. Hood claimed that his losses did not exceed 10,000, Thomas claimed to have captured 13,189 prisoners plus more than 2,000 deserters
Perspectives	
A deliberately planned battle that went almost according to plan and inflicted a shattering defeat on Hood, nearly destroying his army and sending him reeling back across the Tennessee	This comprehensive defeat more or less destroyed the Army of Tennessee and broke Hood

Top: Thomas's offensive sweeps the field. (LC)

Top right: A front-line camp emptied as battle is joined. (M)

Center: Union artillery joining the assault. (M)

Bottom: Guns placed by the victors on the Nashville capitol. (M)

Nashville
Situation c.1 p.m. December 15

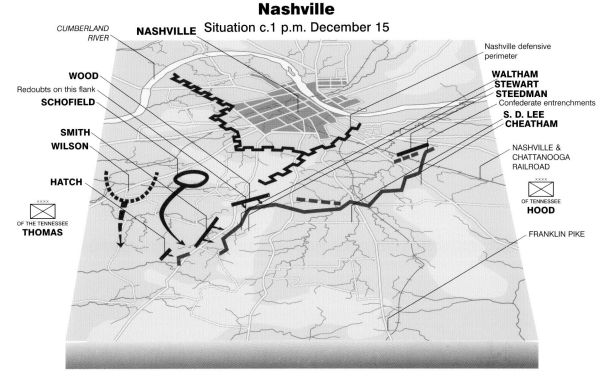

CUMBERLAND RIVER

NASHVILLE

WOOD

Redoubts on this flank

SCHOFIELD

SMITH
WILSON

HATCH

OF THE TENNESSEE
THOMAS

Nashville defensive perimeter

WALTHAM
STEWART
STEEDMAN
Confederate entrenchments

S. D. LEE
CHEATHAM

NASHVILLE &
CHATTANOOGA
RAILROAD

OF TENNESSEE
HOOD

FRANKLIN PIKE

Nashville
Situation c.4 p.m. December 16

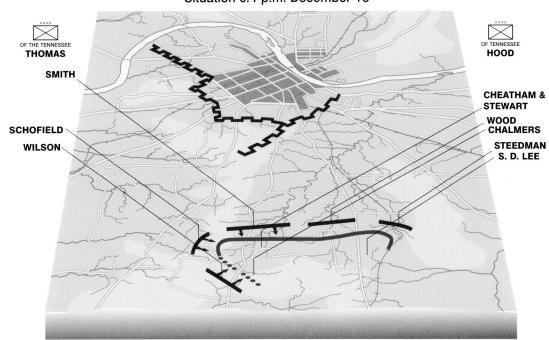

OF THE TENNESSEE
THOMAS

SMITH

SCHOFIELD

WILSON

OF TENNESSEE
HOOD

CHEATHAM &
STEWART

WOOD
CHALMERS

STEEDMAN
S. D. LEE

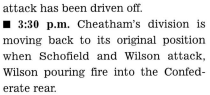

the time it reaches him the Union attack has been driven off.

■ **3:30 p.m.** Cheatham's division is moving back to its original position when Schofield and Wilson attack, Wilson pouring fire into the Confederate rear.

■ Sensing victory, the Union forces charge in. Stewart's corps, seeing the collapse on the left, dissolves; Johnson's division is swallowed whole.

■ Hood's army is only saved from total destruction by Chalmers' pitifully small cavalry division keeping Wilson from the Franklin Pike.

CHRONOLOGY

■ **June 14** Union troops cross the James River via 2,100-foot pontoon bridge.

■ **June 15** Smith's 18th Corps approaches Petersburg cautiously. The defenses are formidable, ten miles long, breastworks 20 feet thick with deep ditches on the attackers' side, 55 redans armed with heavy guns. But, Beauregard has only poor-quality troops with which to defend his works.

■ **Evening** Union forces advance and capture a mile of works and 16 guns before Smith's nerve fails and he halts. Beauregard's surviving troops dig furiously to build a new line and two Confederate divisions are moved from the James to stiffen the defenses.

■ **June 17, 5 p.m.** Vigorous Union assault on lines captures little but empty trenches.

■ **June 18, dawn** 67,000 Union troops advance hesitantly. Many are near the end of their enlistment and are unwilling to sacrifice their lives. Meade loses patience with his generals who each wait for the other to move first. Kershaw's division reaches Petersburg, closely followed by Lee himself. Union assaults continue all day for no gain.

■ **June 25** Work begins to drive a tunnel under Pegram's Salient, initiated by Lieutenant Colonel Henry Pleasants with Burnside's approval.

■ **July 23** The 510ft tunnel is complete and ready to be charged with powder. A division of colored troops has been specially trained to spearhead the assault following the detonation of the mine.

■ **July 29 afternoon** Meade is unsure about the use of the colored troops and the matter is referred to Grant. Grant decides not to use the colored troops in case the assault fails and there are heavy casualties among them. The commanders of three white divisions draw straws to decide which division should head the attack, General Ledlie wins (loses?).

■ Meade now changes the plan: instead of the assaulting troops moving left and right of the crater, they are now to move straight ahead to Cemetery Hill, leaving themselves open to flank attack.

UNION	CONFEDERATES
Commanders	
Lt. Gen. Ulysses S. Grant	Gen. Pierre G.T. Beauregard / Gen. Robert E. Lee
Armies	
of the Potomac of the James of the Shenandoah	of Northern Virginia
Strengths	
c.122,000 max. infantry, cavalry, artillery/engineers	c.67,000 max. infantry, cavalry, artillery/engineers
Casualties	
5,099 dead, 24,879 wounded, 17,576 missing/prisoners	c.30,000 dead, wounded, missing/prisoners
Perspectives	
The fate of the Confederacy was sealed at Petersburg with the virtual destruction of the Army of Northern Virginia	Despite Lee's brilliance and the courage of the Army of Northern Virginia, Grant's stranglehold was too tight and his resources too great

THE CRATER

■ **July 30, 4 a.m.** The mine is sprung late, following a problem with a splice in the fuse. A huge cloud of debris is thrown up and descends on the Union soldiers, causing them to scatter. They take some minutes to reform.

■ The first wave advances but instead of skirting the crater to right and left then advancing on Cemetery Hill, they pause to gaze at the devastation. The second wave comes up and both waves become mixed.

■ The second wave pushes through the crater, climbs to the rim and attempts to re-form.

■ Confederates in trenches right and left of the crater begin to fire into the Union advance, enfilading them and taking them from their rear. The Union troops fall back into the crater.

■ Confederates bring up a battery on their left and sweep the crest of the crater with canister.

■ Ledlie, apprised of the situation, orders the troops in the crater to move forward immediately. (Ledlie is sitting in a bombproof shelter in the Union trenches allegedly drinking rum.)

■ Union reinforcements brought up to ease the situation become lost in the

labyrinthine trenches and end up in the crater which is now full.

■ Further Union advances take the trenches right and left of the crater, but these are held only fleetingly.

■ Ledlie is again apprised of the situation but merely orders the brigade commanders to get their brigades out

Above: The mine explo[ded], earth trembled and hea[ved] and smoke shot upwar[d...] air was filled with earth, caissons, sand-bags an[d] men ..." (Brevet Major [C.] Houghton, 14th New Yo[rk] Artillery.) (B&L)

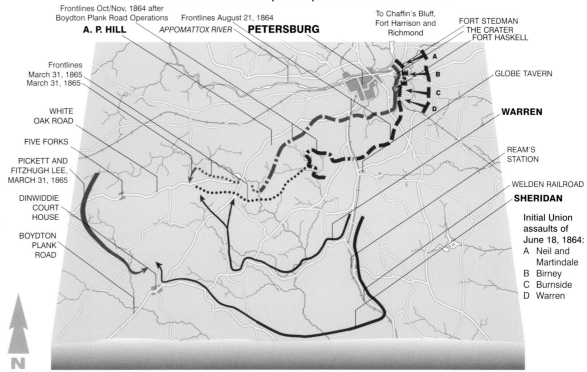

Frontlines Oct/Nov. 1864 after Boydton Plank Road Operations — A. P. HILL

Frontlines August 21, 1864 — APPOMATTOX RIVER — **PETERSBURG**

To Chaffin's Bluff, Fort Harrison and Richmond

FORT STEDMAN
THE CRATER
FORT HASKELL

Frontlines March 31, 1865 March 31, 1865

GLOBE TAVERN

WHITE OAK ROAD

WARREN

FIVE FORKS

REAM'S STATION

PICKETT AND FITZHUGH LEE, MARCH 31, 1865

WELDEN RAILROAD

DINWIDDIE COURT HOUSE

SHERIDAN

BOYDTON PLANK ROAD

Initial Union assaults of June 18, 1864:
A Neil and Martindale
B Birney
C Burnside
D Warren

N

Left top: Surging attacks and counter-attacks that made the Battle of the Crater such a disaster for the Union forces. (LC)

Left center: Union forces in the trenches, waiting for the order to attack. (NA)

of the crater and advance on Cemetery Hill.

■ **7 a.m.** General Ferrero, commanding officer of the colored division of the Ninth Corps is ordered to advance, pass through the troops in the crater and move on to carry Cemetery Hill.

■ The colored troops advance, the leading brigade colliding with a force of Confederates in the hollow beyond the crater. Prisoners and colors are taken but lacking support and subjected to intense fire from flanks and front, they break, falling back to the Union trenches.

■ **2 p.m.** Confederate artillery ceases fire. A column of Confederates advances on the crater despite heavy fire from Union guns, pours into the crater and a murderous hand-to-hand melee ensues in which colored troops who try to surrender are bayoneted.

■ **August 18–21 Globe Tavern** Grant now strikes south-west of Petersburg, overrunning the Weldon Railroad. A. P. Hill counterattacks fiercely but another Confederate lifeline has been cut.

■ **August 25, Reams Station** A force of Union infantry and artillery under Hancock sets out to wreck a Confederate railhead. They are caught in the act by Wade Hampton, rally, drive him back and complete the destruction of several miles of railroad.

■ **September 29–30 Chaffin's Bluff** Two Union corps attack the Richmond side of the lines. Lee, ignoring a demonstration to the south, shuttles some of his garrison from Petersburg. Fort Harrison nonetheless falls to the Union troops; an assault at Peeble's Farm lengthens the Union line to the east.

■ **October 27–28 Boydton Plank Road** A massive effort by Grant to cut off the Confederates' last rail link is repulsed by Hill, at the same time a diversion by Butler to the east of Richmond is defeated by the convalescent Longstreet.

■ Bad weather now halts mobile operations. The besiegers face a well fed and comfortable winter thanks to Grant's 21-mile military railroad. The besieged face semi-starvation and discomfort.

FORT STEDMAN

■ The brainchild of Major General John B. Gordon, this was an attempt to weaken Grant's left so that the Army of Northern Virginia could escape from the trap that Petersburg had become.

■ **March 25, 1865, before 3 a.m.** Taking advantage of an amnesty for deserters (with cash being paid for weapons surrendered), armed Confederate "deserters" overpower the pickets before Fort Stedman.

■ **3 a.m.** Alerted by a minor commotion in the Confederate lines, the garrison of Fort Stedman stand to.

■ Battery X close to Fort Stedman is attacked. In Fort Stedman a gun has been aimed at Battery X and opens fire on the Confederate attackers. The gunners in Battery X defend themselves vigorously.

■ A large force of Confederates has crept up on Fort Stedman, and pours in through embrasures and over parapets. Following a melee in the dark, the Union forces leave the fort to continue the fight from outside.

■ A similar assault on Fort Haskell fails due to the vigilance of a sentry and the Confederates are sharply handled.

■ **7:30 a.m.** With the coming of daylight the situation becomes clear to the Union troops and a series of counterattacks drives the Confederates from the salient with heavy losses.

■ Lee has wagered almost half his available force on this gamble and loses heavily.

Above: Black survivors of the disaster of the Crater, where about 300 colored troops were killed, relax or practise drilling back in camp. (M)

See over for Five Forks and the fall of Petersburg.

■ **March 26** Sheridan, his work in the Shenandoah Valley completed, arrives at Petersburg bringing with him a cavalry and an infantry corps.

DINWIDDIE COURT HOUSE
MARCH 31

■ **Morning** Two corps of Union infantry attack the right of the Confederates at the same time that Sheridan, with his cavalry corps, swings to the west in an attempt at encirclement. Lee's riposte is to send Fitzhugh Lee and Pickett to envelop the encirclers, striking Sheridan's left. The Union forces are driven back. Sheridan then counterattacks.

■ **Evening** Pickett, outnumbered, falls back on Five Forks and entrenches.

CHRONOLOGY

Following the defeat at Dinwiddie Courthouse the previous day, Pickett has withdrawn to Five Forks.

SATURDAY APRIL 1, 1865

■ **10 a.m.** Sheridan receives a message from Grant that he (Sheridan) has complete freedom of action.

■ During the night the Confederates on Sheridan's front have fallen back and there have been lively exchanges with his cavalry.

■ **1 p.m.** Cavalry report Confederates retiring on an entrenched position north of White Oak Road, with an angle in the earthworks to protect their left.

■ Sheridan becomes increasingly agitated as time passes and there is little movement of the infantry. His cavalry are fighting in a dismounted mode and are expending much ammunition "This battle must be fought and won before sundown."

■ **4 p.m.** The Union infantry is in formation and the advance begins. A skirmish line has been thrown out and advances across an open field.

■ On hearing the sounds of the infantry advance, the dismounted cavalry under Merritt begin their advance.

■ The cavalry, armed with breech-loading weapons, either Sharps single-shot carbines or Spencer seven-shot repeaters, demoralize the Confederates with the sheer volume of fire.

■ **Later** As the skirmish line advances, Sheridan rides across the front encour-

aging the troops. An infantryman is hit in the neck and halts. Sheridan tells him he is not hurt and the man continues to advance. After a dozen paces he falls dead.

■ Mackenzie, advancing up the Crump Road under instruction to "whip everything he met," defeats a small detachment of Confederate cavalry.

■ As the Union forces begin to cross boggy, overgrown ground, the advance slows. Sheridan calls for his battle-flag, takes it and personally closes up the wavering ranks. The Union ranks brace themselves and go forward over the earthworks sweeping all before them, capturing or killing all those who had not fled.

■ Sheridan's horse leaps over the earthwork, landing in the midst of a group of Confederate prisoners. This incident restores Sheridan's normal good humor.

■ Following a final sprint, the cavalry are over the earthworks capturing a battery of artillery and scattering the remaining Confederates.

■ The Confederate resistance at the Angle has collapsed and the entire Confederate right wing is exposed.

■ **9:30 p.m.** Grant orders a general assault for 4:00 next morning and orders Union guns to hammer the defenses of Petersburg until the skirmishers advance.

SUNDAY APRIL 2, 1865

■ A general assault is launched all along the lines around Petersburg. A spirited defense at Fort Gregg prevents the Union from capturing the city during the day, but Confederate General A. P. Hill is killed. After dark, the Confederates abandon Petersburg.

Above: Withdrawing after the battle, the Confederate forces had to destroy equipment they could not carry with them. (B&L)

UNION	CONFEDERATES
Commanders	
Lieutenant General Ulysses S. Grant	General George E. Pickett
Armies	
of the Potomac	of Northern Virginia
Strengths	
26,000 Sheridan's cavalry plus the Fifth Corps of infantry	7,000 infantry, cavalry, guns
Perspectives	
This was indeed the beginning of the end for the Confederacy. Since 1861 the Union had tried to capture Richmond and had failed; on April 4 Lincoln entered Richmond	Outnumbered and outgunned. Key commanders including Pickett absent from field when battle starts

Above: At Five Forks, Sheridan's cavalry showed its decisive tactical superiority even against rebel infantry. (LC)

Left: The overwhelming Union victory forced Lee to withdraw from the Richmond–Petersburg lines. (LC)

Five Forks
and the fall of Petersburg

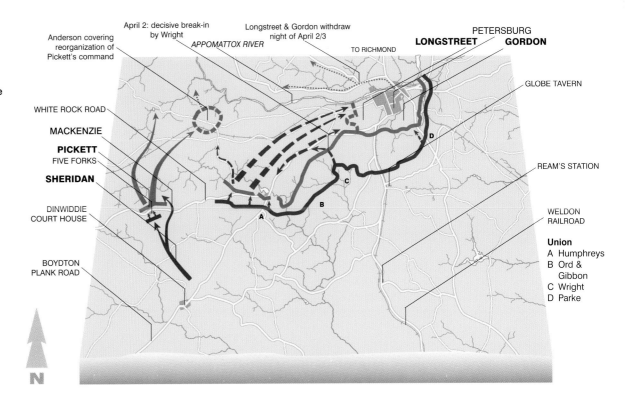

Anderson covering reorganization of Pickett's command

April 2: decisive break-in by Wright

APPOMATTOX RIVER

Longstreet & Gordon withdraw night of April 2/3

TO RICHMOND

PETERSBURG

LONGSTREET **GORDON**

GLOBE TAVERN

WHITE ROCK ROAD

MACKENZIE

PICKETT
FIVE FORKS

SHERIDAN

DINWIDDIE
COURT HOUSE

BOYDTON
PLANK ROAD

REAM'S STATION

WELDON
RAILROAD

Union
A Humphreys
B Ord &
    Gibbon
C Wright
D Parke

N

BATTLEFIELDS

The battlefield sites listed below are state or national park sites that offer public access and interpretive signs and exhibits. For a selection of sites that are of limited access or on private property, see Frances H. Kennedy, ed. *The Civil War Battlefield Guide* (1990).

Antietam National Battlefield, Sharpsburg, Maryland: close to 3,000 acres.

Appomattox Court House National Historical Park, Appomattox, Virginia: 1,325 acres, including the battlefield and reconstructed or restored town buildings.

Chickamauga and Chattanooga National Military Park includes the 5,574-acre Chickamauga Battlefield at Fort Oglethorpe, Georgia; and Lookout Mountain, Missionary Ridge, and Orchard Knob around Chattanooga, Tennessee (an additional 2,493 acres). Corinth Battlefield, Corinth, Mississippi: 5 acres on the grounds of Fort Robinette.

Fort Donelson National Battlefield, Dover, Tennessee: over 500 acres. One can also see the building in town where Grant received his first "unconditional surrender." The site of Fort Henry, some ten miles distant, is now under water, part of an area that was flooded to create a lake.

Fort Sumter National Monument, Charleston, South Carolina: reconstructed fort on 197 acres of public land. Fredericksburg and Spotsylvania National Military Park, Fredericksburg, Virginia: includes Fredericksburg, Chancellorsville, the Wilderness, and Spotsylvania Court House Battlefields, each of them more than a thousand acres.

Gettysburg National Military Park, Gettysburg, Pennsylvania: about 3,800 acres and museum with Cyclorama, a painting in the round.

Grand Gulf Military Monument, Port Gibson, Mississippi: 15 acres.

Harpers Ferry National Historical Park, Harpers Ferry, West Virginia: more than 2,000 acres, including the historic buildings of the town.

Kennesaw Mountain National Battlefield Park, Marietta, Georgia: 2,882 acres.

Above: Artillery in the wooded Shiloh battlefield.

Right: Elk Horn Tavern on the telegraph route at Pea Ridge.

Manassas National Battlefield Park, Manassas, Virginia: close to 5,000 acres encompassing both Battles of Bull Run.

New Market Battlefield Park, New Market, Virginia: 260 acres operated by the Virginia Military Institute whose cadets fought there.

Pea Ridge National Military Park, Pea Ridge, Arkansas: 4,300 acres

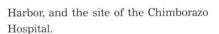

Above: The Dover
house at Fort
Donelson, where
Buckner signed the
document surren-
dering to his old
friend Grant.

Left: Glorieta Pass,
New Mexico,
looking northwest.

(All pictures: Author)

Perryville Battlefield State Historical Site, Perryville, Kentucky: 196 acres.

Petersburg National Battlefield, Petersburg, Virginia: about 2,700 acres: includes original earthworks, the Crater, City Point (the Union supply depot), and Five Forks Battlefield.

Port Hudson State Commemorative Area, Port Hudson, Louisiana: 640 acres.

Richmond National Battlefield Park: several sites around Richmond, Virginia, including Drewry's Bluff, Gaines's Mill, Malvern Hill, Cold Harbor, and the site of the Chimborazo Hospital.

Shiloh National Military Park, Shiloh, Tennessee: 3,838 acres, including an extensive artillery display.

Stones River National Battlefield, Murfreesboro, Tennessee: 405 acres.

Vicksburg National Military Park, Vicksburg, Mississippi: 1,620 acres and the wreck of an ironclad, the U.S.S. *Cairo*.

Wilson's Creek National Battlefield, just southwest of Springfield, Missouri: 1,750 acres.

OTHER SITES OF INTEREST

Confederate Naval Museum, Columbus, Georgia: an overlooked little gem with artifacts and dioramas.

Fort Ward Museum, Alexandria, Virginia: part of the Washington defenses; includes excellent artillery exhibit.

Museum of the Confederacy, Richmond, Virginia: paintings, clothing, and uniforms, weapons, battle flags. The White House of the Confederacy is adjacent.

NOTE: Many of these books have been reprinted several times. Where possible, we provide the publication dates of the first and most recent known editions.

Adams, George W. *Doctors in Blue: The Medical History of the Union Army in the Civil War.* 1952; 1985

Adams, Michael C. *Our Masters the Rebels: A Speculation on Union Military Failure in the East, 1861—1865.* 1978

Anderson, Bern. *By Sea and by River: The Naval History of the Civil War.* 1962; 1989

Annals of the War. 1879; 1996

Arnold, James R. *The Armies of U.S. Grant.* 1995

Ball, Douglas B. *Financial Failure and Confederate Defeat.* 1991

Battles and Leaders of the Civil War. 4 vols. 1887; 1991

Beringer, Richard E., et. al. *Why the South Lost the Civil War.* 1986

Black, Robert C., III. *The Railroads of the Confederacy.* 1952; 1987

Boatner, Mark Mayo, III. *The Civil War Dictionary.* 1959

Brownlee, Richard S. *Gray Ghosts of the Confederacy: Guerrilla Warfare in the West, 1861—1865.* 1958; 1984

Campaigns of the Civil War. 16 vols. 1881—85; 1963

Catton, Bruce. *Mr. Lincoln's Army.* 1951

— *Glory Road.* 1952

— *A Stillness at Appomattox,* 1953

— *The Coming Fury.* 1961

— *Terrible Swift Sword.* 1963

— *Never Call Retreat.* 1965

Coggins, Jack. *Arms and Equipment of the Civil War.* 1962

Commager, Henry Steele, ed. *The Blue and the Gray: The Story of the Civil War as Told By Participants.* 1950; 1982

Connelly, Thomas Lawrence and Archer Jones. *The Politics of Command: Factions and Ideas in Confederate Strategy.* 1973

Craven, Avery O. and Frank E. Vandiver. *The American Tragedy: The Civil War in Retrospect.* 1959

Cunningham, H.H. *Doctors in Gray: The Confederate Medical Service.* 1958; 1993

Cunningham, Sumner A. and Edith D. Pope, eds. *Confederate Veteran.* 40 vols. 1893—1932

Davis, William C. *"A Government of Our Own": The Making of the Confederacy.* 1994

Davis, William C., ed. *The Confederate General.* 6 vols. 1991

— *The Image of War, 1861—1865.* 6 vols. 1981—84

Early, Jubal A. et. al., eds. *Southern Historical Society Papers.* 52 vols. 1876—1959; 1990—92

Eicher, David. *Civil War Battlefields: A Touring Guide.* 1995

— *The Civil War in Books: An Analytical Bibliography.* 1997

Esposito, Vincent J., ed. *The West Point Atlas of American Wars.: Volume I, 1689—1900.* 1959

Foote, Shelby. *The Civil War: A Narrative.* 3 vols. 1958—74

Fox, William F. *Regimental Losses in the American Civil War.* 1898; 1974

Freeman, Douglas Southall. *Lee's Lieutenants: A Study in Command.* 3 vols. 1942—44

Fuller, J.F.C. *Grant and Lee: A Study in Personality and Generalship.* 1933; 1982

Gardner, Alexander. *Gardner's Photographic Sketch Book of the War.* 1865; 1959

Gibbon, John. *The Artillerist's Manual.* 1860; 1991

Goff, Richard D. *Confederate Supply.* 1969

Gosnell, H. Allen. *Guns on the Western Waters: The Story of River Gunboats in the Civil War.* 1949; 1993

Greene, Francis Vinton. *The Mississippi.* 1882; 1989

Griffith, Paddy. *Battle Tactics of the Civil War.* 1989

Hattaway, Herman and Archer Jones. *How the North Won: A Military History of the Civil War.* 1983

Hazlett, James C. et. al. *Field Artillery Weapons of the Civil War.* 1983

Hendrick, Burton. *Statesmen of the Lost Cause: Jefferson Davis and his Cabinet.* 1939

Jones, Archer. *Civil War Command and Strategy: The Process of Victory and Defeat.* 1992

— *Confederate Strategy from Shiloh to Vicksburg.* 1961; 1991

Jones, Virgil Carrington. *The Civil War at Sea.* 3 vols. 1960—62; 1990

Kennedy, Frances H., ed. *The Civil War Battlefield Guide.* 1990

Kerby, Robert L. *Kirby Smith's Confederacy: The Trans-Mississippi South, 1863—1865.* 1972; 1991

Lang, George, Raymond L. Collins, and Gerard F. White, eds. *Medal of Honor Recipients 1863—1994.* 1995

Leslie's Illustrated Civil War. 1992

Livermore, Thomas L. *Numbers and Losses in the Civil War in America, 1861—1865.* 1900; 1986

Long, E.B. and Barbara Long. *The Civil War Day by Day: An Almanac, 1861—1865.* 1971; 1985

Lonn, Ella. *Foreigners in the Confederacy.* 1940

Lord, Francis A. *They Fought For the Union.* 1960

McMurry, Richard M. *Two Great Rebel Armies: An Essay in Confederate Military History.* 1989

McPherson, James M. *Battle Cry of Freedom: The Civil War Era.* 1988.

— *What They Fought For, 1861—1865.* 1994

McWhiney, Grady. *Braxton Bragg and Confederate Defeat.* 2 vols. 1969; 1991

Papers of the Military Order of the Loyal Legion of the United States (MOLLUS). 1991—1995

Miller, Francis Trevelyan, ed. *The Photographic History of the Civil War.* 10 vols. 1911

Moore, Albert Burton. *Conscription and Conflict in the Confederacy.* 1924; 1963

Nelson, Larry E. *Bullets, Ballots, and Rhetoric: Confederate Policy for the United States Presidential Contest of 1864.* 1980

Nevins, Allan. *Ordeal of the Union.* 8 vols. 1947—71

Ordnance Manual for the Use of Officers of the Confederate States Army. 1863; 1976

Owsley, Frank Lawrence. *King Cotton Diplomacy: Foreign Relations of the Confederate States of America.* 1931; 1959

Ramsdell, Charles W. *Behind the Lines in the Southern Confederacy.* 1944

Reed, Rowena. *Combined Operations in the Civil War.* 1978; 1993

Richardson, James D., ed. *A Compilation of the Messages and Papers of the Confederacy 1861—1865.* 2 vols. 1906

Roland, Charles P. *The Confederacy.* 1960

Sears, Stephen W., ed. *The American Heritage Century Collection of Civil War Art.* 1974

Silber, Nina and Mary Beth Sievens, eds., *Yankee Correspondence: Civil War Letters between New England Soldiers and the Home Front.* 1996

Starr, Stephen Z. *The Union Cavalry in the Civil War.* 3 vols. 1979—85

Still, William N., Jr. *Iron Afloat: The Story of the Confederate Armorclads.* 1971; 1985

Trudeau, Noah Andre. *Out of the Storm: The End of the Civil War, April—June 1865.* 1994

Turner, George E. *Victory Rode the Rails: The Strategic Place of Railroads in the Civil War.* 1953; 1992

U.S. Congress. *Report of the Joint Committee on the Conduct of the War.* 6 vols. 1863—66.

U. S. Navy Department. *Official Records of the Union and Confederate Navies in the War of the Rebellion.* 31 vols. 1894—1927

U.S. War Department. *The War of the Rebellion: A Compilation of the Official Records of the Union and Confederate Armies.* 70 vols in 128 parts. 1880—1901 (This set is available on CD-ROM.)

Vandiver, Frank E. *Rebel Brass: The Confederate Command System.* 1956; 1993

Warner, Ezra J. and W. Buck Yearns. *Biographical Register of the Confederate Congress.* 1975

Warner, Ezra J. *Generals in Blue: Lives of the Union Commanders.* 1964

— *Generals in Gray: Lives of the Confederate Commanders.* 1959

Wheeler, Richard. *Lee's Terrible Swift Sword: From Antietam to Chancellorsville, An Eyewitness History.* 1992

— *Voices of the Civil War.* 1976

Wiley, Bell Irvin. *The Life of Johnny Reb: The Common Soldier of the Confederacy.* 1943; 1978

— *The Life of Billy Yank: The Common Soldier of the Union.* 1952; 1993

— *The Plain People of the Confederacy.* 1943

— *The Road to Appomattox.* 1956; 1994

Williams, Kenneth P. *Lincoln Finds a General: A Military Study of the Civil War.* 5 vols. 1949—59

Williams, T. Harry. *Lincoln and His Generals.* 1952

Wise, Stephen R. *Lifeline of the Confederacy: Blockade Runners during the Civil War.* 1989

Woodworth, Steven E. *Jefferson Davis and His Generals: The Failure of Confederate Command in the West.* 1990

Yearns, W. Buck, ed. *The Confederate Governors.* 1985

Campaigns and Battles

Arnold, James R. *Grant Wins the War: Decision at Vicksburg.* 1997

Barrett, John G. *Sherman's March Through the Carolinas.* 1956; 1996

Bearss, Edwin C. *Hardluck Ironclad: The Sinking and Salvage of the Cairo.* 1966; 1980

Brooksher, William R. *Bloody Hill: The Civil War Battle of Wilson's Creek.* 1995

Brown, D. Alexander. *Grierson's Raid: A Cavalry Adventure of the Civil War.* 1954;1981

Carter, Samuel, III. *The Final Fortress: The Campaign for Vicksburg 1862-1863.* 1980

Catton, Bruce. *Grant Moves South.* 1960

— *Grant Takes Command.* 1968

Chamberlain, Joshua Lawrence. *The Passing of the Armies: An Account of the Final Campaign of the Army of the Potomac, Based on Personal Reminiscences of the Fifth Army Corps.* 1915; 1986

Coddington, Edwin B. *The Gettysburg Campaign: A Study in Command.* 1968; 1984

Cooling, Benjamin Franklin. *Forts Henry and Donelson: The Key to the Confederate Heartland.* 1987

Cox, Jacob D. *The Battle of Franklin, Tennessee: November 30, 1864.* 1897; 1983

Cozzens, Peter. *No Better Place to Die: The Battle of Stones River.* 1990

— *This Terrible Sound: The Battle of Chickamauga.* 1992

Davis, William C. *Battle at Bull Run: A History of the First Major Campaign of the Civil War.* 1977

— *The Battle of New Market.* 1975

Dowdey, Clifford. *The Seven Days: The Emergence of Lee.* 1964; 1993

Frank, Joseph Allan and George A. Reaves. *"Seeing the Elephant": Raw Recruits at the Battle of Shiloh.* 1989

Frassanito, William A. *Antietam: The Photographic Legacy of America's Bloodiest Day.* 1978

Frassanito, William A. *Gettysburg: A Journey in Time.* 1975

Gragg, Rod. *Confederate Goliath: The Battle of Fort Fisher.* 1991

Hassler, Warren W., Jr. *Crisis at the Crossroads: The First Day at Gettysburg.* 1970

Hennessy, John J. *Return to Bull Run: The Campaign and Battle of Second Manassas.* 1993

Herdegen, Lance J. and William J.K. Beaudot. *In the Bloody Railroad Cut at Gettysburg.* 1990.

Hoehling, A.A., ed. *Vicksburg: 47 Days of Siege.* 1969

Hughes, Nathaniel C. *The Battle of Belmont: Grant Strikes South.* 1991

Jones, James Pickett. *Yankee Blitzkrieg: Wilson's Raid through Alabama and Georgia.* 1976; 1987

Krick, Robert K. *Stonewall Jackson at Cedar Mountain.* 1990

Luvas, Jay and Harold W. Nelson, eds. *The U.S. Army War College Guide to the Battles of Chancellorsville and Fredericksburg.* 1988

Mahan, Alfred Thayer. *The Gulf and*

Inland Waters. 1883; 1989

McDonough, James Lee. War in Kentucky: From Shiloh to Perryville. 1994

Pfanz, Harry W. Gettysburg: The Second Day. 1987

Priest, John Michael. Into the Fight: Pickett's Charge at Gettysburg. 1998

Sears, Stephen W. Chancellorsville. 1996

— Landscape Turned Red: The Battle of Antietam. 1983

— To the Gates of Richmond: The Peninsula Campaign. 1992

Shea, William L. and Earl J. Hess. Pea Ridge: Civil War Campaign in the West. 1992

Simpson, Harold B. Gaines' Mill to Appomattox. 1963

Sword, Wiley. Shiloh: Bloody April. 1974; 1993

Tanner, Robert G. Stonewall in the Valley: Thomas J. "Stonewall" Jackson's Shenandoah Valley Campaign, Spring 1862. 1976

Wert, Jeffry D. From Winchester to Cedar Creek: The Shenandoah Campaign of 1864. 1987

Wise, Stephen R. Gate of Hell: Campaign for Charleston Harbor, 1863. 1994

Army and Unit Histories

CONFEDERATE

Barber, Flavel C. Holding the Line: The Third Tennessee Infantry 1861–1864. 1994

Bevier, R.S. History of the First and Second Missouri Confederate Brigades, 1861–1865. 1879

Connelly, Thomas Lawrence. Army of the Heartland: The Army of Tennessee, 1861–1862. 1967

— Autumn of Glory: The Army of Tennessee, 1862–1865. 1971

Daniel, Larry J. Cannoneers in Gray: The Field Artillery of the Army of Tennessee, 1861–1865. 1984

— Soldiering in the Army of Tennessee: A Portrait of Life in a Confederate Army. 1991.

Dickert, D. A. History of Kershaw's Brigade. 1899; 1990

Hale, Douglas. The Third Texas Cavalry in the Civil War. 1993

Robertson, James I., Jr. The Stonewall Brigade. 1963; 1987

Simpson, Harold B. Hood's Texas Brigade: Lee's Grenadier Guard. 1970

Tunnard, William H. A Southern Record: The History of the Third Regiment, Louisiana Infantry. 1866; 1988.

Watkins, Sam R. "Co. Aytch": A Side Show of the Big Show. 1882; 1962

Wise, Jennings Cropper. The Long Arm of Lee; or, the History of the Field Artillery, Army of Northern Virginia. 2 vols. 1915; 1991

UNION

Billings, John D. A History of the Tenth Massachusetts Battery of Light Artillery in the War of the Rebellion. 1881; 1987

Curry, William L. Four Years in the Saddle: History of the First Regiment, Ohio Volunteer Cavalry, War of the Rebellion, 1861–1865. 1898; 1984

Curtis, Newton M. From Bull Run to Chancellorsville: The Story of the Sixteenth New York Infantry. 1906

Denison, Frederic. Sabres and Spurs: The First Regiment, Rhode Island Cavalry in the Civil War, 1861—1865. 1876; 1994

Gaff, Alan D. Brave Men's Tears: The Iron Brigade at Brawner Farm. 1985

Huffstodt, Jim. Hard Dying Men: The Story of General W.H.L. Wallace, General T.E.G. Ransom, and their "Old Eleventh" Illinois Infantry in the American Civil War (1861—1865). 1991

Judson, Amos M. History of the Eighty-third Regiment Pennsylvania Volunteers. 1865; 1986

Moe, Richard. The Last Full Measure: The Life and Death of the First Minnesota Volunteers. 1993

Naisawald, L. Van Loan. Grape and Canister: The Story of the Field Artillery of the Army of the Potomac, 1861—1865. 1960; 1992

Nolan, Alan T. The Iron Brigade: A Military History. 1961; 1994

Pullen, John J. The Twentieth Maine: A Volunteer Regiment in the Civil War. 1957; 1991

Rowell, John W. Yankee Artilleryman: Through the Civil War with Eli Lilly's Indiana Battery. 1975

Smith, Donald L. The Twenty-fourth Michigan of the Iron Brigade. 1962

Starr, Stephen Z. Jennison's Jayhawkers: A Civil War Cavalry Regiment and Its Commander. 1973

Stevens, Charles A. Berdan's United States Sharpshooters in the Army of the Potomac. 1892; 1985

Wilkinson, Warren. Mother, May You Never See the Sights I Have Seen: The 57th Massachusetts Veteran Volunteers. 1990

Letters, Memoirs and Biographies

Dana, Charles A. Recollections of the Civil War. 1899; 1963

Fremantle, Arthur J.L. Three Months in the Southern States: April—June 1863. 1863; 1984

Russell, William Howard. My Diary North and South. 1863; 1992

Tapert, Annette. The Brothers' War: Civil War Letters to Their Loved Ones from the Blue and Gray. 1988

Villard, Henry. Memoirs of Henry Villard. 2 vols. 1904

CONFEDERATE

Alexander, Edward Porter. Fighting for the Confederacy: The Personal Recollections of General Edward Porter Alexander. 1989

Anderson, Ephraim M. Memoirs: Historical and Personal. 1972

Andrews, William Hill. Footprints of a Regiment: A Recollection of the 1st Georgia Regulars, 1861—1865. 1992

Ballard, Michael B. Pemberton: A Biography. 1991

Bevens, William E. Reminiscences of a Private: William E. Bevens of the First Arkansas Infantry, C.S.A. 1992

Blackford, William W. War Years with Jeb Stuart. 1945

Bridges, Hal. Lee's Maverick General: Daniel Harvey Hill. 1961; 1991

Buck, Irving A. Cleburne and His Command. 1908; 1985

Casler, John O. Four Years in the Stonewall Brigade. 1893; 1982

Castel, Albert. General Sterling Price and the Civil War in the West. 1968; 1993

Cooke, John Esten. Wearing of the Gray: Being Personal Portraits, Scenes, and Adventures of the War. 1867; 1993

Cumming, Kate. The Journal of a Confederate Nurse. 1866; 1977

Davis, Jefferson. Private Letters. 1966

— The Rise and Fall of the Confederate Government. 2 vols. 1881; 1990

Davis, Varina. Jefferson Davis: Ex-President of the Confederate States of America. A Memoir by his Wife. 2 vols. 1890; 1990

Davis, William C. Breckinridge: Soldier: Statesman, Symbol. 1974; 1992

— Jefferson Davis: The Man and His Hour. 1991

Davis, William C., ed. Diary of a Confederate Soldier: John S. Jackman of the Orphan Brigade. 1990

Dew, Charles B. Ironmaker to the Confederacy: Joseph R. Anderson and the Tredegar Iron Works. 1966.

Douglas, Henry Kyd. I Rode With Stonewall. 1940; 1987

Dowdey, Clifford and Louis Manarin, eds. The Wartime Papers of Robert E. Lee. 1961; 1987

Durkin, Joseph T. Stephen R. Mallory: Confederate Navy Chief. 1954; 1987

Dyer, John P. Fightin' Joe Wheeler. 1941

Early, Jubal A. Autobiographical Sketch and Narrative of the War Between the States. 1912; 1989

Eggleston, George Cary. A Rebel's Recollections. 1875; 1959

Everson, Guy R. and Edward H. Simpson, Jr., eds. "Far, Far from Home": The Wartime Letters of Dick and Tally Simpson Third South Carolina Volunteers. 1994

Ewell, Richard Stoddert. The Making of a Soldier: Letters of General R.S. Ewell. 1935

Freeman, Douglas Southall. R.E. Lee: A Biography. 4 vols. 1934—35

Goree, Thomas J. Longstreet's Aide: The Civil War Letters of Major Thomas J. Goree. 1995

Hattaway, Herman. General Stephen D. Lee. 1976

Heartsill, William W. Fourteen Hundred and 91 Days in the Confederate Army; A Journal Kept by W.W. Heartsill. 1876; 1992

Heth, Henry. The Memoirs of Henry Heth. 1974

Hotchkiss, Jedediah. Make Me a Map of the Valley: The Civil War Journal of Stonewall Jackson's Cartographer. 1973; 1988

Howard, McHenry. Recollections of a Maryland Confederate Soldier and Staff Officer under Johnston, Jackson, and Lee. 1914; 1975

Hughes, Nathaniel Cheairs, Jr. General William J. Hardee: Old Reliable. 1965; 1997

Johnston, Joseph E. Narrative of Military Operations, Directed, during the Late War Between the States, by Joseph E. Johnston, General, C.S.A. 1874; 1990

Jones, John B. A Rebel War Clerk's Diary at the Confederate States

Capital. 1866; 1993

LeConte, Emma. When the World Ended. 1957

Lee, Susan Pendleton. Memoirs of William Nelson Pendleton. 1893; 1991

Longstreet, James. From Manassas to Appomattox: Memoirs of the Civil War in America. 1896; 1992

Manigault, Arthur M. A Carolinian Goes to War: The Civil War Diary of Arthur Middleton Manigault. 1983

Meade, Robert Douthat. Judah P. Benjamin: Confederate Statesman. 1943; 1975

McIntosh, James T. et. al., ed. The Papers of Jefferson Davis. 8 vols. 1971–

McKim, Randolph H. A Soldier's Recollections: Leaves from the Diary of a Young Confederate. 1910; 1984

McMurry, Richard M. John Bell Hood and the War for Southern Independence. 1982;1992

McWhiney, Grady. Braxton Bragg and Confederate Defeat, Volume 1: Field Command. 1969; 1991

Nisbet, James Cooper. Four Years on the Firing Line. 1914; 1991

Nolan, Alan T. Lee Considered: General Robert E. Lee and Civil War History. 1991

Parks, Joseph H. General Edmund Kirby Smith C.S.A. 1954; 1992

— General Leonidas Polk C.S.A. 1962; 1992

— Joseph E. Brown of Georgia. 1977

Pember, Phoebe Yates. A Southern Woman's Story. 1879; 1959

Pemberton, John C. Pemberton: Defender of Vicksburg. 1942

Pender, William Dorsey. The General to His Lady: The Civil War Letters of William Dorsey Pender to Fanny Pender. 1965; 1987

Reagan, John H. Memoirs: With Special Reference to Secession and the Civil War. 1906; 1973

Ripley, Warren, ed. Siege Train: The Journal of a Confederate Artilleryman in the Defense of Charleston. 1986

Robertson, James I., Jr. General A.P. Hill: The Story of a Confederate Warrior. 1987

— Stonewall Jackson: the Man, the Soldier, the Legend. 1997

Roland, Charles P. Albert Sidney Johnston: Soldier of Three Republics. 1964; 1994

Rowland, Dunbar, ed. Jefferson Davis, Constitutionalist: His Letters, Papers and Speeches. 10 vols. 1923

Shingleton, Royce G. John Taylor Wood: Sea Ghost of the Confederacy. 1979

Sorrell, G. Moxley. Recollections of a Confederate Staff Officer. 1905; 1991

Symonds, Craig L. Joseph E. Johnston: A Civil War Biography. 1992

Taylor, Richard. Destruction and Reconstruction: Personal Experiences of the Late War. 1879; 1995

Taylor, Walter H. General Lee, His Campaigns in Virginia, 1861—1865: With Personal Reminiscences. 1906; 1994

Vance, Zebulon B. The Papers of Zebulon Baird Vance. 1963

Vandiver, Frank E. Mighty Stonewall. 1957

— *Ploughshares into Swords: Josiah Gorgas and Confederate Ordnance.* 1952; 1994

Vandiver, Frank E., ed. *The Civil War Diary of General Josiah Gorgas.* 1947

Wert, Jeffry D. *General James Longstreet, the Confederacy's Most Controversial Soldier: A Biography.* 1993

Williams, T. Harry. *P.G.T. Beauregard: Napoleon in Gray.* 1954; 1995

Wills, Brian Steel. *A Battle from the Start: The Life of Nathan Bedford Forrest.* 1992

Woodward, C. Vann. *Mary Chesnut's Civil War.* 1981

Yeary, Mamie, ed. *Reminiscences of the Boys in Gray, 1861—1865.* 1986

Younger, Edward, ed. *Inside the Confederate Government: The Diary of Robert Garlick Hill Kean.* 1957; 1993

UNION

Abbott, Henry Livermore. *Fallen Leaves: The Civil War Letters of Major Henry Livermore Abbott.* 1991

Ambrose, Stephen E. *Upton and the Army.* 1964; 1993

Angle, Paul M., ed. *The Lincoln Reader.* 1947

Basler, Roy P., ed. *The Collected Works of Abraham Lincoln.* 8 vols. 1953—55

Bates, Edward. *The Diary of Edward Bates, 1859—1866.* 1933; 1971

Baumgartner, Richard A. and Larry M. Strayer, eds. *Ralsa C. Rice: Yankee Tigers: Through the Civil War with the 125th Ohio.* 1992

Bellard, Alfred. *Gone for a Soldier: The Civil War Memoirs of Private Alfred Bellard.* 1975

Billings, John D. *Hardtack and Coffee; or, the Unwritten Story of Army Life.* 1887; 1993

Blanchard, Ira. *I Marched with Sherman: Civil War Memoirs of the 20th Illinois Volunteer Infantry.* 1992

Blight, David W. *Frederick Douglass' Civil War: Keeping Faith in Jubilee.* 1989

Brewster, Charles Harvey. *When This Cruel War is Over: The Civil War Letters of Charles Harvey Brewster.* 1992

Brinton, John H. *Personal Memoirs of John H. Brinton, Major and Surgeon U.S.V. 1861—1865.* 1914

Byrne, Frank L. and Jean Powers Soman. *Your True Marcus: The Civil War Letters of a Jewish Colonel.* 1985.

Cadwallader, Sylvanus. *Three Years with Grant.* 1955

Chase, Salmon P. *Inside Lincoln's Cabinet: The Civil War Diaries of Salmon P. Chase.* 1954; 1971

Coffin, Charles Carleton. *Four Years of Fighting.* 1866; 1970

Cox, Florence, ed. *Kiss Josey For Me!.* 1974

Crummer, Wilbur F. *With Grant at Donelson, Shiloh, and Vicksburg.* 1915

Dahlgren, Madeleine Vinton. *Memoir of John A. Dahlgren, Rear-Admiral United States Navy.* 1882

Dawes, Rufus R. *Service With the Sixth Wisconsin Volunteers.* 1890; 1984

DeForest, John William. *A Volunteer's Adventures: A Union Captain's Record of the Civil War.* 1946.

Dewey, George. *Autobiography of George Dewey: Admiral of the Navy.* 1913

DuPont, Samuel Francis. *Samuel Francis DuPont: A Selection from his Civil War Letters.* 3 vols. 1969

Eaton, John. *Grant, Lincoln and the Freedmen: Reminiscences of the Civil War.* 1907

Engle, Stephen D. *Yankee Dutchman: The Life of Franz Sigel.* 1993

Ewing, Joseph H., ed. *Sherman at War.* 1992

Farragut, Loyall. *The Life of David Glasgow Farragut, First Admiral of the United States Navy, Embodying His Journals and Letters.* 1879

Forbes, Edwin. *Thirty Years After: An Artist's Story of the Great War.* 2 vols, 1890; 1993

Fox, Gustavus V. *Confidential Correspondence of Gustavus V. Fox Assistant Secretary of the Navy.* 2 vols. 1919; 1972

Fuller, J.F.C. *The Generalship of U.S. Grant.* 1929

Gibbon, John. *Personal Recollections of the Civil War.* 1928; 1988

Grant, Julia Dent. *The Personal Memoirs of Julia Dent Grant.* 1975; 1988

Grant, Ulysses S. *The Papers of Ulysses S. Grant.* 20 vols. From 1967-

— *Personal Memoirs.* 1885; 1982

Harrington, Fred Harvey. *Fighting Politician, Major General N. P. Banks.* 1948

Haskell, Frank A. *Haskell of Gettysburg: His Life and Civil War Papers.* 1970; 1989

Hay, John. *Lincoln and the Civil War in the Diaries and Letters of John Hay.* 1939; 1988

Hazen, William B. *A Narrative of Military Service.* 1885; 1993

Herbert, Walter H. *Fighting Joe Hooker.* 1944; 1987

Hess, Earl J., ed. *A German in the Yankee Fatherland: The Civil War Letters of Henry A. Kircher.* 1983

Higginson, Thomas Wentworth. *Army Life in a Black Regiment.* 1870; 1982

Johnson, Richard W. *A Soldier's Reminiscences in Peace and War.* 1886

Jones, Jenkin Lloyd. *An Artilleryman's Diary.* 1914

Jordan, David M. *Winfield Scott Hancock: A Soldier's Life.* 1988

Keeler, William F. *Aboard the U.S.S. Monitor, 1862: The Letters of Acting Paymaster William Frederick Keeler, U.S. Navy, to His Wife Anna.* 1964

Kellogg, J.J. *The Vicksburg Campaign and Reminiscences.* 1913

Lamers, William M. *The Edge of Glory: A Biography of General William S. Rosecrans, U.S.A.* 1961

Larimer, Charles F. *Love and Valor: Intimate Civil War Letters Between Captain Jacob and Emeline Ritner.* 2000

Letterman, Jonathan. *Medical Recollections of the Army of the Potomac.* 1866

Lewis, Lloyd. *Captain Sam Grant.* 1950; 1991

Longacre, Edward G. *The Man*

Behind the Guns: A Biography of General Henry J. Hunt, Commander of Artillery, Army of the Potomac. 1977

Lyman, Theodore. *Meade's Headquarters, 1863—1865: Letters of Colonel Theodore Lyman from the Wilderness to Appomattox.* 1922; 1994

Marszalek, John F. *Sherman: A Soldier's Passion for Order.* 1993

Meade, George G. *The Life and Letters of George Gordon Meade.* 2 vols. 1913; 1994

Miles, Nelson A. *Personal Recollections and Observations of General Nelson A. Miles.* 1896; 1992

Nichols, Edward J. *Toward Gettysburg: A Biography of General John F. Reynolds.* 1958; 1988

Nicolay, John G. and John Hay. *Abraham Lincoln: A History.* 10 vols. 1890

Niven, John. *Salmon P. Chase: A Biography.* 1995

Oates, Stephen B. *A Woman of Valor: Clara Barton and the Civil War.* 1994

— *To Purge This Land With Blood: A Biography of John Brown.* 1970

Oldroyd, Osborn H. *A Soldier's Story of the Siege of Vicksburg.* 1885

Palmer, John M. *Personal Recollections of John M. Palmer: The Story of an Earnest Life.* 1901

Patrick, Marsena R. *Inside Lincoln's Army: The Diary of General Marsena Rudolph Patrick, Provost Marshal General, Army of the Potomac.* 1964

Porter, David Dixon. *Incidents and Anecdotes of the Civil War.* 1886

Porter, Horace. *Campaigning with Grant.* 1897; 1986

Reid, Whitelaw. *A Radical View: The Agate Dispatches of Whitelaw Reid, 1861—1865.* 1976

Rhodes, Elisha Hunt. *All For the Union: The Civil War Diary and Letters of Elisha Hunt Rhodes.* 1991

Robertson, James I., ed. *The Civil War Letters of General Robert McAllister.* 1965

Sears, Stephen W. *George B. McClellan: The Young Napoleon.* 1988

Sedgwick, John. *Correspondence of John Sedgwick, Major General.* 2 vols. 1902—3

Selfridge, Thomas O., Jr. *Memoirs of Thomas O. Selfridge, Jr. Rear-Admiral U.S.N.* 1924; 1988

Seward, William Henry. *The Works of William H. Seward.* 5 vols. 1853—84

Shaw, Robert Gould. *Blue-Eyed Child of Fortune: The Civil War Letters of Colonel Robert Gould Shaw.* 1992

Sheridan, Philip H. *Personal Memoirs of P.H. Sheridan.* 2 vols. 1888; 1992

Sherman, John. *John Sherman's Recollections of Forty Years in the House, Senate, and Cabinet: An Autobiography.* 2 vols. 1895

Sherman, William Tecumseh. *Memoirs of General W. T. Sherman.* 1875; 1990

Simon, John Y. and David L. Wilson, eds. *Ulysses S. Grant: Essays, Documents.* 1981

Simpson, Brooks D. *Let Us Have Peace: Ulysses S. Grant and the Politics of War and Reconstruction, 1861—1868.* 1991

Stillwell, Leander. *The Story of a Common Soldier of Army Life in the Civil War 1861—1865.* 1917; 1983

Stockwell, Elisha, Jr. *Private Elisha Stockwell, Jr. Sees the Civil War.* 1958; 1985

Strong, George Templeton. *The Diary of George Templeton Strong.* 4 vols. 1952

Strother, David Hunter. *A Virginia Yankee in the Civil War: The Diaries of David Hunter Strother.* 1961

Swanberg, W.A. *Sickles the Incredible.* 1956

Taylor, Emerson Gifford. *Gouverneur Kemble Warren.* 1932; 1988

Thomas, Benjamin P. and Harold M. Hyman. *Stanton: The Life and Times of Lincoln's Secretary of War.* 1962

Tucker, Spencer C. *Andrew Foote: Civil War Admiral on Western Waters.* 2000

Wainwright, Charles S. *A Diary of Battle: The Personal Journals of Colonel Charles S. Wainwright, 1861—1865.* 1962; 1993

Walke, Henry. *Naval Scenes and Reminiscences of the Civil War in the United States.* 1877.

Weigley, Russell F. *Quartermaster General of the Union Army: A Biography of M.C. Meigs.* 1959

Weld, Stephen Minot, Jr. *War Diary and Letters of Stephen Minot Weld, 1861—1865.* 1912; 1979

Welles, Gideon. *The Diary of Gideon Welles.* 3 vols. 1911; 1960

Williams, Alpheus S. *From the Cannon's Mouth: The Civil War Letters of General Alpheus S. Williams.* 1959; 1995

Wilson, James Harrison. *Under the Old Flag: Recollections of Military Operations in the War for the Union, the Spanish War, the Boxer Rebellion, etc.* 2 vols 1912; 1971

Winslow, Richard Elliott, III. *General John Sedgwick: The Story of a Union Corps Commander.* 1982

The Internet

Web sites come and web sites go, so one hesitates to make specific recommendations. The following guide lists and evaluates numerous sites:

Thomas, William G. *The Civil War on the Web: A Guide to the Very Best Sites.* 2001.

A few sites that exist at this writing (January 2001) and may stand the test of time:

http://memory.loc.gov/ammem/cwphome.html Selected Civil War Photographs in the American Memory Collection; from the Library of Congress

http://valley.vcdh.virginia.edu The Valley of the Shadow: Two Communities in the American Civil War; letters, diaries, and newspaper articles about life in a Pennsylvania community and a Virginia community

http://www.cr.nps.gov/csd/gettex/ Camp Life: Civil War Collections from Gettysburg National Military Park; a National Park Service site with pictures of soldier's possessions

http://www.civilwarletters.com/home.html Letters of an Iowa Soldier in the Civil War